Learning Computer Concepts

A Fundamental Understanding of IC^3 – Technology, Computer Applications, and The Internet

2nd Edition

Shelley O'Hara

Vice President and Publisher: Natalie E. Anderson
Executive Editor: Jennifer Frew
Manufacturing Buyer: Natacha St. Hill Moore
Technical Editors: Joyce Nielsen and Faithe Wempen
Cover Designer: Amy Capuano
Composition: Shu Chen
Printer/Binder: Banta Book Group
Cover Printer: Phoenix Color Corporation

Credits and acknowledgements borrowed from other sources and reproduced, with permission, in this textbook are as follows:

Microsoft, Windows, and/or other Microsoft products referenced herein are either trademarks or registered trademarks of Microsoft Corporation in the U.S.A. and other countries. This book is not sponsored or endorsed by or affiliated with Microsoft Corporation.

Copyright © 2006 by Pearson Education, Inc., Upper Saddle River, New Jersey, 07458. All rights reserved. Printed in the United States of America. This publication is protected by Copyright and permission should by obtained from the publisher prior to any prohibited reproduction, storage in a retrieval system, or transmission in any form or by any means, electronic, mechanical, photocopying, recording, or likewise. For information regarding permission(s), write to the Rights and Permissions Department.

10 9 8 7 6 5 4 3 2
ISBN: 0-13-186889-6

Contents

INTRODUCTION v

IC³ COMPUTING FUNDAMENTALS - 2005 EXAM CORRELATION viii

IC³ KEY APPLICATIONS - 2005 EXAM CORRELATION ix

IC³ LIVING ONLINE - 2005 EXAM CORRELATION xi

IC³ AND CERTIPORT INFORMATION .... xiii-xv

PART I: COMPUTING FUNDAMENTALS

Lesson 1: Defining A Computer 1
- Review the history of computing
- List the types of computers
- Define a computer
- Describe the parts of a computer
- Understand the differences among computers
- Define computer processors
- Explain types of memory
- Buy, upgrade, and maintain your computer
- Troubleshoot computer problems

Lesson 2: Storing Data 37
- Define hard drives
- Use a floppy drive
- Learn about CD and DVD drives
- Familiarize yourself with other storage devices

Lesson 3: Using Input and Output Devices 51
- Use the keyboard
- Use a mouse
- Use other input devices
- Create digital images with a scanner or camera
- Define types of monitors
- Use a printer and other output devices

Lesson 4: Defining Software 72
- Understand how software works
- Describe what to consider when purchasing or upgrading software
- Define word processing and identify the main word processing programs and features
- Describe spreadsheet programs and identify spreadsheet programs and basic features
- Describe database programs
- Define presentation programs
- Describe publishing
- Define graphics programs
- Discuss other program types

Lesson 5: Defining Operating Systems 99
- Define an operating system
- Distinguish between DOS and Windows
- Identify other operating systems
- Work with the desktop and windows
- Shutdown and restart the computer
- Manage files
- Install new programs
- Customize Windows using the control panels

PART II: KEY APPLICATIONS

Lesson 6: Working with Applications 122
- Start and exit programs
- Work with documents
- Type and edit text
- Print documents

Lesson 7: Formatting Documents 140
- Format text
- Format paragraphs
- Format pages
- Add graphics and tables
- Work with multiple collaborators

Lesson 8: Creating Worksheets **158**
- Enter data
- Create formulas
- Format data
- Create charts
- Use your spreadsheet as a database
- Use other financial programs

Lesson 9: Presentations **177**
- Design presentations
- Create presentations
- Create slides
- Edit and reorder slides
- Format slides
- Preview the slide show presentation
- Print speaker notes and handouts

PART III: LIVING ONLINE

Lesson 10: Networking **189**
- Understand the concepts and terminology of networking
- Become familiar with types of networks
- Learn the benefits and risks of networking
- Understand the fundamental principles of network security
- Understand the similarities and relationships among different telecommunications networks
- Learn about networking hardware and software
- Understand different Internet connection methods and transmission rates
- Become familiar with the responsibilities of an Internet Service Provider (ISP)
- Learn how computers and the Internet are used to collect, organize, evaluate, and share information
- Understand how computer technology works behind the scenes in everyday activities
- Learn about the impact of electronic commerce (e-commerce) on business, individuals and governments

iii

Lesson 11: E-mail 209
- Define e-mail
- Send and receive messages
- Handle e-mail
- Work with attachments
- Create an Address Book
- Set up mail options
- Troubleshoot e-mail problems
- Follow e-mail etiquette rules
- Use other Internet communication methods

Lesson 12: The Internet 230
- Define the Internet
- Get connected
- Browse Web pages
- Work with Web Pages
- Search the Internet
- Internet Communications

Lesson 13: Security and Privacy 250
- Know how to keep yourself safe
- Learn about computer crime
- Keep safe from computer viruses
- Learn how to browse the Internet safely
- Learn environmental-friendly computing

IC[3]-1: COMPUTING FUNDAMENTALS EXERCISES 266

IC[3]-2: KEY APPLICATIONS EXERCISES 274

IC[3]-3: LIVING ONLINE EXERCISES 302

GLOSSARY 308

INDEX 336

INTRODUCTION

You may not think of it, but you are living during a time of revolution. Just like the Industrial Revolution changed how people worked and lived, the computer revolution is doing the same. Personal computers weren't even sold until the start of the 1980s. Now they are in businesses and homes across the world.

Computers affect every area of our lives, and they will continue to do so in existing and new ways. Computers have also changed how we work. This applies not just to the equipment we use (typewriters vs. computers, memos vs. e-mail), but also to work style. Consider these other elements:

- The introduction of the computer has made flexible work situations possible. More people can telecommute (work from home). Small businesses are booming.
- Workers have more ways to stay in touch: e-mail, pagers, cell phones, faxes.
- Portable computers, including notebooks or handheld (palm) devices, let you take your work with you.
- The Internet has opened an entire world of opportunity for promoting services and selling goods.

Computers and Work

No matter what industry you work in now or wish to work in sometime in the future, you can find some common tasks that are aided by computers. Here are some of the common tasks that a computer can help you manage:

- *Write*. You can jot notes about a project or idea. You can also use your computer to create documents — reports, term papers, manuscripts, letters, proposals, memos, outlines, and more.
- *Communicate.* You have several means of communicating with a computer, including via fax (if you have a fax modem) or through e-mail.
- *Manage contacts.* You can keep track of friends, clients, customers, and business associates using contact management software and your computer.
- *Manage money.* You can track expenses, tally income, plan for taxes, and more using your computer and a spreadsheet program or a specialized program like Quicken.
- *Plan and manage your schedule.* You can enter meetings, classes, and to-do items on a schedule, keeping track of not only the date and time, but also the results of activities.
- *Plan and manage a project with a variety of schedules and deadlines.* You can keep track of key project dates and plan the entire timeline for a project.

Introduction

Having an understanding of computers, therefore, becomes imperative to any kind of success. To start, you need to know what a computer is and the basics of how it operates. Then you need some background information about computer programs, what kinds there are, and what they are used for. Computers and the Internet are so intertwined that to use the Internet you need to understand not only the computer, but you also need to understand Internet concepts, such as Web browsing and electronic mail (e-mail). The goal of this book is to provide you with this information so that you are well versed in all the main computer concepts.

What This Book Contains

The book is divided into three parts. The three sections correspond to the three parts of the IC³ Exam. (You'll find more on IC³ is below.) You'll find these parts:

- **Part I: COMPUTING FUNDAMENTALS**, starts with an explanation of computers and how they are put to use. This part also includes lessons on the hardware, or physical, components of a computer, including the processor, memory, keyboard, mouse, printer, modem, and drives.
- **Part II: KEY APPLICATIONS**, focuses on the programs you use on the computer. These programs are what make the computer such a versatile tool. Starting with the system software (called operating system), this part also covers word processing, spreadsheets, databases, graphics, presentations and publishing, and programming.
- **Part 3: LIVING ONLINE**, explains how you can expand a single PC to a world of PCs and covers both Internet basics and networking.

What is IC³?

The IC³ standards is an internationally developed and recognized symbol of digital literacy. The objectives are created by subject-area specialists from around the world. The IC³ standards represents the skills you need to get ahead in today's fast-paced technological world. The skills that IC³ standards cover are perfect for anyone entering current job markets or higher education programs.

Once you have mastered the IC³ skills covered in this text, you can take the IC³ Exam. Receiving this certification is a validation of your computer and Internet literacy skills. Visit **www.certiport.com** for information on locating a testing center.

Introduction

How This Book Helps You

This book contains several features to help you master the key concepts of computing. In particular, you'll find these elements:

- *Short, concise lessons.* Each lesson has several clearly defined objectives and focuses on a single topic. Figures illustrate key concepts, and the ending summary helps you to review what you've learned.
- *Up-to-date content.* The book covers the latest technology and programs so that you are well prepared as you further your education or get ready for the
- *Helpful tips.* Each lesson also includes tips, how-to advice, troubleshooting information, or interesting asides that add another layer of knowledge.
- *Covers all IC³ objectives.* All of the IC³ skills and concepts are covered. Refer to the Exam Correlation starting on page viii.
- *Prepares students to take the IC³ Exam.* Additional correlated hands-on exercises are included starting on page 266. Skills are mastered through repetition.

Instructor's Resource Material

In addition to the student text, an Instructor's Resource CD-ROM is available. The CD contains teaching material, including teaching tips, hints, strategies, and shortcuts. The CD also includes tests that can be printed out and distributed and PowerPoint slides correlated to the text. (ISBN: 0-13-186892-6)

IC³ EXAM OBJECTIVES

Following is a list of the exam objectives with reference to where the objectives are covered. In addition to the lessons referenced below, turn to the correlated exam exercises beginning on page 266 for additional practice.

IC³ Computing Fundamentals - 2005 Exam Correlation

Domain 1.0: Computer Hardware This domain includes the knowledge and skills required to identify different types of computers and computing devices, the components of a personal computer (including internal components such as microprocessors) and how these components function and interact. The domain also includes the knowledge and skills relating to computer storage, performance and maintenance procedures.

- **Objective 1.1** Identify types of computers, how they process information and how individual computers interact with other computing systems and devices.

    Reference: Lessons 1 - 3

- **Objective 1.2** Identify the function of computer hardware components.

    Reference: Lessons 1 - 3

- **Objective 1.3** Identify the factors that go into an individual or organizational decision on how to purchase computer equipment.

    Reference: Lessons 1 - 3

- **Objective 1.4** Identify how to maintain computer equipment and solve common problems relating to computer hardware.

    Reference: Lessons 1 - 3

Domain 2.0: Computer Software This domain includes the knowledge and skills required to identify how software works, software categories such as operating systems, applications and utilities, fundamental concepts and best uses of each type of software, and which application is best used for a specific purpose.

- **Objective 2.1** Identify how software and hardware work together to perform computing tasks and how software is developed and upgraded.

    Reference: Lesson 4

- **Objective 2.2** Identify different types of software, general concepts relating to software categories, and the tasks to which each type of software is most suited or not suited.

    Reference: Lesson 4

IC³ Exam Objectives

Domain 3.0: Using an Operating System This domain includes the knowledge and skills required to perform the most frequently used functions of an operating system. Elements include the ability to install and run software, control the workspace (desktop), perform file management and change system settings (display, date and time settings, etc.). For purposes of this domain, the operating system used as an example for performance based questions is Windows, the most popular PC operating system.

- **Objective 3.1** Identify what an operating system is and how it works, and solve common problems related to operating systems.

  Reference: Lesson 5

- **Objective 3.2** Manipulate and control the Windows desktop, files and disks.

  Reference: Lesson 5

- **Objective 3.3** Identify how to change system settings, install and remove software.

  Reference: Lesson 5

IC³ Key Applications - 2005 Exam Correlation

Domain 1.0: Common Program Functions This domain includes the knowledge and skills required to perform functions common to all Windows applications with an emphasis on the common functionality of the Microsoft Office applications Word, Excel and PowerPoint. Skills and knowledge covered in this domain will concentrate on those features considered basic and — to the largest extent possible — applicable to all Windows-based word processors, spreadsheets and presentation programs. Elements include the ability to start and exit either the Word or Excel application, modify the display of toolbars and other on-screen elements, use online help, and perform file management, editing, formatting and printing functions common to Word, Excel, PowerPoint and most Windows applications.

- **Objective 1.1** Be able to start and exit a Windows application and utilize sources of online help.

  Reference: Lesson 6

- **Objective 1.2** Identify common on-screen elements of Windows applications, change application settings and manage files within an application.

  Reference: Lesson 6

- **Objective 1.3** Perform common editing and formatting functions.

  Reference: Lesson 6

- **Objective 1.4** Perform common printing functions.

  Reference: Lesson 6

IC³ Exam Objectives

Domain 2.0: Word Processing Functions This domain includes the knowledge and skills required to perform functions specific to creating documents with a word processor (as opposed to common functions such as those identified in Domain 1: Common Program Functions). Elements include paragraph formatting (including line spacing, indenting and creating bulleted or numbered lists), document formatting (including headers and footers), applying styles and other automatic formatting options, creating tables, applying borders and shading to text and tables

- **Objective 2.1** Be able to format text and documents including the ability to use automatic formatting tools.

  Reference: Lesson 7

- **Objective 2.2** Be able to insert, edit, and format tables in a document.

  Reference: Lesson 7

Domain 3.0: Spreadsheet Functions This domain includes the knowledge and skills required to analyze information in an electronic spreadsheet and to format information using functions specific to spreadsheet formatting (as opposed to common formatting functions included in Domain 1). Elements include the ability to use formulas and functions, sort data, modify the structure of an electronic worksheet, and edit and format data in worksheet cells. Elements also include the ability to display information graphically using charts, and to analyze worksheet data as it appears in tables or graphs.

- **Objective 3.1** Be able to modify worksheet data and structure and format data in a worksheet.

  Reference: Lesson 8

- **Objective 3.2** Be able to sort data, manipulate data using formulas and functions and add and modify charts in a worksheet.

  Reference: Lesson 8

Domain 4.0: Communicating with Presentation Software This domain includes the knowledge and skills required to communicate effectively with presentation software such as Microsoft PowerPoint, and to use simple functions specific to creating and editing presentations (as opposed to common functions included in Domain 1: Common Program Functions). Elements include the ability to create and modify slides in a presentation, create different types of presentation output and identify the most effective ways to use a presentation program to communicate with others

- **Objective 4.1** Be able to create and format simple presentations.

  Reference: Lesson 9

IC³ Living Online - 2005 Exam Correlation

Domain 1.0: Networks and the Internet This domain includes the knowledge of common terminology associated with computer networks and the Internet, components and benefits of networked computers, the difference between different types of networks (for example, LAN and WAN), and how computer networks fit into other communications networks (like the telephone network and the Internet).

- **Objective 1.1** Identify network fundamentals and the benefits and risks of network computing.

  Reference: Lesson 10

- **Objective 1.2** Identify the relationship between computer networks, other communications networks (like the telephone network) and the Internet.

  Reference: Lesson 10

Domain 2.0: Electronic Mail This domain includes the knowledge and skills required to identify how electronic mail works, the makeup of an e-mail address and other communications methods such as instant messaging. The domain also includes the ability to use an electronic mail software package and to identify the rules of the road (i.e., netiquette) regarding the use of electronic mail.

- **Objective 2.1** Identify how electronic mail works.

  Reference: Lesson 11

- **Objective 2.2** Identify how to use an electronic mail application.

  Reference: Lesson 11

- **Objective 2.3** Identify the appropriate use of e-mail and e-mail related netiquette.

  Reference: Lesson 11

Domain 3.0: Using the Internet This domain includes the knowledge and skills required to identify information and resources that are available on the Internet and use a Web browsing application. Elements include the ability to identify elements of Web pages and Web sites and how to determine the quality of information found online. Elements also include the ability to use a Web browsing application such as Microsoft Internet Explorer® to browse the Internet.

- **Objective 3.1** Identify different types of information sources on the Internet.

  Reference: Lesson 12

- **Objective 3.2** Be able to use a Web browsing application.

  Reference: Lesson 12

- **Objective 3.3** Be able to search the Internet for information.

  Reference: Lesson 12

Domain 4.0: The Impact of Computing and the Internet on Society This domain includes the knowledge and skills required to identify the benefits and risks of computing and the role of the Internet in many areas of society, from home and work to school and recreation. Elements include the ability to identify how computers and the Internet are used in different aspects of work, school, and home and how these areas of society are impacted by the availability of computer technology and online resources.

- **Objective 4.1** Identify how computers are used in different areas of work, school and home.

    Reference: Lesson 10

- **Objective 4.2** Identify the risks of using computer hardware and software.

    Reference: Lesson 13

- **Objective 4.3** Identify how to use computers and the Internet safely, legally, ethically, and responsibly.

    Reference: Lesson 13

IC³ and Certiport Information

 INTERNET AND COMPUTING CORE CERTIFICATION

YOUR FUTURE STARTS WITH IC³

IC³ ... WHAT IS IT?

IC³, or the Internet and Computing Core Certification program, is a global training and certification program providing proof to the world that you are:

- Equipped with the needed computer skills to excel in a digital world.
- Capable of using a broad range of computer technology - from basic hardware and software, to operating systems, applications and the Internet.
- Ready for the work employers, colleges and universities want to throw your way.
- Positioned to advance your career through additional computer certifications such as CompTIA's A+, and other desktop application exams.

IC³ ... WHY DO YOU NEED IT?

Employers, Colleges and Universities now realize that exposure to computers does not equal an understanding of computers. So now, more than ever, basic computer and Internet skills are being considered prerequisites for employment and higher education.

THIS IS WHERE IC³ HELPS!

IC³ provides specific guidelines for the knowledge and skills required to be a functional user of computer hardware, software, networks, and the Internet. It does this through three exams:

- Computing Fundamentals
- Key Applications
- Living Online

By passing the three IC³ exams, you have initiated yourself into today's digital world. You have also given yourself a globally accepted and validated credential that provides the proof employers or higher education institutions need.

Earn your IC³ certification today - visit www.certiport.com/ic3 to learn how.

Achieve • Distinguish • Advance

Certiport is a registered trademark of Certiport, Inc. in the United States and other countries.

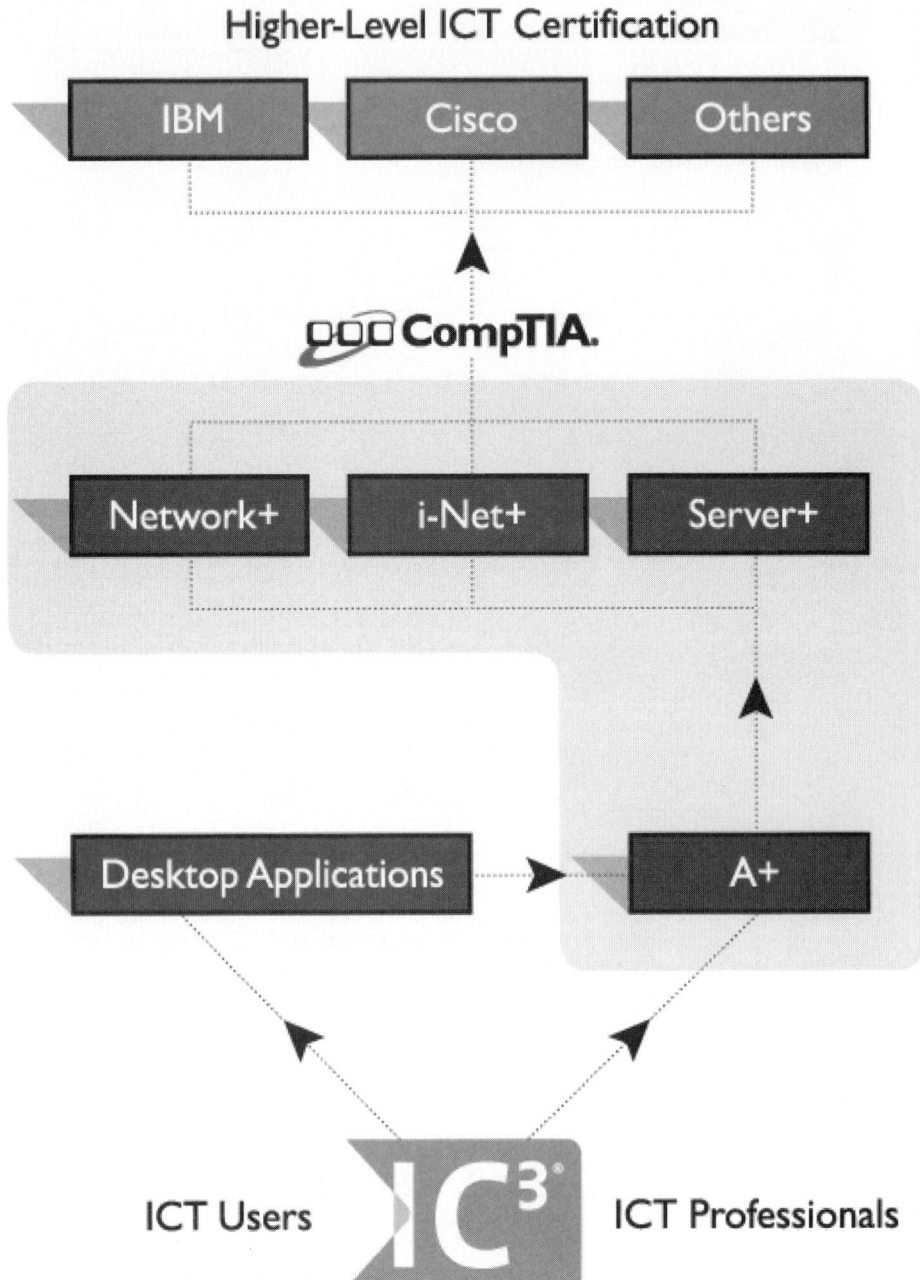

IC3 and Certiport Information

LESSON 1: DEFINING A COMPUTER

Objectives

➢ Review the history of computing
➢ List the types of computers
➢ Define a computer
➢ Describe the parts of a computer
➢ Understand the differences among computers
➢ Define computer processors
➢ Explain types of memory
➢ Buy, upgrade, and maintain your computer
➢ Troubleshoot computer problems

The Evolution of a Personal Computer

A hobbyist named Edward Roberts built the first personal computer. A picture of his Altair homemade computer appeared on the cover of *Popular Mechanics* and excited budding computer enthusiasts everywhere (see Figure 1.1). Roberts formed a company (MITS) and sold the first PC for $397. It came as a mail-order kit; you had to put it together. The system boasted 1K of memory, a processor with speed up to 2MHz, and didn't have a monitor or keyboard. You could flip switches and make lights blink. That was 1975, just 30 years ago.

Figure 1.1. The Altair 8800 computer.

Lesson 1
Defining a Computer

When IBM entered the picture and started selling its first personal computer (1981), the personal computer became a little easier to use. A standard computer had 64K of RAM, a 5¼" floppy drive, a monitor (monochrome), a keyboard, and a 20M hard drive. These computers cost anywhere from $3,000 to $15,000. Computers did not have sound cards or mice (at least not IBM PCs), and DOS was the main operating system. This was just 24 years ago.

 Before hard disks: The hard disk was a novelty. Before hard disks, programs came on floppy disks, and you had to swap disks in and out to use the program and save your data. A hard disk was not standard equipment.

Let's jump ahead to the year 2005, where a typical computer system has 256M or more of RAM, an 80G (or larger) hard drive, 19" monitor, modem, sound card and speakers, and speeds up to 3.6 GHz. And computer technology continues to evolve and at this quick speed. New technology is constantly being introduced to the market to make computers faster, more reliable, more affordable, and more user-friendly. Let's take a look at the different types of computers and how they are used.

Types of Computers

One way computers vary is size, and you will encounter many different types of computers, as described in this section.

PERSONAL OR MICROCOMPUTERS

Most homes and businesses have personal computers, also called PCs or microcomputers. In this category, you may find models that sit on your desktop and are horizontal (see Figure 1.2). Or you can find tower models that sit on the floor and are upright (vertical).

Figure 1.2. Desktop and tower PCs are the most popular today.

PORTABLE OR LAPTOP COMPUTERS

Many people travel or work outside an office. For these people, portable computers are popular. This type of computer runs on batteries and can be carried with you. Portable computers encompass a variety of computer types, which vary by size. Here are the most common types:

- *Notebook.* As its name implies, notebook computers are roughly the size of a notebook. They differ in size and weight. The keyboard and display are connected, the keyboard is smaller, and the notebook may use a special pointing device such as a touchpad. This type of computer may also be called a laptop (see Figure 1.3).

- *PowerBook and iBook.* These are the names of the most popular Macintosh portables.

Figure 1.3. Notebook PCs are portable, weighing anywhere from 5 to 10 pounds.

 Smaller is not cheaper: Just because a notebook computer is smaller does not mean it is less expensive. In fact, this type of computer costs more than a comparable desktop model. Why? The components used are more expensive.

- *PDAs (personal digital assistants).* This type of computer is a handheld device and is often used in conjunction with a desktop or other PC. For instance, you might use a PDA to keep track of appointments and notes. You can then download (copy) the information from your PDA to your desktop or notebook computer. This device may have a special keyboard; some use a pen or stylus for entering data. You may also hear this type of computer called a palmtop. Figure 1.4 shows a PDA.

Lesson 1
Defining a Computer
Learning Computer Concepts

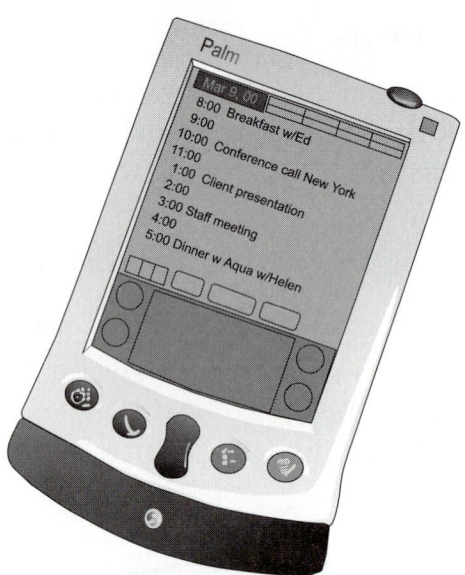

Figure 1.4. PDAs are useful for special-purpose applications, such as for keeping track of appointments or notes.

 Phone, e-mail, and fax: Many PDAs include capabilities that let it function as a cell phone, pager, fax, or even scanner. You may also be able to send and receive e-mail. This type of PDA uses infrared light to communicate with other computer systems.

 Cell phones. Many cell phones are also integrating other features such as the ability to take pictures, download weather or other information from the Internet, and store information.

NETWORKS

To share information and programs, computers can be linked together into a network. Networks that are housed in a small geographic area (such as within one office) are called LANs (local area networks). These may be connected via cabling or telephone wires. Networks that span a wide geographic area (perhaps across several sites, even states) are called WANs (wide area networks). Wireless networking has also become very popular. Rather than connect the computer via cabling, you can set up a wireless hub that can communicate without being physically connected, but instead through wireless transmission. You can find more about the different types of networks in Lesson 10.

The main computer of a network is called the server. This computer is the most powerful, houses common programs and data files, and may provide access to shared devices, such as a network printer. The server also stores the network operating system that controls access to the programs, files, and devices on the network. Computers connected to the server are called clients.

Learning Computer Concepts Lesson 1
Defining a Computer

WORKSTATIONS

A more powerful type of desktop or PC may be referred to as a workstation. Popular workstation manufacturers include Sun, IBM, Silicon Graphics, and Hewlett-Packard. These computers are a step up from a microcomputer but not quite as powerful as a minicomputer. They are commonly used by professionals whose jobs require a lot of computation power, including engineers, scientists, and graphic artists.

MINI AND MAINFRAMES

A mainframe is a large computer that is capable of processing large amounts of data very quickly. A minicomputer is similar to a mainframe, only it cannot handle as much data. Both provide data capabilities for storage and handling beyond those of a desktop PC.

You can find mini and mainframe computers in government and business. For instance, the IRS has a mainframe for tax information. Your state driver's license branch houses its information on a mainframe. University computers are often mainframes. Banks, science labs, insurance companies, and other large businesses use mainframes.

Other computers, called terminals, are networked to the mainframe or minicomputer. You can gain access to the information on the mainframe or minicomputer through these terminals. These might be regular desktop computers, laptops, or plain terminals (not a standalone computer).

SUPERCOMPUTERS

The biggest and most expensive computer is called a supercomputer, and it exponentially expands the speed, power, and storage capacity of even mainframe computers. You'll find these computers in high-tech areas, such as the military, nuclear weapons, space programs, weather forecasting, and similar fields.

What is a Computer?

A computer is an appliance. What makes it different than other appliances, say like a refrigerator, is that there's not one single use for a computer. It's a versatile tool that can be used for many tasks.

WHAT CAN YOU DO WITH A COMPUTER?

Consider just some of the things you can do with a computer:

- *Create documents*. You can use your computer to create any number of documents: letters, memos, newsletters, brochures, presentations, budgets, income and profit statements, invitations, greeting cards, stationery, invoices, order forms, recipes, term papers, grading lists, phone lists, grocery lists, reports, manuscripts, illustrations, photographs, blueprints, design plans, advertisements, and many, many other types of documents. Document creation is probably the most common use for a computer.

- *Manage data.* Computers simplify the entry, update, and maintenance of data. This may be anything from a simple address book to a complex data order system including products, inventory, orders, and customers. Any collection of information (class schedule, student list, product inventory, video collection, etc.) can best be managed with a computer.

- *Connect to the Internet.* The Internet is a network of networks, and you can connect to this resource and send electronic messages (e-mail), chat with other people, display Web sites (information presented in a graphic format so that it is inviting, easy to browse, and linked to related information), participate in discussions, and more. For more information on connecting to the Internet, see Lesson 12.

- *Play games.* You can use computers to have fun, whether that be playing an arcade game like pinball or a card game like Solitaire. You might enjoy role-playing games, or you might fancy flight simulators. You can find games for just about any activity.

- *Get information.* The computer can also be a resource for information. You might use a computer encyclopedia to research data or look up articles and maps in an atlas. In addition to resources in programs or CDs, you can also find a wealth of information on the Internet, including current news, stock prices, articles, tips and advice, job hunting resources, homework help, and more.

- *Learn a new skill.* You can use a computer to learn how to type or learn a foreign language. You can find educational software geared toward children, teaching a child to read, for instance, as well as software geared for adults.

- *Shopping.* Use of the Internet for commerce and shopping is changing the retail sales marketplace. You can search for any type of item, purchase it, and have it delivered to your home. You can comparison shop and make sure you get the best deal.

WHAT BENEFITS DO YOU GET FROM COMPUTERS?

Computers can be used for many types of tasks, and they offer some specific benefits over the paper method for accomplishing these tasks. In general, a computer offers these benefits:

- *Error-free calculations.* A computer has incredible computing power. Not only can it quickly compute calculations, but it will not make a mistake when doing so. Whether calculating the total of a company's sales or computing precise measurements for an entire building, a computer simplifies any type of calculation. Note, though, that if you enter an incorrect value, that *will* cause inaccurate results.

- *Speed.* Not only does the computer not make mistakes, but it can perform computations in milliseconds, much quicker than a blink of an eye. It can also perform several tasks at once.

- *Flexibility*. A computer is flexible because it can be used for a variety of tasks. And a computer provides you a great deal of flexibility in working with the data you enter. As an example, consider an address list. With a computer, you can easily sort the list in any order. You can delete entries you no longer need and add new entries. You can quickly find a particular entry, and you can update an entry to keep the information current. The computer provides flexibility and versatility in working with the data you enter.
- *Expandability*. A computer also enables you to expand its current components by adding new features such as better sound, TV reception, a network, and more.
- *Storage*. A computer can store information digitally. One computer can store entire filing systems of paper data. Saving space is one benefit, but you can also find and retrieve data quickly from a computer.
- *Consistency and repetition*. A computer can handle repetitive tasks easily, accurately, and quickly. It won't get bored or distracted. It will provide the same quality on the first task as on the ten thousandth.

How a Computer Works

The great thing about a computer is that you don't really have to know how it works to use a computer. You don't know what makes a car work, do you? Many beginning users are intimidated by computers because they don't know how it works, and they think they will break it. Not true.

You don't need to know complex programming information to use a computer. You do not need mechanical information about how the components inside work. You simply have to understand a few key concepts of computing.

Two things work together to make a computer: the hardware and the software, as described in this section.

 Understand binary information. A computer is basically a collection of electronic circuits, and these circuits can be on or off (open or closed). The two states of the circuit are represented by two digits, 0 and 1. Hence you may hear the term binary system when referring to a computer. It may seem impossible to take two states and use it to effect, but by combining multiple bits (0 or 1), you can represent any character or number.

HARDWARE

Hardware consists of the physical components that make up a computer. Most common systems have a monitor (the TV-like thing), a keyboard (which you type on), a mouse (for selecting items), speakers, and a system unit (see Figure 1.5). The system unit is the box, and inside this box is where you find the electronic wizardry like the CPU and memory. You'll read more about the system unit and other hardware components later in this lesson.

Lesson 1
Defining a Computer

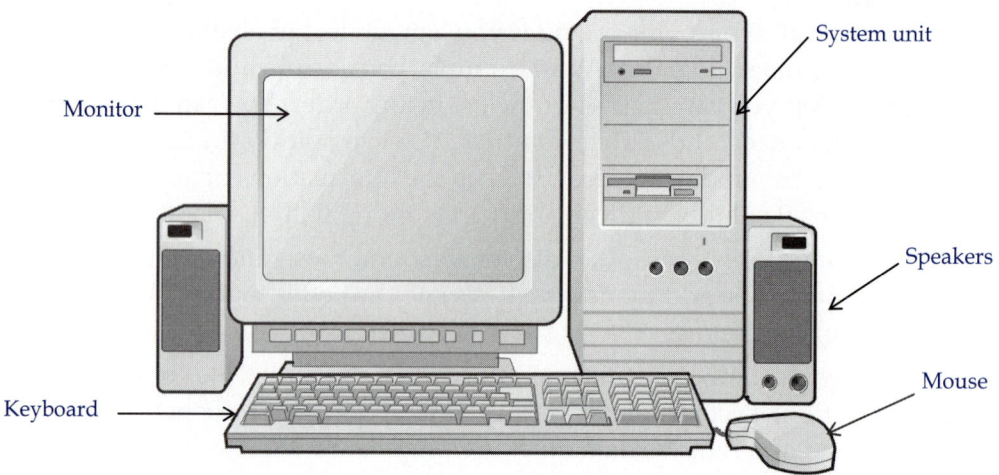

Figure 1.5. A computer system consists of a system unit, monitor, keyboard, and mouse.

SOFTWARE

The hardware can't do much without software. Software is a set of programming instructions that you use to accomplish a certain task. When referring to software, you may hear the terms program, application, software, or any combination of these terms (software application, for instance). They all mean the same thing.

Programs are designed for different purposes. For example, a word processing program is designed to facilitate creating documents (letters, memos, reports, and so on). A spreadsheet program is used to create worksheets, such as budgets, expense records, and other documents dealing mostly with some type of numeric value. A database program is used to store, edit, and manipulate data, such as an address list or a schedule of classes. There are many other types of software for different functions as well. For instance, system software runs the computer, and antivirus software guards against virus contamination. You learn more about application software in Lessons 4 and 6.

When dealing with software, keep these main concepts in mind:

- All computers come with an operating system, a special type of software described in the next section.
- New computers may also come bundled with application software. The programs that are provided will vary from system to system.
- You can purchase new programs and install them onto your computer. When you install a program, you copy the necessary program files from the program discs (from a CD) to your hard drive. You also set up access to these programs. For Windows systems, you add the program to your Start menu and/or create a shortcut icon to the program.

OPERATING SYSTEM

All computers require an operating system to work. New computers come with an operating system. You can also upgrade the operating system on your computer.

The operating system handles common tasks of using a computer, including starting the computer, starting a program, printing a document, and storing a file. The operating system takes your commands and translates them into language that the hardware can understand. As an example, you select the Save command to save a document; the operating system then handles the process of actually writing the document to a disk and also keeping track of where it is stored.

The most popular operating system is Microsoft Windows. Windows XP Home is the most common operating system for home computers. Windows XP also has a Professional edition that provides features for businesses and other more advanced users.

If you have a Macintosh computer, your computer will use the Macintosh operating system; the most current edition is called Mac OS X Panther.

WEB: Get information on the latest versions of Microsoft Windows at www.microsoft.com/windows. For information on Macintosh products and its operating system, see www.apple.com.

You can read more about Windows and other popular operating systems in Lesson 5.

Hardware Defined

As mentioned, most computer systems consist of these key hardware components:

- The system unit
- CPU
- The monitor
- The keyboard
- The mouse
- Speakers

This section describes each of these elements.

OUTSIDE THE SYSTEM UNIT: POWER BUTTONS AND DRIVE ACCESS

The system unit is the box-like item that usually sits on your desktop or stands on the floor. All of the other components are connected to the system unit via cables. Also, the system unit has a power plug, which you plug into an electrical outlet.

If you take a look at the outside of the system unit, you see buttons for turning on and resetting the computer as well as slots. These slots provide access to the drives on your system; you can access your floppy drive, CD or DVD drive, and any other drives you may have, such as a ZIP drive or tape backup drive (see Figure 1.6).

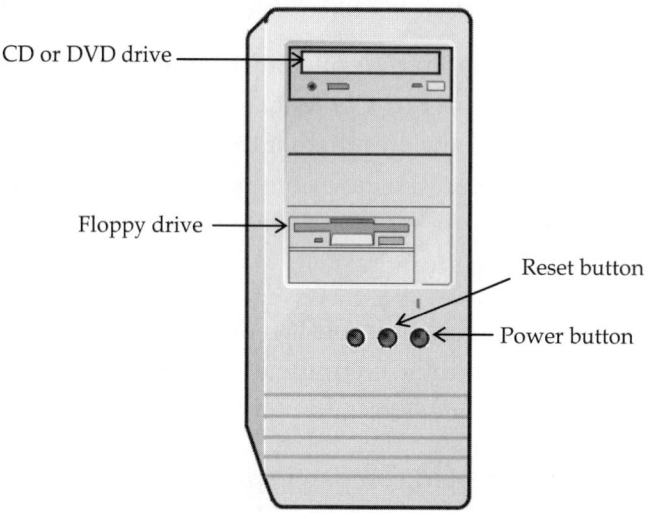

Figure 1.6. The front of the system unit has access to your floppy drive and CD or DVD drive.

In addition to these drives, most computers have at least one hard drive inside the system unit. (The next section describes this drive.) Drives provide a place to store programs and data. The floppy drives are used mostly to transport and backup files. For instance, you can copy a document onto a floppy drive from work to take home. Newer computers do not come with a floppy drive, but instead use CD discs for storing data. (You learn more about different drive types in Lesson 2.) You can select to add a floppy drive as part of a new computer, and you might do this if you often share files or have used floppy disks to store information.

CD and DVD drives are used to store programs and collections of information. Most programs are distributed on a CD disc. You can also find collections of information (such as an encyclopedia or collection of clip art) on CDs. You can insert the CD into the drive, and then run the programs on the CD, access the information, and copy files from the CD, as needed.

 Read and write: Initially most CD-ROM drives were for reading information only; they could be used to access information and copy that information, but you could not write information to them (save a document to a CD for instance). Now most CDs allow both reading and writing. You can read more about different types of CDs in Lesson 2.

The outside of the computer also provides access to ports (think plugs). The type of ports you have and their use varies depending on your system. Here are the most common port types:

- *Keyboard and mouse ports.* These ports are used to connect these input devices (covered in Lesson 3). If you have an optical mouse, your computer will have an infrared port so that the mouse can communicate with the computer.
- *Monitor port.* This port is used to plug your monitor into the system unit. Monitors are covered in more detail in Lesson 3.
- *Parallel port.* This port is the biggest and has lots of pins. Usually your printer connects to your computer with a cable. One end of the cable plugs into the printer, and the other end plugs into the parallel port.

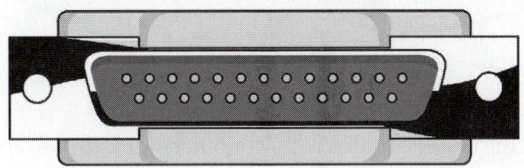

Figure 1.7. This is called a parallel port because communications go both ways along the cable.

- *Serial port.* A serial port is smaller and doesn't have as many pins as a parallel port. Some printers connect to your computer via a serial port. You may also connect other devices such as a joystick (for playing games).
- *USB port.* The newest type of port is a USB port, and this is a small slot-like port. You may have several USB ports on the front and/or back of your computer. Some printers connect via a USB port. You can also attach other devices such as a digital camera, MP3 (music) player, and others.
- *Ethernet ports.* This type of port is used to connect your computer to a network. For more information on networking, see Lesson 10.
- *Telephone port.* If you have an internal modem, that card will have a telephone port. You can use this to connect to the Internet through the phone lines.
- *MIDI port.* This is a special type of port used to connect musical instruments to the computer.

INSIDE THE SYSTEM UNIT: CPU, MEMORY, DRIVES, AND SPEAKERS

Inside the system unit is where the most important components of a computer are stored. These are stored in a case because they are sensitive electrical components that you don't need to handle. You'll find the CPU or central processing unit, memory, drives, and other electronic components inside the system unit (see Figure 1.8).

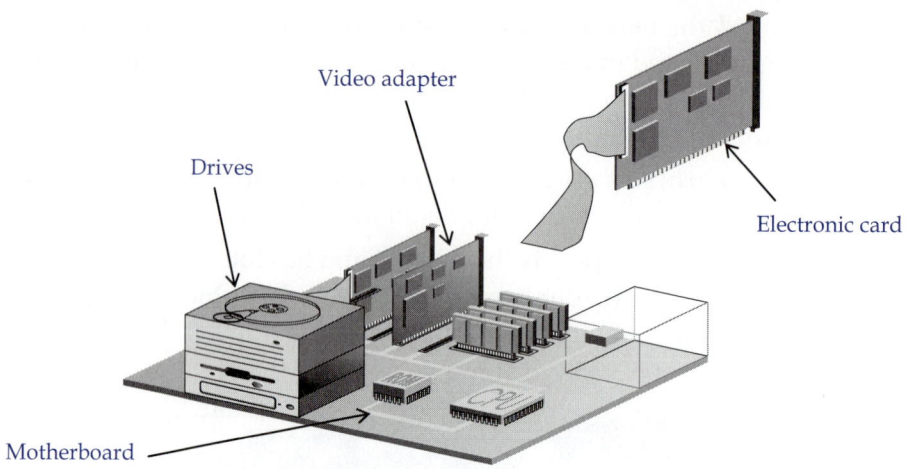

Figure 1.8. The inside of the system unit stores the motherboard, drives, and other electronic cards.

The brain of a computer is called the CPU or central processing unit or simply processor. This is a small wafer-size chip; you've probably heard of the most common chip maker (Intel). The processor is stored on the motherboard inside the system unit, and the processor determines the speed and power of your computer. Figure 1.9 shows an illustration of a motherboard. You can read more about processors later in this lesson.

 WEB: Visit the site for Intel (www.intel.com) to get the latest information on Intel's processors. Another popular company that makes processors is AMD. You can visit their site at www.amd.com.

Figure 1.9. The motherboard houses the processor and memory; other components are connected to the motherboard via cables.

The motherboard is the main electronic board inside the system unit, and all the devices for a computer are connected to this motherboard (see Figure 1.9). In addition to the processor, the motherboard also houses the memory. These are also electronic chips. Memory is the temporary storage place for programs and documents that are open, that is, those you are currently working on. Systems vary in the type and amount of memory.

Add memory: A common system upgrade is to add more memory. You can find more information on types of memory and how it affects system performance later in this lesson.

You gain access to some drives from the front of the PC, but the drives themselves are housed inside the system unit. In addition to a floppy drive and CD or DVD drive, most computers have at least one hard drive. This is the primary storage space for programs and data. Some systems have more than one hard drive. All drives are connected to the motherboard via a cable.

The motherboard includes slots into which you insert electronic cards (also called add-on cards, expansion cards or boards, adapter cards, or interface cards). These cards expand the capabilities of your system. Here are some examples of expansion cards:

- *Video card.* For your PC to display programs and data, you need a monitor (for the actual display) and a video card. The video card handles the communication from the processor to the monitor. This card is plugged into the motherboard and has a port, which you can access from the back of the system unit. You connect the card to the monitor via a cable.
- *Modem card.* Modems are used to communicate via the telephone with other computers (most commonly, the Internet). While you can purchase external modems, most modems are internal devices, electronic cards inserted into an expansion slot in your computer. Part of the card is accessible from the back of the system unit. You can plug your phone line into the phone jack on this accessible part of the card.
- *Sound card and speakers.* To play sound on a PC, you need a sound card and speakers. A sound card is plugged into an expansion slot. Speakers are hooked up through the part of the card that fits through the back of the system unit.

The system unit also includes a power supply, which provides the power to these electronic components. You don't have to mess too much with a power supply, but one thing you should do is be sure you have some type of power protector to handle electrical spikes or power surges. To protect your PC from these, consider using a surge protector to protect against power spikes. Businesses may take this protection one step further and use an uninterruptible power supply (UPS). A UPS runs your PC from a battery, which is continually recharged by the electrical outlet. This type of power supply protects against power outages. A UPS is often used with a network server.

INPUT: KEYBOARD AND MOUSE

You need a way to communicate with your computer and you usually do that with two input devices: a keyboard and a mouse. A keyboard is pretty simple to understand (see Figure 1.10). You press the letters or numbers on the keyboard. You type not only to enter text but also to select commands, such as Save, Print, or Exit. There are other input devices, such as a light pen.

Lesson 1
Defining a Computer   **Learning Computer Concepts**

Figure 1.10. A keyboard includes numbers, letters, symbols, and other special keys.

When computers were initially introduced, the interface (what you saw and how you used them) was text- or command-based. You had to type commands to get the computer to do what you wanted. The operating system Microsoft Windows changed all that. Windows and Windows programs use a graphical user interface (called a GUI and pronounced "gooey"). Instead of typing commands, you can point to what you want. To enable pointing, a mouse was established as a standard component on a computer. A mouse is a pointing device, and you use it to select commands and data, start programs, and perform other tasks. Figure 1.11 shows an illustration of a mouse. You can learn more about the keyboard, mouse, and other input devices (such as digital cameras and touch screens) in Lesson 3.

 Macintosh sets standard: Macintosh computers have always had a graphical user interface and included a mouse. Windows, in fact, imitated the Macintosh.

Figure 1.11. You use the mouse as a pointing device to select commands and text.

OUTPUT: MONITORS AND PRINTERS

Believe it or not, the first computer did not have a display. It was a box with a series of lights and switches on the front. You programmed the computer by flipping switches, and you could tell what was happening by the flashing of the lights. Of course, a display or monitor was soon added and is now an integral part of a computer. The monitor screen displays programs, error messages, and results of your input from the keyboard and/or mouse.

A monitor is actually two components: the TV-like thing and the electronic card housed inside the system unit. You may hear this card referred to as a graphics adapter.

To make paper copies of the documents you create, you need a printer. The printer is connected to the PC via a cable. You plug the printer into one of the ports (parallel, serial, or USB depending on the type of printer). Monitors and printers, as well as other output devices (projectors, for instance), are covered in more detail in Lesson 3.

What Makes a Computer Different

Now that you know what pieces and parts make up a computer, you may wonder how can they be so different? Why does one computer cost $500 and another $3,000? This section describes some of the ways that computers differ.

SYSTEM TYPE

The two most common types of computers are IBM and compatibles (often referred to generically as PCs) and Macintosh computers. The first PC was created by IBM, but other companies immediately began making the same computer. These were called clones or IBM-compatibles. While IBM may have initially dominated the personal computing market, it no longer does. Now the market is shared by companies such as Dell, Micron, Compaq, Gateway, and others. Most computers sold today are PCs.

 WEB: Visit some computer sites such as Dell (www.dell.com) or Gateway (www.gateway.com). Look at the resources they provide for computer buyers as well as current computer users.

At the dawn of the computing era, another company offered a different type of computer, one that did not look like the original PCs and did not have any clones. This type of computer is called Macintosh and was created by a company called Apple. Macintosh computers still have a small share of the entire personal computing market. These computers are especially popular in graphics-intensive fields such as desktop publishing, illustrations, and other publishing fields.

PCs and Macs don't differ in how they work or what you can do with them. They differ in the operating system. PCs, as mentioned, most often run Microsoft Windows. Macs use an operating system called simply System (the version name varies). It used to be that you could not open PC files on a Macintosh and vice versa, but the two have become more compatible and some systems may be able to read both types of disks.

POWER AND SPEED

If you price new computers, you'll find they vary in price even though two models may look exactly the same. Why? Because computers can vary in their processing power and speed.

Speed is determined by several factors including the type of processor, amount of memory, and other technical elements. Power is also determined by the processor. You can get a better understanding of speed and power by reading the sections on processors and memory.

ADD-ONS

Computers also vary in the other types of components they include. For instance, a computer may include a modem (for connecting to the Internet), sound card and speakers, and special drives such as CD or DVD drive. As a component becomes popular, it usually becomes a standard part of a PC. For instance, initially computers were not sold with modems, CD drives, or sound cards. You could purchase and add these components. Because a modem, sound card, and CD or DVD drive are so integral to computer use now, most new computers are sold with them as part of the standard package.

Newer add-ons include a digital camera, video or cable connections, scanners, and special game ports and devices (joystick or flight yoke for instance). You can learn more about these features in later lessons in this book.

SIZE

Another way computers differ is in size. Desktop computers fit on your desktop and are the most common system type sold. For portable computers, you can purchase notebook or handheld computers.

Processors in More Detail

A processor is the main electronic chip in a computer. The processor determines the speed and power of a PC. It is, in effect, the computer's "brain." This chip is part of the motherboard, the main circuit board inside the system unit. For all the pertinent facts about processors, read this section.

HOW PROCESSORS WORK

A processor is several millions of transistors etched onto a computer chip. The processor determines how the computer processes data and handles instructions (see Figure 1.12). Computers recognize the state of each transistor as on or off. This system is called binary because it uses two digits to represent the two states: 0 for off and 1 for on. One switch is called a bit (binary digit) and is the smallest unit of data.

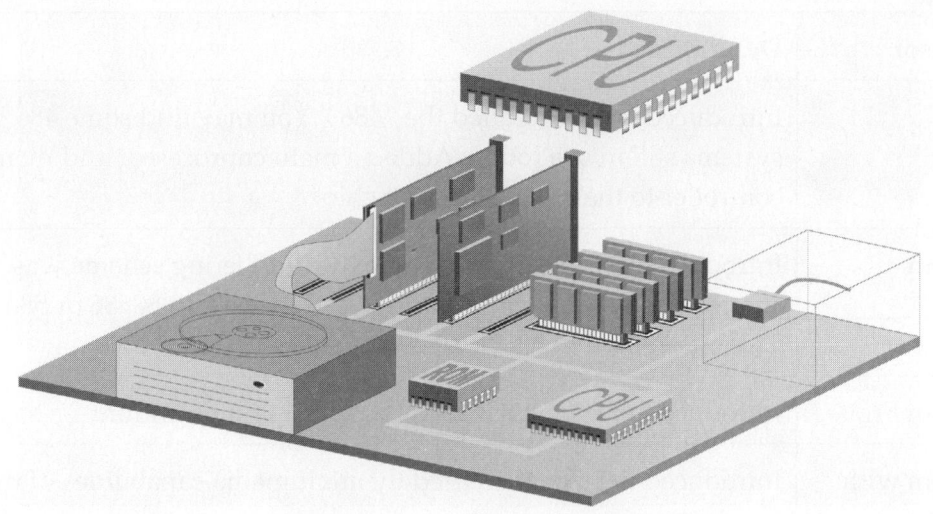

Figure 1.12. A computer processor.

 Base 2: Computers use a Base 2 number system, combining digits to represent numbers greater than or equal to 2. People use a Base 10 numbering system (1-10). When a number is greater than or equal to 10, we use more than one digit to represent that number.

To represent data, such as a letter, the computer groups together bits. A group of 8 bits is called a byte. You can arrange these 8 bits (one byte) into 256 possible combinations. This is important because each character in the alphabet (upper- and lowercase), number, and symbol on the keyboard (!, #, @, and so on) can be represented with one byte.

TYPES OF PROCESSORS

The first computers used processors manufactured by Intel; Intel is still the dominant processor manufacturer in the industry. Intel initially used a numbering scheme to name its processors; the higher the number, the more powerful the processor. Numbers were used until recently, when Intel started using a name. Learning the different types will help you determine the age and speed of any PCs you use. You can also use this information if you are thinking of purchasing a new or used PC.

Here's a brief rundown of the history of processor development:

Processor	Description
8086	Introduced in 1978 and used in the first PCs.
8088	Introduced in 1979 and used in the first IBM PCs.
80286	Introduced in 1982. Called the "286." Obsolete now.
80386	Introduced in 1985. Called the "386." Also obsolete.

Lesson 1
Defining a Computer

Processor	Description
80486	Introduced in 1989. Called the "486." You may find some 486 systems still in use today. Added a math coprocessor and memory controller to the main processor chip.
Pentium	Introduced in 1993. This is where the numbering scheme was changed to a name. The Pentium is effectively an 80586 or 586 chip. This chip is five times faster than a 486.
Pentium Pro	Introduced in 1996. Increased the speed of the Pentium.
Pentium with MMX	Introduced in 1997. Increased the multimedia capabilities of the Pentium.
Pentium II	Introduced in 1997. Increased the speed and added MMX technology to the Pentium.
Pentium III	Introduced in 1999, this chip offers speeds up to 800MHz. (See the section on speed.)
Pentium 4	The most current version of Intel's processors. You'll find that there are a variety of categories within the Pentium that detail technical information about the chipset, speed, and other elements, indicated with a complex numbering system. (Visit www.intel.com if you want complete information on all the various processors and technical details.) Just keep in mind that the higher performance of the processor, the higher the price of the computer.
Celeron	Provides features of the Pentium 4, but at a little slower speed. This chip is more affordable and less powerful.

 WEB: New processors are introduced periodically. For all the latest information, you can visit Intel's Web site at www.intel.com.

Intel used to be practically the only processor supplier, but now it's not uncommon to find computers that use processors (equally as good as the Pentium) from other companies (in particular AMD with its Athlon processor).

SPEED OF PROCESSORS

Older processors were measured in megahertz (millions of cycles per second). This speed is abbreviated MHz. Computers now are much faster and are measured in gigahertz GHz (billions of cycles per second). Just keep in mind the higher the number, the faster the clock speed (and the more expensive the computer). One of the ways that processors differ is in the maximum speed you can achieve. Here's a breakdown of clock speeds by processors:

Processor	Speeds
Pentium II	233MHz, 266MHz, 300MHz, 350MHz, and 400MHz
Celeron	400MHz, 433MHz, 466MHz, 500MHz, 533MHz
Pentium III	450MHz, 500MHz, 533MHz, 550MHz, 600MHz, 650MHz, and 1000MHz (also abbreviated 1 G Hz)
Pentium 4	From 2 GHz up to roughly 3.6 GHz. Expect this speed to keep increasing and for new Pentium chips to have even higher speeds.

Moore's Law: The evolution of processors is summed up by Moore's Law. Basically, the CPU power doubles every 18 months. This fact was observed by Intel founder Gordon Moore.

You'll see this speed and other processor features advertised in brochures, Web sites, and print ads for new computers. Just keep this in mind (from Intel's Web site): "A higher number within a processor family can indicate more processor features, more of a specific processor feature, or a change in architecture."

Clock speed doesn't keep time: A system clock is not used to keep time, but is a crystal that pulsates at a fixed interval. These digital pulses time and synchronize the tasks performed by the processor.

OTHER WAYS PROCESSORS DIFFER

Speed is probably the most hyped feature of a processor, and the one consumers focus on, but processors differ in other ways, as listed here:

- *Design or architecture of the chip.* The design of the chip is called the architecture and at its most basic is a measure of the number of transistors on the chip. To compare, the 386 computers had 320,000 transistors, and the 486 included 1.2 million. The Pentium has 3.1 million, and Pentium II includes 7.5 million! The more transistors, the faster the processing.
- *Cache.* A temporary storage area for frequently accessed or recently accessed data. Cache size is measured in megabytes (MB) or kilobytes (KB), and the bigger the cache size the better the performance/speed of the computer.
- *Front side bus.* The processor is connected via a set of wires (called the address bus) to the memory and other key components in your system. This speed is measured in GHz or MHz.
- *Chipset.* Intel defines the chipset in this way: "The chipset is the heart of the PC. It connects the processor, memory and other components, and moves data throughout the system, directly affecting overall system performance."

The chipset includes lots of technical details about the system bus, for instance. Again, keep in mind that the more complex the chipset, the better the performance (and the more expensive the computer).

OTHER CHIP MAKERS

Intel is the most popular processor manufacturer, but it has gotten competition in recent years. You can also find systems with processors from AMD (Advanced Micro Devices) and other companies. These companies offer processors similar in speed and features to those of Intel.

As mentioned, Macintosh computers use a different type of processor, initially made by Motorola. Motorola used a different numbering scheme, but the basic measurements of speed and registers apply. The first chips were named 68000, 68010, and 68030 and were introduced in 1979, 1983, and 1984, respectively. These chips had a 32-bit register size. In the early 1990s more features were added, speed was increased, and the register size was increased to 64-bit. Models 68040 and 68060 were introduced at this time. Then came models MPC 740 and MPC 860 with a 128-bit register size.

Current Mac systems use a PowerPC G5 processor with speeds up to 4 GHz and built-in graphic enhancements.

WEB: For information on chips used in Macintosh systems, visit www.apple.com.

Memory in Detail

Next to processors, the most important component of a computer is memory. Memory is another determining factor in speed and performance. The more memory, the faster the computer (and the more expensive). This section explains the different types of memory and how it works.

HOW MEMORY WORKS

The processor stores basic instructions, but it cannot store programs or data. To store this information, the processor needs a working area; this working area is the computer's memory, called RAM. Memory are chips on the motherboard or on a small circuit board that is plugged into the motherboard (see Figure 1.13).

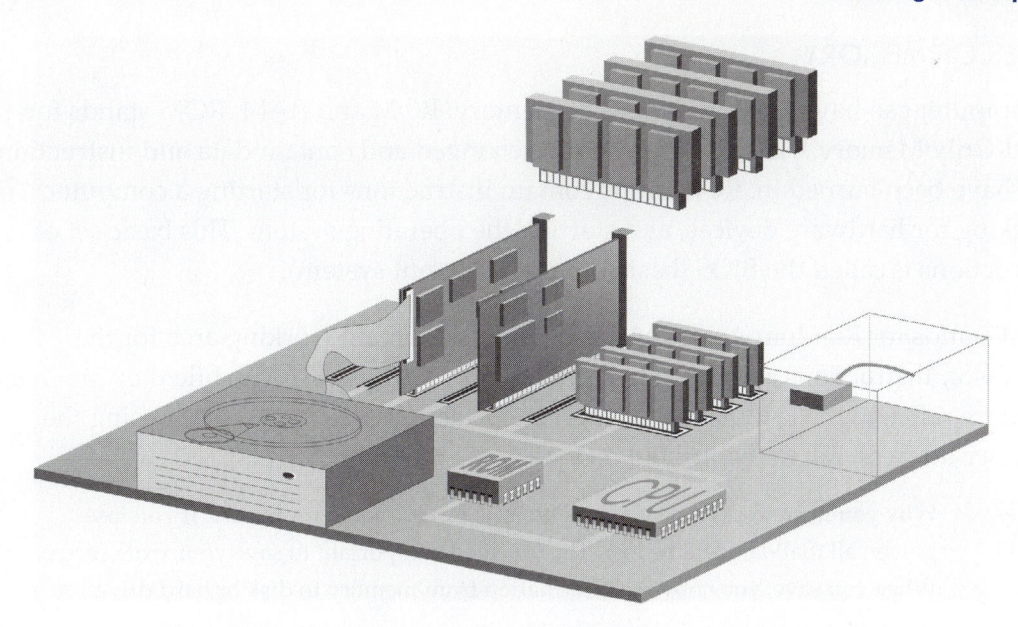

Figure 1.13. Memory is housed on the motherboard as chips or as a separate circuit board connected to the motherboard.

Data and information are stored in memory at specific locations, identified by a memory address. Using the address, the processor can store, retrieve, and release data from the different memory addresses. The amount of data that can be stored at one address varies, but you can generally estimate the storage to be one byte (about one character).

The processor sends requests for data (the memory address) along the address bus to memory. Data is then sent back to the processor through the data bus (see Figure 1.14). As a simple example, here's how this request works: the processor says; "Send me what's in mailbox 2," and then memory sends back the contents of that mailbox.

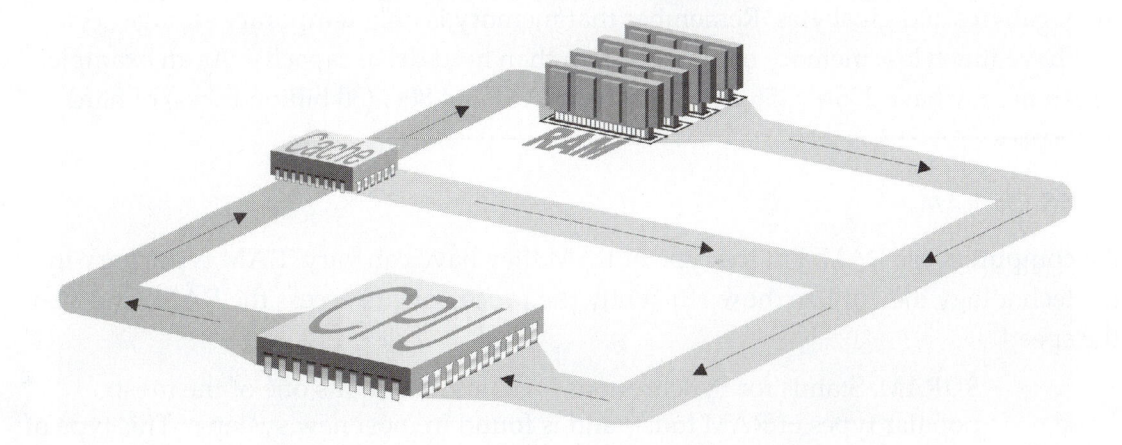

Figure 1.14. Memory requests travel back and forth from the processor to memory via the address and data buses.

TYPES OF MEMORY

A computer can have two main types of memory: ROM and RAM. ROM stands for Read-Only Memory. These chips cannot be changed and contain data and instructions that have been burned in. ROM chips contain instructions for starting a computer, checking for hardware devices, and starting the operating system. This basic set of instructions is called the BIOS (basic input and output system).

RAM stands for Random Access Memory, and is the main working area for the processor. Instructions and data are stored (temporarily) in RAM while they are in use. Random refers to the fact that the processor can access each byte of data using the memory address, not necessarily in order.

> **Why you need to save:** Data in memory is stored only temporarily. If you lose power, all that data will be lost. That's why it's important to save your work often. When you save, you copy the information from memory to disk or hard drive.

RAM SIZE AND SPEED

New computers come with a set amount of RAM, which is measured in megabytes (M or MB). (Remember that one megabyte equals one million bytes and one gigabyte equals one billion bytes.) In addition to the RAM that comes with a system, you can always add more memory. Most new computers have memory in the range from 256M to 1024M (or 1G).

The speed of this type of memory is measured in nanoseconds (ns). The smaller the number, the faster the speed. You can expect to find speeds ranging from 60 to 100 ns.

A common mistake is to confuse memory size with hard disk size. Both are measured in megabytes and gigabytes. Remember that memory is only temporary storage. You will have much less memory on your system than hard drive capacity. As an example, a system may have 256M (256 million bytes) RAM and 80G (80 billion bytes) of hard disk space.

TYPES OF RAM

All computers use RAM, but the type of RAM they have can vary. RAM types vary in the technology they utilize (how efficiently the processor can access the RAM) and also the speed.

- **SDRAM.** Stands for Synchronous Dynamic RAM. It's one of the most popular types of RAM today and is found in most new systems. This type of memory provides data at fast speeds.
- **DDR-SDRAM.** Stands for Double Data Rate - Synchronous Dynamic RAM. This type of memory is an improvement over regular SDRAM and can increase the memory speed. One thing that makes this type of memory so popular is that memory makers are free to manufacture it because it is an open standard.

- *RDRAM*. Stands for Rambus Dynamic RAM. It improves performance by allocating memory in a new way.
- *Rambus DRAM* (RDRAM). This memory was developed by Rambus, Inc. and like DDR-SDRAM increases the memory bus and the speed. Despite the speed, RDRAM hasn't been very popular because of price, as well as compatibility and other problem issues (heat).

MORE MEMORY TERMS AND CONCEPTS

You know the basics of how memory operates, but when reading system reviews or checking out new systems, you can also find other terms that relate to memory (and hence performance). Here are some other concepts you should understand:

- *Flash memory*. If you lose power, anything stored in RAM is lost. Flash memory stores data even when the PC is off. ROM, for instance, is a form of flash memory. Digital cameras also use flash memory.
- *Cache*. The processor and memory are constantly moving instructions and data back and forth. To help speed this process, processors include cache (pronounced "cash") memory. This memory is much faster than RAM and is used to store frequently used instructions and data. Rather than send requests via the address and data bus, the processor checks its cache first. The size of the processor cache is measured in kilobytes (K or KB).

    Clear Internet cache: The Internet can use a lot of cache space. You can clear this space by deleting temporary Internet files.

- *Video memory*. You'll learn more about video cards and monitors later in this lesson. To speed the display of images, most video cards also come with special video memory.

GETTING SYSTEM INFORMATION

If you don't remember what type processor or how much memory you have, you can get detailed system information using Microsoft Windows.

Follow these steps to get system information on a PC:

1. Click Start and then right-click the My Computer icon. Or if you have a desktop icon for My Computer, you can right-click this icon.
2. Select Properties. You see the System Properties dialog box (see Figure 1.14).

Lesson 1
Defining a Computer

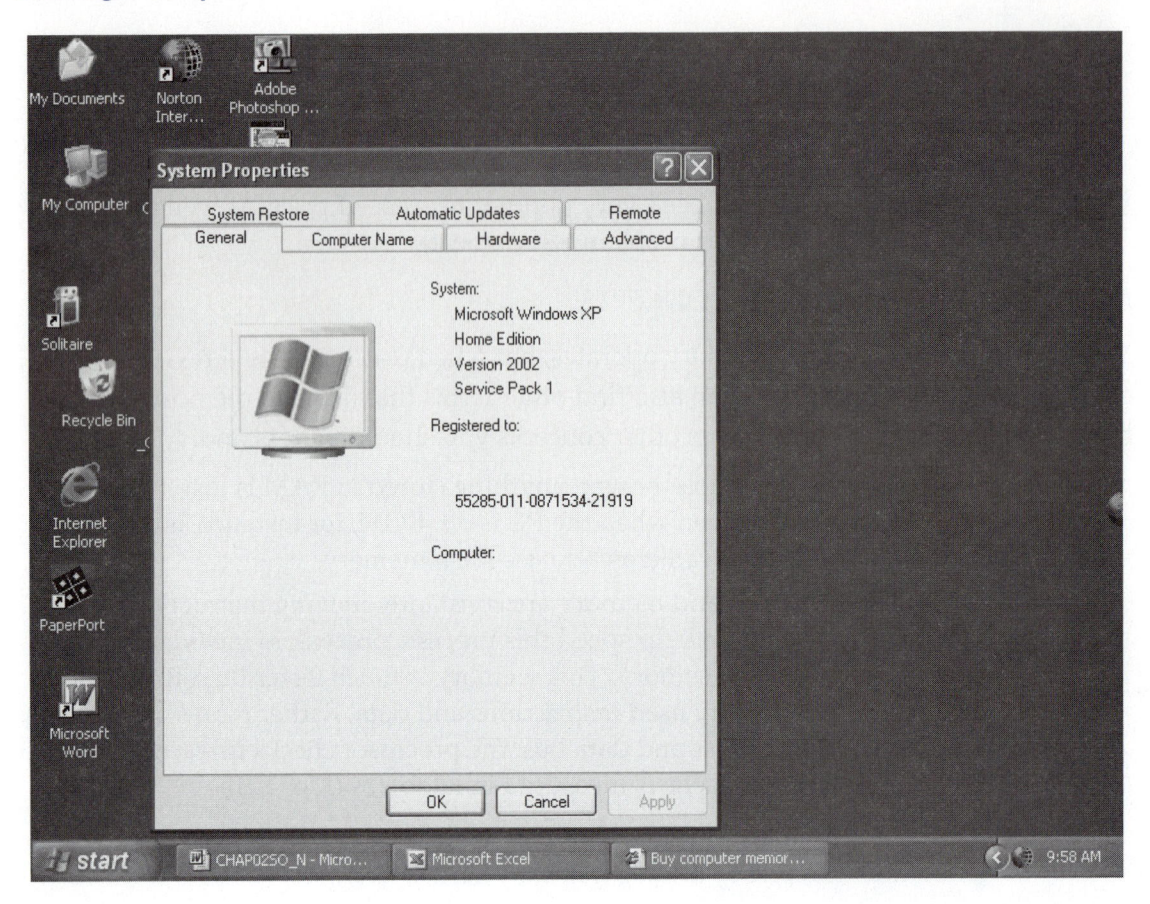

Learning Computer Concepts

Figure 1.14. You can use this dialog box to get detailed system information.

2. On the General tab, review the information about the current operating system version, computer type, and amount of memory.

3. Click OK to close the dialog box.

Purchasing, Upgrading, and Maintaining a Computer

If you don't have a computer, you may consider buying one. If you have an older computer, you may consider upgrading it (adding new components). And, finally, you should also ensure the safety and "life" of your computer by performing some maintenance. This section discusses these topics.

BUYING A COMPUTER

If you are thinking of buying a computer, you need to do a little preparatory work to ensure you get a computer that best matches your needs and at the best deal. This section gives you some step-by-step directions.

Follow these steps to research buying a computer:

1. Make a list of what tasks you want to do with your computer. The biggest mistake when purchasing a computer is buying a computer for price. The first factor has to be your needs. You

should have a clear idea of what you want to use the computer for.

2. Make a list of the features you need. You can use the list of uses to help determine the features. Do you need sound cards? Modem? Special monitor? What kind of printer? What applications do you need?

3. Investigate places that sell computers. You can purchase computers through computer or electronic superstores, online, or even through office supply stores and discount retailers such as SAM'S CLUB. Visit some stores. Collect product information sheets. If you have access to the Internet, visit some of the big computer makers, including Gateway (www.gateway.com), Dell (www.dell.com), Micron (www.micron.com), or Compaq (www.compaq.com). Print product information sheets. Purchase a computer magazine; most include numerous ads for systems, plus articles.

4. Make sure you understand all the technical terms, in the product sheets. You'll find lots of acronyms and technical terms, such as Intel Pentium 4 Processor, 2.8GHz, and USB ports. You should understand what each of these means. Use this book if you need help decoding the list. If you aren't sure about a particular item in a product spec sheet, ask.

5. Look into what extras are included with the computer. Some computers come with a printer or digital camera or other devices. Also, while all computers come with an operating system, some include other software (bundled software). This may include antivirus programs, word processing programs, or even complete suites of applications such as Microsoft Office. Use this information to compare different systems, but keep your needs in mind. If a computer has a photo editing program but you don't need this program, don't let the "free" programs detract you from getting a computer suited to your needs.

6. Comparison shop. Once you collect all this information, you should be able to define the system you want. You can then compare prices. Another factor to consider is service, support, warranties, and reliability of the computer manufacturer. You can research these factors in computer magazines or online at popular computer resources.

UPGRADING A COMPUTER

As your needs expand, you may want to consider upgrading your computer. You can upgrade just about every major component. But first consider the benefits you will get from that upgrade. Some upgrades will extend the life of your computer, making its speed and power acceptable for a longer timeframe. Others may not be worth the cost and effort. You may be better off purchasing a new PC. Review this list of upgrading tips:

- *Upgrade the processor*. You can upgrade the processor, but keep in mind that it's not the only thing that determines performance. If the other components cannot take advantage of the speed and features of this processor, you may not gain anything. It's similar to putting a racing engine into a Volkswagen. You'll only get so much performance gain. Also, your system must offer a processor that can be upgraded.

- *Add more memory*. Memory is a fairly straightforward upgrade, easy to do and offering a pretty good performance gain. This type of upgrade is especially useful if you use more than one application at a time.

    WEB: You can get upgrade information for memory at Buy Computer Memory (www.buycomputermemory.com).

- *Add more disk space*. Programs and data files quickly consume your hard drive. You can gain more storage space by adding another disk drive. You may also want to add other drives, such as a ZIP drive (higher-capacity floppy drive). For more information on disk drives, see Lesson 2.

- *Upgrade your monitor*. You can purchase a newer (bigger, better) monitor for your PC. Or you might add a graphics card to speed performance. A newer graphics card is most useful for game fanatics. A bigger monitor might be suited for those in any type of graphics or desktop publishing field.

You may also add other hardware devices such as a new printer, digital camera, scanner, joystick, MP3 player, and others. To add new hardware, you connect the device and then run Windows Add New Hardware Wizard. Lesson 5 on operating systems covers adding hardware in more detail.

MAINTAINING A COMPUTER

You make a big investment when you purchase a computer, and therefore, you should ensure its safety and reliability. You can perform many of the most common (and simple) maintenance tasks yourself. The most important maintenance points to keep in mind follow:

- *Protect your computer*. You should take care to protect your computer from theft and damage. Make sure you place it in a safe place (away from extreme fluctuations in heat and cold). If you have a laptop, don't leave it unattended.

- *Protect from power fluctuations*. Power spikes, surges, blackouts (loss of power), and brown outs (partial loss of power) can damage your computer equipment. Remember the computer uses electricity, and the components inside are connected to the computer's power supply and also use electricity. This makes the computer and computer components susceptible to power spikes. Also, lightning can travel through anything that's plugged into a power outlet and wreak havoc with your computer. And, your documents can be damaged if a power failure or surge occurs when you are working on a file or a file is open. (Some programs offer an automatic recovery feature that may enable you to retrieve some of your document.) To protect from power surges or fluctuations, buy and use a power surge suppressor or UPS (uninterrupted power supply) strip and plug your equipment into one of these devices. Also, during really bad electrical storms, you may want to unplug your computer from its power supply. (Don't just turn off your UPS strip.)

- *Protect your data*. To protect your data, you should make periodic backups (extra copies of your data). You can use a backup program, or you can copy important files to a CD or other type of disk. Businesses, for instance, may back up to a tape drive. Also periodically check your disk for problems. (See the next section for how to check your disk with Windows XP.) Often Windows disk check program can fix the problem automatically. Finally, don't leave floppy, CD, or DVD discs out in extreme heat or cold.

- *Improve your performance*. To improve the speed of your computer, you should perform periodic (once a month or more depending on how much you use your computer) maintenance tasks. You can defragment your drive as well as get rid of unnecessary files. These tasks are covered in Lesson 2.

- *Keep your machine clean*. This means cleaning your mouse and keyboard. You can purchase canned air to spray your keyboard to clean out in between the keys. (You can also try turning it upside down and shake sometimes works to dislodge some items). You shouldn't eat or drink by your computer, but if you spill something, make sure you clean it up immediately.

- *Protect against viruses*. If you use your computer online or share disks with someone else, you need to take precautions about viruses spread through email, Internet access, and file sharing. Lesson 13 goes into more detail about these safety issues.

CHECKING A DISK FOR PROBLEMS

You should periodically check your disk to make sure you don't have problems. For instance, sometimes part of a file gets misplaced when you save it. Or your drive may develop bad sections (called sectors). If your drive has a few bad sectors, don't worry. That's somewhat common. If your drive has several bad sectors or is making noises, your drive may be going bad. In that case, back up your data and then get some professional troubleshooting advice on repairing or replacing the drive.

Follow these steps to check a disk for problems:

1. Double-click on the My Computer icon on your desktop. If you don't have this icon, click Start and then click My Computer.

2. Right-click on the hard drive you want to check and then click Properties.

3. Click on the Tools tab (see Figure 1.15).

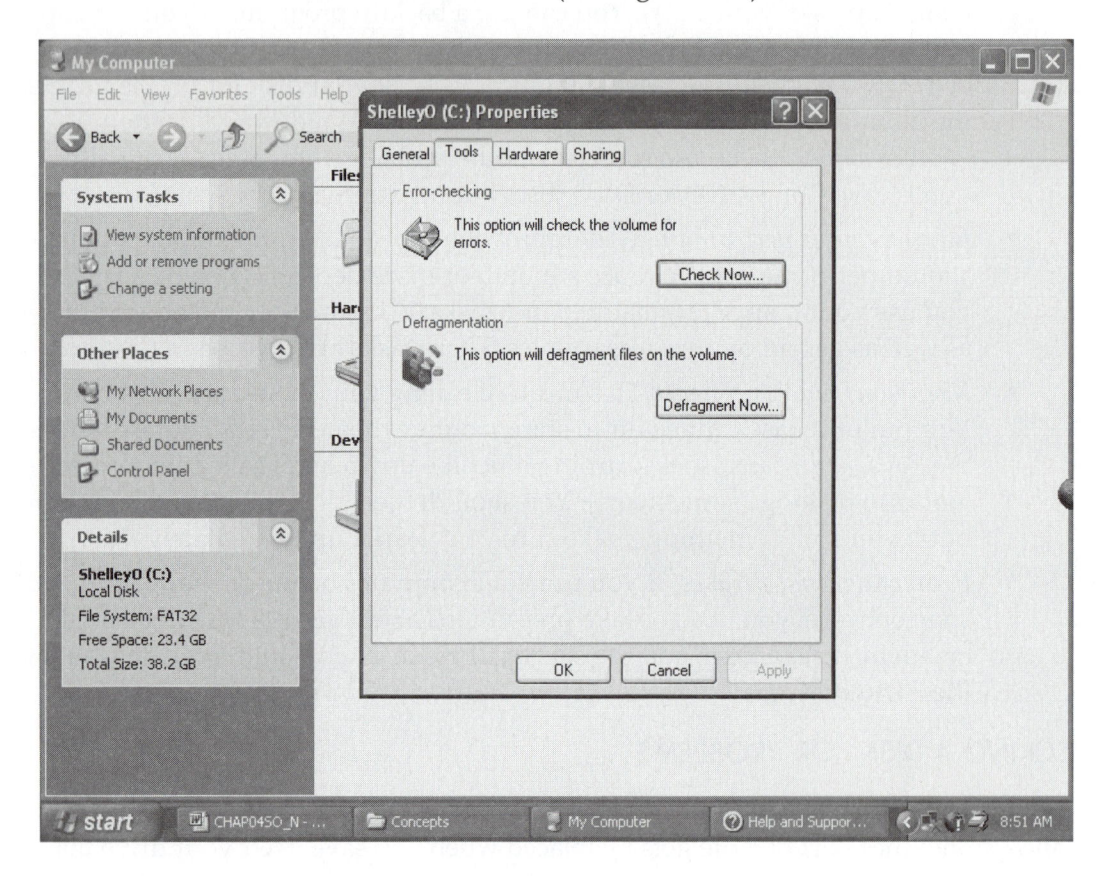

Figure 1.15. You can check a disk for errors.

4. Click the Check Now button.

5. If you want Windows to repair errors automatically, click the check box Automatically fix file system errors.

6. Click Start. Windows checks your hard drive and then displays a message. Click OK to close the message box.

Troubleshooting

Hardware components can develop problems over time, and you can take steps to prevent problems as well as troubleshoot and fix problems when they do occur. Note that problems are best solved by following a step-by-step approach, trying one thing at a time to see if that fix works and then moving on to another possible fix. It's also a good idea to keep notes about what you did and what happened, especially noting any error messages.

In general, follow these basic steps to approach a problem:

1. If you have a problem, try to remember exactly what preceded the problem and what happened afterward. Did you install something new? A new program? A new hardware device? Did you get an error message? If so, record the message exactly.

2. See if you can replicate the problem. Can you perform the same steps and get the same problem consistently?

3. Try some basic fixes. Some problems can be resolved by restarting the computer. Or make sure that the computer is plugged in and all the cables (mouse cable, printer cable, keyboard cable, and so on) are securely connected.

4. If you can't solve the problem, find available help or advice. You can use Windows troubleshooting help. (Lesson 5 covers getting help in Windows.) You may also need to call for professional technical support. Depending on your support agreement, you should be able to get technical support from your computer manufacturer.

5. When calling, be sure you can document the program (noting what happened before and after as well as any error messages). Communicate the problem and your results to fix the problem accurately and thoroughly.

6. If the problem is fixed, note how the problem was solved (in case it occurs again.) And if possible, avoid whatever caused the problem!

HARDWARE PROBLEMS

This section covers common hardware problems. Note that you can perform many of these tasks yourself, although there are some maintenance tasks and troubleshooting problems that should be done by experienced professionals. These include things such as replacing malfunctioning hardware, upgrading internal hardware components, and working with any electrical equipment. This section does mention some of these advanced techniques so that you know what to expect if you encounter this problem (or if you are experienced enough to perform these tasks yourself).

DRIVE PROBLEMS

Your hard drive, floppy drive, or CD or DVD drive may encounter problems. (Drives are the topic of Lesson 2.) You may find that files don't open quickly or that they are scrambled. You may hear a whining or rattling sound from the drive. To check the disk for problems, you can run a disk check (covered in the preceding section). If the disk has significant problems, you'll probably need to purchase a new drive.

First, backup all your data. (You should be doing this all along since data on a bad disk can be corrupt. But even if you haven't done a backup, do so as soon as you suspect problems to salvage what data you can.)

Second, purchase and install a new drive. You'll need to reinstall your programs, set up your email and Internet connection, and transfer all your data to the new drive. (Getting a new hard drive is a lot like getting a new computer.)

Floppy, CD, or DVD drives don't require as much set up because they are use temporary, removable disks for storage. You can simply replace the drive.

If your drive becomes too full or its performance is sluggish, you can try a few fixes. First, delete any files or programs you don't need. (Make backup copies of files if you think you'll need them. You may also backup files you want to keep but don't need to access on the computer, such as old reports or e-mails.)

Second, empty your Recycle Bin. These files take storage space, and you can regain the space by emptying the Recycle Bin. (Recycle Bin files are recommended for deletion when you use the Disk Cleanup wizard, covered next.)

Third, use Window XP's features for handling disk clutter. You can run the Disk Cleanup wizard (open the My Computer window, right-click the hard drive you want to clean, and then click Properties). Use the Disk Cleanup button to identify possible files for deletion. You can also defragment your drive (covered in Lesson 2). You access this feature from the drive properties dialog box (refer to Figure 1.15).

MONITOR PROBLEMS

If your monitor is not working properly (the display is blurry or you see garbage or leftover images from menus or programs), you need to troubleshoot your monitor. First, make sure that all the connections are secure. Is the monitor plugged into a power outlet? Are the cables (both ends) that connect the monitor to the computer plugged in?

Also, check for monitor controls for adjusting the color, sharpness, and placement of the images on-screen. (How you access these varies from monitor to monitor.) Look for buttons on the front of the monitor or check your monitor manual.

You may also need to reinstall the driver (the file that tells Windows the specific details about your monitor). See the section "Driver Problems."

PRINTER PROBLEMS

If your printer isn't working properly, check that it's plugged in, is online, and the cable is connected securely both to the computer and to the printer. You can also try turning off and on the printer; this sometimes clears problems.

Also, most computers display error messages to indicate common problems (such as a printer jam). If the printer isn't working properly, check for paper jams. Also, make sure the printer has paper (usually you'll receive an error message or see an error light on the printer when the printer is out of paper).

Finally, check the toner. If the printout is light, smeared, or not printed in the proper colors (for color printers), it might be a problem with the toner. Try installing a new printer cartridge(s).

For maintenance, keep the printer clear from dust and dirt, periodically cleaning out any accumulated dirt. (And again, don't drink or eat near your computer.) A dirty printer may in fact be the cause of the problems!

OTHER COMPONENT PROBLEMS

If you add new hardware (such as a modem, printer, or a new sound card), and it doesn't work, the first step is to check the obvious. Is it connected to a power source? Is it connected to the computer? Is the card securely inserted into the slot into the motherboard? If the connections are secure and the component has problem, you should check the driver (covered next). You should also make sure that you have configured the device as specified in the installation instructions. (For instance, for some adapter cards, you may have to flip a switch on the card.) Check the manual for your particular device as these situations and setup can vary wildly.

DRIVER PROBLEMS

Checking the driver is a common troubleshooting process for all hardware component problems. You can review, troubleshoot, and update your driver using the Device Manager.

Follow these steps to check a disk for problems:

1 Right-click the My Computer icon.
2 Click Properties.
3 In the System Properties dialog box, click the Hardware tab.
4 Click the Device Manager button (see Figure 1.16).

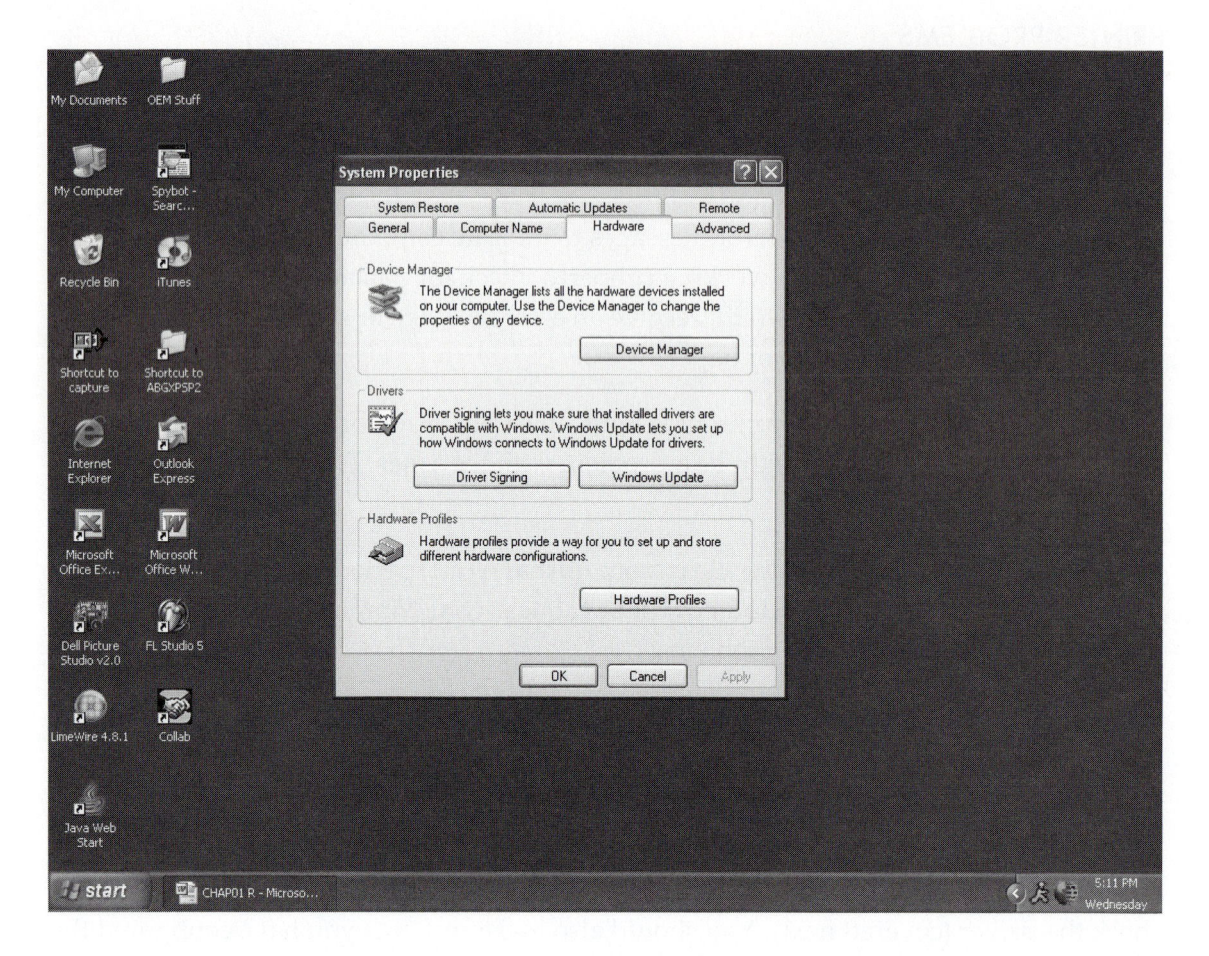

Lesson 1   **Learning Computer Concepts**
Defining a Computer

Figure 1.16. You can use the Device Manager to view a list of components on your system.

5   In the Device Manager list, click the plus sign next to the type of hardware component. For instance, to view monitors, click the plus sign next to monitors. You see the monitors installed on your system (see Figure 1.17).

Learning Computer Concepts

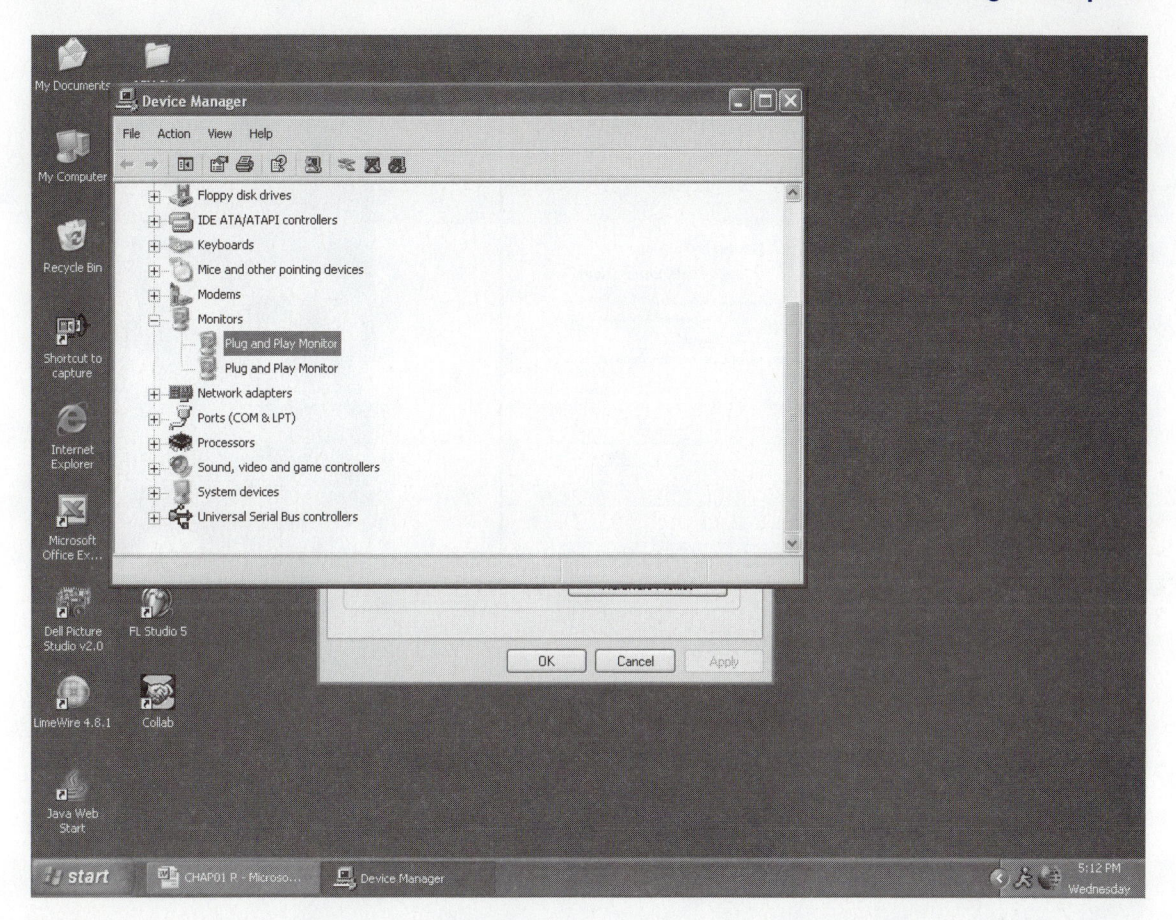

**Lesson 1
Defining a Computer**

Figure 1.17. To troubleshoot a specific device, display the device in the list.

6   Right-click the device you want to troubleshoot and then click Properties. You can then use the features in the device properties dialog box, shown in Figure 1.18, to troubleshoot the device, update the driver, scan for changes, and make other device driver changes.

Lesson 1
Defining a Computer

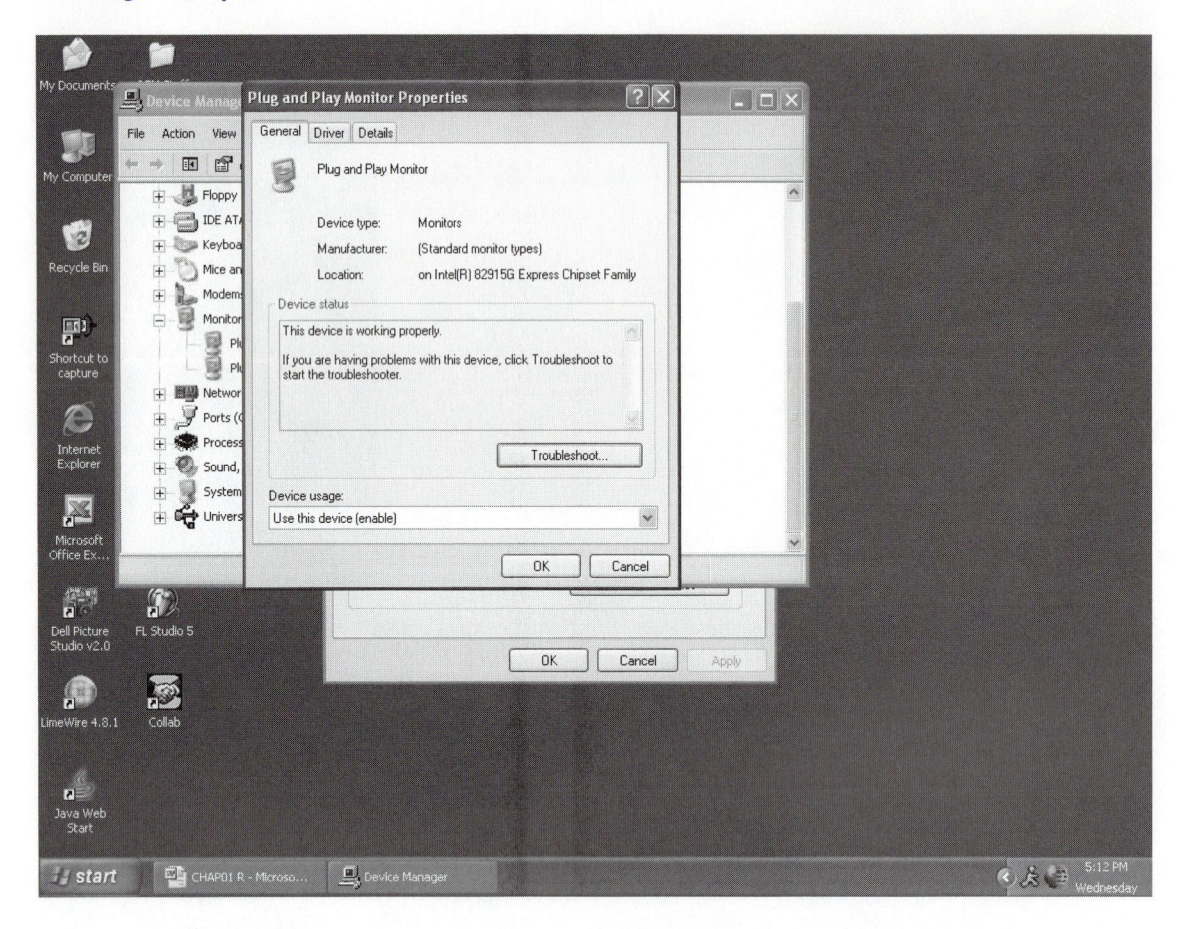

Learning Computer Concepts

Figure 1.18. Use the properties dialog box to get troubleshooting advice, update the driver, and more.

Summary

- A computer is a tool you can use for a variety of tasks including creating documents, storing information, playing games, learning a new skill, and connecting to the Internet.

- The most common type of computer is a microcomputer. This type of computer is most often referred to as a PC or personal computer. In addition to this type of computer, you may encounter minicomputers, mainframes, workstations, or portable computers.

- Computers are accurate, flexible, reliable, and quick. They help automate routine tasks and facilitate data storage.

- The physical components of a computer are the hardware. Most systems consist of a monitor, keyboard, mouse, and system unit. You may also have a printer and speakers.

- The system unit houses the electronic components of your computer including the motherboard (holds the processor and memory), video adapter, drives, power supply, and slots for adding components.

- All systems need a special type of software called an operating system. The most commonly used operating system is Microsoft Windows.
- Input devices enable you to enter information, select commands, and type text. You use keyboards for entering text. A mouse is used to select commands, start programs, and select text and objects.
- Output devices enable you to see or print the data you enter. A monitor displays programs as well as text or data you enter. A printer prints hard-copy versions of your documents.
- Computers vary in price, size, power, speed, and system type.
- A processor is the brain of a computer and determines its speed and power. A processor consists of millions of transistors etched on a chip. Intel is the most popular manufacturer of computer processors.
- The clock speed of a processor is measured in gigahertz (GHz) or megahertz MHz for older computers. The higher the number, the faster the computer. Top speeds are currently in the range of 3-4 GHz.
- A computer has two types of memory: ROM and RAM. ROM stands for Read-Only Memory; this memory stores unchanging data such as the BIOS. RAM stands for Random Access Memory and is the computer's working area, a place to temporarily store program instructions and data.
- RAM is measured in megabytes. Most new systems have at least 256M of RAM.
- To extend the life of a computer, you may consider upgrading some of the components. Before you upgrade, be sure the performance gain will be worth the price and effort. Sometimes it's better simply to purchase a new computer.

Lesson 1
Defining a Computer

Q&A

Multiple Choice

1. The system unit houses
    a. Monitor
    b. Keyboard
    c. Motherboard
    d. All of the above

2. The set of programming instructions that are used to accomplish tasks is called
    a. Hardware
    b. Software
    c. Input device
    d. Output device

3. The speed of a computer is measured in
    a. Kilobytes
    b. Megabytes
    c. Mega- or gigahertz
    d. Meters

4. The main chip in a computer is the
    a. Processor
    b. Circuit board
    c. Operating system
    d. Floppy drive

Fill in the Blank

1. RAM is measured in _____.
2. _____ devices allow you to enter information or select commands.
3. A(n) _____ is an example of an output device.
4. _____ is the most popular processor manufacturer.

Short Essay

1. Describe the different ways that computers vary.
2. Name the most common components of a computer.

LESSON 2: STORING DATA

Objectives

➢ Define hard drives
➢ Use a floppy drive
➢ Learn about CD and DVD drives
➢ Familiarize yourself with other storage devices

Defining Hard Drives

To use a computer effectively, you need a permanent place to store your data and programs. This storage space is provided by a hard disk, a magnetic storage device inside your system unit. This section explains how hard disks vary, how they work, and how you use them to keep data and programs organized.

HOW HARD DRIVES VARY

Hard disks vary in three main ways: capacity (size), speed, and drive standard. The capacity of a drive is measured in megabytes (M or MB), and more commonly gigabytes (G or GB). A few years ago a 500M drive was considered big. Now most new computers come with drives that start at 80G and go up from there to several hundred gigabyte drives. The bigger the drive, the more data and programs you can store. You'll be surprised how quickly a hard drive fills up, with your data and with programs.

M/MB and G/GB: M stands for megabyte and is roughly 1 million bytes. You may also see this measurement abbreviated MB. G or GB stands for gigabyte and is roughly one billion bytes.

Check drive size: If you aren't sure how big your drive is in Windows, click Start and then click My Computer. (If you have a desktop icon for My Computer, you can double-click this icon to open My Compter.) Right-click your hard drive and select Properties. You can see the capacity as well as the used and free space on your drive.

The second way that hard disks vary is speed, and you'll find two measurements of speed: seek time and transfer time. The seek time is the amount of time starting from the time the computer requests the file up to the second that the drive delivers the first byte of the file. Seek time is measured in milliseconds (ms); most hard drives have access times in the range of 10 to 20 milliseconds.

The transfer time (also called data rate), the other indicator of hard drive performance, is how quickly the drive can transfer the data, that is, read or write data to the disk. This speed is measured in megabytes per second (MBps) or kilobytes per second (KBps). You can find speeds from 5MBps up to 40MBps. The higher the number, the faster the drive.

Lesson 2
Storing Data

To communicate with the processor, a hard drive uses a controller, which is connected to the motherboard either as a built-in part of the motherboard or as an expansion card (see Figure 2.1). Controllers follow different standards, and you'll also see the standard as a way to distinguish drives.

Figure 2.1. The hard drive is housed inside the system unit and is connected to the processor via a controller.

HOW A HARD DRIVE WORKS

A hard disk is sealed in a vacuum chamber and consists of several aluminum platters coated with a magnetically sensitive material (usually iron oxide). This coating enables the data to be polarized by an electromagnet. Like processor data, the magnetic bit can be on or off, but unlike a processor, it does not require electricity to maintain its current state (on/off). Drives have read/write heads that move over the disk surface and change the polarity of the magnet (see Figure 2.2). That's how data is written to and read from the disk. Read heads relay the information from disk; write heads record the information to disk.

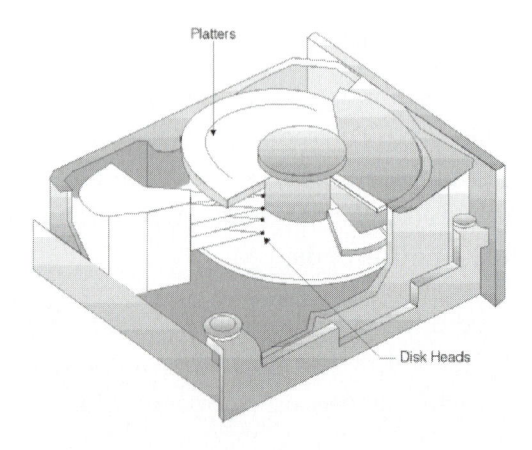

Figure 2.2. A drive stores data by charging magnetic particles.

To prepare a disk for use, you need to format it. Formatting a disk writes a series of concentric circles around each platter (like a phonograph, but each circle is separate rather than continuous). These tracks are numbered, and the number of tracks on a disk depends on the drive type.

Tracks are then divided into pie-like sections called sectors (see Figure 2.3). Sectors are also numbered. So now the drive is divided into little areas, each with a unique number. (Think about a running track, divided into lanes. Each lane may have dividers to indicate the distance or the starting place for runners. These lanes are similar to the tracks on the disk. If the running track was divided into equal segments, these are similar to sectors.)

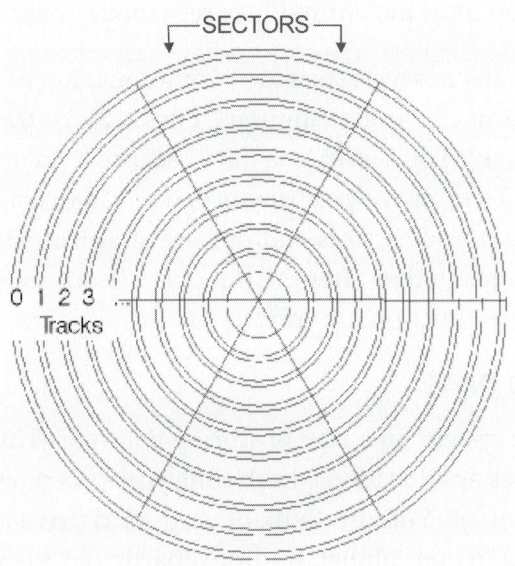

Figure 2.3. A drive is divided into tracks and sectors.

Depending on the drive type, the size of the sector can vary. Also, you'll find that the number of sectors per track varies. As an end user, you don't need to worry about the number of sectors and tracks. However, this information is useful if you ever hear or read about this specification; you'll understand what they refer to. Also, you need a basic understanding of how data is stored so you can grasp drive performance issues, such as defragmenting (covered later).

HOW A DRIVE STORES DATA

You now know how the data physically is written to and read from the disk, but how does it work mechanically? How does the drive know where to find data and where to write new data?

As mentioned, each track and sector is numbered. The operating system uses this numbering scheme to find areas that are not used for writing or saving data and also to find data to retrieve (reading data). The operating system stores this information in a table. In previous versions of Windows, this was called the file allocation table (FAT or

FAT32). Newer versions use NTFS, which provides more reliability, better performance, more security, and other advanced features.

When you save a file, the operating system finds space that is available. The drive goes to the first area (called cluster) and fills it up. If the file is too big to fit in one cluster, the operating system goes to the next available cluster and writes data to that area. This continues until the entire file is stored. Note that the file may be stored in several clusters and that the clusters may not be next to each other.

When you want to open a file, the operating system finds the various sectors that store that file. Then the drive goes to the first cluster to retrieve the first part of the file, goes to the next cluster, and so on until the entire file is retrieved.

Initially, on a new drive, the open clusters are contiguous, but over time as you add and delete files, the file areas may be noncontiguous. Files may be fragmented (stored in clusters all around the disk). You won't lose data because they are fragmented, but it does slow performance. To improve performance, you can defragment the drive, basically rearranging the stored clusters and putting all full clusters at the start of the drive and all open clusters together after the full ones. There are programs that automatically perform this function for you.

ORGANIZING A HARD DRIVE

The drive and operating system take care of storing and retrieving data. You only need to keep track of file names and locations. Each time you save a new file, you assign a name and a location or folder. You can think of your hard drive as one big filing cabinet. If all the files were stored in one cabinet, finding a particular file would be cumbersome. Instead, a cabinet is divided into folders. Likewise, your hard drive is divided into folders, including folders created by programs and folders you create. To keep your data organized, you need to give some thought to your folder structure. Keep these pointers in mind:

- Each drive has a name, which consists of the drive letter and a colon. If you have a floppy drive, it is named drive A:. The first hard drive is drive C:. If you have more than one hard drive, they are named D:, E:, and so on. The CD or DVD drive, if you have one, uses the next free letter. If you have only one hard drive, the hard drive is drive C: and the CD drive would then be named D:. If you have two hard drives (C: and D:), then the CD drive would be drive E:.

- In a Windows environment the main folder on each drive is called the root. This folder contains all the other folders on your computer. This folder does not have a name, but is indicated with the backslash key (\).

- You can have folders within folders. These nested folders are sometimes called subfolders.

- Windows sets up several folders. The tools and programs needed to use Windows are stored within a main folder called Windows. This folder contains several folders within the main Windows folder.

- Windows also sets up a special My Documents folder. It's a good idea to include all of your data within this folder because it's easy to access this folder and with all of your data within one main folder, backing up your data is also quicker.

- Within the My Documents folder, you'll find folders for My Pictures, My Music, and My Videos. These folders help store these special file types together in one location.

- In addition to the folders Windows sets up, you can create your own folders. You should spend some time thinking of an organizational strategy for your work. You might include folders for each type of document (artwork, letters, databases, and so on). You might set up folders by project. If several people use the computer, you might set up folders for each person.

- When you install a new program, the installation program will set up a separate folder for its files. This folder may also contain subfolders (folders within folders). Most applications have a built-in installation program that leads you through the installation process.

Access My Documents folder: You can quickly access the My Documents folder by clicking Start and then clicking My Documents. You may also add a shortcut icon to this folder to your desktop.

- When you save a file, you assign a file name and a folder. The combination of folder and name is called the path. For instance, if you save a file named CHAP01.DOC on drive C: in a folder named CONCEPTS, the path to this file would be C:\CONCEPTS\CHAP01.DOC. Note that the drive, folder, and file name are separated by backslashes. With Windows, you don't need to type the path. Instead, you can browse through the folder structure to have Windows supply the path name for you.

DISPLAYING THE CONTENTS OF YOUR HARD DRIVE

To see the contents of your drives in Windows, you use the My Computer icon. You can then open any of the drives and then open any of the folders.

Follow these steps to see the contents of your drives in Windows:

1. Click Start and then click My Computer. Or if you have a desktop shortcut to My Computer, double-click this icon. You see drive icons for each drive on your system (see Figure 2.4).

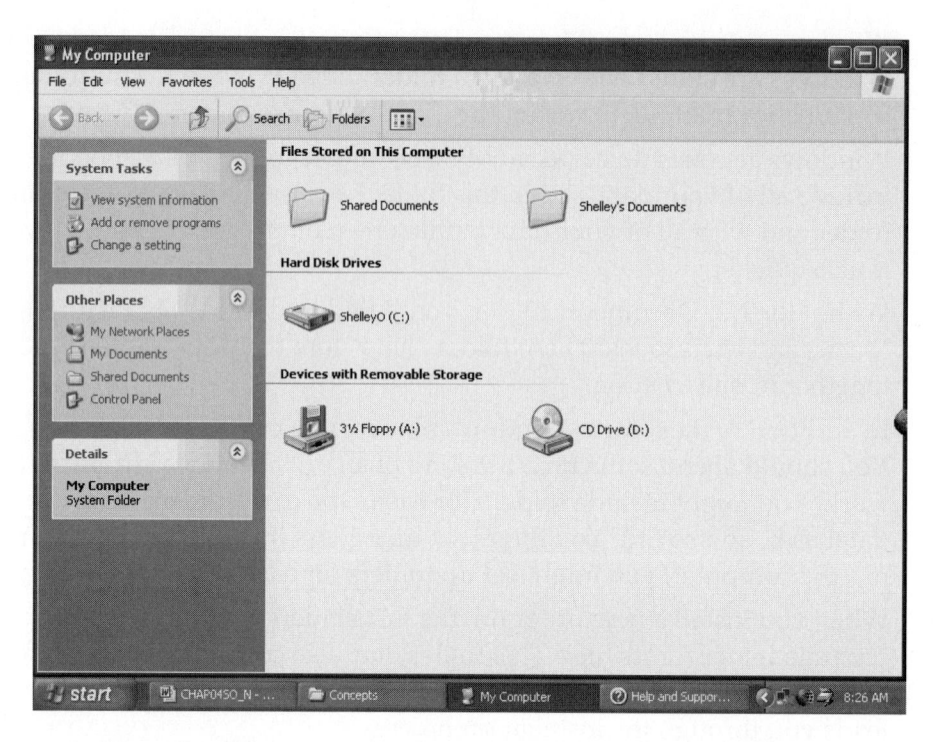

Lesson 2
Storing Data   **Learning Computer Concepts**

Figure 2.4. My Computer displays icons for each drive on your system.

2. Double-click the drive you want to open. For instance, double-click drive C:. You see the contents of that drive. Notice that folders are indicated with a folder icon (see Figure 2.5). Windows also uses different data icons for different file types as well as programs.

Figure 2.5. You can display the contents of the drives on your system.

3   Continue opening folders until you find the file or folder you are looking for.

4   When you are done browsing your system, click the Close (X) button to close the folder window.

CHECKING, BACKING UP, AND OPTIMIZING YOUR DRIVES

To keep your drive performing in top shape, you should perform some routine maintenance. Windows includes tools for checking your disk for errors. You can also use special tools to defragment the files (reorganize them so that opening and accessing files is quicker) and improve performance. Keep the following guidelines in mind:

- Clean out unneeded files. One way to improve performance is to get rid of unnecessary files. You can delete files manually or use the Disk Cleanup feature of Windows (see Figure 2.6). To access this tool, open My Computer and then right-click the disk you want to tidy up. Select Properties. Click the Disk Cleanup button to start the wizard. From here, you can check for unnecessary files and then select/confirm which of these targeted files are deleted.

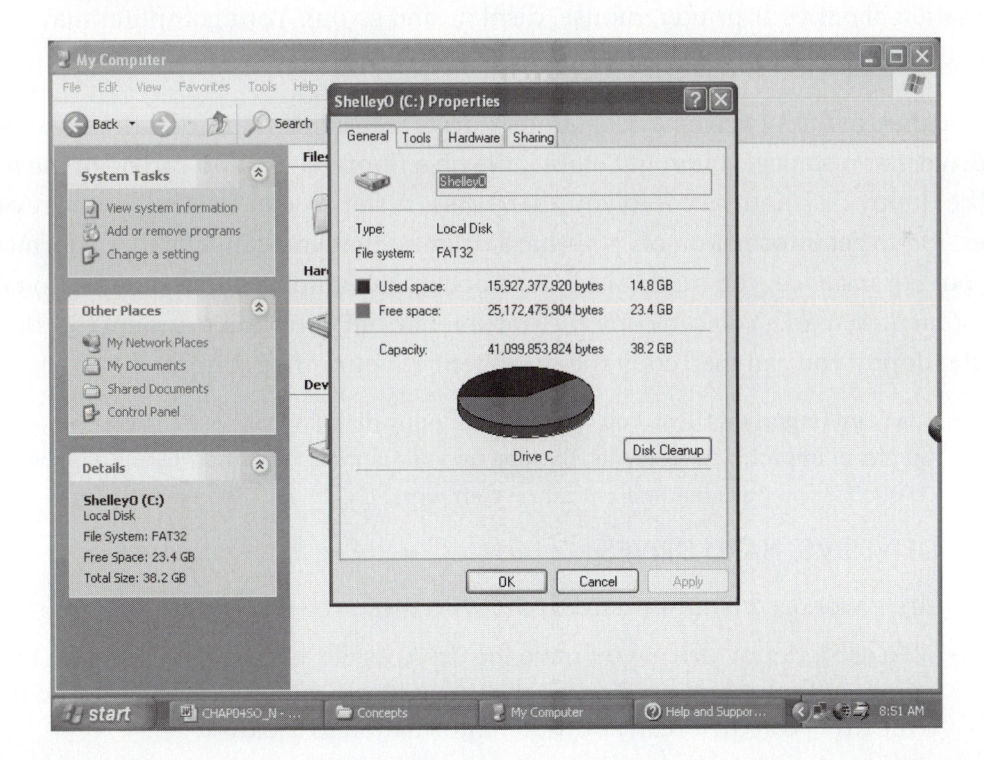

Figure 2.6. You can clean up (delete) unnecessary files on your system.

- Check the drive for errors. You should also periodically scan your drive for errors using the program included with Windows. Lesson 1 covered how to perform this task.
- Over time, all drives become fragmented. If your drive has become fragmented, you can use the Disk Defragmenter included with Windows to defragment the drive. You can access this from the Tools tab (see Figure 2.6).

Click the Defragment Now button to start the process. (Note that defragmenting can take a while.)

- Back up your work. Hard drives and computers develop problems. To safeguard your data, you should periodically make a spare or backup copy of your files. You can do so manually by copying files from your hard drive to a CD, for instance. Or you can use special backup software and special storage devices for your backup needs. (Other backup options are covered later in this lesson.)

- Protect your computer. If you have an Internet connection or share files with others, your system needs to be safeguarded against viruses. You should install an antivirus application to check your system for viruses. (This type of software is covered in Lesson 13.)

Using Your Floppy Drive

Hard drives are the primary storage of a computer. Hard drives store your data files and your program files, as well as important information about your computer setup (information about your printer, mouse, display, and so on). Your computer may also have another type of drive: a floppy drive.

What use does a floppy drive have? A floppy drive is used to get information onto your hard drive. For instance, you might store a file on a floppy disk. You can open the file from the floppy disk and save it to your hard disk. A floppy drive also does the reverse: enables you to get information off your hard drive so that you can take that information with you. For instance, you might work on a document at home and then want to take the document to work. You can copy the document from your home system to a floppy. From the floppy you can then copy the document to your office computer.

Back up important files: You can also use floppy disks to make extra backup copies of important documents. Backing up your work is very important. You'll be best off if you learn this *before* you lose your work.

FLOPPY DRIVES VS. HARD DRIVES

A floppy drive works similar to a hard drive, with these key differences:

- To use a floppy drive, you have the drive itself (accessed via a slot on the front of the system unit) and a disk. You insert the disk into the slot so that the drive can then read and write information to the disk.

- Hard drives store much more data than a floppy drive and are also faster. Most floppy disks can store a maximum of 1.44M of data. Compare that to hard drives that can store 80G or more of data.

- A hard drive comes formatted, and you usually never, ever want to reformat a hard drive. You do this only in the most extreme circumstances. Most floppy disks come preformatted. If not, you need to format them to prepare them for use. You can reformat a floppy disk, but doing so erases all the data on that disk.

> **Floppy is not floppy:** Many beginning users are confused when they hear the term "floppy" disk because the disk is not floppy. But it used to be! Older systems used a different disk type, which was floppy. These disks measured 5¼" in size (compared to the 3½" size of common floppy disks now) and could not store as much data.

FLOPPY DISK CARE AND MAINTENANCE

Because you can physically handle a floppy disk, you need to take some precaution in handling this type of disk. Here are some points to keep in mind:

- As mentioned, before you can use a floppy disk, it must be formatted. Some disks are sold preformatted or you can use your system to format the disk. If you format a disk that contains data, all that data will be erased.
- If you don't want someone to be able to save data to a disk or format a disk, you can write-protect it. To do so, slide the write-protect tab up. Figure 2.7 shows the anatomy of a floppy disk, including the write-protect tab.

← write protect tab

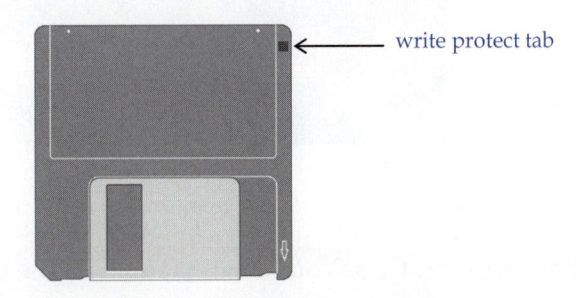

Figure 2.7. A floppy disk is 3½" in size and includes a tab for protecting the disk.

- To keep your disks organized, put labels on them and write the contents of each disk on the label. You might also include the date. Store the disks in a safe place.
- Keep your floppy disk out of extreme heat or cold.

Floppy disks used to be the only way to easily transport data, and floppy drives were standard equipment on computers. With the advent of CD and DVD drives that enable you to both read and write data, floppy disks are not always needed. (CD and DVD drives are covered next.) If you purchase a new computer, you may not have a floppy drive. Instead, you can use your CD or DVD drive to copy, share, and back up files.

Using CD and DVD Drives

A floppy disk is limited in the amount of data it can store. As programs got larger and multimedia became so popular, a new type of storage device was introduced: the CD drive (see Figure 2.8). This drive uses a different method for storing data; lasers are used to read and write data. These discs can store much more data than a floppy drive. Typically, a CD can store 700M of data. Compare that to 1.44M of data on a floppy disk. A CD is the equivalent of more than 450 floppy disks.

Lesson 2   **Learning Computer Concepts**
Storing Data

Figure 2.8. A CD can store much more data than a floppy disk.

Most programs come on CDs. You install them from the CD to your hard drive. You can also find collections of information on CDs, such as encyclopedias, clip art, fonts, and other information. You can also play audio CDs on your computer, and you can use your computer to create audio CDs.

> **Play your music CDs:** You can play music CDs on your computer, although the sound quality will only be as good as your computer speakers allow. To do so, use Windows Media Player (included with Windows) or any of the other popular music players.

DRIVE SPEED

CD drives differ in speed and type. Speed is measured in kilobytes per second (KBps), and the read and write speeds of a CD are slower than those of a hard drive. Speed is indicated as a measure of how much faster the CD is than the original speed of the CD drive. 8X means 8 times faster. 24X means 24 times faster. 48X means 48 times faster. These measurements can be deceiving, though, because you aren't sure what X indicates. The X roughly equals 150 kilobytes per second, but this isn't standardized. If purchasing a new system, get the exact CD access and transfer times.

TYPES OF CD DRIVES

Initially, only CD-ROM drives were available. With these drives, you could only read data from the disc. (ROM stands for Read Only Memory.) Newer drives enable you to read and write data. Here's a breakdown of the various drive types:

- *CD-ROM.* The original CD drive. With this drive, you can only read information.
- *CD-R.* Stands for CD Recordable. With this type of drive, you can read information and also record your own CD-ROM discs. The information that is written to disc cannot be changed.
- *CD-RW.* Stands for CD Rewritable. You can not only read and write data to disc, but you can also rewrite and erase data on the disc. The speed for rewriting data is slower than reading or recording.

DVD

In addition to CD drives, DVD (digital versatile disc) drives have also become common on computers. You are probably familiar with DVD discs and drives for viewing movies. You can also find this type of drive on newer PCs.

DVD uses a different technique for storing data on the disc and can store a lot more data in the same amount of space as a CD, up to 7 times more data than a CD. This type of disc can store from 4.3G up to 17G of data. Speed is measured the same as CD drives; common speeds include 4X and higher. DVD drives are slower at reading and writing data than CD drives. Also DVD drives can read CD discs.

Like CD drives, you'll find different types of DVD drives:

- *DVD-R.* With this type of drive, you can read information and also record data to the DVD once. The information that is written to disc cannot be changed.
- *DVD-RW.* DVD Rewritable. You can not only read and write data to disc, but you can also rewrite and erase data on the disc. The speed for rewriting data is slower than reading or recording.
- *DVD-R or DVD +/-R+.* New in 2002, you can write once with this type of drive which offers enhanced compatibility and performance.
- *DVD-R or DVD+/-RWW+.* Includes added technical advantages to the traditional DVD-RW drive.

Other Storage Options

You can find still more storage options. You are likely to see these in use with networks or businesses that require frequent backups. If you need to store and move large amounts of data, you may need a larger-capacity portable drive. For instance, artists or multimedia creators often create files that are huge. If they need to send these files to someone else, they may use a higher-capacity drive, such as a Zip drive or a Jaz drive. Another popular drive type is a flash memory drive

One type of drive that provides more storage capacity is magnetic disk cartridge drives. These drives use cartridges that can store up to 150M of data. The Bernoulli box was a popular type of this drive. Next came the SyQuest drive, and in 1995, the Iomega Zip drive was introduced. This drive can store 100M, 250M, or 750M, depending on the drive. Zip drives can be internal or external. The internal drives will operate faster. The disk is about the same size and looks like a floppy disk, but you cannot use floppy disks in the Zip drive or vice versa. A Zip disk is a bit thicker and heavier than a floppy disk.

These drives vary in how data is stored and the medium used to store the data (disk, cartridges, etc.). You can use only the medium designed for that drive and you cannot mix media. That is, you cannot, for instance, use a floppy disk in a Zip drive. The person to whom you are sending the data must have the same drive type. For instance, if you store a presentation on a Zip disk and send it to a client, that client must also have a Zip drive in order to access the information on the disk.

Iomega also offers a REV drive designed as a replacement for tape backup drives (covered next). These drives, which can also be used as removable storage, are faster than tape and can store up to 35G (or up to 90G if you compress the data).

WEB: Visit Iomega (www.iomega.com) to get information on the different storage devices they offer.

TAPE DRIVES

You may find another type of drive used mainly for backups. This type of drive stores the information sequentially on a tape (like a cassette tape). Because of the sequential storage method, these drives are not useful for storing data you need to retrieve quickly. They do provide an inexpensive and quick method of making a copy of all the data on your system for backup and can be set to automatically back up at a given time. This drive is often used to back up network servers.

Tape drives differ in the type of tape cartridge they use and the amount of data that can be stored on a tape. The highest capacity use digital audio tape (DAT).

Size doesn't matter: The size of the cartridge is no indication of the capacity.

You must use the type of medium designed for your particular tape drive. Also, you cannot use that medium on tape drives not designed for your medium. That means a tape drive is usually used for one system, to store and if needed restore data from that system onto tapes. This type of drive is not used to transport data, for instance, from one computer system to another.

USB FLASH MEMORY DRIVES

This new type of portable device is about the size of a car key and connects to your computer's USB port. You can use it to share your data by saving the files (photos, music, documents) to the device and then plugging it into another computer. Drives vary depending on capacity (amount the device can store); you can find 128M, 256M, 512M, and 1G mini drives. This type of drive also differs in physical size. For instance, Iomega offers a mini and micro drive; the micro drive is about the size of a thumbnail!

NETWORK DRIVES

If you are hooked up to a network, you may have storage space on the network (in addition to your space on the hard drive on the computer that's connected to the network). Often you include shared files on the network drive, but you may also store other work or files. For more information on accessing and using a network drive, see Lesson 10.

Summary

- To store data permanently, your system includes a hard drive. Hard drives vary in size or capacity, speed, and standard.
- Size is measured in gigabytes (G or GB).
- To use a disk, it must be formatted. Formatting divides the disk into tracks and sectors, each area with a unique number. The operating system uses this number to keep track of where data is stored.
- Windows sets up a My Documents folder with subfolders to encourage you to keep your documents organized. In addition to using these folders, you need to create new folders for storing your data.
- A floppy drive provides a way to take data and documents with you from one computer to another.
- For more data storage, most new systems include a CD drive that you can both record (and possibly rerecord) data to. These drives vary in speed and type. CDs can store as much as 700M of data.
- DVD stands for digital versatile disc and was originally designed to distribute films. DVD drives are also found on newer systems and these drives can read DVDs as well as CDs.
- If you need a higher-capacity portable drive, you can purchase one of several types, including a Zip drive.
- Tape backup drives are useful for backing up data, especially on network servers. These drives store data sequentially like a tape cassette.
- If you need a small portable device, you may consider one of the new flash memory drives that connect to your computer via a USB port.

Lesson 2
Storing Data

Q&A

Multiple Choice

1. The hard drive:
    a. Determines the amount of RAM or memory you have
    b. Connects to the Internet using phone lines
    c. Provides a place to permanently store your data
    d. Houses the graphics card for the monitor

2. This type of drive enables you to read and write to the disc as well as rewrite and erase data:
    a. CD-ROM
    b. CD-R
    c. DVD
    d. CD-RW

3. This type of disc stores more data than a CD and uses a different storage method:
    a. CD-ROM
    b. DVD
    c. CD-R
    d. Floppy

4. The name of your primary hard drive is usually:
    a. A:\
    b. B:\
    c. C:\
    d. D:\

Fill in the Blank

1. Preparing a disk for use is called _____.
2. Tape drives are mostly used for making _____.
3. Rearranging the data on a disk for more optimal performance is called _____.
4. _____ stands for file allocation table and is one method of keeping track of where data is stored.

Short Essay

1. List the things you need for your hard drive to do to safeguard your data and maintain your system.
2. Name the ways that hard drives vary.

LESSON 3: USING INPUT AND OUTPUT DEVICES

Objectives

- ➢ Use the keyboard
- ➢ Use a mouse
- ➢ Use other input devices
- ➢ Create digital images with a scanner or camera
- ➢ Define types of monitors
- ➢ Use a printer and other output devices

Using Your Keyboard

Devices used to enter data are often called input devices, and the most common input devices are a keyboard (covered here) and mouse (covered next). Your computer has a keyboard, which you use to enter data, select commands, and move around in a document. In addition to the alphanumeric keys, the keyboard has other special keys. This section describes the typical keyboard.

TYPICAL KEYBOARD LAYOUTS

Most keyboards use a layout called QWERTY, named for the keys in the upper-left corner of the keyboard. Figure 3.1 shows a typical keyboard layout. The letter and number keys are easy to recognize. You also have keys for special characters such as ! or @. In addition, a keyboard includes these special keys:

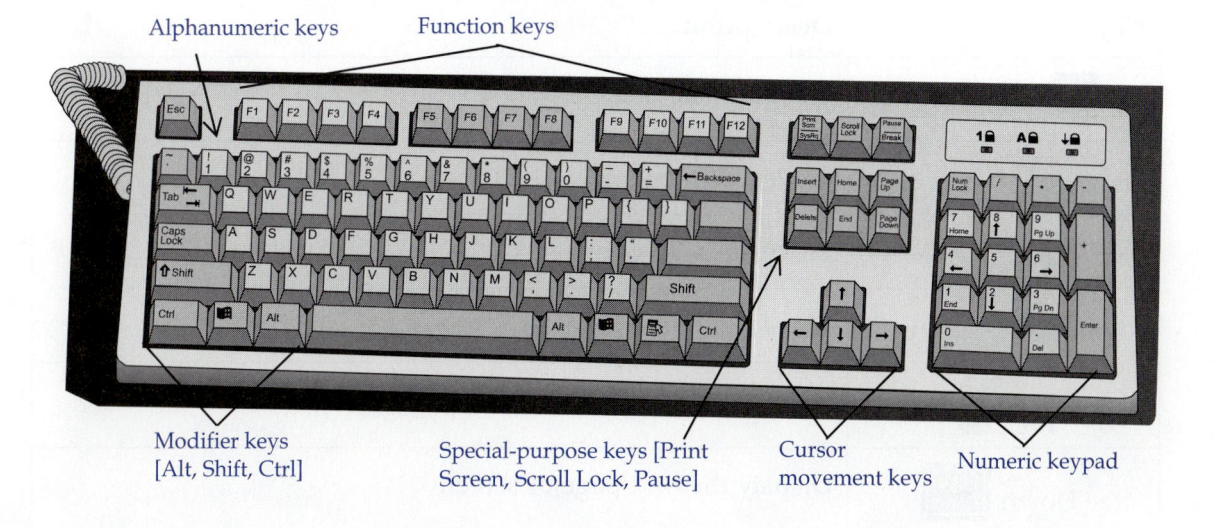

Figure 3.1. A typical keyboard includes alphanumeric keys, a numeric keypad, and function keys.

- *Function keys.* The function keys are labeled F1 through F12 and usually appear on the top row of the keyboard. Some keyboards include two sets of function keys at the top and left. Before the popularity of Windows and a graphical interface, function keys provided access to program features. For instance, you may press F1 to get help or F7 to start the speller. Function keys are still used as keyboard shortcuts.
- *Movement keys.* To move around a document, you can use the movement keys. (See the next section on movement keys.)
- *Modifier keys.* You can use the Shift, Alt, and Ctrl keys in conjunction with other keys to perform a different task. As a simple example, press the Shift key to type a capital letter. Alt and Ctrl are usually used for keyboard shortcuts. For instance, in Windows press Ctrl+X as a shortcut for selecting the Edit, Cut command.
- *Numeric keypad.* To simplify the entry of numbers, most keyboards include a numeric keypad. You can press the Num Lock key and use this keypad to enter numbers. If Num Lock is not pressed, you can use these keys for cursor movement.

> **Turn Num Lock on:** To turn Num Lock on, press the Num Lock key. Press the key again to turn it off. You can tell when Num Lock is on because you should see an indicator light on the keyboard.

- *Special-purpose keys.* Your keyboard also includes some special-purpose keys including Print Screen (used for printing the current screen), Scroll Lock (used for special cursor movements in different programs), and Pause (used for pausing a program, usually some type of batch program).

MOVING AROUND A DOCUMENT

The movement keys enable you to move around in a document. This set of keys also includes two editing keys (Insert and Delete). Here's a common list of movement keys and their associated action.

Key	Description
Up ↑	Move up one line
Down ↓	Move down one line
Left ←	Move left one character
Right →	Move right one character
Page Up	Display the previous page or screen
Page Down	Display the next page or screen

Key	Description
Home [Home]	Move to the beginning of the line or document
End [End]	Move to the end of the line or document
Insert [Ins]	Change editing modes from Insert to Typeover
Delete [Del]	Delete the selected item

Backspace vs. Delete: You can use either Backspace or Delete to delete selected text or graphics. You can also delete individual characters. Backspace deletes characters to the left of the insertion point. Delete removes characters to the right of the insertion point.

AVOIDING INJURY

While it may seem ridiculous that you can get injured typing, you can. Repetitive movements, such as typing on a keyboard, can cause repetitive stress injuries (RSI), such as carpal tunnel syndrome. To protect yourself, consider these tips:

- *Type with your hands in the proper position.* Your hands should be parallel to the floor when typing. That is, you shouldn't have to bend your wrists up or down to type.
- *Use a wrist rest.* You can purchase a wrist rest to support your wrists when typing. You can also purchase bracelets to wear as a support.
- *Purchase a special keyboard.* Companies have created new ergonomic keyboards to prevent injury. For instance, Microsoft sells a special keyboard with a layout more suited for typing (see Figure 3.2). This keyboard is contoured, allowing a more natural movement for typing.

Figure 3.2. You can purchase ergonomic keyboards.

WEB: Visit http://www.microsoft.com/hardware/mouseandkeyboard to get information about the keyboards (and mice) Microsoft offers.

- *Take breaks and do stretching exercises.* You can also avoid injury by doing exercises to stretch and relax your wrists and fingers. Also, take a break if you have long spells of typing.

Lesson 3   **Learning Computer Concepts**
Using Input and Output Devices

Using a Mouse

Initially all a computer had for input was a keyboard, which was fine because all computing was command-based. You had to type a command to get the computer to do anything. Macintosh and Windows programs changed all that. Windows changed from a command-based computing system to a graphical user interface. That is, instead of typing a command to start a program, you could use an icon. You can double-click a program shortcut icon to start the program or use the Start menu. While you can do these actions with the keyboard, they are most easily done with a mouse.

> **Macs and mice:** Macintosh computers always used a graphical interface and included a mouse. In fact, Windows (some say) was modeled on the Macintosh or at least on technology employed by the Mac.

Now a mouse is standard equipment on a computer, and you use a mouse to perform these common tasks:

- *Start programs.* As mentioned, you use a mouse to start a program. You can double-click a program icon or click the commands in the Start menu.
- *Select text.* When you want to modify text, you start by selecting the text you want to edit, format, or otherwise change. You can select text with a mouse by dragging across it. You can also use the mouse to select data in other programs, for instance, a range in a worksheet or entries in a database.
- *Move and resize items.* You can use the mouse to resize a window or to move a window around on the desktop. You can also use a mouse to move and resize graphics. Figure 3.3, for instance, shows a picture selected. Note the selection handles around the picture. You can use these to resize this picture.

Figure 3.3. You can use a mouse to select and move or resize a graphic object.

TYPES OF MICE

When you purchase a new computer, it comes with a mouse. Different manufacturers offer different mice, but most look similar to one illustrated in Figure 3.4. The mouse may be shaped differently (to best suit your hand); it may come in designer colors. Most mice include at least two buttons (a right and a left button). Some may offer a third button. The IntelliMouse by Microsoft includes a scrolling button in the middle of the mouse. You can use this to scroll through a document. Macintosh mice may have only one button.

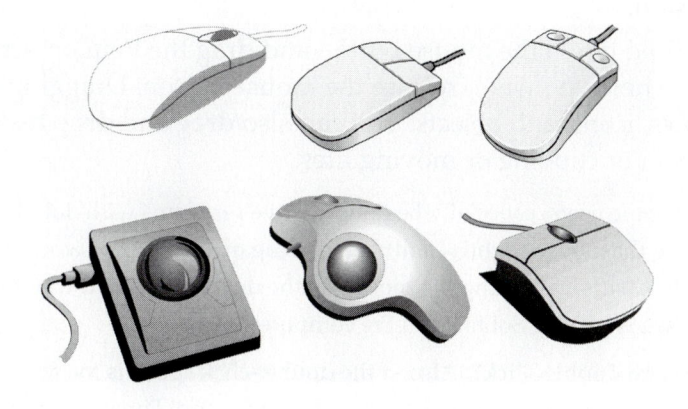

Figure 3.4. Most mice include at least two buttons.

Newer systems may have an optical mouse. Introduced in 1999, optical mice have a light emitting device (LED); this displays a red light that bounces light off the service and then sends information to the computer telling it where to move to. The cursor appears to move very smoothly, one reason for its popularity. Also, because it doesn't have any moving parts, the mouse is less likely to develop problems, including dirt getting inside the mouse and affecting its tracking sensors. Finally, this type of mouse does not require a mouse pad.

WEB: Visit www.logitech.com, a popular mouse maker. Take a look at the different types of mice and keyboards offered. Note the other products this company makes.

Regular mice connect via a cable to the system unit. Newer optical mice use infrared technology, and they are not connected with a cable. You also have a special file on your system called a mouse driver. This file tells your operating system the type of mouse and how to work with the mouse.

Change mouse drivers: If you are having problems with your mouse or get a new driver or new mouse, you can update the mouse information. In Windows, click the Start button, right-click My Computer, and select Properties. Click the Hardware tab and then click the Device Manager button. Then expand the listing for Mice and other pointing devices so that you can see your mouse listed. Right-click your mouse and then click Properties. Click the Driver tab. You can use the options in this dialog box (including other tabs) to review driver information and update the driver.

Lesson 3
Using Input and Output Devices

COMMON MOUSE ACTIONS

To use a mouse, you need to learn these common mouse actions:

- *Point.* To point with the mouse, you move the mouse on the desktop until the corresponding pointer on-screen points to the item you want.
- *Click.* To click, you press the mouse button once. Most often you click the left mouse button. For shortcuts, you may be instructed to click the right mouse button. This is called right-clicking.
- *Double-click.* To double-click, you press the left mouse button twice in rapid succession.
- *Drag.* Hold down the mouse button and drag the item on-screen. When the item is where you want, release the mouse button. Dragging is used to move windows, icons, and objects. You can also drag and drop text when editing a document or copying or moving files.

Practice. Some users, especially beginners, have problems with double-click. They click, move the mouse slightly, and then click again. This won't work. You have to double-click without moving the mouse on the desktop. A good way to practice mouse tasks is playing Solitaire on the computer.

Trouble with double-click? Also, if the double-click speed is too fast or too slow, you can change it. To do so, click Start and then Control Panel. Open the Mouse Control Panel. (In Classic view, double-click the Mouse icon. In Category view, click on Printers and Other Hardware and then click on Mouse in the lower half of the screen.) Adjust the double-click speed as needed.

Using Other Input Devices

Mice and keyboards aren't the only type of input devices. You can also find trackballs, joysticks, game pads, and others, as covered here.

TRACKBALLS

A trackball looks like an upside-down mouse. On a mouse, you'll find a little ball underneath that rolls along the desktop. In a trackball, this ball is on top, and you move the pointer by rolling the ball. Because it takes less space, a trackball is sometimes found on notebook computers.

Giving presentations: You can purchase a special kind of trackball useful for presentations. Rather than stand at the computer to display the presentation, the presenter can move around the room and move from slide to slide with the remote-control trackball.

Other notebook computers use a trackpad or touchpad for moving the mouse. For instance, IBM's popular notebook ThinkPad uses a trackpad (see Figure 3.5). You move the mouse by moving your finger around on the pad. To click, use the left button beneath the trackpad. To right-click, click the right-button.

Figure 3.5. As another alternative, a notebook computer may include a trackpad, used for moving the mouse pointer.

JOYSTICKS AND OTHER GAME DEVICES

If you play a lot of games, you may want a more arcade-like control. In this case, you can use a joystick, flight yoke, or other game device (like a steering wheel). The joystick includes a lever for moving around as well as buttons (see Figure 3.6).

Figure 3.6. For games, you might use a joystick, which connects to a special game port on the back of the computer.

PENS

If you've ever signed for a package electronically, you've used a type of electronic pen. Some computers provide this type of input device. You can use the pen not only to write notes but also to select commands. Many PDAs (personal digital assistants) include an electronic pen. Because handwriting varies so much, a pen isn't that useful for typing data. It's appropriate for notes and signatures, but not for longer documents.

Graphic artists and engineers often use a special type of light pen with a drawing or digitizing table for drawing or creating blueprints. With a graphics tablet, for instance, an artist can sketch, trace, or work with existing drawings by using a light pen to draw on the tablet.

TOUCH SCREENS

Another popular type of input device is a touch screen. Every time you take money out of an ATM, you use this type of entry. You touch the screen to select commands and enter data. Many libraries include this type of entry system because it is easy to use. As another example, you may come across an information kiosk at the shopping mall that provides access to information via a touch screen.

ENVIRONMENTAL AND SCIENTIFIC PROBES

In special workplaces and industries, probes and sensors may be hooked up to the computer to input data. For instance, a sensor may conduct pH and temperature tests and input the data to the computer. Or an environmental probe many measure humidity or electronic currents.

VOICE RECOGNITION

Typing and entering data are the most repetitive, error-prone, and tedious tasks for using a computer. New ways of getting data onto the computer are introduced, perfected, and adapted all the time. For instance, voice recognition is another way to enter data. Currently, this type of input isn't mainstream; you may find it in some programs, but it's probably not accurate enough to use it for entering lots of data.

This type of input device works by translating spoken words into text, using a sound card, a microphone, and voice recognition software. You can use this setup not only to enter text, but also to select commands. Most programs come with commands they recognize. Because voices differ, you must speak clearly and spend some time training the software to recognize your unique pronunciation.

Getting Digital Images

In addition to input devices for selecting commands and entering text, you can also use special input devices to create digital images. You can do so using a scanner or a digital camera.

Before the arrival of digital cameras, the only way to convert a photograph into a digital file type was using a scanner. A scanner works like a copy machine, but instead of making a copy, the scanner converts the image into a digital file. You can use a scanner for photographs or any type of illustration.

More recently, digital cameras have become popular. This type of camera stores the image as a digital file. You can then copy or move the file from the camera's memory to the computer via a cable. Some cameras have a disk (or similar media like a card) as the storage device, and you can move pictures from your camera to other sources (the computer, a multifunction printer, or printing kiosks, for instance).

Also, you can get traditional files developed as digital files on a photo CD (in addition to having the film developed as traditional pictures). Most film developers offer this option. You can then open these digital photo files and display and edit the photograph. Figure 3.7 shows a photograph from Kodak's PhotoCD (or PCD).

Figure 3.7. You can manipulate photographs.

USING A SCANNER

As mentioned, one way to get data into the computer is using a scanner. This type of input device is most commonly used to scan in pictures or illustrations. You can also use a scanner to scan text, but this requires special software. You can find special-purpose scanners, such as a bar code reader.

You can use a scanner to create an electronic file (and image) from a paper image. For instance, you can sell items at online auctions at eBay. To provide pictures of the items for sale, you can scan them. Scanners range in price from $100 on up. You can find two basic types of scanners: handheld scanners and flatbed scanners. (You can also get a multifunction printer that provides fax capabilities. These are covered later in this lesson.)

WEB: Visit www.hp.com or www.epson.com. Use the links to navigate to the pages that cover the various scanners sold. Note the different models and price range.

Handheld scanners are the least expensive. You create the image by taking the scanner and running it over the image or item. Flatbed scanners work like copy machines. You place the image on the scanner and then scan or copy the image. Figure 3.8 shows a

Lesson 3
Using Input and Output Devices

flatbed scanner. Grayscale scanners can create images in black and white. Color scanners can process color images.

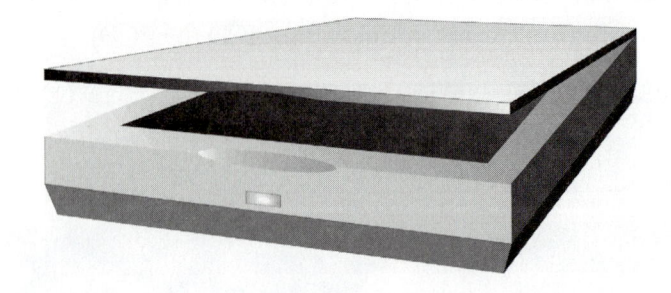

Figure 3.8. You place the image on the scanner and then scan it, much like making a copy on a copy machine.

Once an image is scanned, you can include it in documents or on Web pages. You can print it using your printer. You can also use special software to edit or enhance the image.

You can also use a scanner to scan text. This task requires not only the scanner but also special software to translate the scanned characters into text that you can edit. This type of software is called optical character recognition (OCR) and can be quite expensive. The software allows you to edit the text as though it were word processing text. Without OCR software the text would scan as one whole picture. Usually you have to check the resulting text to be sure the results are accurate. As technology advances, you'll find OCR software that works better and is less expensive.

Scan it: When you shop at a store, the cashier may use a special bar code reader to scan the items you want to purchase. This type of scanner reads a special bar code (a pattern printed on products) and then enters the item and price. Bar code is also used with a remote-control wand to access tracks on a laser disc player.

DIGITAL CAMERAS

Another source of digital images is the digital camera. Rather than take a picture and then send the film out to be developed, you can use a digital camera. Then, with your computer and printer, you can print the resulting photographs. (Note that the quality depends on your printer.) You can also copy the digital photographs to your PC and insert them into documents or Web pages. With special editing software, you can even edit the photographs.

WEB: For information on digital cameras, visit www.kodak.com. Note the differences between cameras (as well as the prices). You can also visit other popular camera makers to find out about their digital models: Cannon (www.canon.com), Nikon (www.nikon.com), Sony (www.sony.com), Olympus (www.olympus.com), and others.

Digital cameras cost from $200 to $1800 or more. Here are some pointers for working with this type of camera:

- The quality of the image is measured by its resolution (the number of pixels). The higher the resolution, the better the image quality. Cameras vary in the minimum and maximum resolutions they offer. High-end cameras offer resolution from 5-megapixel up to 8-megapixel. Lower-end cameras are usually in the 2 to 3.2 megapixel range.
- Digital cameras vary in the number of images they can store. You can expect to be able to store anywhere from 40 to 100 or more images.
- Images are stored in the camera's memory (a special card or disk). Most cameras have 4M to 8M of memory.
- You can take the images from a camera and have them printed at a traditional film developer. You can also print the images on your printer at home. Using special paper will help give you better quality. You can save money by selecting which images to develop or print. (You can delete any out-of-focus or otherwise "bad" pictures.) As another option, you can purchase special photo printers and print on traditional paper and size, with good results.
- To copy the images from the camera to the computer, you most often use a cable (connected via serial or USB port). The time it takes to copy the images (called the download time) varies. Some cameras include media cards, memory sticks, or disks that you can eject and then transfer to your computer, to printers with slots for these cards, or to printing kiosks.
- Digital cameras operate on batteries, and the cost and battery life vary from camera to camera.
- A good way to store pictures is to copy them to a CD. You can do this yourself. Or you can ask a local film developer to do this (copy your pictures from either actual photos or from digital images to a CD for safekeeping).
- Like traditional cameras, digital cameras vary in the features they offer such as focal range, controls for aperture, and so on. If you are a fairly advanced photographer, you may investigate these camera features.

Photo printer: You can purchase special printers for printing photographs, including HP PhotoSmart, Kodak Personal Picture Maker, and Sony Digital Photo Printer. These range in cost from $200 to $500.

VIDEO CAMERAS

In addition to photographs, you can also create, edit, and play back videos using a video camera and video software. You can create your own home movies or include video clips on a Web site. Some digital cameras enable you to shoot videos with audio. Keep in mind that the video features of a camera are basic; if you want to create home movies or other productions, you'll most likely want a video camera.

Lesson 3
Using Input and Output Devices

As another option, you might have a Web cam. You can transmit live video images via the Internet. A common application of this type of input device is for videoconferencing. You can also shoot video with a digital video camera and then download the video to your computer for editing.

> **WEB:** Go to www.logitech.com and see what video cameras this company offers. Consider how you might use this type of computer component.

Making Sense of Monitors

In addition to input devices, you also have key output devices for your computer. You have output devices that enable you to display data (the monitor) and print data (the printer). These are common output devices that you use daily. Other output devices, such as plotters, are used for specialized purposes.

To display programs and see data, your system has a monitor. The monitor is actually two components: the TV-like thing that sits on your desktop and an electronic card housed in your system unit (see Figure 3.9). (This card is sometimes called the video adapter or video card.) This section will explain the important concepts about a monitor and adapter.

Figure 3.9. The monitor displays programs and data.

HOW MONITORS VARY

Monitors differ in image quality, size, and performance. Here are just a few of the factors to consider when evaluating monitors:

- *Size.* Monitors, like TVs, are measured diagonally. Common monitor sizes include 15" up to 21". The bigger the monitor, the larger the working area or display.

Learning Computer Concepts
Lesson 3
Using Input and Output Devices

> **Graphics work:** People who work with graphics or detailed CAD (technical drawing software) programs often benefit from a bigger monitor. You can also purchase side-by-side monitors for displaying two pages at once.

- *Resolution.* Resolution is a measure of the number of pixels (picture elements) that can be displayed. The higher the number, the more detailed the image. Most monitors let you select from several resolutions. Common resolutions include 800 x 600 (800 pixels by 600 pixels) and 1024 x 768. To understand the difference, compare Figure 3.10, which shows 800 x 600, and Figure 3.11, which shows 1024 x 768.

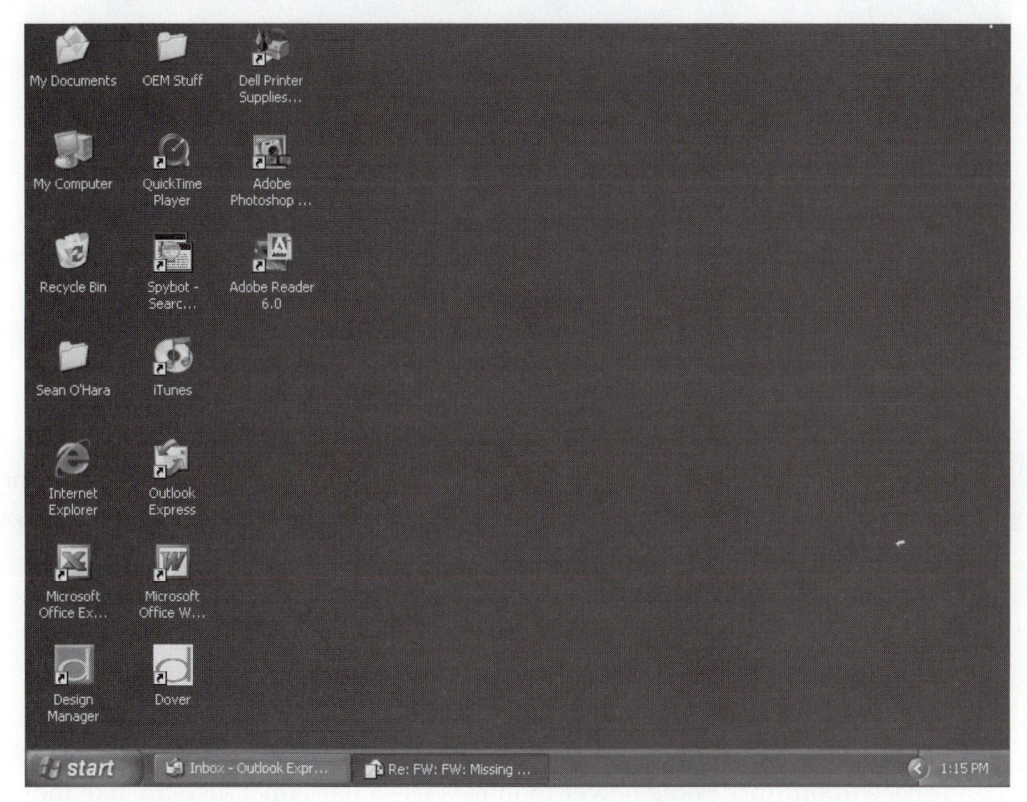

Figure 3.10. In 800 x 600 resolution, the image is bigger, and the image details are not as fine.

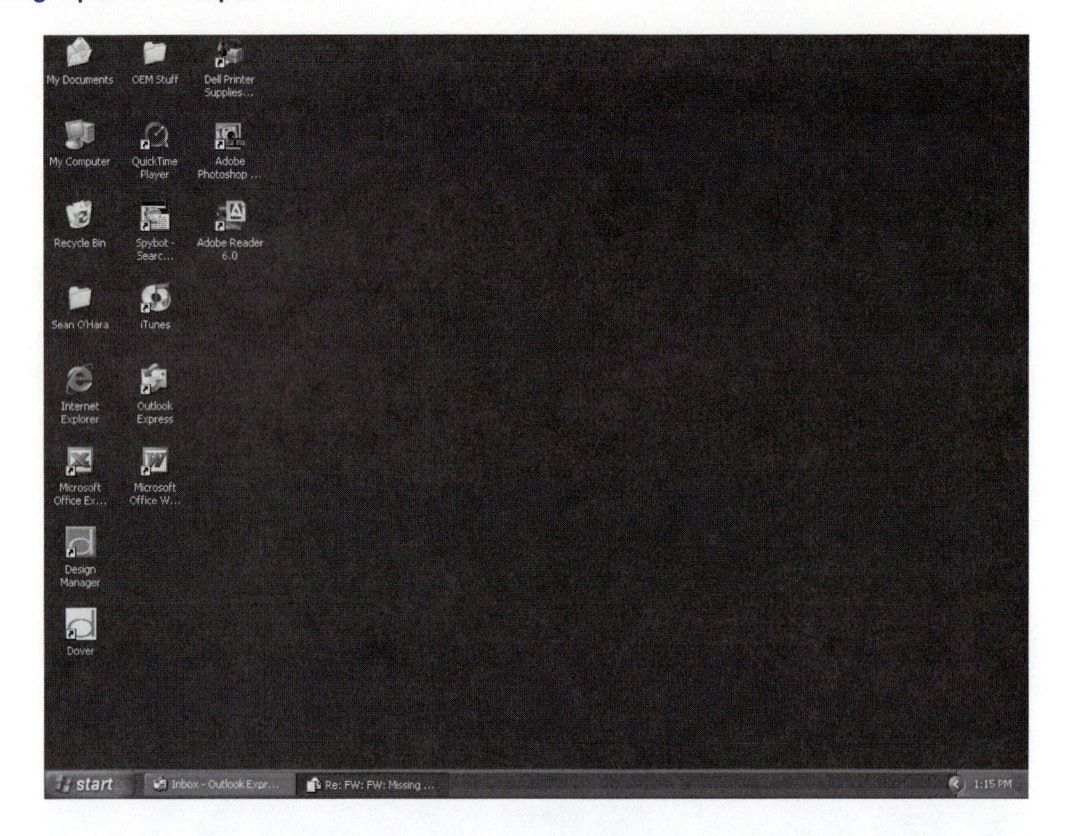

Lesson 3
Using Input and Output Devices
Learning Computer Concepts

Figure 3.11. In 1024 x 768 resolution, the image is smaller, but the quality is better.

> **Select your resolution:** You can change the resolution of your monitor. To do so, right-click a blank part of the Windows desktop and then select Properties. Click the Settings tab and then select the resolution by dragging the Screen resolution slider bar.

- *Colors*. Monitors also differ in the number of colors they can display. Like resolution, you can usually switch among different color settings.
- *Display standard*. Older monitors may use a different standard for the display. This is no longer an issue.
- *Footprint size.* Monitors tend to be big and bulky and take quite a bit of desk space (footprint). Some newer monitors use a flat-panel display, like those used for notebooks.

> **Monitors and TV.** You can also get monitors with special features for displaying HDTV on your computer monitor. You can also get a TV within a window if you have the Windows Media Center edition on their PC.

GRAPHICS CARD

The quality of your image is determined in part by the actual monitor, but also by the video card. The video card is housed inside your system unit; your monitor is connected to the card via a cable. The monitor and the video card are a set. That is, when you purchase a new computer, it comes with a graphics card. If you purchase a new monitor, you can use the existing graphics card (if you buy a compatible monitor) or get a new graphics card. As another combination, you can purchase a new graphics card that extends the capabilities of your current monitor. The graphics card must support the type of monitor you own.

Most graphics cards include memory to help speed the processing of the data image. This memory is called video RAM, or VRAM. The more memory, the faster your computer can process and display the image. You can also find special graphics accelerator cards, which greatly enhance your graphics capabilities. The average user doesn't need a speedier card. If you use your computer for extensive multimedia (creating videos, playing graphics-intensive games, creating multimedia), you may want to consider a graphics accelerator card.

LAPTOP MONITORS

Laptops (notebooks) use a different type of monitor. The regular monitor type is too bulky, so laptops use a flat-panel monitor that's usually about ½" thick. Most laptops use a liquid crystal display (LCD). Calculators use the same type of display. You can find two types of LCDs: active matrix and passive matrix. These differ in the technical details of how the transistors and pixels are aligned. Basically, active matrix displays are better quality, but more expensive.

Purchasing a laptop? Monitors for a laptop can vary greatly and may be the most important consideration when purchasing this type of computer. What's the best way to evaluate them? Look at the display yourself. You can see which laptop has the crisper display.

PROJECTORS

If you use your computer to display a presentation or to share data such as sales figures, you can also hook up a projector to your computer and then display the screen onto a screen or wall. For instance teachers may lead the class through a computer exercise using a projector to display the actions on a projected screen. Sales representatives may give a presentation and use a projector to show sales information.

When evaluating projectors, look into these factors: brightness (measured in ANSI lumens), portability, resolution, uniformity, and features. For brightness, 800-1000 lumens is acceptable for lights-off presentations in classroom-size rooms. If you want to show a presentation in bright light in a training or conference room, look for a projector in the 2500-5000 lumens range. For the best resolution, match the projector's resolution to the resolution of your monitor. Look for a uniformity rating of 85% or better for the most consistent images. Features depend on your needs. You can find projectors that connect via a cable or are wireless, that provide wireless control, and also have video inputs, to name the most common features.

Printing

The printer is the other most common output device. Printers let you print hard-copy versions of documents. Printers vary in cost, quality, speed, and special features. Cost is directly related to the quality and speed. You can find printers starting at $100 and costing up to several thousand dollars. Quality is a measure of the resolution similar to a monitor's quality, only printer resolution is a measure of the number of dots per inch (dpi). Speed is measured by the number of pages printed per minute (ppm). Slow printers print around 2 pages per minute. Speedier (and more expensive printers) may be able to print 30 pages or more. Printers may also have extra memory to speed processing of pages.

Printers also vary in how the image is created on the page. You can find three basic types of printers: dot-matrix, inkjet, and laser.

DOT-MATRIX PRINTERS

Dot-matrix printers were once a popular choice because they were inexpensive. These printers work by firing a series of pins against a ribbon to create dots. Think about an impressionist painting, composed all of dots. A printout from a dot-matrix printer is the same. Each character, number, or illustration is composed of lots of little dots. The quality of the printout ranges from OK to pretty bad. This type of printer is pretty much obsolete, although you will find it in companies that need to print multipart forms. For example, car service stations often print their receipts (multipart forms) on a dot-matrix printer.

INKJET PRINTERS

Inkjets are probably the most common type of printer today. They offer a good mix of quality and affordability. This type of printer includes cartridges that squirt ink onto the page (see Figure 3.12). Most inkjet printers print in color as well as black and white. (Inkjets offer the most affordable way to have a color printer. See the section on color printers later in this lesson.) Prices range from entry-level inkjet printers at the very low end at around $40 up to $250 or more.

Figure 3.12. An inkjet printer is a popular model, especially for low-cost color printing.

LASER PRINTERS

Laser printers create an image using technology similar to a copy machine. The paper is rolled around a drum, and toner is applied from the drum to the paper. This type of printer may be more expensive than a comparable inkjet, but it is reliable, durable, and provides great quality. Laser printers are especially useful as network printers. You can expect speeds ranging from 4 to 16 pages per minute for black and white low-end laser printers; more expensive models may be able to print from 15 to 50 pages per minute. Prices begin around $200. Figure 3.13 shows an illustration of a laser printer.

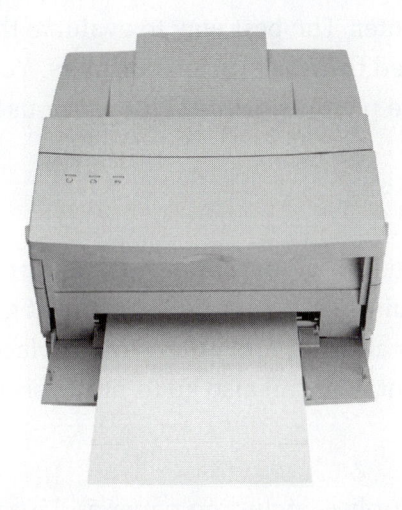

Figure 3.13. A laser printer provides great quality and good printing speed.

COLOR PRINTERS

It used to be that you could purchase only high-end (expensive) color printers, but the introduction of color inkjet printers changed all that. This type of printer offers color at an affordable price. (Expect to pay a little more for a color inkjet vs. the same quality black-and-white printer.) You can find color inkjet printers as cheap as $40 to $100.

If you purchase a color printer, the specifications may include two speeds: one for printing in black and white and one for printing in color. (Color takes more time, as do documents with lots of graphics.)

You can also purchase color laser printers, but these are more expensive than their black-and-white counterparts and much more expensive than inkjet color printers.

COMBINATION PRINTERS/FAXES/COPY MACHINES

You can also find printers that combine several features; these are usually called multifunction printers. Designed for small businesses and home offices, this printer type can function as a printer, a fax, and a copy machine. The printer may also be able to function as a scanner. Inexpensive models of this type of printer can cost as little as $100. You can also find printers with more features and better quality in the higher price range.

Lesson 3
Using Input and Output Devices

> **WEB:** Visit www.hp.com. Use the links to view the various types of printers that this popular printer manufacturer sells as well as the pricing and various technical differences among the different printers.

PHOTO PRINTERS

As digital cameras have become more popular, special photo printers were introduced to the market. You can find small photo printers that print on traditional size and quality photo paper. You can also print from other printers to special printer paper. If you plan to print photos, check out the photo features of a general purpose printer (if that's your choice) or a special photo printer. The best way to evaluate them is to visit a retail store and view actual photos printed from the various printers. You can also find photo printer reviews which include pictures printed from various printers to get a good idea of each printer's quality.

PLOTTERS

Another special type of printer is a plotter. This is used to print large documents such as banners or blueprints for a building. You may find these at graphic design houses, architectural and constructional firms, and other similar places. If you only occasionally need to print a large document, you can also go to print service bureaus such as Kinkos.

PRINTING SUPPLIES

To use a printer, you need supplies, including paper and ink. The ink will depend on the type of printer and specific model. Some may use a ribbon, similar to a typewriter ribbon. Others use cartridges. For instance, most laser printers use toner cartridges. The price of the ink can get expensive. You may pay as much as $80 for a toner cartridge for a laser printer. (How long these supplies last depends on how much and what you print. If you print a lot of graphics, for instance, the toner will run out sooner. If you print mostly text, your toner will last longer.)

If you have a color printer—for instance, an inkjet color printer—you'll have two cartridges: one for black and one for color. Inkjet cartridges aren't cheap either; you can pay between $20 to $40 depending on the type of cartridge you need for your computer. And, as mentioned, if you have a color laser printer, you'll have to purchase two cartridges.

PRINTER PORTS

A printer is connected to your system unit via a cable. One end of the cable plugs into the printer and one into the back of the system unit. Some printers connect to the LPT port (often called the printer port or parallel). You may find some printers that connect to the serial port, and many newer printers connect to the USB port.

Printing a document in most applications follows the same basic set of steps.

Follow these basic steps to print a document:

1 Open the document you want to print.

2 Select the Print command. Usually, you select File, Print. You can also look for a Print button in the toolbar or in Windows use the keyboard shortcut (Ctrl+P). You see the Print dialog box (see Figure 3.14).

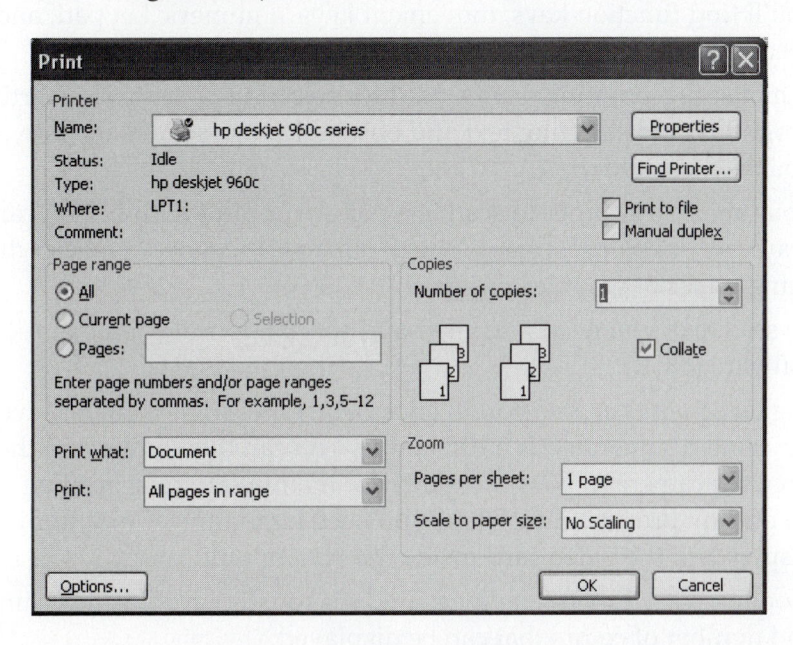

Figure 3.14. Select options for printing this document.

3 Make any changes to the options for printing the document, including the number of copies, pages printed, and so on.

4 Click OK. The document is printed.

Save time and paper: You can save time and paper by previewing your document before printing. Look for a Print Preview command in the File menu.

Lesson 3   **Learning Computer Concepts**
Using Input and Output Devices

Summary

- To enter data into the computer, you need input devices. Common input devices include keyboards, mice, trackballs, and pens. Newer technology includes voice recognition capabilities.
- Most keyboards use the QWERTY layout. In addition to alphanumeric keys, you'll find function keys, movement keys, a numeric keypad, and other special-purpose keys.
- A mouse is a pointing device used for selecting commands, starting programs, and selecting text and objects. Mouse actions include point, click, double-click, and drag.
- You can use a scanner to scan in a picture or photograph. You can purchase a grayscale or color scanner. Once the image is scanned, you can then edit it using a special graphics program.
- To scan text, you need a scanner and special optical character recognition software (OCR).
- Digital cameras enable you to take pictures with the camera, saving them in the camera's memory as a digital file. You can then download the images from the camera to your computer for manipulating or printing.
- To display programs and data, you need a monitor. A monitor is both the display and the video card inside the system unit.
- Monitors vary in the size (measured diagonally), resolution or image quality, and number of colors that can be displayed.
- Laptops use a special type of monitor; most are LCDs, or liquid crystal displays. You can buy flat-panel monitors for your computer that take up less space; this type of monitor costs more.
- The newest type of mouse is an optical mouse which doesn't have any moving parts and uses a LED to position the mouse cursor on the screen.
- To print hard-copy versions of your documents, you need a printer. The two most popular printer types are inkjet and laser printers. These printers vary in cost, quality of image, and speed (measured in pages printed per minute).
- To print a document, use the File, Print command.

Learning Computer Concepts — Lesson 3: Using Input and Output Devices

Q&A

Multiple Choice

1. Keyboards include:
    a. Function keys
    b. Movement keys
    c. Numeric keys
    d. All of the above

2. Resolution for a monitor is a measure of the number of:
    a. Pixels
    b. Inches
    c. Centimeters
    d. Megabytes

3. This type of printer works like a copier:
    a. Inkjet
    b. Laser
    c. Dot-matrix
    d. Photo printer

4. Typing with your hands in the proper position is one way to avoid this type of injury:
    a. Eye strain
    b. Headaches
    c. Repetitive stress injury
    d. Back spasms

Fill in the Blank

1. A(n) _____ mouse does not require a cable; it uses infrared signals to move the pointer on-screen.
2. A(n) _____ is a common input device for playing games.
3. _____ printers work by squirting ink onto the page.
4. The quality of your monitor is determined by the monitor and also the _____ which is housed inside the system unit.

Short Essay

1. Explain the key mouse actions: point, click, double-click, right-click, and drag.
2. Name the different ways that you can create digital images.

LESSON 4: DEFINING SOFTWARE

Objectives

- Understand how software works
- Describe what to consider when purchasing or upgrading software
- Define word processing and identify the main word processing programs and features
- Describe spreadsheet programs and identify spreadsheet programs and basic features
- Describe database programs
- Define presentation programs
- Describe publishing
- Define graphics programs
- Discuss other program types

Understanding Software

Most of your time spent using a computer will be spent within a program, such as a word processing program or a game. As described in Lesson 1, software is a set of programming instructions that you use to accomplish a certain task. Programs are designed for different purposes. For example, you use a word processing program to create documents such as reports, memos, letters, manuscripts, and so on. Another common program is a spreadsheet; you use this to create mostly numeric documents such as budgets, expense records, income statements, loan payments, and so on.

> **Many names:** When referring to software, you may hear the terms program, application, software, or any combination of these terms (software application, for instance). They all mean the same thing.

This section starts by discussing how software and hardware work together and how to purchase and install software. You then learn about some different types of programs.

UNDERSTANDING HOW SOFTWARE WORKS

Software is a set of instructions that communicates with your hardware and performs certain actions (such as displaying a character on-screen). You interact with the software in a variety of ways: you type on the keyboard, and you select commands from the menu (using the mouse or the keyboard). The software then translates these actions into language the hardware can understand, and the appropriate action occurs. For instance, you press the letter "P," and the letter "P" appears in a document on-screen.

Your interaction with the software is called input, and you use certain input devices such as a keyboard for typing characters and numbers, a mouse for selecting commands and items on-screen, a scanner for converting an illustration into a digital file, a microphone for recording sound, a digital camera for taking pictures, and others. (Input devices are covered in Chapter 3.)

The computer takes the input and translates it to output (displaying a character on a screen, printing a document, for instance). The computer processes all of these data and requests using complex rules called algorithms.

UNDERSTANDING HOW SOFTWARE IS CREATED

Programs are created by programmers writing lines of code in a programming language. This language tells the computer how to handle input from the user (and other sources) and how to create output (display characters, print, for instance). For new programs, a plan is created that determines what features the program will have, how it will look, and other design details. Marketing and sales people, product manager, customers, and other provide feedback and suggestions for this process.

New programs (or upgraded versions of existing programs) go through a testing process. The programmers and testers are looking for bugs (problems, inconsistencies, and other things). The testing phase is often called the beta review and is often open to advanced users who test the program in real-world situations and provide feedback. These quality control tests help ensure that when the final program is complete, it has been thoroughly reviewed and many bugs (problems) have been fixed. (Bugs are difficult to get rid of, so most software still have bugs. Periodically bug patches are released when a bug is discovered; these patches fix the bug.)

BUYING A PROGRAM

Your computer may have come bundled with certain software programs. In addition, you may decide to purchase additional programs. First, decide what you need the software to do: create reports, manage your money, layout a newsletter. Then you can find a software program that matches your needs. You'll find there are several programs that suit your purposes. How do you decide? You can read reviews online or in computer magazines. Also, ask other computer users what programs they prefer. You can also visit computer, office supply, or electronic stores and review the program details to help you make your decision. You can purchase programs at computer or electronic stores (also some department stores such as Target or Wal-Mart carry some software), through online stores, or by calling any of the mail-order software companies.

Programs vary in price from free (called freeware) to expensive. You might spend thousands of dollars on a custom program. Most retail programs range in price from $25 up to several hundred dollars. The more sophisticated the program, the higher the price.

Lesson 4   Learning Computer Concepts
Defining Software

When purchasing a program, be sure to get the most current version. Also, if you require more than a word processing program, consider a suite, such as Microsoft Office. This package bundles together several popular programs. For instance, in one version of Microsoft Office, you receive Word, Excel, Outlook, Publisher, and some other programs for small businesses. Check out the bundle deals if you are shopping for new programs.

Finally, make sure your computer can run the software. You can find a list of requirement—the required disk space, processor type, memory, and so on—on the package or in the program description.

UPGRADING A PROGRAM

New versions of programs are introduced every 2-3 years. New features are often added, the software may be updated to take advantage of new technology (such as digital camera handling), or the software may be updated when a new version of an operating system is introduced. You'll often see new versions advertised in magazines, TV, and other media. New versions are also often previewed in computer publications. Finally, you may receive e-mail or regular mail from the software companies introducing the new program.

You will then have to decide whether to upgrade. If the new version has features that will be useful to you (save time, expand its use, and so on), you should upgrade. Another reason to upgrade is if your office or co-workers are upgrading; you want to have the same version that everyone else uses to avoid compatibility programs. Also, you may upgrade to take advantage of the being able to use new hardware and software functionality (as mentioned).

On the other hand, if you are content with your current program, you may not want to upgrade. When you upgrade a computer, you may find that it doesn't work well with your other programs or hardware. You may spend some time troubleshooting or tweaking problems to get the system features to be compatible.

If you choose to upgrade, you may do so by buying an upgrade version at a computer or other retailer that sells software. Most often, you pay less to upgrade than you do to purchase the program new. The installation program will check to be sure you have an existing version of the software, so don't try to purchase the upgrade if you don't actually have the software. A more recent method of upgrading is through the Internet. If you have a fast Internet connection, you can download the new program version files and install the new program from these files.

Some program manufacturers even set up automatic installations. For instance, this is common with anti-virus program where you want to keep up-to-date on any new viruses. Therefore, it's key you check for and install new program features often. These programs often schedule automatic updates.

Minor updates: Sometimes minor updates are released to a program. These may fix a software problem (a bug), add a new feature, or correct any security problems with the program. You can find and download these types of updates from the software company's site.

The rest of this lesson discusses different kinds of common programs.

What is Word Processing?

The most common type of computer program and the program used in most homes and offices is a word processing program. You can use a word processing program to create any type of text-based documents, including letters, memos, faxes, reports, manuscripts, newsletters, brochures, contracts, resumes, and manuals. Figure 4.1 shows a document created with a word processing program.

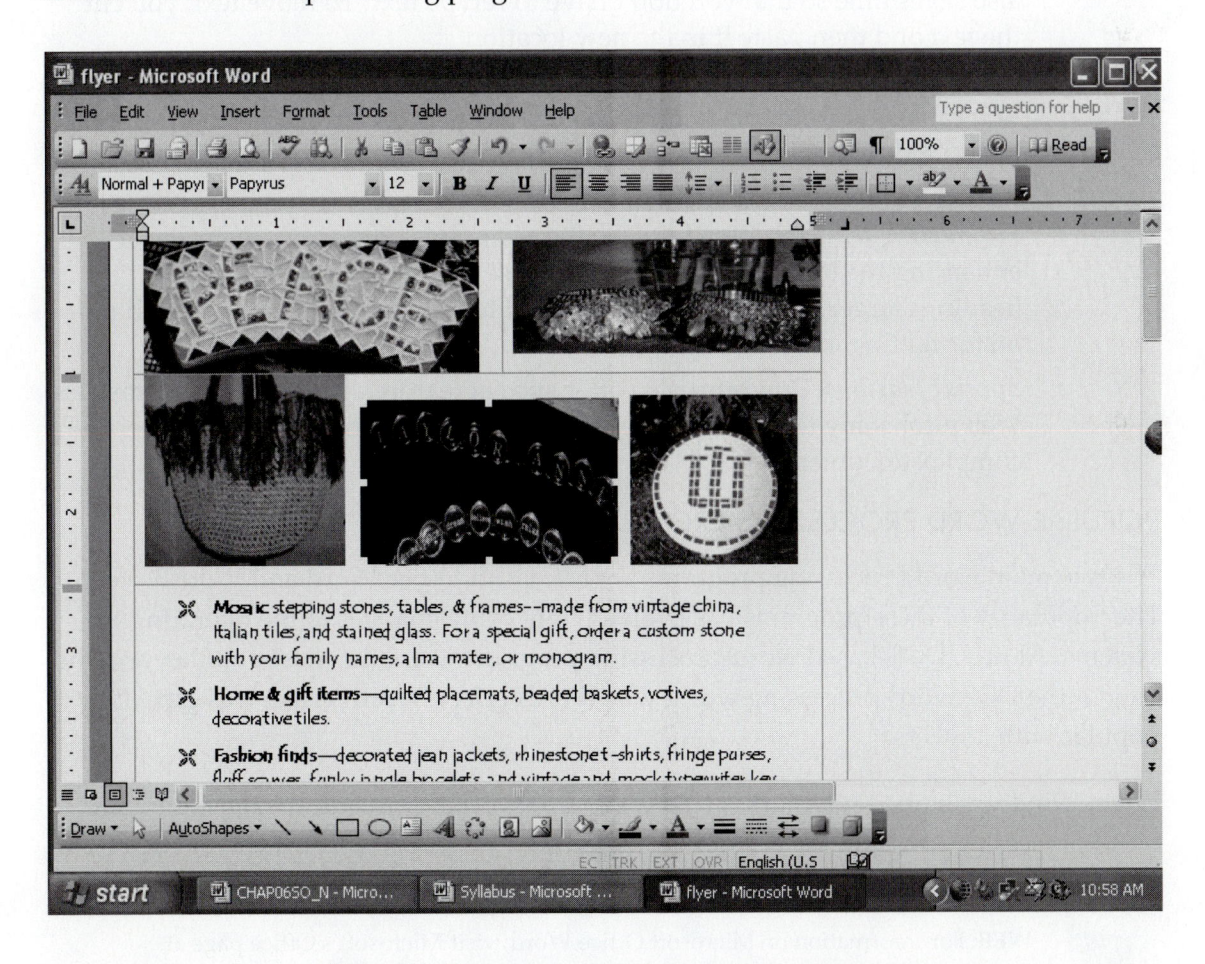

Figure 4.1. You can use a word processing program to create any type of document, including a flyer.

A word processing program offers many benefits. First, you can see the words on-screen as you type, so you can easily correct errors. You can backspace to delete and retype an incorrect word. Second, you can easily add text to any part of the document. Simply click where you want the new text and type. The new text is inserted, and the existing text moves over. And finally, you can delete text easily. You can select the text and press the Delete key to delete it. The existing text moves up to fill in the gap. (For more information on using this type of program, see Lessons 6 and 7.)

FEATURES AND BENEFITS OF WORD PROCESSING PROGRAMS

In addition to making typing and correcting text easier, a word processing program offers many features to simplify document creation. The following lists the basic features of word processing programs:

- *Editing features*. In addition to being able to insert and delete text, you can also copy and move text. You can copy and move within a document or from one document to another. You can even copy and move text from one program to another program. This copy and paste makes editing easier and also saves time so that you don't have to retype text. To move text, you cut the text and then paste it in the new location.
- *Checking features*. Most word processing programs have a spelling program. You can use this feature to check your document for errors. Some programs have a grammar checker for checking grammar and a thesaurus for looking up synonyms.
- *Formatting features*. Word processing programs offer many features for enhancing the look of the text. You can use a different typeface, make headings larger, change the text color, set tabs, and more. (You can find more on formatting in Lesson 7.)
- *Special features*. Programs also offer special features, such as tables, graphics, Web publishing tools, and more. You can use these special features to create complex documents.

POPULAR WORD PROCESSING PROGRAMS

The two main word processing programs are Microsoft Office Word and WordPerfect. The popularity of these programs has evolved, mirroring changes to the operating systems. At first, DOS-based word-processing programs were the most popular, and the king of the DOS word processing world was WordPerfect. WordPerfect was especially popular with lawyers.

When Windows gained popularity, so did Windows programs, and the most popular word processing program for Windows is Microsoft Word. This is now the most popular and commonly used word processing program.

> **WEB:** For information on Microsoft Office Word, visit Microsoft's Office page at www.office.microsoft.com. For information on WordPerect, visit Corel's Web site at www.corel.com and then look for links for information on WordPerfect.

Both Word and WordPerfect are top-of-the line, full-powered word processing programs and have comparable features. In addition to these programs, you can find simple versions of word processing programs. Windows, for instance, includes a word processing accessory called WordPad. Microsoft Works also includes a simpler version of a word processing program. If you use a Macintosh, you can use ClarisWorks, another integrated program.

What is a Spreadsheet?

A spreadsheet is probably the most common application next to word processing. If you need to work with any kind of numbers (financial data or statistical information), you'll benefit from a spreadsheet program. Spreadsheet programs are used to create documents called worksheets, which are set up like accounting paper. (For information on how to create worksheets, see Lesson 8.) You'll find rows and columns, used mostly for entering figures. Here are some examples of different worksheets you might create or work with:

- *Sales.* If you work in sales or perhaps sell some product yourself, you might use a worksheet to total sales. Businesses often use worksheets not only to total sales, but to forecast sales, to spot trends, to pinpoint sales problems, and to break down sales into meaningful categories. For instance, a company might total sales by division to see which division leads in sales. As another example, the same company might also total sales by quarter to see when sales peak (see Figure 4.2).

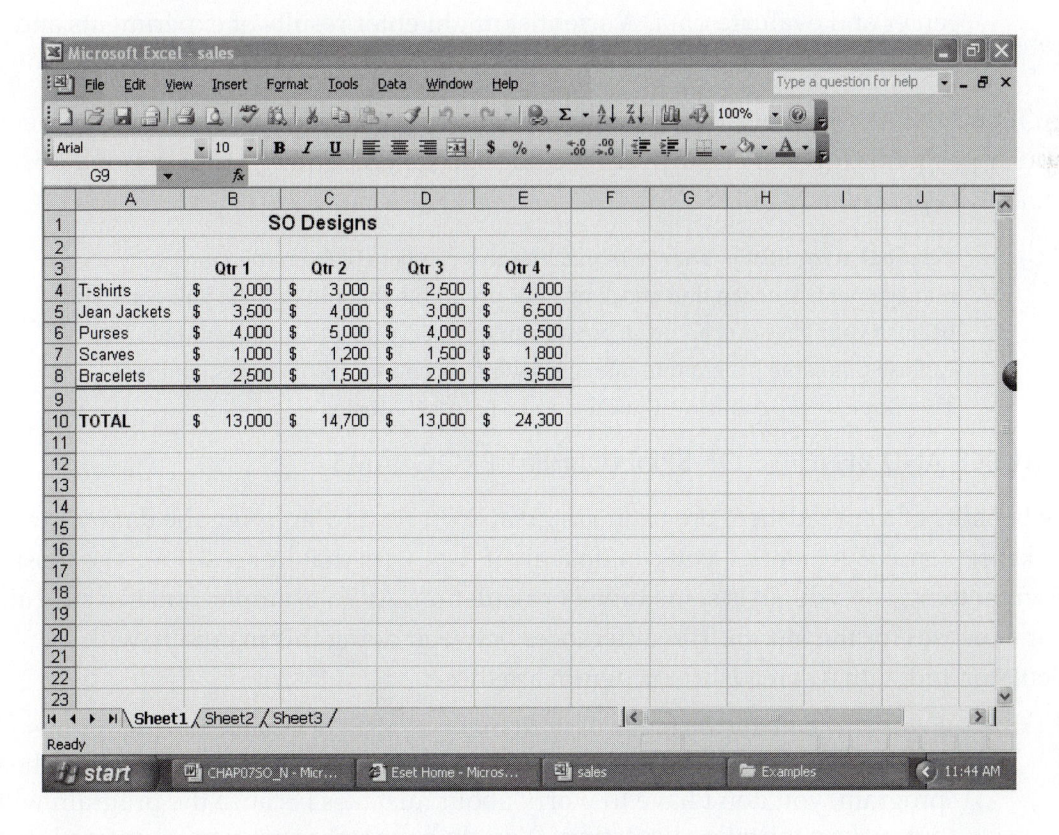

Figure 4.2. You can use a worksheet to total sales.

- *Budget.* You can list your expenses and create a budget. You can project what you think you'll spend, track what you actually spend, and compare the two.
- *Income.* If you have several sources of income, you can total your income with a worksheet. You might also use a worksheet to keep track of expenses and to prepare for tax time. As another example, small and large businesses use spreadsheet programs to prepare and analyze income and expense information.
- *Invoice.* You can set up a worksheet to list and total services for an invoice. To manage the finances of a business, the company financial person may keep a list of vendors and pay bills (accounts payable), keep track of customers and what they owe (accounts receivable), send invoices, and create reports (for instance, create aging reports to see which accounts are past due and how far past due they are).
- *Project management.* To keep track of projects, you can list goals or milestones and then track progress. As another example, contractors use worksheets to prepare bids. For instance, a roofing company might create a worksheet listing the work and materials and associated costs.
- *Data list.* Although a spreadsheet is not a full-featured database program, you can use it to keep track of simple lists, such as products, inventory, or collections.
- *Scientific data.* For certain science projects, you might use a worksheet to enter and evaluate data. A scientist might enter results of experiments and analyze data using some of the more sophisticated features of the program.

You'll find that spreadsheets are a popular program for handling financial data; other popular programs for similar purposes include special accounting programs and tax preparation programs.

Personal accounting: Your personal finances can benefit from this same type of management. You can find check register programs that not only let you enter and balance your checking account, but also help you create and track a budget. You can use this same program to manage savings accounts, print checks, and more. Two popular programs are Quicken and Microsoft Money.

FEATURES AND BENEFITS OF SPREADSHEET PROGRAMS

The benefits of a spreadsheet program are great. You start by entering the data into a worksheet; once it is entered, you can do a great deal with that information. The most common thing you will do is some type of calculation. As an example, you can sum all your expenses for the month. The differences between doing this manually with a calculator and with a spreadsheet program are these:

- *Error-free calculations.* It's easy to make a mistake when entering figures using a calculator. You might mistype or forget an entry. With a spreadsheet program, you don't have to worry about mistakes because the program will not make a mistake calculating. (You do have to be sure you've entered the correct values.)

- *Fast recalculations.* If you forget an entry, an entry changes, or an entry is no longer valid, you can make a change. You don't have to redo the calculation: the program does it for you. You can easily add new rows and columns within an existing worksheet if, for instance, you forget something.

- *Data entry shortcuts.* You can use shortcuts to enter data, especially formulas. You can create a formula and then copy it to other places in the worksheet. Because of how cells are referenced, the same formula will work in other places.

- *More analysis.* Once the data is entered, you can manipulate it. You might sort entries from largest to smallest. You might find the average of your monthly food expenses. You can use the data to make forecasts. For instance, what if you received a 6% raise? What would your yearly income be? Your monthly income?

- *Special functions.* In addition to common mathematical operations, such as addition, subtraction, multiplication, and division, you can use special formulas called *functions*. You can find functions for figuring a loan payment to calculating the return on an investment.

- *Charts.* You can chart the data. Sometimes a chart shows a relationship or trend that the values themselves don't readily show. For instance, if you chart your expenses in a pie chart, you might notice that the largest chunk of your income is spent on CDs.

POPULAR SPREADSHEET PROGRAMS

The most popular spreadsheet program is Microsoft Office Excel. This program is sold as a separate package and also as part of Microsoft Office (a bundle of common business applications). If you use a spreadsheet program, you will most likely be using Excel.

If you have a home computer, you might have Microsoft Works. This program, often bundled with home computers, is an integrated program with a word processing, a spreadsheet, and a database module. Works and Excel are similar, although Excel includes many more features.

Spreadsheet history: One of the first programs created for a computer was a spreadsheet program. Lotus created its spreadsheet program which it named 1-2-3. If you have used computers for a long time, you may remember this popular program.

WEB: If you do not have a program but would like to purchase one, you can get information on Excel by visiting Microsoft's Office site at www.office.microsoft.com.

What is a Database?

A database program is used to keep track of information about people, products, events, transactions, or other items. Think about a simple Rolodex, which you use to keep name and address information organized. The list includes all the pertinent information (name, address, phone numbers, etc.) on one card, and the cards are organized alphabetically. That's the basic concept behind a database program; only a database program offers much more sophistication and flexibility than a Rolodex.

To understand the usefulness of a database program, let's take a look at some types of databases that are used:

- *Contacts.* At its simplest, a database can be used to track people. In addition to names, addresses, and phone information, you can also keep other dates, such as business information. Contact management is critical in business. You might need to keep track of clients, customers, vendors, competitors, members, or any other group of individuals. Figure 4.3 shows a contact screen for a popular database program called Access.

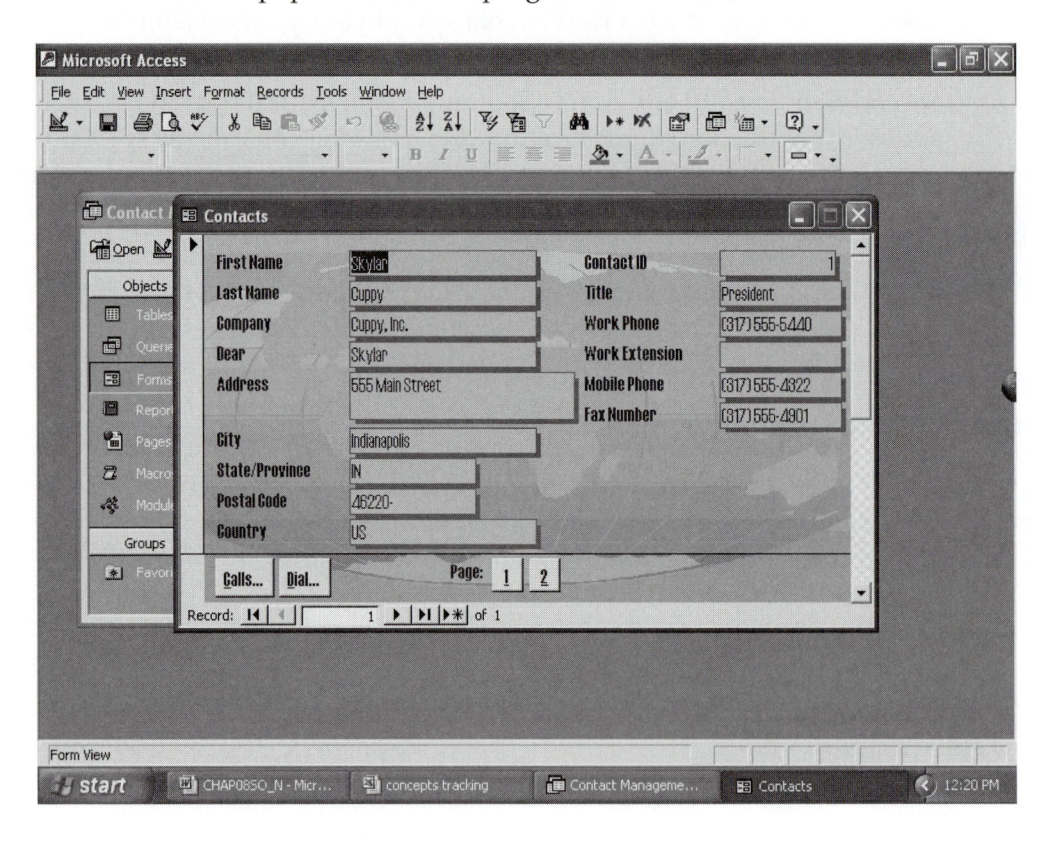

Figure 4.3. One of the most common applications of a database program is to keep track of contacts.

- *Products.* If a company sells some type of product, a database is an ideal way to organize information about that product or to keep an inventory. This type of database might store the product number, description, number sold, number in inventory, and so on. With most programs, you can create several databases with multiple tables in each and link them. For example, you might have one database table that lists basic product information and then another that tracks sales and inventory.

- *Transactions.* Databases are often used to keep track of transactions—sales or rentals, for instance. Banks also use very large databases to keep track of transactions.

- *Billing.* Businesses use databases or accounting programs that function similar to a database program to keep track of various accounts, such as accounts payable and accounts receivable. Doing so makes it easy to generate invoices, track expenses, and total income.

- *Personnel.* To keep track of employees, businesses often use a database for personnel. This database can store not only information about that person, but also hiring, salary, and tax information. Schools and universities also use databases to keep track of student information.

- *Schedules.* Databases can be used to track schedules, but they also make planning a schedule easier. Think about a school or university and all its classes. Imagine planning not only when the classes were held, but also where they were held, who was teaching them, and who was signed up—without the help of a computer. Databases simplify the scheduling of classes and other events.

- *Collections.* Similar to a product database, a collection database keeps track of the items in a collection. This might be a simple list of the CDs you own or a sophisticated and detailed list of the pieces in a museum with acquisition information, value, location, and other key data.

- *Scientific and other research data.* Scientists and other researchers use databases to store information about a particular project. As a simple example, think about a marketing company that has a database of current and potential customers with all the related information.

This list gives you just a few examples of the many types of databases. Anytime you come across a collection of facts or data pieces that need to be organized, think of a database. As a final example, think about renting a movie from your local video store. That store not only uses a database to track which movies it stocks, but also has a database for its customers. The store also has a database that keeps track of the rentals, who rented what, when it's due, who owes late fees, and so on. The store might also have a database of vendors from which they order videos. And it probably has a database to keep track of employees and payroll information. So a database allows you to search for information in a variety of ways.

DBMS: When discussing databases, you might see the designation DBMS (database management system). You'll also hear terms such as database programmer, database engineer, and others used to refer to people who create customized databases.

FEATURES AND BENEFITS OF DATABASE PROGRAMS

The benefits of a database program are immense, especially if you consider the paper method of keeping track of data. Imagine keeping track of customers on paper. What if the information changed? What if a name was not filed or spelled correctly? Imagine again the nightmare of trying to arrange something as simple as a schedule of classes for a school on paper. Indeed, a database program provides many advantages, including the following:

- *Enter data simply.* Although the hardest part of a database program is actually getting the data entered, once it's entered you have so much control. Also, most programs provide shortcuts for entering data. With a standard form, you ensure you are keeping track of the same information. You can easily spot missing data.
- *Find data easily.* The paper method for finding a certain piece of information is tedious. With a database, you can quickly pull up the information you need, and you have a variety of methods for finding that information. For instance, suppose you can't remember a customer's name. You can look up the customer by the city or state. Or you might remember that the name starts with *Tr*. You can search for customers whose last names match this entry.
- *Keep data updated.* One look at anyone's address book will tell you how messy it is to keep track of data manually. People move. Numbers change. With a database, you can quickly and easily find and update any of the information.
- *Track more detailed information*. A database makes it easy to keep related information together. If you have to track data manually, you may not want to go to the effort to note someone's birthday or gift preference. With a database, you can easily track this information. Doing so provides you with the pertinent information you need.
- *Sort data.* You can rearrange the data in a database to suit your needs. For instance, for a mailing, you might want to sort by ZIP Code. You can sort names in alphabetical order. For a product database, you might organize the database by price to see how the products stack up price wise. Then you can re-sort by past sales to view which product has sold the most. Re-sort again to see which products are running low on inventory. With a few commands, you can change the order to view the data in the organization that makes most sense for your particular purpose.
- *Query data.* With a database program, you can also query or question the database. You might create a query that says, "Show me all customers in South Carolina." In a product database, you might say, "Show me all products that have less than five items in stock. " In a video database, you might query, "Show me the most rented movie this week. " The possibilities are endless.
- *Create reports.* With sorting and querying, you can also create printed reports for analysis or distribution.
- *Transfer the information from a database into a spreadsheet.* This offers more ways to work with the database information.
- *Connect and keep data streamlined by using a relational database.* A relational database consists of tables, and each table can be linked by a unique key. For instance, a customer table may include a customer ID. When a customer places an order, rather than repeat all the customer data, the order table can simply refer to the customer by the ID. This type of database structure makes it easy to maintain and keep information up-to-date; it also enables you to focus on the particular task (the order, for instance, rather than the customer details).

POPULAR DATABASE PROGRAMS

The most popular full-featured database program is Microsoft Office Access. This program is sold as a separate package and also as part of Microsoft Office (a bundle of common business applications). Other popular programs include Corel's Paradox and Lotus Approach.

In addition to the full-featured programs, you can find special-purpose programs, especially for contact management. ACT! is a popular program for keeping track of contact information for businesses.

Also, keep in mind that you can find customized database programs. These might be unique programs, designed for a particular business or office. Or they might be customized versions of a popular database. For instance, a developer might use Access to create a program for sales or inventory for a particular company.

> **WEB:** Visit www.office.microsoft.com for product information on Access. For information on ACT!, go to www.act.com. For information on Approach, visit www.lotus.com and look for information on their SmartSuite package, which includes Approach.

Using Presentation Programs

If you are a speaker or need to make any kind of presentation, you'll most likely use a presentation program. For instance, you can find presentations for training, presenting a business plan, and selling a product. You can create presentations for an employee orientation, company meeting, financial overview, or project overview.

Traditionally, a presentation is done with a slide show and screen. Presentation software has simplified the creation of slide shows and expanded the way presentations can be given. You can create presentations designed for the computer or the Web. (Lesson 9 covers creating presentations in more detail.)

FEATURES OF PRESENTATION PROGRAMS

Presentation programs include features that help you in creating a presentation. But they go beyond that to add other elements:

- *Wizards.* Giving presentations is usually part of a job, not the entire job. Therefore, most people do not spend day in and day out creating presentations. Thus, the creators of this type of program provide wizards to help get you started. PowerPoint, for instance, includes wizards for popular presentation types (see Figure 4.4).

Lesson 4
Defining Software

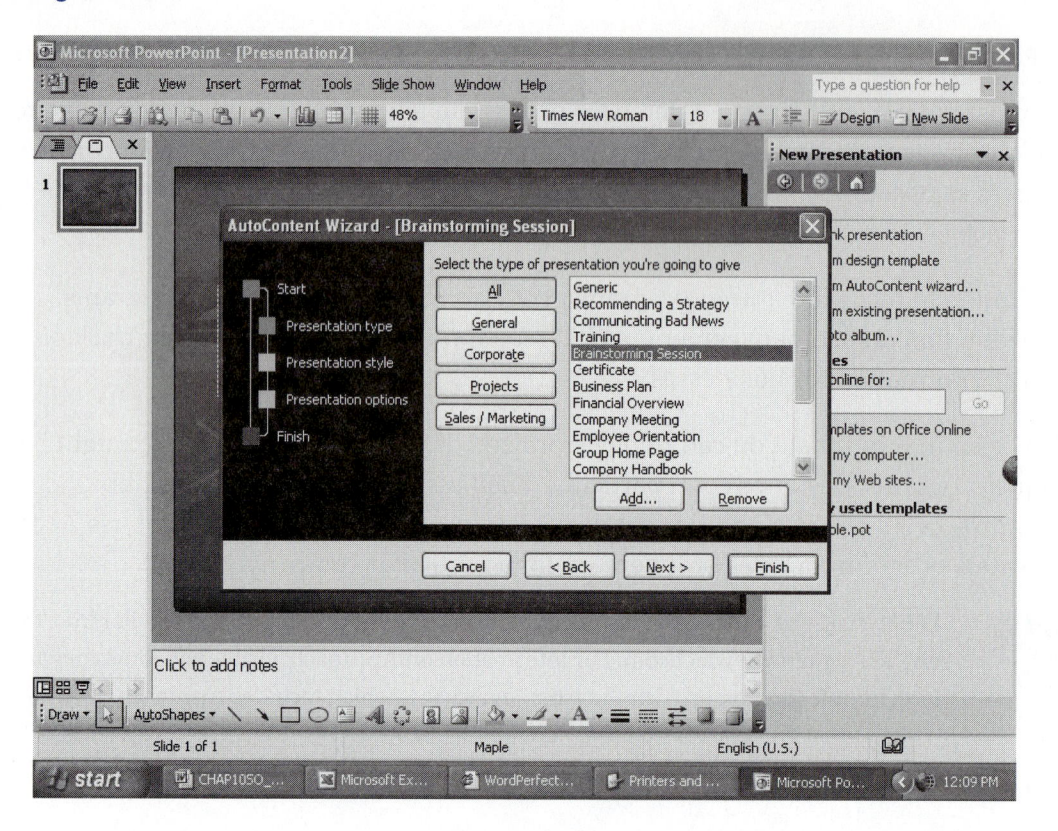

Learning Computer Concepts

Figure 4.4. You can use the AutoContent Wizard in Microsoft Office PowerPoint to create common presentation types.

- **Templates.** You can also select design themes to apply consistent formatting (background, headers and footers, logos, and so on) to your presentation.
- **Consistent design.** In addition to templates, you can select from some predefined slide types. For instance, you can select slides with placeholders for graphics, tables, bulleted lists, and so on.
- **Audience handouts.** Most programs enable you to create audience handouts, most often using the slides from the presentation. Your audience can use these handouts to follow along and to take notes.
- **Speaker notes.** To help the presenter, most programs enable you to create speaker notes. The note includes the slide as well as comments or points you may want to remember.
- **Special types of information.** In addition to text, you can create slides that contain graphics, animations, charts, tables, and organization charts.
- **Special effects.** You can add special effects, such as transitions or animations. Transitions add special effects when moving from slide to slide.

POPULAR PRESENTATION PROGRAMS

Popular presentation programs include Microsoft Office PowerPoint, Corel Presentations, and Lotus Freelance Graphics.

WEB: Visit www.corel.com and display the product information for Corel Presentations. You can also get information about Lotus Freelance Graphics at www.lotus.com. For info on Microsoft Office PowerPoint, visit www.microsoft.com. At all of these sites, you'll have to navigate to the product page for that particular product. Also note that these programs are often included in program suites. For instance, Microsoft Office PowerPoint is included with most versions of Microsoft Office.

Using Desktop and Web Publishing Programs

In addition to presentations, you can create other types of documents that you want to display or print. This section covers programs for desktop publishing (printed documents) and Web publishing (documents displayed on a Web site).

USING DESKTOP PUBLISHING PROGRAMS

You can use a desktop publishing program to create a wide variety of documents including:

- *Newsletters.* You can create, print, and distribute newsletters. They might be a simple two-page document (printed on both sides) or several pages. You can include articles, pictures, illustrations, and other elements.
- *Advertisements.* You can create a wide variety of advertisements, including flyers, signs, banners, and print ads.
- *Brochures and booklets.* You can create brochures describing a product or service. You can make booklets on any topic imaginable.
- *Manuals.* Most how-to manuals are desktop published. The manual may include steps, technical information, tables, and other elements.
- *Business forms.* With a desktop publishing program, you can create professional business forms. For instance, you can make invoices or even your own business cards.
- *Personal stationery.* You can design your own stationery. Having a party? You can desktop publish an invitation. You can also create postcards and greeting cards.

Most programs, especially the low-end programs, were designed under the assumption that you may not be a layout expert. Therefore, they provide lots of templates for common publications. For example, Figure 4.5 shows just some of the templates and wizards you can use in Microsoft Office Publisher.

Lesson 4
Defining Software

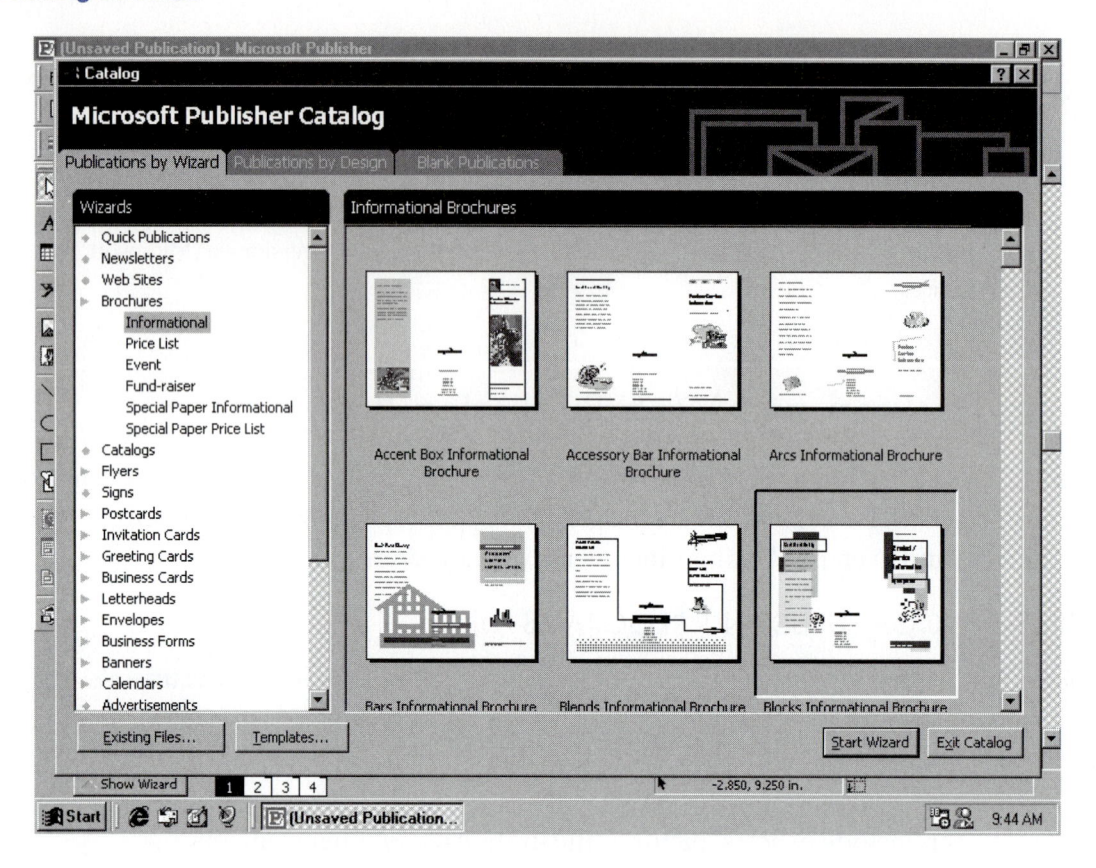

Figure 4.5. Desktop programs simplify creation by providing predesigned templates and wizards for a variety of publication formats.

As desktop publishing has become more popular, common applications, such as word processing and spreadsheets, have added desktop features to their programs. For simple documents, you may not even need a separate program. You may be able to use your word processing program. With a program such as Word, you can incorporate graphics, use columns, and add headers and footers. You can create a pretty sophisticated layout with the features of this program.

If the word processing program does not provide enough control or features to suit your publication, you can purchase a desktop publishing program. You can find programs ranging from the simple (Microsoft Office Publisher or PrintMaster) to the complex (Aldus PageMaker, QuarkXpress, Adobe FrameMaker).

> **WEB:** To get an idea of the various programs, visit the Web sites for PageMaker (http://www.adobe.com/products/pagemaker/main.html) and QuarkXpress (http://www.quark.com/products/xpress/). Compare the features and prices of these programs.
>
> Visit the sites for the low-end programs (www.microsoft.com) for Microsoft Office Publisher and (www.broderbund.com) for PrintMaster.

> **Arts and Crafts:** Broderbund also offers special-purpose printing programs for creating greeting cards, banners, scrapbook pages, and more.

You'll find desktop publishing programs in small businesses that do their own publishing. For instance, a company may design its own forms, letterheads, and publications (internal newsletters, product catalogs, brochures, and so on). You'll also find this type of program used in publishing fields (publishers, editors, writers, advertising agencies, journalists and so on).

What does this type of program provide beyond a word processing program? It provides a great deal of control for handling text and graphics. Here are just a few of the features of this type of program:

- *Greater text control.* For simple one-column documents, your word processing program is great. You may also find features for adding columns and text boxes; but to place text anywhere on the page with utmost control, you need a desktop publishing program. As an example, think about a newsletter with stories that start on page 1 and then continue on another page. Think about two- or even three-column documents. Consider pull-quotes (quotations set off from the main body of text) or separate areas for a table of contents. While you can add these items using a word processing program, doing so would be cumbersome. Desktop publishing programs, on the other hand, are designed to work for just these types of layout features.

    Still need a word processing program: Most desktop publishing programs concentrate on layout rather than text creation. Whereas you can type text, you will most likely create the text in your word processing program and then import it into the desktop publishing program. Why? Because your word processing program will provide much better features for editing and creating text.

- *More text formatting options.* Desktop publishing features offer more formatting options for text, including kerning (setting the spacing between characters) and hyphenation.
- *Better graphics placement.* While you won't use your program to create graphics, you will use a desktop publishing program to place a graphic in the publication. Not only can you place the graphic in the exact spot you want, but you can also control how text wraps around the graphic, add captions, use borders for the graphic, change the size, and so on.
- *Better output.* Desktop publishing programs offer the best output. You can print on your own printer, or you may prepare the publication and then send it to a service bureau or printing press. Desktop publishing programs offer great control for this type of printing. As an example, the program can prepare color separations for color documents.
- *Automatic references.* Because these programs are designed to handle long publications, you'll find features for automating the creation of indexes and table of contents. You can also generate lists of tables or figures.
- *Style consistency.* To ensure consistency with the formatting, you can create and assign styles. (Word processing programs offer the same style features.)

Using styles also makes changing the design easier. You can update the style and all text formatted with that style will be updated.

Learn the lingo: If you work with desktop publishing, you will need to learn the lingo for measurements. Publishers use points to measure type; there are 72 points to an inch. Twelve points make one pica, another measurement commonly used in desktop publishing.

WEB: For more information, visit this site: www.microsoft.com and display the product information for Microsoft Office Publisher. You can find product information as well as design advice.

USING WEB PUBLISHING PROGRAMS

The popularity of the World Wide Web has opened another avenue for publishing: the Web. You don't have to be a business to have a Web site. You can create your own personal Web site, listing your favorite things or displaying your resume, for example. You can find programs to help you create and manage your Web site. You can also find services to publish your Web site (place it on the Web so that others can visit the site). For instance, you might be involved in a project for setting up a Web site for someone. Perhaps your school has a Web site (or is thinking of creating one). Maybe you just want a forum to express your thoughts. Perhaps you have some business or service you want to advertise. Whatever the reason, you can create a Web site.

To publish a Web site, you need the following: a program for creating Web pages and a provider that will publish your Web site. You may also need programs for creating other special multimedia Web page elements, such as animations, videos, or graphics.

Web pages are most often a special type of document called HTML. This stands for HyperText Markup Language, the special formatting language used to define the look and contents of a Web page. Don't panic and think you have to learn programming. You can find programs that simplify the creation of HTML documents.

For simple pages, you may be able to use your word processing programs. As Web publishing has become more popular, more programs are incorporating features to aid in designing and publishing Web pages. For instance, Microsoft Office Word includes Web wizards. You can also create and save any document as an HTML file.

If your needs go beyond the capabilities of a word processing program, you can purchase Web publishing programs such as Microsoft Office FrontPage.

You can also find Web sites that provide templates and allow you to customize your own Web page, for instance Yahoo!'s GeoCities and Homestead. You can also place your page on site for little or no charge.

WEB: Visit the sites for publishing simple Web sites include Yahoo!'s GeoCities (http://geocities.yahoo.com/) and Homestead (www.homestead.com).

In addition to the program, you need a way to take the documents you create and make them accessible from the Web. To do so, you need an Internet or online provider. If you have Internet access, you already have an account with an Internet provider. Most provide some type of Web hosting or publishing service. For instance, America Online (AOL) offers this service, as does EarthLink. Some offer free hosting services. For others, you may pay a fee. Also, the free sites may be limited to a certain size. If you go beyond this size, you may have to pay. For business sites, you may also be able to hire designers or programmers to help create and maintain the site.

What can you do with a Web publishing program? Why do you need this type of program? The following list gives you an idea of some of the key features:

- *Wizards and templates*. Like other publishing programs, most users need some help in creating a publication, especially if it's not something they do full-time. To aid in creating sites, most programs provide wizards and templates. For instance, FrontPage includes a wizard for creating a personal Web site. You make selections for the content, and it creates a layout with pertinent sections. You then edit these sections to include your own information.
- *Links.* Your Web site should contain links to other sites. A link is an image or text that, when clicked, takes you to another Web page or Web site. You can find features for inserting, formatting, and managing the links (also called hyperlinks) in your program.
- *Graphics and other media.* To create an inviting Web site, you want to include more than just text. Your program should simplify adding graphics, banners, forms, pictures, animations, and other multimedia elements. The most popular format for graphic images are JPEG and GIF. You may also add animations or video clips.
- *Preview and publish.* The program should include commands that enable you to preview the page, to see it as it will appear in a Web browser. You should also find commands for publishing the site on your Web server. You may have to request the specifications from your Internet Service Provider (ISP).
- *File management.* A Web site may consist of several pages and several types of documents, including text, graphics, photographs, tables, charts, animations, sounds, and other elements. Most programs offer features to help you keep track of these elements.
- *Navigation*. If your Web site contains several pages, you want an easy way for your visitors to navigate from page to page. You can find tools for adding navigation panes. You can also view a roadmap of the site so that you see how pages are interconnected. You can make changes to the organization or flow of the pages.
- *Reports.* To keep track of all the page elements, you can use the reporting feature. In FrontPage, the site summary report includes the number of pictures, linked files, unlinked files, older files, recently added files, hyperlinks, broken links, errors, and tasks. You can use this feature to troubleshoot problems with the site.

Lesson 4
Defining Software

Using Graphics Programs

Graphics software is a category that encompasses several programs, all dealing with images. You can use this type of program to create illustrations, edit images, and create special types of drawings, such as architectural drawings. This section explains the types of things you can do with these programs and also defines the various program types.

While word processing programs, spreadsheets, and databases may be used by a wide variety of people, you will find graphics programs are more specialized. That is, artists, photographers, illustrators, designers, architects, desktop publishers, and others use this type of program. This list gives you a general idea of the types of things you can create with graphics programs:

- *Artwork.* Artists use graphics programs to create artwork, logos, advertisements, and illustrations. For instance, a graphic artist created the line drawings in this book using computer programs (see Figure 4.6).

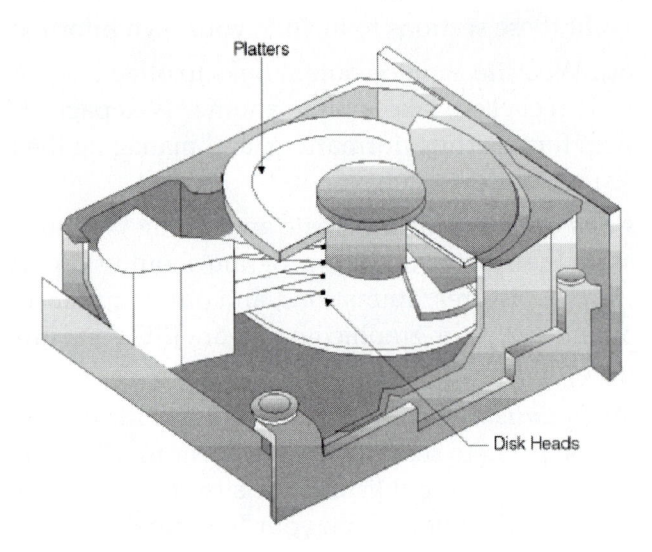

Figure 4.6. This illustration was created with Adobe Illustrator.

- *Photographs.* You can also display and manipulate photographs using graphics software. Photographers, designers, and artists use photo-manipulation software to take, store, and work with photos. For instance, the portrait in Figure 4.7 was created by a graphic artist (Kathy Hanley) from a photograph.

Figure 4.7. You can manipulate photographs.

- *Architectural drawings.* Architects, engineers, and designers use a special type of program called CAD (Computer-Aided Design) to create blueprints and other planning documents. For instance, clothing and package design can be done with this type of program.
- *Web graphics.* A Web page includes all kinds of graphics. In addition to photographs and illustrations, you may find buttons, logos, navigation tools, and animation on a Web page. These graphic parts of the page are created with graphics programs.
- *Animation.* Computers have made animation much easier than the original process of drawing each image. You'll find animation in films, cartoons, Web sites, games, and virtual tours.

TYPES OF GRAPHICS PROGRAMS

As mentioned, the term "graphics programs" actually covers several types of programs, broken down into these main program types:

- *Paint programs.* Even if you are not an artist, you may still use paint programs to create illustrations. Paint programs include a palette of artist tools (paintbrush, pencil, eraser, for instance) that you can use to draw on the page (see Figure 4.8). Popular paint programs include Paint Shop Pro (JASC Software), Adobe SuperPaint, and Paint (included with Microsoft Windows).

Lesson 4
Defining Software

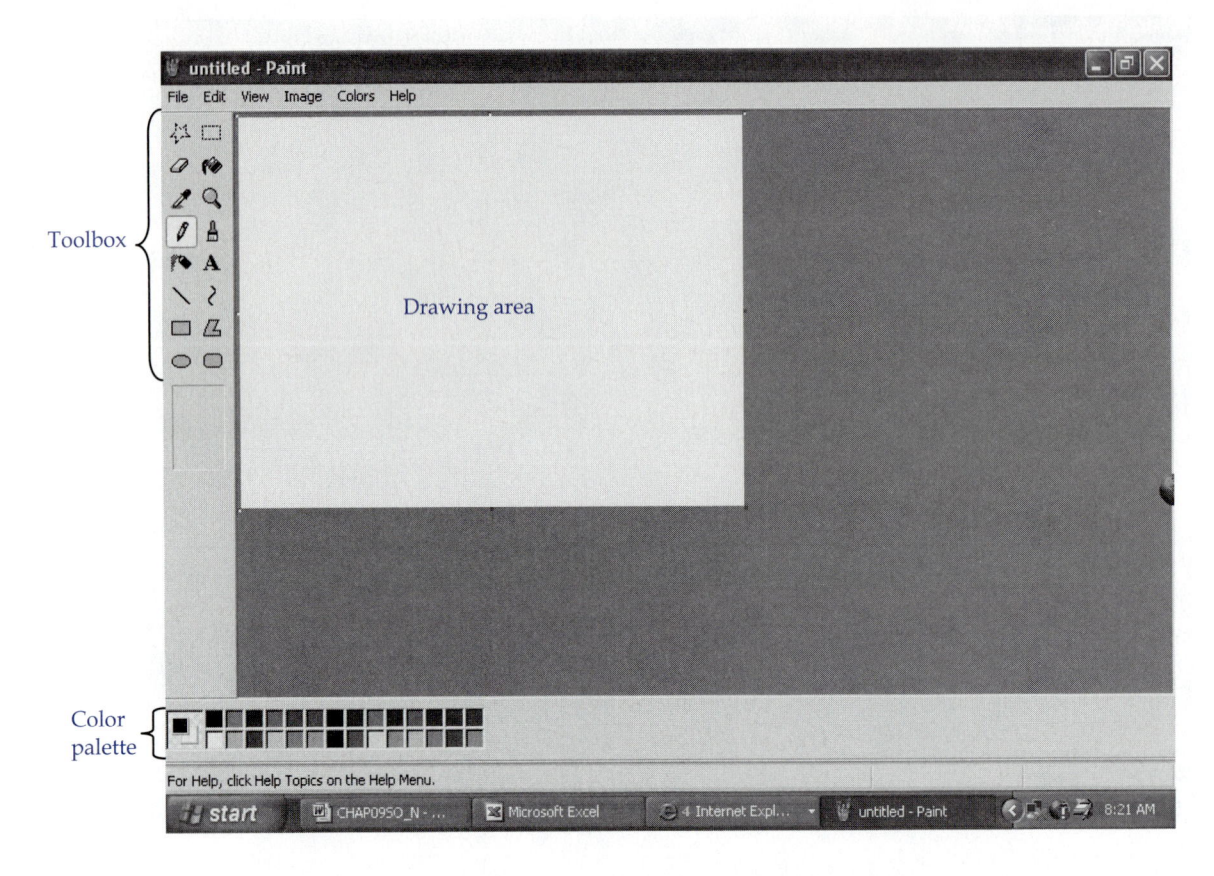

Figure 4.8. Paint, included with Windows, is a fun way to experiment with your drawing skills.

- *Draw programs.* Drawing programs create images using mathematics. The programs use equations to define a line drawn from one point to another. The equation also determines the thickness and color. Each item is a discrete object, distinct from other objects. Because the image is a discrete object, you can move, select, copy, and edit it. Drawing programs are also better for handling text. Popular drawing programs include Adobe Illustrator, CorelDraw, and Visio. You'll also find that other types of programs may include a drawing component you can use to add objects. For instance, in Word you can use the drawing toolbar to draw objects, such as lines or circles in a document. You can also do the same in Excel, PowerPoint, and Publisher.

   WEB: Visit Adobe's Web site at www.adobe.com. Notice the range of programs it includes for drawing and illustrating. Note the different features of programs, from the low-end for beginners or dabblers to the high-end for professional artists.

- *Photo manipulation software.* You can use scanners and digital cameras to create a digital file from a photograph. Then you can use this type of program to manipulate that photo. You may want to crop the image, sharpen the focus, change the lighting, or add a moustache to your Aunt Martha. Popular programs include Adobe Photoshop and JASC Paint Shop Pro. Figure 4.9 shows a photograph opened in Paint Shop Pro.

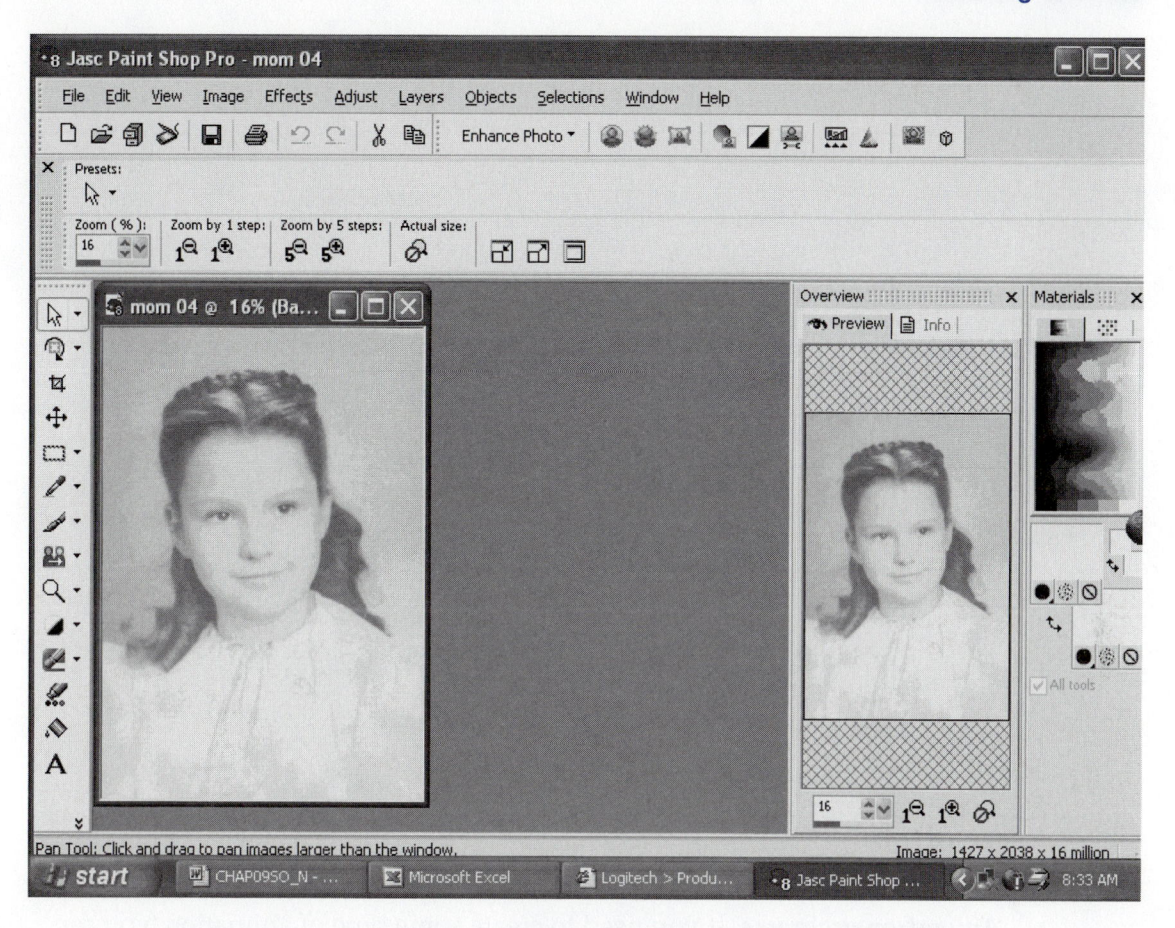

Figure 4.9. You can open and edit photographs using special graphics software.

> **No more disorganized photos:** Photo CDs enable you to easily store photos and to quickly review and select photos you want.

- *CAD programs.* For technical drawings for blueprints or product design, you can use a special type of program called CAD. CAD can mean Computer-Aided Drawing, Computer-Aided Design, or Computer-Aided Drafting. These programs take the place of drafting tables, rulers, and mechanical pencils. Instead of drawing a blueprint, you can create one using a CAD program (see Figure 4.10). Architects use these programs to create blueprints. Carpenters, electricians, and other construction workers use these documents to plan and create buildings. Engineers at a manufacturing plant can use this type of program to plan new products. The most popular CAD program is AutoCAD from AutoDesk.

Lesson 4
Defining Software

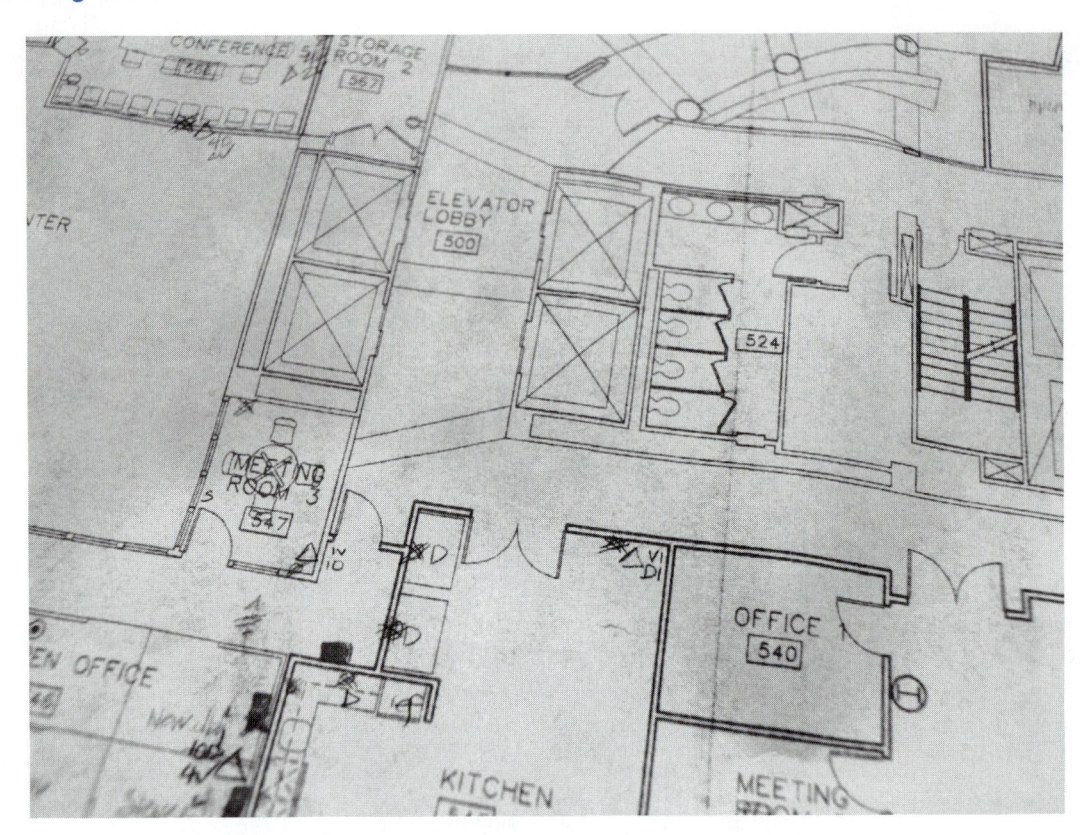

Learning Computer Concepts

Figure 4.10. CAD programs can be used to create blueprints.

- *Animation programs.* If you need to create some type of animation, you can use this type of program to create, edit, display, and print your animations. You'll find this type of software in film and television, as well as other fields. For instance, a realtor may provide a walk-through or virtual tour of a house using the same concept. Video games rely heavily on animation. Another type of animation is used in multimedia programs, such as HyperStudio, or presentation programs, such as PowerPoint.

WEB: Visit www.shockwave.com. Look at some of the examples and programs it includes for animations.

- *Clip art.* If you are not an artist, don't despair. You can still add illustrations to your documents. To do so, you can use clip art. This type of artwork is created by professionals and then sold for your use. You can find a variety of clip-art images in themes from cooking to business, sports to plants. You can purchase clip-art libraries on CDs. You can also find clip art online. Also, many programs, such as Microsoft Office Word and Microsoft Office Publisher, come with some clip art. Figure 4.11 shows the Clip Art task pane in Microsoft Office Word.

Learning Computer Concepts

Lesson 4
Defining Software

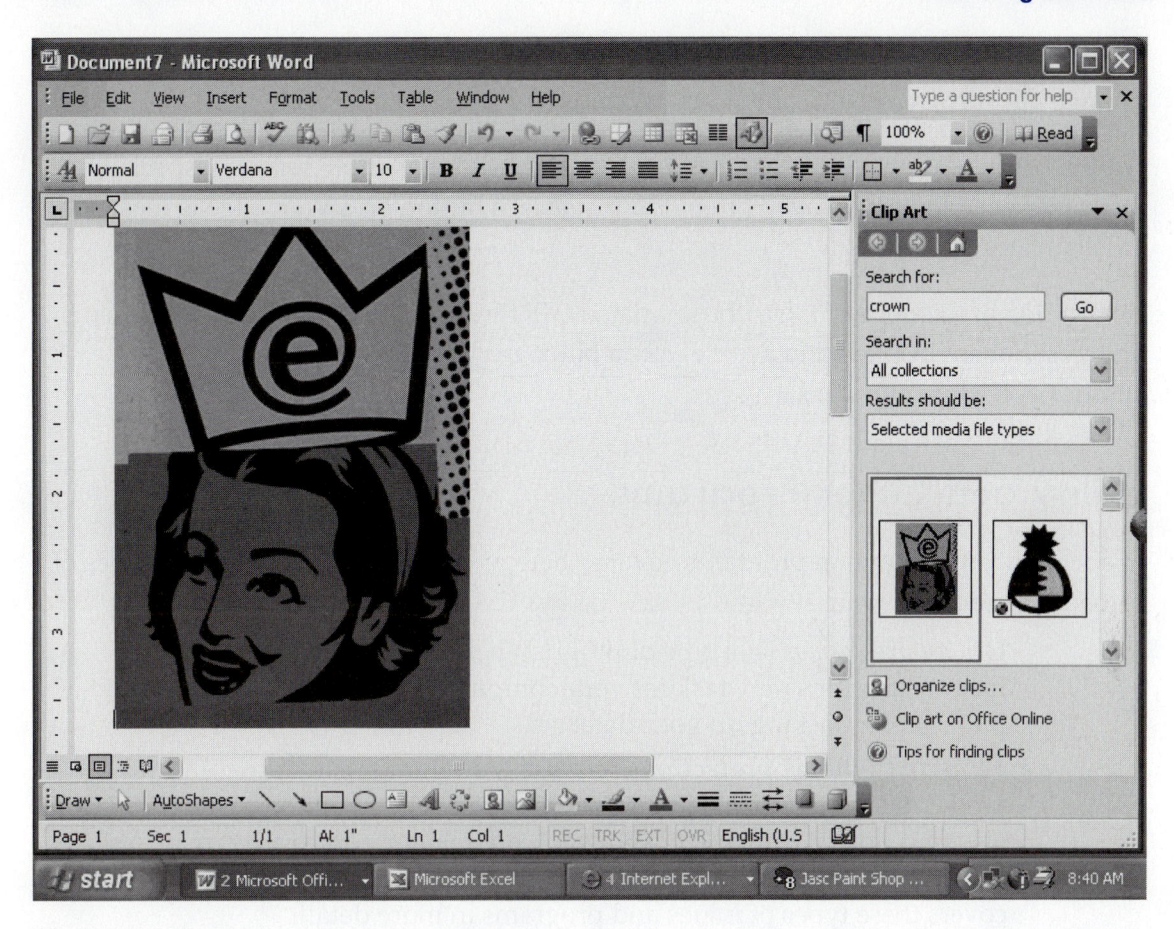

Figure 4.11. You can find precanned art called clip art and insert it into your document.

WEB: Visit www.clipart.com to view a list of sites that offer free clip art. Think about how you might use clip art in your work or home.

Check clip art use rights. Most often clip art is licensed for your use. You can use it as often as you want. Other images are usually not provided free for your use. For instance, you cannot scan an image from a book and use it as your own without getting copyright permission. You also cannot copy a picture from a Web site that is copyrighted and use it without permission, even if you modify it.

UNDERSTANDING GRAPHICS FILES

When you work with images, you have a great deal of flexibility in how you save the file, that is, the file type. For instance, if you build a Web site, you should be familiar with the most common type of graphic images. You'll find graphic images in a variety of file formats, and some are more suited than others for special purposes. Let's take a quick look at the various types of graphics file types.

Two graphics file formats emerged as the most often used on the Web. These file formats are JPEG (or JPG) and GIF file formats. JPEG stands for Joint Photographic Experts Group and is a bitmap file format. Photographs or complex images are usually in this file format because it works well for displaying colors and changes in colors. They are a popular file format because of the quality and file size.

GIF stands for Graphic Interchange Format and is used for simple images, especially those that need to be displayed often. For instance, a button on a Web page is most likely a GIF image.

A variation of this type of file is the animated GIF file. You see these in advertisements or logos that are displayed in a cycle (like a billboard that flips from one image to another every few minutes).

Utility and Other Programs

In addition to the common programs covered here, you'll also find many other types of software including:

- *Utility programs*. This type of program helps you perform some maintenance or safety task for your computer. For instance, you may buy a program for backing up your data.
- *Virus and Internet protection software*. You'll find many programs for protecting against viruses and unauthorized use of your computer. You can also find programs that block unwanted e-mail or popup advertising. Many Internet programs include all of these features in one program. Lesson 13 covers these types of issues and programs in more detail.
- *Checkbook managers*. Rather than keep a paper version of your checks, you can use a checkbook manager to keep track of and write checks. In addition to automatically calculating your balance, you can also categorize your expenses and print reports, create a budget, and more. Popular checkbook programs include Quicken and Microsoft Money.
- *Games and hobbies*. If you enjoy a particular game or hobby, you can find a program designed for it. You can usually find popular versions or similar versions of game station (PlayStation, Xbox, and so on) games as well as arcade games, card games, and more. You can also find programs for designing a cross-stitch pattern, making greeting cards, and other craft and hobby pastimes.
- *Educational software*. You can use programs to teach you to type, to learn a foreign language, and more.

Summary

- Word processing is the most commonly used productivity program. Microsoft Office Word is the best-selling program in this category. This type of program helps you to create any type of document. Features help edit, change the appearance, check spelling, and print documents.

- Spreadsheets are the second most commonly used productivity programs. Microsoft Office Excel is the best-selling program in this category. You use this type of program to create worksheets. Most worksheets consist of text entries, numeric entries, and formulas.

- Databases, although complex programs, are found in many types of businesses. Databases are used to keep track of information about a person, place, event, item, or transaction. You can create databases with programs such as Access or Approach. You can also hire a database programmer to create a customized database.

- Presentation programs simplify the creation of a presentation. Most programs provide some templates and wizards to help you get started. Popular presentation programs include Microsoft Office PowerPoint, Lotus Freelance Graphics, and Corel Presentations. These programs are included within program suites from each company.

- Desktop publishing revolutionized the print industry, making it less expensive and easier to create professional-quality publications from a computer. Popular desktop publishing programs include Adobe PageMaker, QuarkXpress, and Microsoft Publisher.

- Another popular form of publishing is Web publishing. To do this, you need software to create the Web documents and also a server on which to publish the content.

- Graphics programs encompass several types of programs. They all enable you to create, edit, and print some type of image. Paint and draw programs are used to create illustrations. Paint programs work by filling in pixels (picture elements) to create the image. Draw programs are mathematically based; an image is defined as a mathematical equation.

- The two most popular file formats for Web graphics are JPG and GIF. JPG is used for more complex images; GIF is used for simple illustrations and pictures that need to be displayed often (and therefore quickly).

Lesson 4
Defining Software

Q&A

Multiple Choice

1. Which of the following are features of most word processing programs?
    a. Editing
    b. Spell checking
    c. Formatting
    d. All of the above

2. This type of program is used to keep track of information about people, products, events, transactions, or other items:
    a. Database
    b. Presentation
    c. Animation
    d. CAD

3. In addition to slides, you can also print these to go along with your presentation:
    a. Speaker notes
    b. Animations
    c. Transitions
    d. Recipes

4. Popular desktop publishing programs include:
    a. Freelance Graphics
    b. PowerPoint
    c. PageMaker
    d. All of the above

Fill in the Blank

1. _____ images are illustrations created by professionals and distributed for your use.
2. In a spreadsheet program, you can create _____ to represent numeric values visually.
3. _____ and _____ are two of the most popular graphic file formats.
4. Web pages use a special type of language called _____.

Short Essay

1. Describe the issues you should consider when buying or upgrading new software.
2. Discuss the ways you can use a photo editing program to alter a photograph.

LESSON 5: DEFINING OPERATING SYSTEMS

Objectives

- ➢ Define an operating system
- ➢ Distinguish between DOS and Windows
- ➢ Identify other operating systems
- ➢ Work with the desktop and windows
- ➢ Shutdown and restart the computer
- ➢ Manage files
- ➢ Install new programs
- ➢ Customize Windows using the control panels

What is an Operating System?

The operating system is a special kind of software that all computer systems must have to operate. The operating system handles and manages all system operations including booting (starting) up the system, displaying information on your monitor, starting programs, printing files, storing files, opening files, managing keyboard and mouse input, and more. The operating system takes these common user actions (such as double-clicking the mouse) and communicates that action to the appropriate hardware component, getting that component to do the requested action (for instance, start a program).

The most common operating system, especially for consumers, is Microsoft Windows. You will also find other operating systems for Macintosh and high-end systems, such as workstations. This lesson explains the key concepts of dealing with this critical system software.

DOS and Windows

People who have used computers for a long time remember DOS. (DOS stands for "disk operating system" and was developed by Microsoft for IBM for use on the first PCs. This particular brand of DOS was called MS-DOS.) This operating system was command-based. To get the computer to do anything, you had to type a command. And the interface—what you saw when you used your computer—had a black screen and a C:\ prompt. Figure 5.1 shows a DOS window.

Figure 5.1. To make the computer perform a task, you had to type commands in the proper format (called syntax).

To copy files, start a program, or do anything else, you had to type commands in the proper format, as in this example:

COPY *.DOC C:\MEMO\

This command would copy all of the document files (*.DOC) in the current folder to the folder MEMO on drive C. Using DOS was not easy.

MORE DOS DIFFICULTIES

DOS programs, which are now virtually obsolete, were a little easier to use than DOS itself because most provided menus, which you could use to select commands. DOS programs also often used function keys. The disadvantage is that each DOS program looked and worked differently. Just because you could use one DOS program didn't mean those skills would work in another program. Using DOS and DOS programs was like trying to communicate with people from France, Italy, Germany, and Spain, each with its own language, customs, standards, and so on.

Also, DOS did not centralize key system information, such as the printer or the mouse. You had to use batch files to set up the mouse (special mini-programs) and in some cases you had to set up the printer to work with each program you used.

Here were some other disadvantages of DOS:
- You could run only one program at a time.
- Your system could handle only 640K of RAM. To use RAM beyond that point, you had to use special memory software.
- File names were limited to 8 characters.
- Using the operating system was not intuitive.

Learning Computer Concepts
Lesson 5
Defining Operating Systems

INTRODUCING WINDOWS

Windows changed the PC computing world by providing a different operating system with a more user-friendly interface. Introduced in the mid-1980s, Windows used a graphical user interface (GUI, pronounced "gooey") that imitated the Macintosh. Rather than type commands, you could point to little pictures called icons. Figure 5.2 shows the desktop of a current version of Windows.

Figure 5.2. Windows uses a graphical user interface.

Windows (all versions considered here) provided these benefits:

- *Better interface*. The graphical user interface made using a computer much easier, especially for beginners.
- *Consistent program design*. Windows programs must follow a standard design. Most programs look and operate in a similar fashion. For instance, selecting a menu command is the same throughout most Windows programs. Getting help in programs works the same way. This change benefited the user. Once you learn one Windows program, you can use the same basic skills in other Windows programs.
- *Multitasking*. With Windows, you can open and work with more than one program at a time.

- *Shared system resources and information.* This operating system not only shares resources, such as the printer, but also stores this key information in one location. Once you set up your printer in Windows, you can use that same printer in any Windows program without modification.
- *Simplified program setup.* Installing and starting programs are easier.
- *Customized desktop.* You can customize the desktop (what you see when you start Windows), plus many other features of Windows.

WINDOWS VERSIONS

The first version of Windows was introduced in 1985 and was not successful. Newer versions were subsequently introduced, and with Windows 3.0, Windows became a success. In 1995, Microsoft released Windows 95, which was a complete overhaul of Windows, dramatically improving the user interface as well as technical details that helped optimize the performance of Windows.

Windows 98 was introduced in 1998. A newer version of Windows, Windows Millennium edition, was released in September of 2000. Some of the new features of Windows Me include advanced digital media functions. With these tools you can create, edit, and share digital pictures, movie clips, and audio files. Using these new features, users can create a video, including animated graphics, edit the video, and then post it to the Internet. Also, in response to the number of homes that have multiple computers, Windows Me includes home-networking capabilities.

In addition to these consumer-oriented Windows versions, Microsoft also developed an operating system for higher-end systems and especially for networks. The first network version was called Windows for Workgroups. Then came Windows NT. (You can find different versions of Windows NT, as this product has evolved.) In 2000, Windows released Windows 2000, an operating system in between NT and regular Windows designed for businesses.

The most current version of Windows is Windows XP. This version of Windows included a big change to the look of Windows, aimed at making it even easier to use. Windows XP also added features that provided more reliability, higher performance, and greater customization.

Windows XP comes in Home and Professional editions. There's also a version called Windows Media Center edition which is based on Windows XP. This version includes more multimedia capabilities, including a TV tuner. Most new computers come with Windows XP Home. If you are hooked up to a network or are a small business, you may want to use Windows XP Professional.

WINDOWS UPDATES

Microsoft is working on yet another upgrade to Windows. In the meantime, Microsoft periodically adds small updates to Windows to improve features and fix problems (such as holes in security). You can download and install these updates at www.microsoft.com. After awhile, Windows makes available a complete set of these updates as a service pack. You can download and install these service packs to update your version of Windows. Currently, Service Pack 2 for Windows XP is the most recent Service Pack.

Other Operating Systems

While Windows is the most common operating system, it isn't the only operating system available. You can find other operating systems, especially on special system types. For instance, the Macintosh uses a different operating system. Workstations often use a different operating system, and networks may also employ something other than Windows. This section discusses some of the other common operating systems.

MACINTOSH SYSTEM

Macintosh computers have always had a graphical user interface. In fact, much of Windows was copied (or imitated) from the Macintosh operating system. This operating system is called "System," and the current version is System OS X Panther.

If you've used Windows, you won't have any trouble using a Macintosh because tasks and features are similar. Both use a mouse to point to and open icons. Both enable you to set up your desktop with features you most often use. Menus and program windows look similar. The Macintosh includes a group of programs called the Control Panel for managing components such as the keyboard and mouse. Given these (and other) similarities, most of the contents of the section "Working with Windows" will apply to the Mac as well.

> **WEB:** Visit www.apple.com to get information about the latest Mac operating system.

UNIX

Unix is the granddad of all operating systems and was initially popular in university settings. This operating system is most often found on high-end systems and workstations, and it has features that are uniquely suited to this environment. Unix can run on many different types of computers, including mainframe and minicomputers. It is a multitasking, multiprocessing operating system.

The downside? Unix is command-driven like DOS. (DOS was somewhat based on Unix, so you'll find that some DOS commands are pulled directly from Unix.)

LINUX

Linux is another popular operating system. It is like Unix in many ways: it can run on almost any computer and it has Unix-like commands. The difference is that Linux is free and therefore has been successful in the computer industry and mainstream media.

> **Finland student:** Linux was developed in 1991 by a 21-year-old college student named Linus Torvalds from Finland. Torvalds did not like DOS, so he decided to write his own operating system.

PALMTOP OPERATING SYSTEMS

Because palmtop and other handheld computers are limited in size, they cannot store a complete operating system. Therefore, they need a simpler version of system software. Windows developed an operating system for these types of devices. Called Windows CE, this operating system can be found in palmtop computers, handheld computers, and household devices. In addition to Windows CE, you can find other popular operating systems including the Palm operating system by Palm Pilot.

Working with Windows

To get an idea of what you can do (and how to do it), you can review this primer on key Windows tasks, including displaying files, starting programs, and more.

UNDERSTANDING THE DESKTOP

When you start a Windows computer, you see the Windows desktop (see Figure 5.3). Like your physical desktop, the Windows desktop includes tools to get you started using your computer. Here are the key elements usually found on the desktop:

> **Customize:** Keep in mind that you can customize your desktop, adding program icons, changing the background image or color, and arranging the icons. Your desktop, then, probably looks different than the ones shown in this book's figures. You will find, though, that many of the icons (such as the Recycle Bin) are almost always displayed on the desktop.

Learning Computer Concepts

Lesson 5
Defining Operating Systems

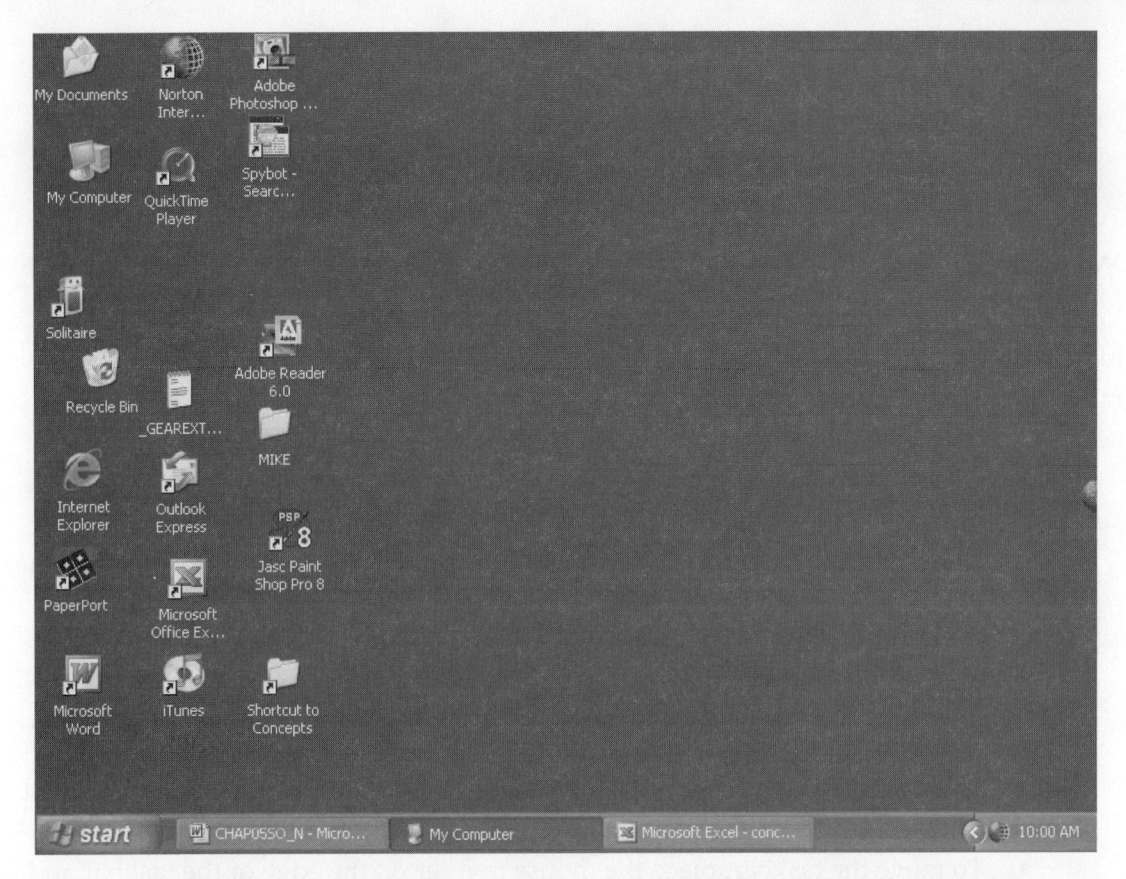

Figure 5.3. The Windows desktop is your starting point for all PC tasks.

- *Start button.* You use this button to start programs, but also to access other commands for using Windows, including getting help and accessing the Control Panel.

- *Taskbar.* The Start button is displayed on the taskbar. This taskbar also displays buttons for all open programs and windows, providing you an easy method for switching between programs. The taskbar also includes icons for tasks. As an example, if you are printing, you will see a printer icon on the taskbar (far right part of the taskbar).

- *Icons.* The little pictures on the desktop are called icons. You'll have some special Windows icons (covered in this list), plus any icons you have added. You can create icons for programs, files, folders, or devices so that you have fast access to them. Some programs, when you install them, automatically create desktop icons.

- *My Computer.* This is a special Windows icon. You can open this icon to view the drives on your system and their contents. If you don't have a shortcut icon to My Computer on the desktop, you can access this icon from the Start menu.

- *Recycle Bin.* Another special Windows icon, this system folder contains all the files you have deleted. When you delete a file, it is not deleted, but moved to this special folder. You can retrieve the file if needed or delete it from the bin permanently.

- ***My Documents.*** Yet another Windows icon, this is a folder that is often used to store all your documents. You can add a shortcut icon to the desktop as well as access this folder from the Start menu.
- ***Program icons.*** You may also see program icons on your desktop. You can double-click the program icon to start the program.

WORKING WITH DESKTOP ICONS

You can move the icons on your desktop around, perhaps grouping certain icons together or placing icons you use less often apart from those you do use. You can also move the taskbar. Finally, you can open icons. Depending on the type of icon, different actions will occur. Review this list of things you can do with desktop items:

- You can double-click an icon to open it. If that icon is a folder, you see the contents of the folder. If the icon is a shortcut icon to a program (covered later), that program starts. If the icon is a shortcut to your printer, you see the print queue. To close any open windows, click the Close (X) button in the upper-right corner.
- If you want to rearrange the icons, place the mouse pointer on an icon and then drag it to a new location. You can automatically arrange all of the icons into columns by right-clicking the desktop and selecting Arrange Icons By. Select an order (name or type, for instance). Windows aligns the icons in that order.
- To move the taskbar, place the mouse pointer on the edge of the taskbar and drag it to its new location. You might, for instance, place the taskbar along the right edge of the window.

   Taskbar won't move? If the taskbar won't move, it may be locked. To unlock it so that you can move the taskbar, right-click the taskbar and then click Properties. Uncheck the Lock the taskbar check box and then click OK.
- To display a shortcut menu of desktop commands, right-click the desktop. You can do this, as you just learned, to arrange icons. You can also display the Display Properties dialog box for changing the appearance of the desktop (covered later).

RESIZING, MOVING, AND CLOSING WINDOWS

Everything in Windows is displayed in a window on the screen. That window may contain a program or content (list of files or folders). When you open an icon, you see the contents. As an example, when you open My Computer, you see the drives on your system. If you start a program, that program is opened in a window. All windows have the same set of controls which you can use to move and resize the window. Figure 5.4 identifies these controls. You can move and resize the windows as needed (similar to rearranging papers on your physical desktop). You can do any of the following:

Learning Computer Concepts

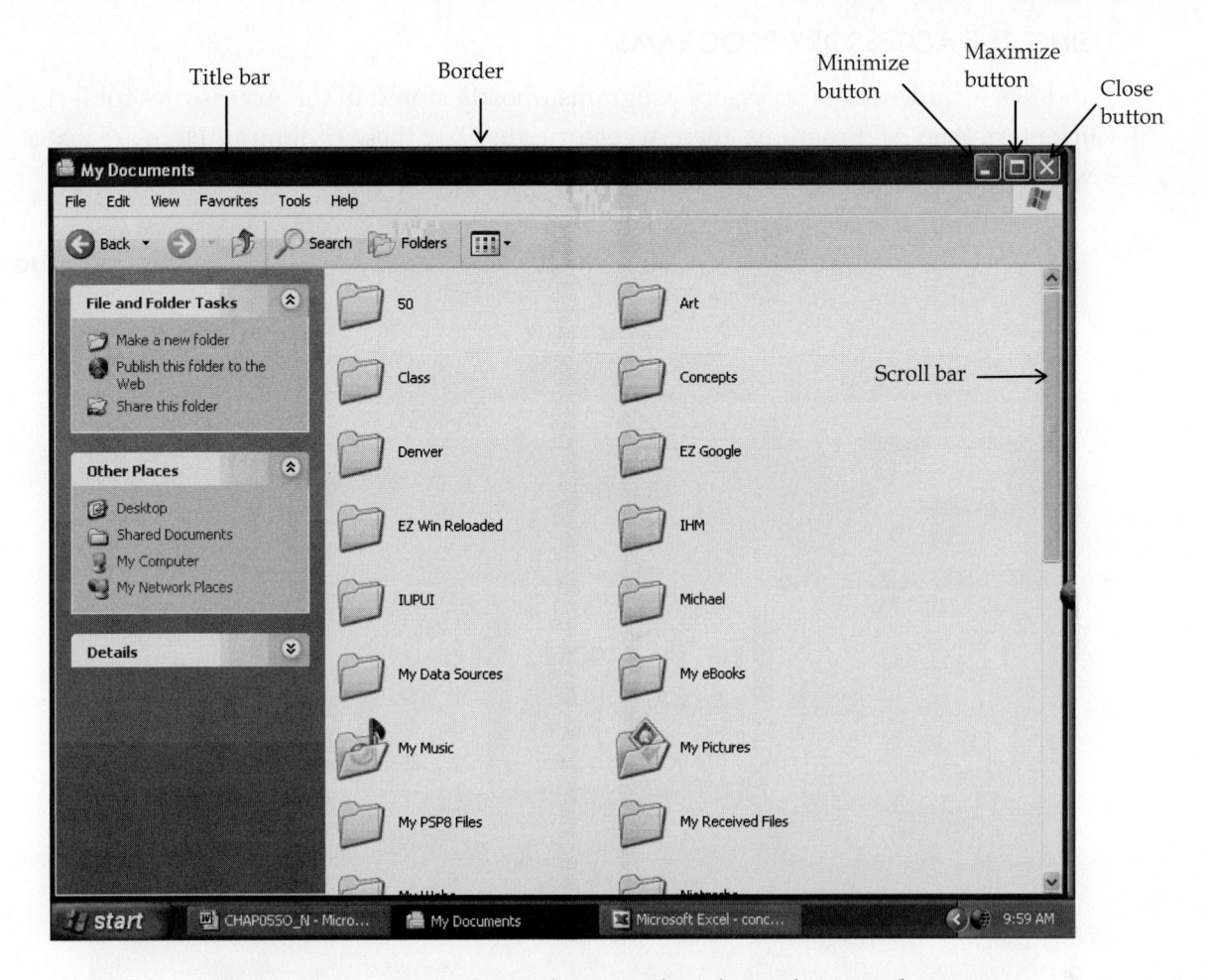

Lesson 5
Defining Operating Systems

Figure 5.4. You can use the window controls to change the size and shape of the window as well as close the window.

- To close the window, click its Close button or choose Close from the File menu.
- To minimize a window (keep it open, but shrink it to a button on the taskbar), click the Minimize button.
- To expand a window to fill the entire screen, click the Maximize button. When a window is maximized, you cannot resize or move it. Also, the Maximize button changes to a Restore button. Click this button to restore the window to its previous size and location.
- To move a window, drag the title bar.
- To resize a window, put the pointer on any of the window borders or corners and drag the border.
- To scroll through a window, click the scroll bars. You can find scroll bars along the right or bottom of the window (if not all of the contents of the window can be displayed within the window).
- All open windows have a taskbar button for the window. To change to another window, click its button in the taskbar.

Lesson 5
Defining Operating Systems

USING THE ACCESSORY PROGRAMS

Windows includes some accessory programs (mostly stored in the Accessories folder). Click Start, then All Programs, then Accessories to view these programs. Here are just a few highlights of these accessory programs and program folders:

- *Solitaire* (see Figure 5.5). Solitaire is a good way to relax or pass the time. Solitaire is also any excellent way for new users to master the mouse (learn to click, drag, double-click, etc.).

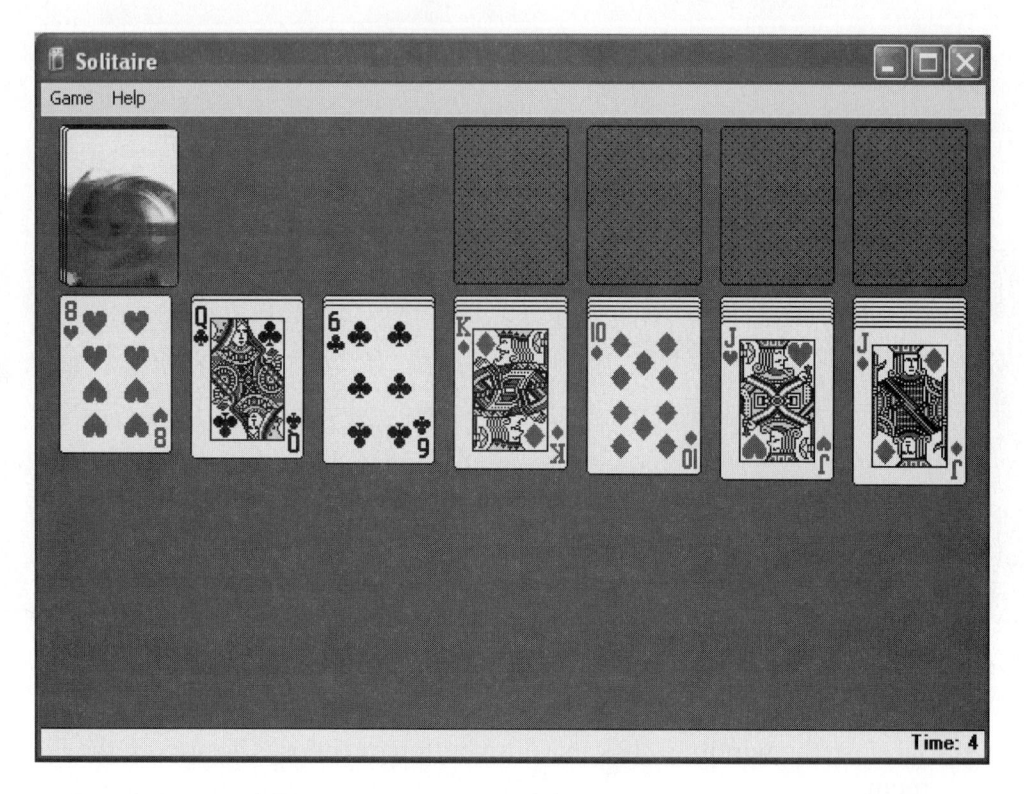

Figure 5.5. Be careful! You can get addicted to playing the computer version of Solitaire.

- *Calculator.* Use this simple program to perform calculations.
- *Entertainment programs.* In the Entertainment folder, you can find programs for playing sounds, media files, and audio CDs. You can also control the volume.
- *System tools.* For access to system tools, check out this folder. You can also scan a disk for errors, defragment a disk, and schedule maintenance tasks using the programs in this folder.
- *Paint.* You can create simple illustrations with this paint program, shown in Figure 5.6.

Figure 5.6. Express your creativity with this paint program.

- *WordPad.* You can use this simple word processing program to create documents.

GETTING HELP

Another handy Windows feature is its online help system. If you have a question about a topic, if you need troubleshooting advice, or if you forget how to perform a task, you can use Windows help.

> **Follow these steps to get help in Windows:**
>
> 1 Click the Start button and then click Help and Support. You see the Windows help center (see Figure 5.7).

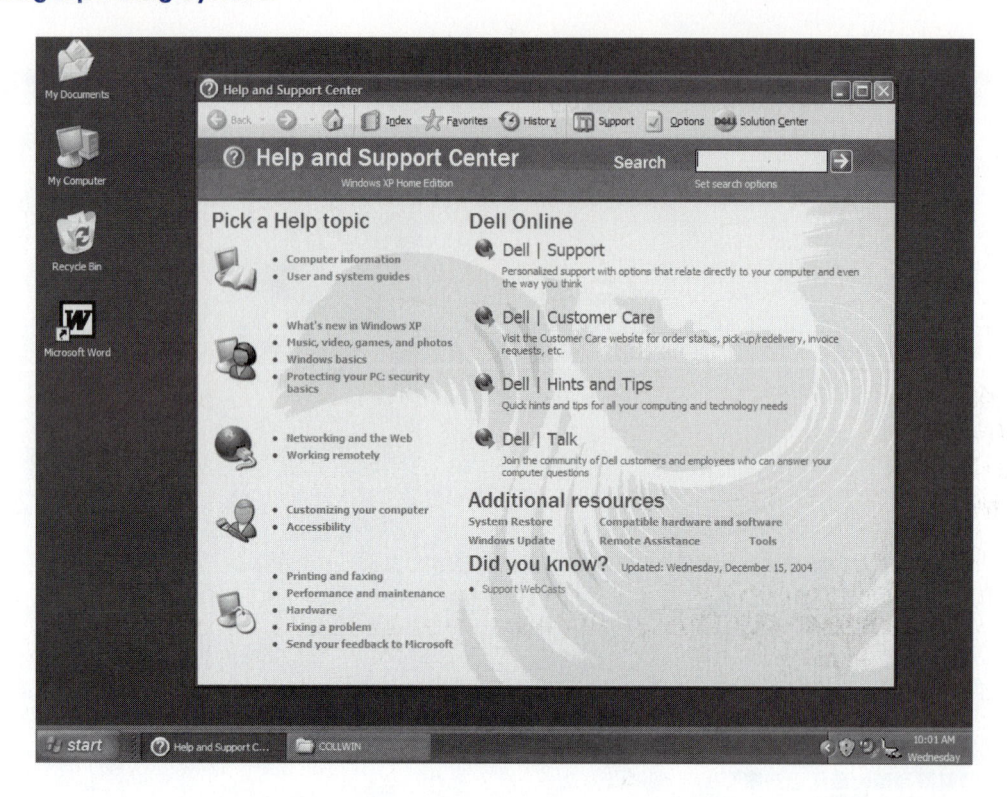

Lesson 5
Defining Operating Systems   **Learning Computer Concepts**

Figure 5.7. You can use the Windows Help Center to look up answers to questions and find steps for common tasks.

2   Select a topic from the list on the left. (You can also search for a topic by typing the question or topic in the Search box and clicking the Go arrow.) You see a list of subtopics for the main category.

3   Select the topic on which you want help. Do this until you see tasks, overviews, articles, and tutorials listed in the right pane.

4   Click the appropriate task, article, or tutorial from this pane.

5   Review the help information and then click its Close (X) button to close the Help and Support Center.

RESTARTING AND SHUTTING DOWN

When you are done working with your computer, you shouldn't just turn off your computer. Instead, you need to use a command. First, exit all programs, saving any documents that are open. Then click Start and then Turn Off Computer. Click Turn Off.

If your computer gets stuck (won't respond), you can restart. You may also need to restart if you make a change to the setup of the computer (add a new hardware component, for instance, or make a change). Click Start and then Turn Off Computer. Click the Restart button.

If you are unable to display the Start menu (the computer isn't responding at all), you may have to reset the computer by turning it off and then back on using the Power or Reset button. Turn off the computer, wait a minute or two, and then turn the computer back on.

> **Stuck?** If your computer gets stuck (won't respond), you can sometimes close the problem program. Press Ctrl+Alt+Delete to display the Task Manager, which lists all open programs. Select the program you want to exit and click End Task.

If you are connected to a network, you may perform a different procedure for logging off and shutting down the PC. Check with the system administrator or class instructor.

Managing Files

One of the main tasks of an operating system is file management. The operating system will handle the storing and opening of files. You also will need to do some file maintenance, and to do so, you can use Windows. Most common tasks are listed in the task pane (at the left edge of all file windows); you can use these commands to copy, rename, delete, and perform other file maintenance tasks. This section covers common file maintenance tasks.

VIEWING AND SORTING FILES

To start, you need to display the drive, folder, or files you want to work with. To do so, you can use the My Computer icon. It displays icons for each of the drives on your system as well as special system folders (see Figure 5.8). To open the icon and display the contents of your system, click Start and then click My Computer. If you have a desktop shortcut icon for My Computer, you can also double-click the icon to display its contents. Once opened, you can do any of the following:

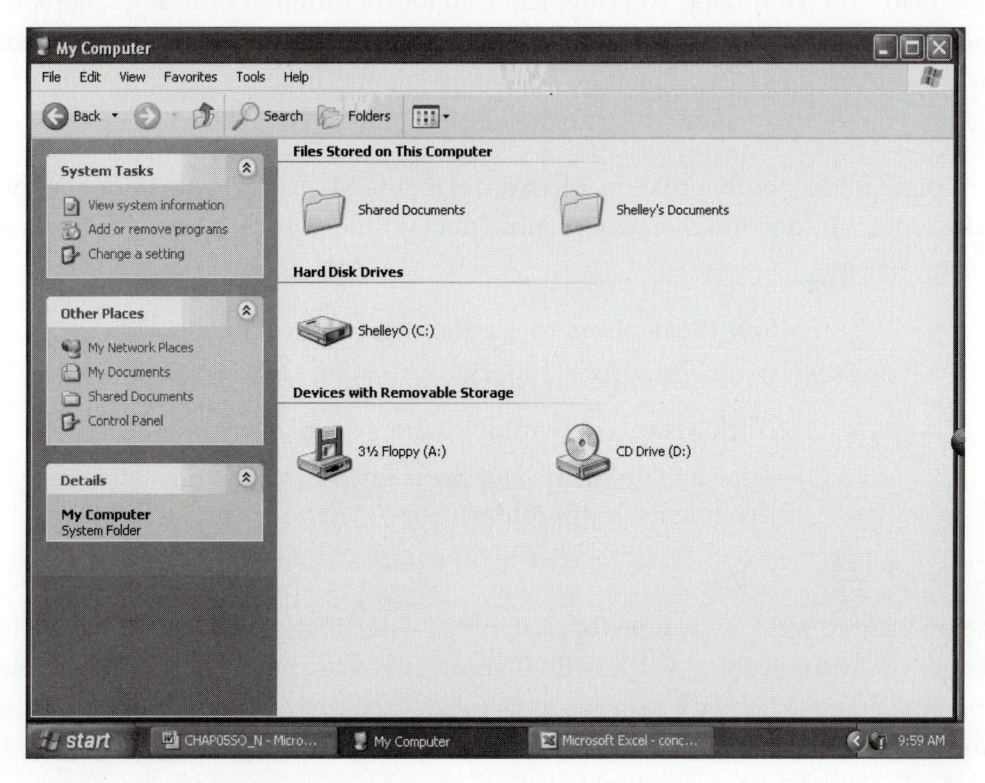

Figure 5.8. Use My Computer to display the drives on your computer.

- You can double-click a drive icon to open the drive. You may be looking for a folder or file to copy, move, or delete. Or you might be looking for a program file so that you can create a shortcut to the program.
- Select common tasks from the task pane (the left part of the window). For instance, you can view system information or change system settings.
- You can get information about the drives. For instance, you might want to see the amount of free space on your hard drive. Right-click the drive and select Properties.
- You can access system tools, such as commands, to scan a disk for errors, format a floppy disk, or start a backup program. To display a list of commands and tools for drives, right-click the drive. Then select the command you want.
- The toolbar buttons and task pane also enable you to navigate to other drives and folders on your computer. You can click any of the folders or drives listed under Other Places. You can also use the Up button in the toolbar to move up through the folder structure.
- If you want to sort files, you can do so by date, size, name, or type. Click View and then click Arrange Icons by and select your sort order. Sorting may help you find a file that you've lost or may help you select a group of related files (for instance, all files with names that start with CHAP).

CREATING A NEW FOLDER

One of the key things you need to do to keep your computer organized is to set up and use folders to store your data. You can pick from lots of different ordering schemes: you may put all chapters from a manuscript in one folder, you may store all memos together, or you may put all files related to a project in one folder. The choice is yours, but do make sure you set up a folder structure that is easy to use.

You can place folders within folders. Most users let the My Documents folder be the main documents folder and then create subfolders within. You also may want to use this organizing scheme.

Follow these steps to create a new folder:

1. Open the folder in which you want to place the new folder.
2. Click **Make a new folder** in the task pane.
3. Type a folder name and press Enter. You can now store new documents in this folder.

SELECTING FILES

When you want to work with a file (open it, copy it, delete it, and so on), the first step is to select the item you want to work with. If you want to copy a file, for instance, select that file by clicking it. You can select a single file, a group of files in a row, a set of files that are not in a row, or all files. You can also select a folder by clicking it. Here are the basics of selecting a single or multiple files:

- To select a single file or folder, click it.
- To select the contents of the entire folder, click Edit in the menu bar and then click the Select All command.
- To select files that are in a row next to each other, click the first file and then hold down the Shift key and click the last file. All files—including the first and last—are selected.
- To select files that are not next to each other, hold down the Ctrl key and click on each file you want to select. (You can do the same thing to select multiple folders.)

RENAMING FILES

If you don't like the original name you used for the file, you can rename it, using a more descriptive name. You can also rename folders.

Follow these steps to rename a file or folder:

1. Select the file or folder you want to rename.
2. In the task pane, click **Rename this file** or **Rename this folder**. (The command will vary depending on what you have selected.)
3. Type a new name and press Enter. The file (or folder) is renamed.

MOVING AND COPYING FILES

You can move or copy files as needed. You might move a file if you want to store it on a different drive or in a different folder. You can copy files if you want to keep an extra copy or perhaps you want to keep the original, but modify the copy.

Follow these steps to move or copy a file:

1. Select the file or folder you want to move or copy.
2. Click **Move this file** or **Copy this file** in the task pane. (The command will vary if you have several files selected—Copy the selected items, for instance—or if you have a folder selected—Copy this folder.) Windows displays a dialog box that lists the drives and folders on your computer.
3. Select the appropriate folder from this list. You can click the plus sign next to a folder to display subfolders within. Figure 5.9, for instance, displays the Move Items dialog box.

Lesson 5
Defining Operating Systems

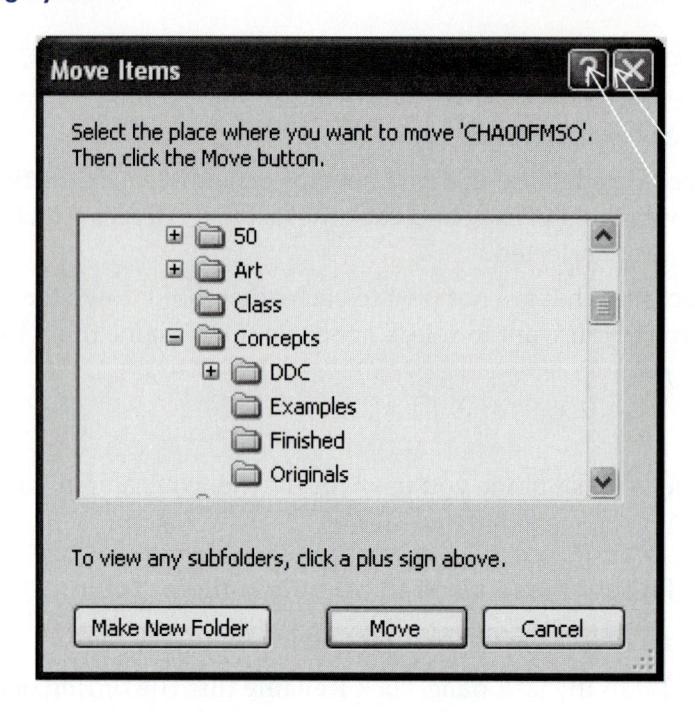

Figure 5.9. You can select the folder to which to move (or copy) the selected items.

    4   Click the Move button to move or the Copy button to copy.

DELETING AND UNDELETING FILES

In addition to renaming, moving, and copying files, you should also delete files you no longer need so that you can free up that disk space. Note that deleted files are not really deleted, but moved to the Recycle Bin. You can undelete them if needed.

Follow these steps to delete a file:

1. Select the file or folder you want to delete.
2. Click **Delete this file** in the task pane. The file is deleted.

Follow these steps to undelete a file:

1. Double-click the Recycle Bin to open it.
2. Select the file you want to restore.
3. Click **Restore this item**. The file is restored to its original folder.

Empty Recycle Bin. If you really want to get rid of a file, you can empty the Recycle Bin. To do so, click the Empty Recycle Bin command.

Can't find a file? If you cannot find a file by browsing, search for it using the Search command. Click the Start button and then select Search. Follow the prompts in the task pane to select the type of file you want to search for, enter the search criteria (you can search by name, date, content, and other file features), and start the search.

> **Back up work:** Your documents are the most valuable items on your computer. You may have some documents that you are unable to re-create. Therefore, it's important that you save your work while you create documents. It's also critical that you keep an extra copy (backup) of your data files. You can copy files manually to a CD. Or you can use a backup program. You should backup often!

HANDLING FILE PROBLEMS

When you work with files, you can occasionally experience difficulties in finding files, in having enough disk space, and in being denied file access. Use the following list to review common problems and their fixes:

- If you cannot find a file, try searching for it using Windows Search command. (Click Start and then Search. Follow the prompts for selecting what type of file to search for, entering the search criteria, and reviewing the search results.)
- You can avoid losing files by setting up a good organizational structure for your files, creating folders and storing like files together. Also, use descriptive names so that you can easily identify a file by its name.
- You should also make period backups of your documents. In this case if you lose a file, you can always go back to the spare copy.
- As you use the computer more and more, your disk will become full of files. You should periodically delete files you no longer need.
- If you are denied access to a file, it may be password protected, or you may not have permission to access the file on that network. In this case, check with your system administrator.

Installing Software

Lesson 4 discussed how to purchase new software or upgrade your software. When you do so, you need to install it using Windows. Most programs come with an automated installation program. Usually you insert the program CD and the installation will start automatically. If this doesn't work, you can use the Add or Remove Programs feature to add new programs or uninstall programs. Click Start and then click Control Panel. In Category view, click the Add or Remove Programs link. (In Classic view, double-click the Add or Remove Programs icon.)

When you install a new program, the installation program should add a program icon to the Start menu. (It may also add a program shortcut to your desktop.) Lesson 6 covers starting and working in applications.

Sometimes you'll encounter problems installing software: the installation program won't start, the installation doesn't finish, the program once installed doesn't work, or other programs don't work once the new program is installed. Pinpointing the exact problem can be tricky and you may need to call for technical support since every system varies, and it's hard to determine exactly what may cause the problem on your particular system.

If the installation program won't start, try opening My Computer and then double-clicking on the icon that contains the program disk. See if you can find an installation or setup file. Double-click that and see if that works. Or try using the Run command (click Start and then Run), type the name of the installation program, and click OK. If that doesn't work, contact the software company and see whether they can send you a new disc. You may have a defective program.

> **Permission:** For networked systems or systems that have user accounts set up, you may not have the authority to install new software. In this case, check with your system administrator.

If the installation doesn't complete, note when it stopped. Check the program manual to see if it provides any troubleshooting advice for installation that isn't completed. Do the same if the installation completes, but the program won't start. Or if the new program causes problems with existing programs.

Most software programs are set up so that you can easily open and work with previous versions of that program's files. If your files are quite a bit older (it's been a while since you've upgraded), you may have to save your original files into a format that the new program can read. Check with your program manufacturer about handling previous file versions.

Just as you can install programs, you can also uninstall or delete them. When you do so, you remove the program files, and you will then not be able to run this program from your computer.

Customizing Windows with Control Panels

One of the other benefits of Windows is that you can customize it to work and look just the way you want. Windows provides Control Panel icons that control the settings for common hardware and system settings. To display these control panels, follow these steps:

Follow these steps to display Control Panels:
1   Click the Start button.
2   Click Control Panel.

The Control Panel has two different views: category and classic view. In category view, you can select by task. For instance, to access the Display Control panel, click the Appearance and Themes category icon and then select the option for changing the display. Classic view (used in previous versions of Windows) simply displays the various icons for the system Control Panels. Figures 5.10 and 5.11 show both views. You

Learning Computer Concepts
Lesson 5
Defining Operating Systems

can switch the views by clicking the command in the task pane. (The command varies depending on the current view.)

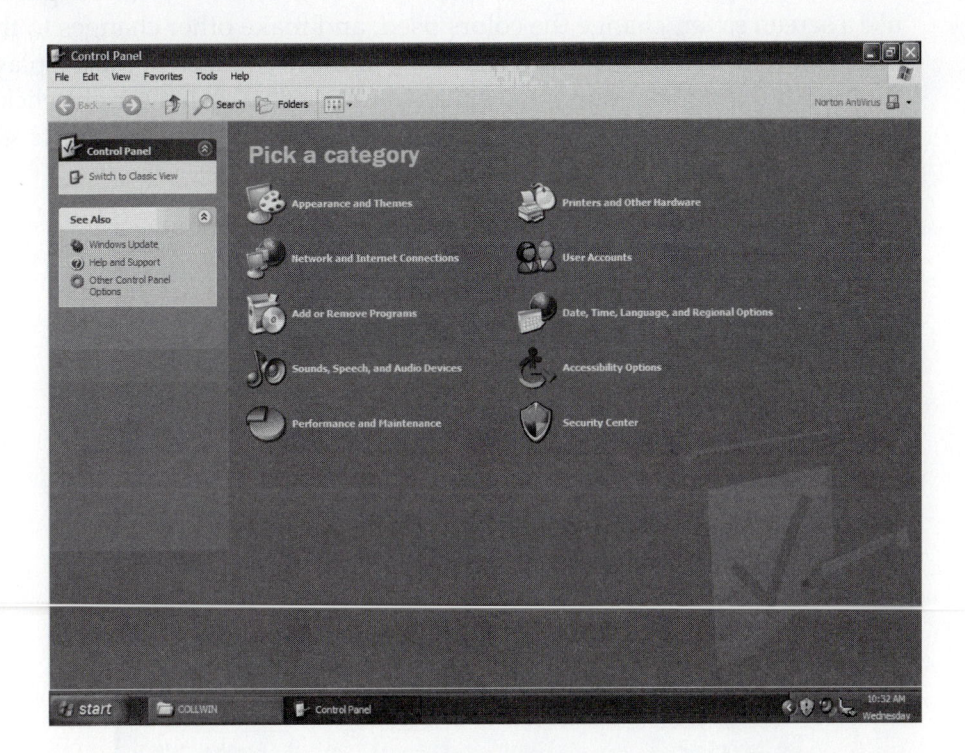

Figure 5.10. In Category view, you can select what you want to change by selecting a task.

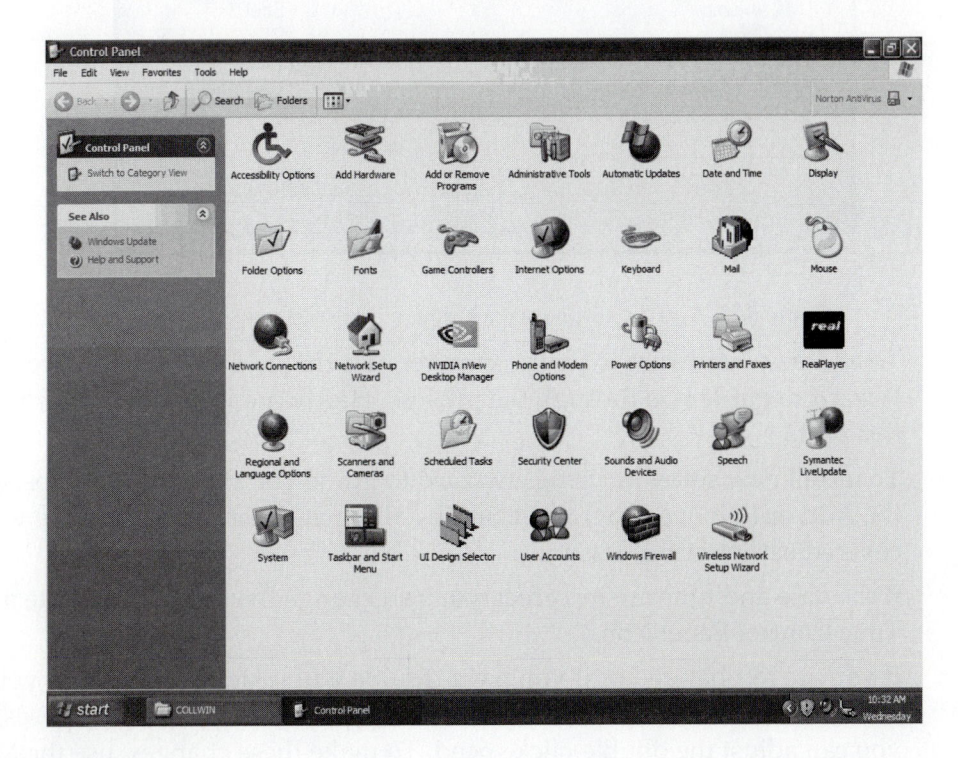

Figure 5.11. In Classic view, you see the icons for each Control Panel option.

117

Lesson 5
Defining Operating Systems

The following provides just a few of the features you can change:

- You can change the image that is displayed on your desktop (see Figure 5.12), use a screen saver, change the colors used, and make other changes to the appearance of Windows. You make most of these changes in the Display Properties dialog box. Use the Display Control Panel icon. Or right-click a blank area of the desktop and then click Properties. Use the various tabs to make changes.

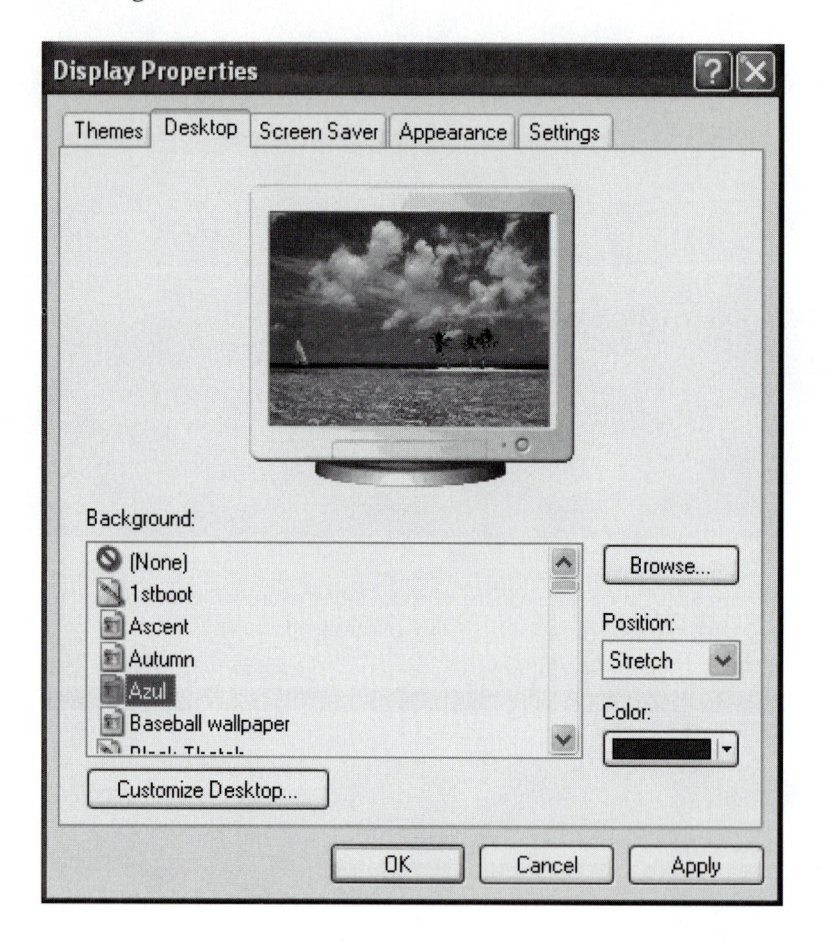

Figure 5.12. You can display a background image on your desktop.

- To add new hardware to your computer, use the Add New Hardware Wizard to guide you through the process. Hardware was covered earlier in this part.
- To install new software using a wizard to guide you through the steps, use the Add or Remove Programs icon. Installing and removing software was covered earlier in this lesson.
- If the date and time are incorrect, you can change them using the Date and Time Control Panel icon.
- If you are left-handed or if you have trouble with using your mouse, you can customize the mouse. You can switch the right and left button purposes, and you can adjust the double-click speed. To make these changes, use the Mouse Control Panel icon.

Learning Computer Concepts
Lesson 5
Defining Operating Systems

- To install a new printer or to make changes to your current printer's settings, use the Printers and Faxes icon.
- If you want to change the appearance of the Start menu or taskbar, look at the options available in the Taskbar and Start Menu Control Panel.
- If more than one person uses your computer, you can set up User Accounts; each person will then be able to save his or her own screen saver settings, Internet favorites list, and more. Use the User Accounts icon to make this change.

These are just a few of the many, many ways you can adapt Windows so that it suits your preferences.

Changing System Settings

Note that there are other system settings that are more complex such as how Windows handles memory or the details in key system files such as the Registry. Usually only very experienced computer users, such as system administrators, make these types of changes. In fact, on some computers, you cannot even make these types of changes. Careless changes can wreak havoc on a system, adding the wrong date and time stamp on files, preventing programs from working, and other problems.

If you know what you are doing and intend to make a major system change, make sure you understand the purpose (how the change will affect the computer and why you need to make this change) and the consequences of making the change (what can go wrong). Make sure you know how to undo the change if you have problems after effecting the change. You may want to take detailed notes so that you can remember exactly what you did and what changes you made so that you can reverse the process if needed.

Troubleshooting Windows Problems

As you work with Windows, especially as you need new hardware and software, you may encounter some problems. Because the system is complex and everything must work together, compatibility problems are common. For instance, the printer must work with Windows XP. The software program must be able to work with other programs and hardware installed. If you have compatibility issues with hardware, try reinstalling the hardware driver. If you used the Windows-supplied driver, try using the driver supplied with the hardware component. If that doesn't work, try searching online for a newer driver (the file that tells Windows the details about the program). For software compatibility, check with the software manufacturer for suggestions on how to handle problems.

In addition to compatibility problems, sometimes system files become corrupt. Perhaps the computer wasn't shut down properly or the program has a bug. You may notice that your computer gets stuck and that you need to reboot more often. Or you may receive frequent error messages. In this case, you should investigate whether your operating system has a problem.

Often, you can often fix these problems by restarting and checking the disk for errors. If that doesn't work, you can restart in safe mode and troubleshoot problems from this bare-bones startup. In some cases, you may need to reinstall the operating system, or you may install an upgraded version of the operating system. This may involve a patch (a small addition that fixes known problems) or a service pack (put out roughly once a year). The service pack combines all the updates, bug fixes, and patches that have been created up to that time. Currently Service Pack 2 is the most current version.

Log on permission: Some systems require a specific logon procedure. If you don't follow the correct steps (for instance, mistype your password), you may be locked out of the system. In this case, check with your system adminstrator on how to get properly logged onto the computer.

Summary

- All computer systems require an operating system to work. This special system software handles common tasks, such as starting programs, saving files, displaying things on the monitor, and more.
- The most popular operating system is Microsoft Windows. You can find several Windows products, each designed for a specific market (consumers, businesses, networks). Windows XP is the current version.
- Other popular operating systems include the Macintosh operating system, Unix (used on high-end computers and workstations), and Linux (a free version of a high-end operating system similar to Unix).
- Windows uses a graphical user interface that enables users to point to what they want. Most Windows programs follow a standard design so that once you learn one Windows programs you can transfer these skills (selecting a menu command, saving a document, copying text, for instance) to other Windows programs.
- When you start Windows you see the Windows desktop, which includes the Start menu, taskbar, and icons.
- Everything in Windows is displayed in a window. You can move, resize, open, and close windows as needed.
- You can use Windows to perform common file maintenance tasks, such as copying a file, creating a new folder, deleting files, and renaming a file.
- You can use Control Panel settings to install new software, display a list of installed printers (and add new printers), customize the mouse, and more. To display Control Panel settings, click on Start and then click Control Panel.

Learning Computer Concepts

Lesson 5
Defining Operating Systems

Q&A

Multiple Choice

1. DOS stands for:
    a. Digital Over Satellite
    b. Disk Omnipresent Star
    c. Disk Operating System
    d. Disk Organizing System

2. When you delete a file it is not really deleted but moved to the:
    a. Recycle Bin
    b. Hard drive
    c. Email window
    d. CD-R drive

3. Windows includes this icon to provide access to view the drives on your computer:
    a. Recycle Bin
    b. Taskbar
    c. Run command
    d. My Computer

4. The name of the operating system for Macintosh computers is:
    a. MacDaddy
    b. System
    c. Cipher
    d. DOS

Fill in the Blank

1. To make a change to a system setting, use Windows _____.

2. The _____ is what you first see after Windows starts; it displays icons for programs and folders.

3. This system folder enables you to store all of your documents in one folder called _____.

4. When your computer is stuck, you need to _____ it.

Short Essay

1. List the different file management tasks you can perform with Windows.

2. Explain the advantages of a graphical user interface like Windows over a command-based one like DOS.

LESSON 6: WORKING WITH APPLICATIONS

Objectives:

- ➤ Start and exit programs
- ➤ Work with documents
- ➤ Type and edit text
- ➤ Print documents

Working in Programs

One of the great advantages of Windows is program consistency. Most programs look and operate similarly. Skills you learn in one program are transferable to other programs. As an example, you select a menu command the same way in most Windows programs: click the menu name and then click the menu command. Many programs include the same menus (File, Edit, View, Help) and same commands in those menus (Save, Open, Copy, Paste). This section covers the basics of starting and exiting programs, getting familiar with common on-screen tools, and getting help.

STARTING A PROGRAM

Windows provides several ways to start a program:

- The most often used programs are listed on the opening Start menu (as well as programs for accessing the Internet and e-mail). If your program is listed here, you can click Start and then click the program name without having to display and select from the complete list.
- All of the programs installed on your computer should be listed on the complete list of Start menu items. You can display this list by clicking All Programs. Sometimes they are stored within folders, and you have to display the folder to access the program icon.
- You can add desktop shortcuts to commonly used programs. You can then double-click the program icon to start the program.
- You can double-click a file icon on the desktop to open that file in that file's associated program. For instance, if you double-click a Word document, Windows will start Word and open that document. (If Windows doesn't know which program to use to open the file, you'll be prompted to select one.)

Follow these steps to start a program from the Start menu:

1. Click Start and then All Programs (see Figure 6.1).
2. If you see the program name, click it to start the program. Some programs, like the accessory programs, are stored within folders

on the Start menu. Click or point to the folder name until you see the program. Then click the program name to start it.

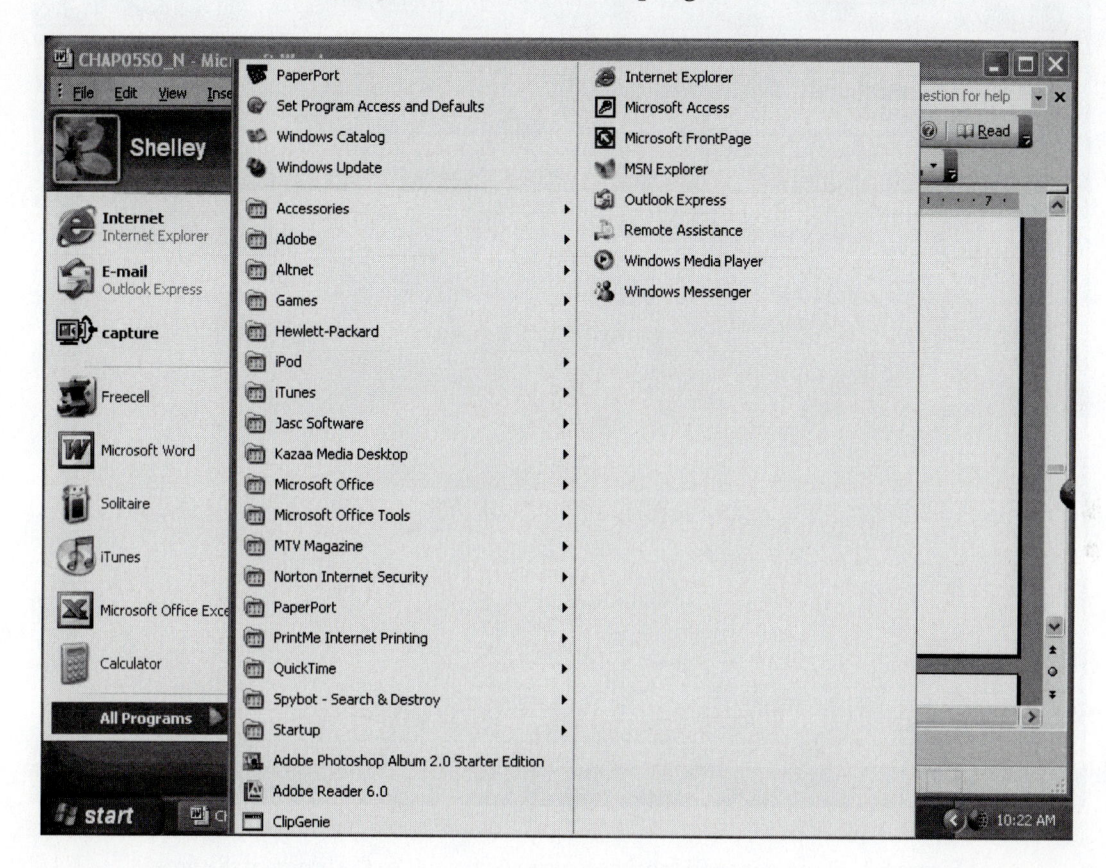

Figure 6.1. You can start programs from the Start menu.

EXITING A PROGRAM

When you are done working in a program, exit the program. Doing so frees up system resources. You can exit by selecting the File, Exit command, by clicking the Close button, or by pressing the keyboard shortcut key (Alt+F4). Before exiting, be sure to save any documents you have created. (If you forget, most programs will prompt you to save the document when you exit, but you should still get in the habit of saving.) Saving a document is covered later in this lesson.

UNDERSTANDING THE PROGRAM TOOLS

Most Windows programs look similar. For instance, take a look at Figure 6.2, a blank document in Microsoft Office Word. This window shows the key elements you can expect to find in most programs:

Lesson 6
Working with Applications

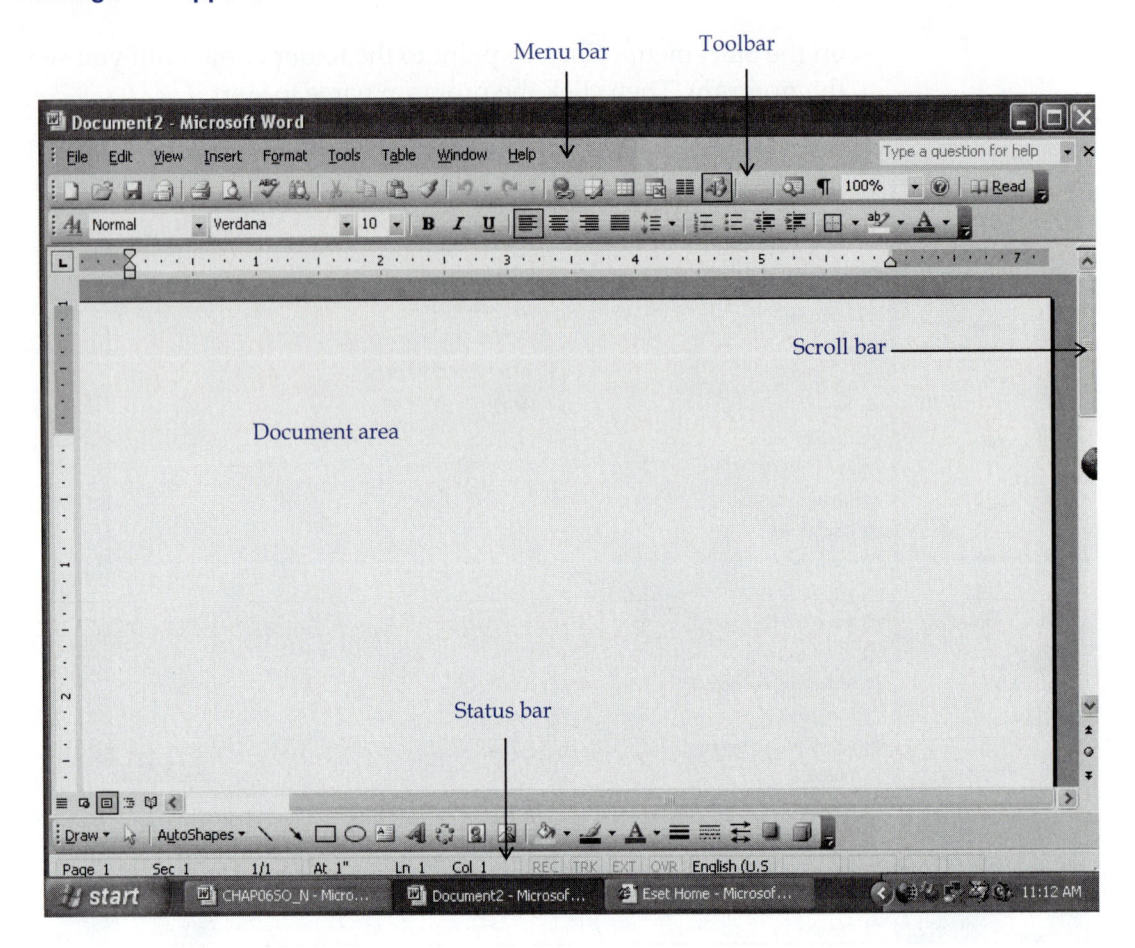

Figure 6.2. A program window has tools to help you use the program features.

- *Menu bar.* The menu bar lists the names of the menu. To open a menu, click its name. You see a list of commands. To select a command, click that command.

- *Toolbars.* Toolbars are rows of buttons; each button is a shortcut to a frequently used command. For instance, click the Bold button (the one with a B) to make text bold. If you aren't sure what a toolbar button does, place the mouse pointer on the edge of the button and the button name (called a ScreenTip) should popup.

  Display or hide toolbars: If you don't use the toolbars, you can hide them. Click View and then Toolbars. Then uncheck any toolbars that are displayed (indicated with a checkmark). On the other hand, you may want to display additional toolbars. In this case, click View and then Toolbars and then check the toolbars you want to display.

- *Document area.* The area where your text will appear when you type is the big blank area. In a spreadsheet program, this appears as a grid of rows and columns.

- *Status bar.* For information about the current document, check the status bar.

- *Window controls.* You also have control buttons for opening and closing the document and program windows. If you see scroll bars along the right and bottom, you can use this to scroll through the document.

Learning Computer Concepts

Lesson 6
Working with Applications

GETTING HELP

Just as you can get help with Windows features, most programs also include online help systems. You can use these to look up tasks, search for information, or find a topic in an index. Use online help if you forget how to do something or if you run into a problem. Usually you can find an answer or solution.

Follow these steps to get help from within an application:

1. Click Help and then the Help command. The name will vary depending on the program.

2. Type a question or description of what you want to do and then click Search. You see matching help topics. The pane on the right lists the top topic (see Figure 6.3).

3. If needed, click the help topic that best matches your query.

4. Review the help information in the pane on the right.

5. When you are done reviewing the information, click the help window's Close (X) button.

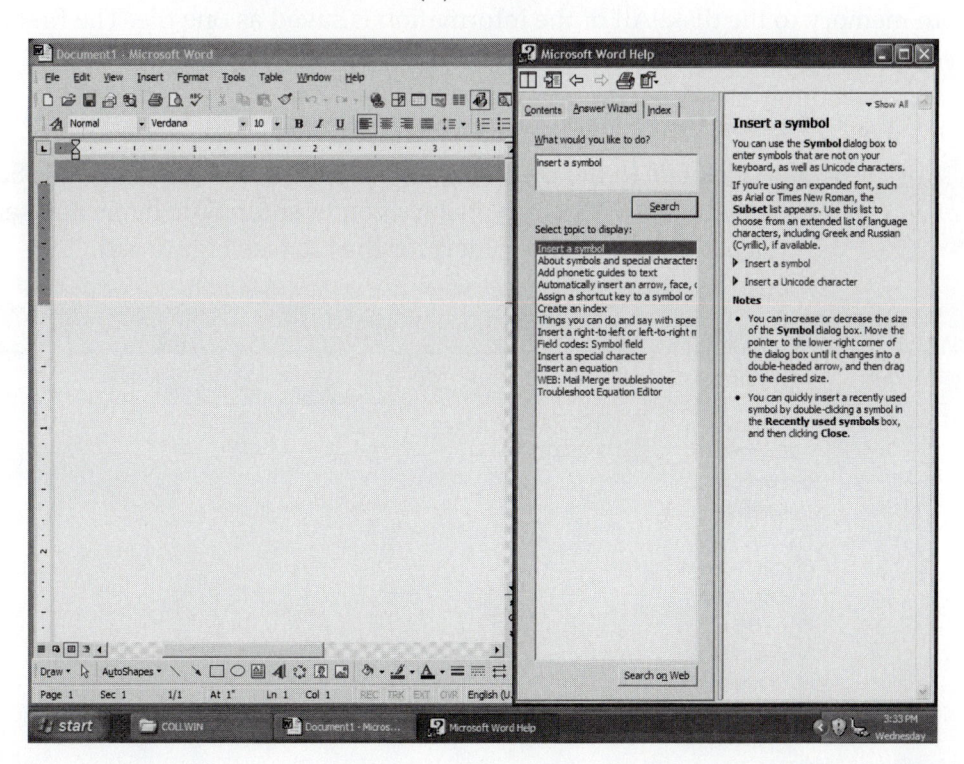

Figure 6.3. You can review the help information and then close the window when you are finished.

Other help methods: Your school or workplace may also provide support; these are sometimes called help desks. You can contact one of these staff members to also get help (especially for complex hardware problems). And some programs include tutorials. You can start these from the Help menu and follow along getting an overview of the program from the tutorial.

Lesson 6
Working with Applications

Working with Documents

When you work in programs, the result is most often a document. That might be a report, a memo, a picture, a budget, a presentation, a database, and so on. Part of learning to use a computer effectively is learning to save and to save often. You save so that you don't lose all the work that you've created. Work that appears on-screen is stored only temporarily in the computer's memory. If you lose power or someone messes with your document, all that work is lost. That's why it's so important to save.

You save also so that you can go back and open the document again. You may need to finish it, fine-tune it, edit it, print it, add images, or anything else. This section covers saving, closing, opening, creating new documents, and printing.

SAVING A DOCUMENT

As you know, when you type or enter data, it is stored in memory, which is not permanent. If you exit the program or turn off the computer, all that data is lost. To make a permanent copy of the data, you save it to your hard drive or a disk. Doing so copies the data from memory to the disk. All of the information is saved as one file. The first time you save a document, you assign a file name and a location (folder and drive).

Follow these steps to save a document:

1. Click File in the menu bar and then click Save. You see the Save As dialog box, which enables you to enter a file name and select a location (drive and folder) for the file (see Figure 6.4).

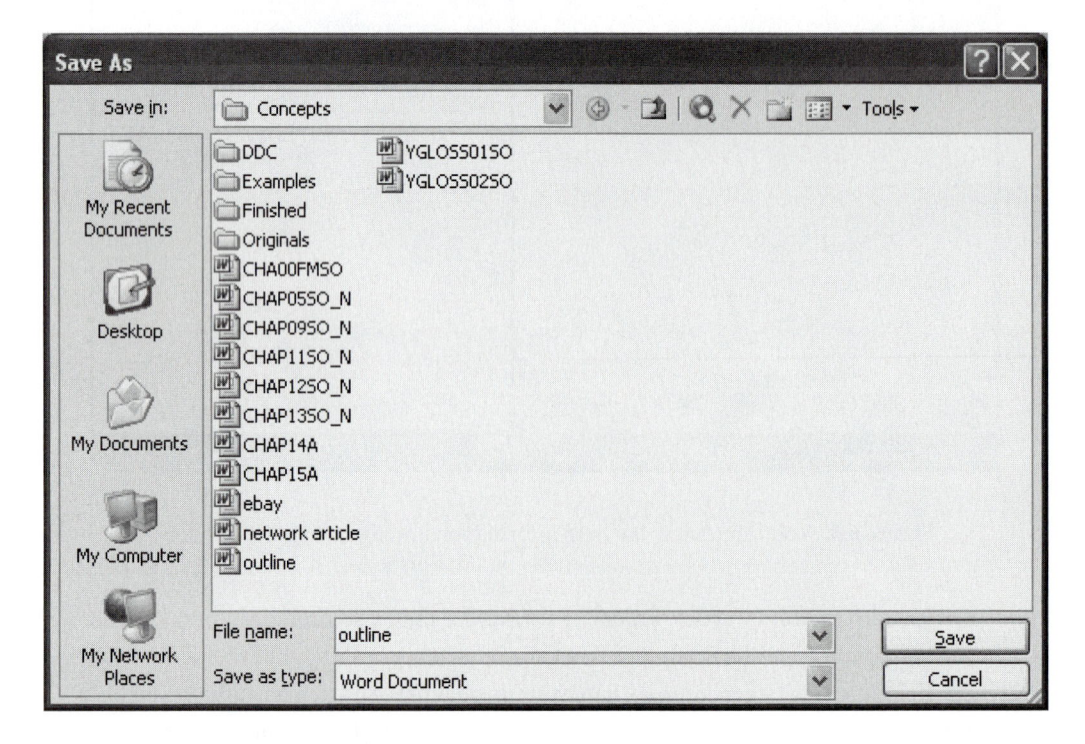

Figure 6.4. Use this dialog box to save a document.

2. If necessary, change to the drive and folder where you want to save the document. You can use the Save in drop-down list to select another drive or folder. You can also move up through the folder structure by clicking the Up One Level button.

3. Type a file name for the document.

4. Click the Save button. The document is saved with that name; most programs display the file name in the title bar of the document window.

You shouldn't just save once, but instead save periodically as you make changes to the file. The disk version includes only the additions you have made up to saving the file. Any changes or additions after you saved are not saved until you save again. (Some programs have Automatic Save feature that saves a document at set intervals, but it's best to remember to save yourself and not rely exclusively on this automatic save to save your work.) To save a file again, use the File, Save command, press Ctrl+S, or click the Save toolbar button. When you save again, you do not have to type the name and select the location. When you select File, Save, you save the file with the same file name and location as before.

Save to new location: If you want to save a document to another location or with a different name, you can use the File, Save As command. Type a new name or select a new location. The original remains intact.

Here are some pointers when naming documents:

- Use a descriptive name, something that will remind you of the contents. MEMO may sound OK today, but a few weeks from now, you won't remember what MEMO contains.

- Consider setting up a folder for your word processing documents within the My Documents folder. You might have several folders, one for each project or one for each type of document (memos, reports, letters). See Lesson 5 for help on creating new folders.

- Each program has a default file format. (Check your program to find yours.) You can use this file on another computer if that computer has the same program. If it does not, you may need to save the file in another file format. Common file formats that any program can read are TXT (text) and RTF (rich text format). Use the File, Save As command and then select a file type from the dialog box.

- You should periodically get rid of documents you no longer need. First make a backup copy and then delete the files. Doing so will free up disk space and keep the files you do need less cluttered. See "Deleting Files" in Lesson 5 for more information.

- You can also save a document to a disk. To do so, select this drive when you save and name the document.

OPENING A DOCUMENT

When you save a document, it is then available for you to open and work on again. Most work is an ongoing process, so you may need to refer to the document, make changes to the document, print the document, or change the appearance of the document.

Follow these steps to open a document:

1. Click File in the menu bar and then click Open. You see a dialog box similar to the Open dialog box shown in Figure 6.5.

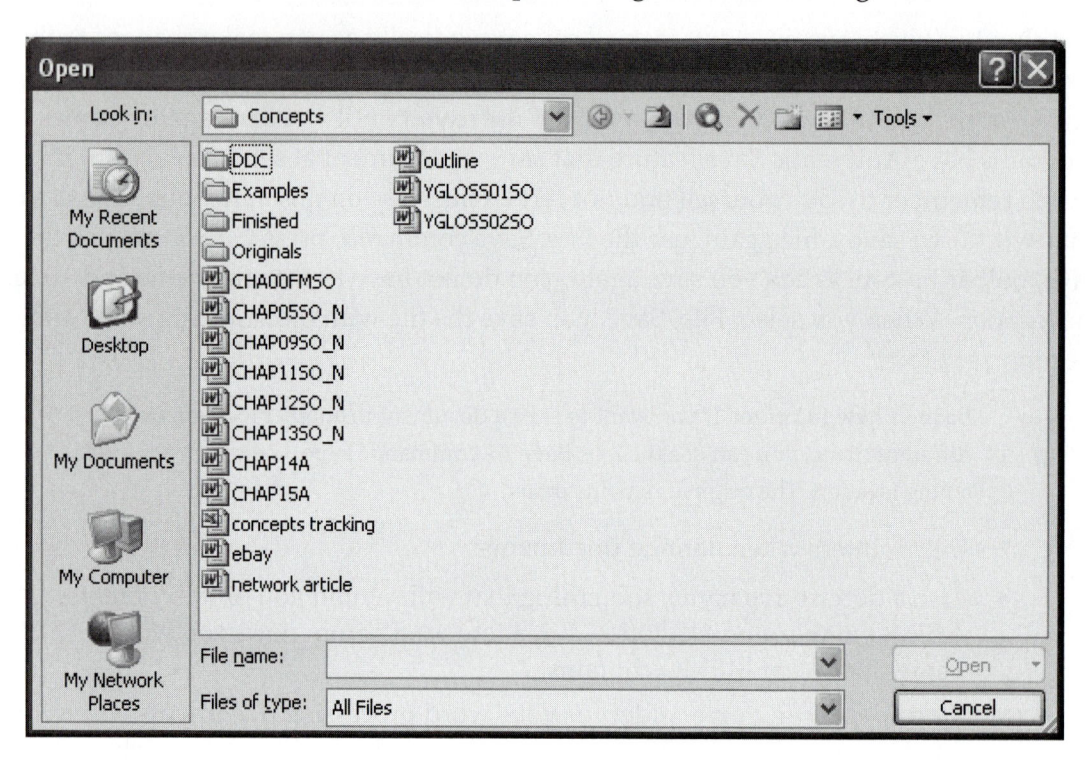

Figure 6.5. Open documents you have saved from this dialog box.

2. Display the file you want to open. If the file is not listed, you can change to another drive or folder by displaying the Look in drop-down list and selecting another drive or folder or by clicking the Up One Level button to move up through the folder structure.

3. Double-click the file or click it to select it and then click the Open button. The file is opened.

DEALING WITH PROBLEMS OPENING DOCUMENTS

In some cases, you may have problems opening a document. Usually this occurs if you are trying to open a document that is in another file format. For instance, you may try to open a WordPerfect document in Word. Or you may try to open an older version of a program file. A lot of progress has been made to make file sharing easier, even among different types of computers (Macs and PCs). So these compatibility problems are not as common.

Still if you have problems, see if your program has a converter tool that can convert the file to a file type you can open. Also, check to see if the person can save the file in a different file type. Most programs enable you to save a file in different file formats, including some simple, common file types that are compatible with most programs (TXT and RTF files for word processing files, for instance).

As another possibility the file may become corrupt (develop problems). This is especially common with files saved on floppy disks because they are susceptible to the wear and tear of traveling, being inserted into different machines, and often left in the sun or cold.

> **Open from file window:** You can double-click a file from a file window and Windows should start the program and open the file. If this doesn't happen, it means that file type is not registered to a particular program. Instead, start the program and open the document from the program. (Or use Windows help to learn how to set program and file associations.)

VIEWING A DOCUMENT

Many programs enable you to view the document in different ways. For instance, in PowerPoint, you can display a view that shows miniature versions of all your slides, or you can view just one slide at a time. In Microsoft Office Word, you can display just the text of the document, or you can display the document in page layout view (which shows headers, footers, and page numbers, for instance). To change to a different view, click View in the menu bar and then click the view you want.

In addition to changing the view, some programs enable you to work on more than one document at a time. For instance, you might have an outline of a chapter open in one document and one chapter open in another. You can switch among the open document windows as needed. To do so, click Windows in the menu bar. The current document has a checkmark next to it. To view another document, click its name. You can also use the Windows taskbar to switch among open documents (even documents from other programs). Click the button for the window that you want to display.

Yet another view option is to zoom in or out on a document. If you have very tiny print, you may want to enlarge the view so that you can better read the text. For this option, click View in the menu bar and then look for a Zoom command. Select the magnification level you want.

One last word of advice on viewing: Keep in mind that different programs have different view options. If you aren't sure what you can do, try searching for view, zoom, or display in that program's help system.

CLOSING A DOCUMENT

When you are done working with a document, you should close it. Doing so frees up resources. You can click File in the menu bar and then click Close. Or you can click the Close (X) button for the document window. Be sure you click the one for the document window—not the program window. Clicking the program window's Close box will exit the program.

Lesson 6   **Learning Computer Concepts**
Working with Applications

CREATING A NEW DOCUMENT

When you start a new program, a new document is displayed so that you can start working. If you need to, you can also create a new document at any time. To do so, click File in the menu bar and then click New. Depending on the program, you may need to select a template. A template is a predesigned document that may contain text and formatting to get you started. Consult online help or your program manual for more information on using templates.

Typing and Editing Text

The easiest part of most programs is typing and editing text. To type text, you simply press the keys on the keyboard. As you type, the character appears on-screen, and the flashing vertical line (called the *insertion point*) moves right.

In a word processing line, when you reach the end of the line, the program will wrap the word to the next line, so you do not have to press Enter. In fact, a common error for beginners is to press Enter at the end of each line. Don't. It *does* matter if you press Enter. Doing so inserts hard line breaks. If you add or delete text, the text will not adjust correctly. That's why you should just let the text break where it will. You can press Enter when you want to end one paragraph and again if you want to insert a blank line.

Another mistake beginners often make is pressing the spacebar twice at the end of each sentence. Just use one space. Also, don't use the spacebar to indent text. Use the Tab key instead or set indents (more on this later).

In a spreadsheet program, you type your entry into a cell and then press Tab or Enter to move to the next cell. You can type numbers or letters (words or phrases). You learn more about entering text into this type of document in Lesson 8. In a presentation program, you type text into a text box. Lesson 9 covers the basics of typing text in this type of program.

MOVING AROUND THE DOCUMENT

In a word processing program, the insertion point indicates where text will appear when you type. You can move this pointer to another spot in the document using the keyboard or the mouse.

To use the keyboard, press the cursor movement keys:

- ← Left one character
- → Right one character
- ↑ Up one line
- ↓ Down one line

Most programs offer several other keyboard combinations for moving around. Learn these to save time. For instance, pressing Home usually moves the insertion point to the beginning of the line, whereas pressing End usually moves the insertion point to the end of the current line.

To use the mouse, move the mouse pointer (which looks like an I-beam in some applications) to the spot you want. Then click to place the insertion point.

MAKING SIMPLE CHANGES

You can easily correct simple mistakes as you type. Press Backspace to delete characters to the left of the insertion point. Press Delete to delete characters to the right of the insertion point. To add text, move to where you want to place new text and start typing.

UNDOING MISTAKES AND REPEATING COMMANDS

If you accidentally make a mistake—for instance, delete text that you need—you can undo the change. Click Edit in the menu bar and then click Undo. You can also click the Undo button in the toolbar. You can undo several of the last changes you've made including editing and formatting changes.

If you change your mind again and want to redo what you've undone, use the Edit, Redo command or click the Redo button.

Another handy feature is the Repeat command (found in many programs). If you want to execute the same command again, you can click Edit, Repeat or press the shortcut key (F4).

MOVING AND COPYING TEXT

If you enter data in the wrong order or if you need to use the same data again, you can move or copy it. For instance, you can move text in a word processing program from one location to another. You might rearrange the sentences in a paragraph so that they flow better. You might move whole sections around in a document. You can even move text from one document to another. In a worksheet, you may move data over to make room for new information. Moving and copying data in worksheets is covered in Lesson 8.

Copying is also a part of editing. You might want to repeat the same text in another location in a document. Or sometimes you need to repeat the same idea, but worded differently. Don't retype. Copy the text instead and then modify the copy. Worksheets provide lots of shortcuts for copying and filling data. Again, you'll find this information in Lesson 8.

Copying and moving use a similar process and the same analogy: cut and paste. To move text, you cut it from its original location and then paste it in the new. To copy, you copy and then paste. When you cut and paste, the original text is deleted from that location and moved to the new location. When you copy and paste, the original and the copy appear in the document.

Look for Cut, Copy, and Paste commands in the Edit menu. Most programs also have keyboard shortcuts and toolbar buttons for these features.

Follow these steps to copy or move text:

1. Select the text you want to copy or move.
2. Select the command (Edit, Cut to cut or Edit, Copy to copy).
3. Move to where you want to place the text. Be sure to click the mouse to place the insertion point.
4. Select the Edit, Paste command to paste the text.

SELECTING TEXT

To perform most editing and formatting tasks, you start by selecting text. If you are using most programs, you'll find that concept often: "Select the text and then… Select the file and then… Select the image you want and then…"

Selecting identifies the thing that you want to modify. In a word processing program, most often that is text. You can select text by dragging across it with the mouse button or by holding down the Shift key and highlighting the text using the arrow keys. Figure 6.6 shows text selected.

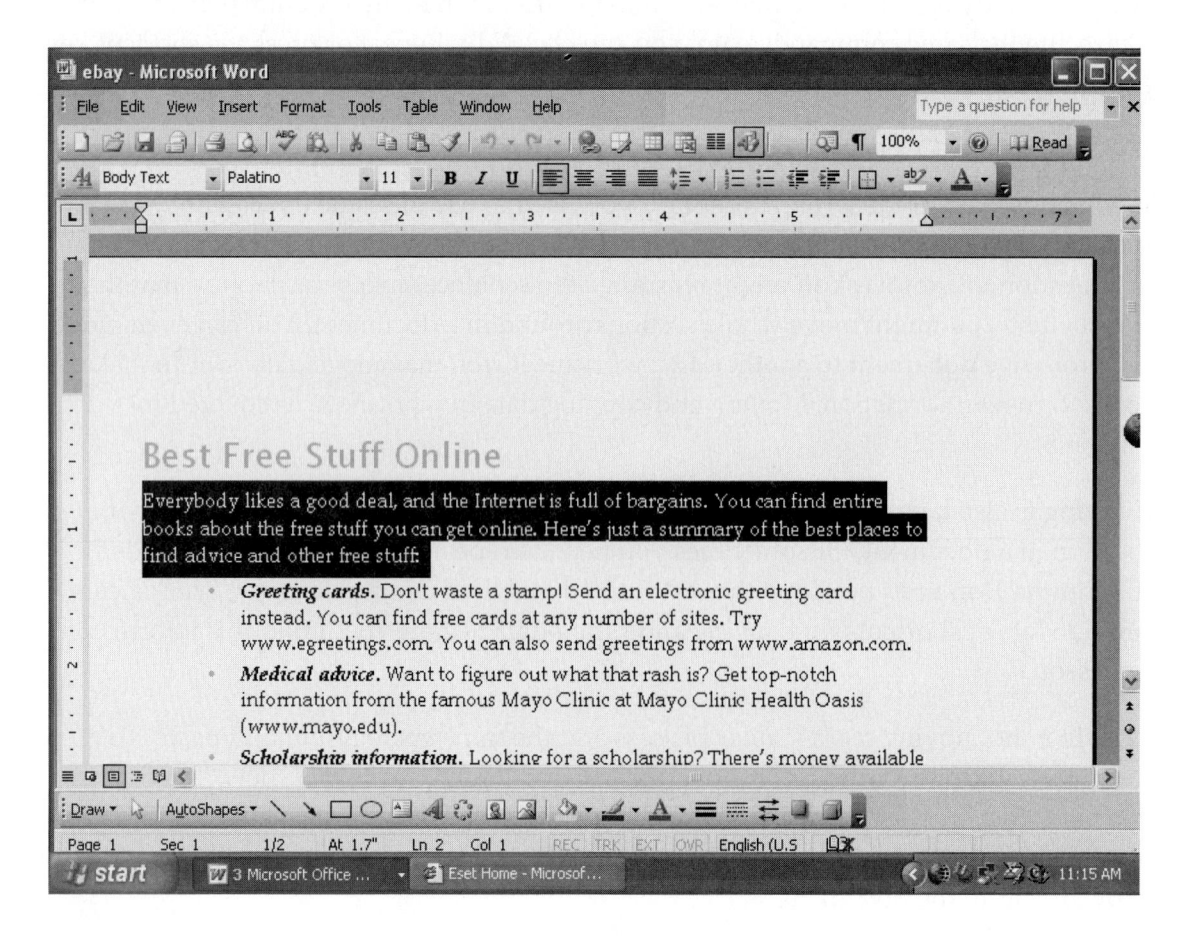

Figure 6.6. Most editing and formatting tasks start with selecting the text.

Learning Computer Concepts

Lesson 6
Working with Applications

INSERTING THE DATE, SYMBOLS, AND PAGE BREAKS

In a word processing document, you may need to insert the date or time as well as symbols. When a page fills up with text, the program will automatically create a page break, but at times, you may want to force a page break at a certain spot. For instance, when you create a title page, you may insert a page break. For inserting these special elements, consider these suggestions:

- You can type the date and time, but most programs also provide a quick command for inserting this information. For instance, in Microsoft Office Word, click Insert and then Date and Time. You can select from a variety of formats. You also have the option of inserting a coded date or time entry; this field will be updated every time you open the document. You might use this in templates when you want to always insert the current date. To use this feature, check the Update automatically check box.

- You can also insert a wide variety of symbols from typographical symbols such as the em dash to smiley faces or trademark symbols. To insert a symbol, click Insert and then Symbol. You can select from any of the symbols displayed (see Figure 6.7). To view other available symbols, display the Font drop-down list and select a symbol font. Then select the symbol you want and click the Insert button.

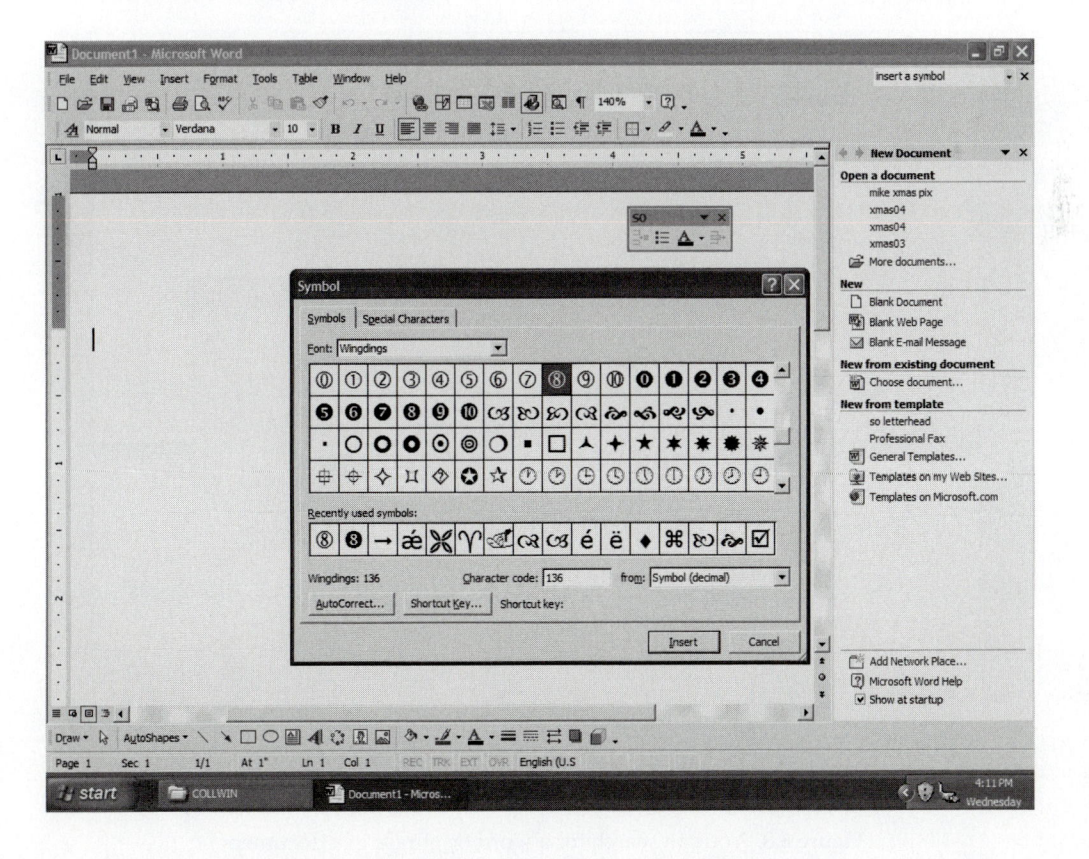

Figure 6.7. You can select from a wide variety of symbols to insert in your document.

- To insert a page break, press Ctrl+Enter. Or use the command Insert, Break and select Page break.

Lesson 6
Working with Applications

FINDING AND REPLACING DATA

As mentioned, you can move around a document using the scroll bars or arrow keys. You can also use shortcut keys designed to move quickly to the top or end of a document. You also have other methods for moving to a certain part of the text. You can search for a word or phrase. You might do this to move to that section, or you might need to check a reference you made. In any case, most programs enable you to search for a word or phrase (or partial word or phrase) using the Find command.

Follow these steps to find text:

1. Click Edit in the menu bar and then click Find.
2. Type the word or phrase you want to find.
3. Click Find Next. The program moves to the first match and highlights it (see Figure 6.8). You can continue searching until you find the location you want.
4. To stop the search, click Cancel.

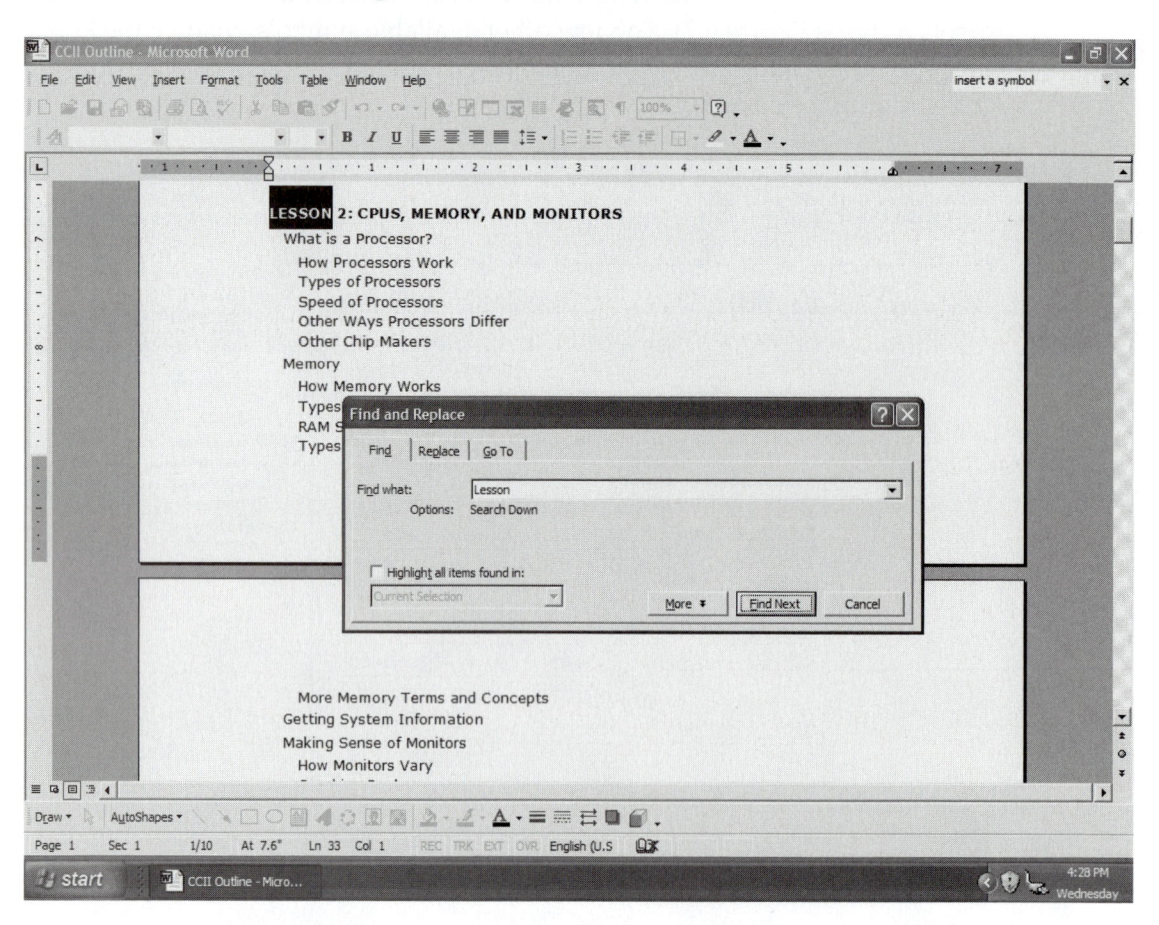

Figure 6.8. You can search for a word or phrase in a document.

The companion to the Find command is the Replace command. You can use this to make replacements to words or phrases in your document. For instance, if you typed "Chapter" and your editor prefers "Lesson," you can search for and replace all the times chapter appears, using lesson in its place.

Follow these steps to replace text:

1. Click Edit in the menu bar and then click Replace.
2. Type the word or phrase you want to find.
3. Type the word or phrase to use as the replacement.
4. Click Find Next. The program moves to the first match and highlights it (see Figure 6.9). You can do any of the following:

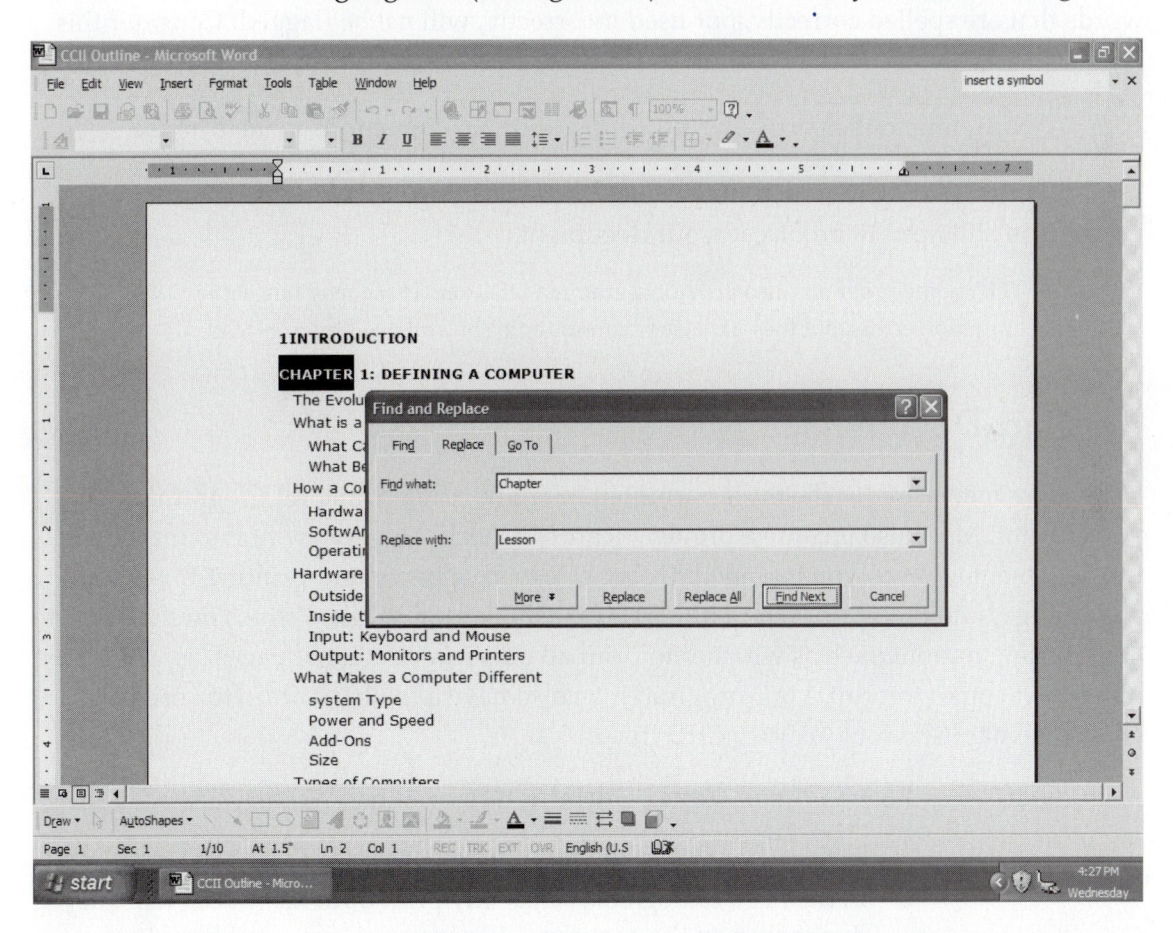

Figure 6.9. You can search for and replace text in your document.

5. Click Replace to replace this occurrence.
6. Click Replace All to replace all occurrences.
7. Click Find Next to skip making this replacement and go to the next match.
8. Click Cancel to stop the search and replace.

Lesson 6
Working with Applications

CHECKING SPELLING

Many programs include a spell checker. You should use this program to check the words in your document. Before you think you can quit worrying about spelling forever, understand how the speller works.

The speller works by comparing the words in your document to the words in its dictionary. It then flags any words it cannot find. That does not necessarily mean that the word is misspelled. Proper names or terms may not be found in the dictionary. For this type of flag, you can ignore the misspelling or add the word to your dictionary so that it is not flagged again.

If the speller finds the word in its dictionary, the word will not be flagged. That means words that are spelled correctly, but used incorrectly, will *not* be flagged. Consider this sentence:

> *Their* going to the party, but they don't know the directions to *there* house.

The speller won't flag any spelling mistakes, but your English teacher will find the errors. You still need to proofread your document.

TIP: Some programs also provide a grammar checker. These may flag some common errors, but they are also not foolproof. You still need to proofread.

Printing Documents

Many documents are for the most part intended to be printed, and all programs enable you to print. Most also include a preview feature. Check the preview first to make sure the document looks as you intended. Doing so can save paper and printing time. Make any changes and then print. The command to print is usually File, Print. You then select any printing options such as whether to print all pages or a range of pages, as well as the number of copies to print. Your program may also have a toolbar button for printing and a keyboard shortcut (usually Ctrl+P).

Follow these steps to print a document:

1. Click File in the menu bar and then click Print.
2. In the Print dialog box, select any print options. (These will vary depending on the program.) For instance, you may be able to select the number of copies to print, the print range, and other options (see Figure 6.10).

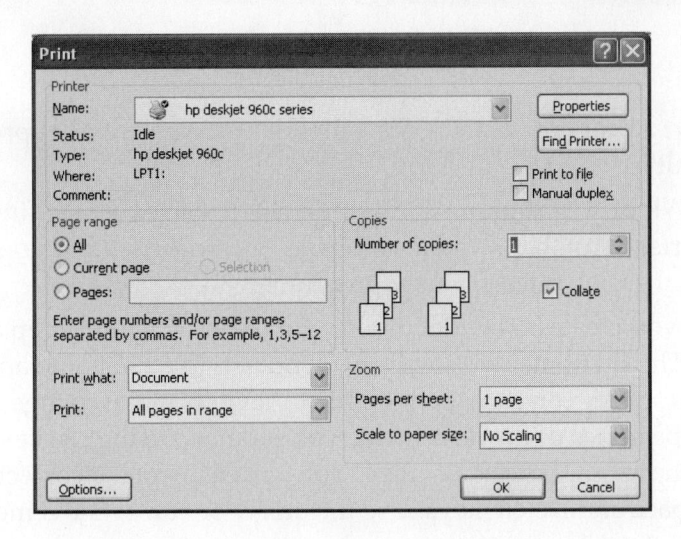

Figure 6.10. Select your printing options and then click OK.

3   Click OK. The document is printed.

When printing keep these troubleshooting tips in mind:

- If you want to stop or pause a print job, open the print queue. You can do so by double-clicking the print icon in the Windows taskbar. You can also click Start and then Control Panel. Open the Printer Control Panel and double-click the icon for your printer. You can then use the commands in the print queue to stop, pause, restart, or cancel a particular print job or all print jobs.

- Sometimes the document is sent to the printer so quickly that you don't have time to view the print queue. In this case, you can just let the document print.

- If the printer isn't working, make sure the cables are securely connected (the one that connects to the printer as well as the one that connects to the computer). Also, make sure the printer has power and is turned on.

- If the printer has a problem, you should see some type of indicator on the printer (like a flashing light). The computer may also display a message telling you, for instance, that the printer is out of paper or ink. In this case, fix the problem by adding paper or a new ink cartridge.

- If your printer is acting funny (printing garbage), try unplugging it from its power source for a few minutes and then plugging it back in. If that doesn't work, you may need to reinstall the printer driver. Consult Windows troubleshooter printer help for the steps on checking and reinstalling drivers.

Lesson 6
Working with Applications

Summary

- To start a program, use the Start menu. You can also start programs from shortcut icons on the desktop.

- Most Windows programs look similar. You can expect to find a menu bar, toolbar(s), scroll bars, and a status bar. Including similar on-screen tools makes it easier to learn a new program.

- When you create a new document, you must save it to keep a permanent copy. The first time you save a file, you assign a file name and location. Once a file is saved, you can open the file to review, make changes, print, or change the appearance of the document. You type text using the keyboard. As you type, the text appears on-screen. You can easily make corrections using the Backspace and Delete keys. Use the arrow or cursor movement keys to move around the document. You can also move the mouse pointer and click to place the insertion point within the document.

- If you accidentally make a mistake—for instance, delete text that you need—you can undo the change using the Undo command or Undo button.

- You can select text with the mouse or the keyboard. Selecting text is usually the first step when you want to make a change (copy text, move text, change the look of text, etc.).

- Many programs include a spell checker. You should use this program to check the words in your document. You still need to proofread your work.

- You can print your documents using the File, Print command.

Learning Computer Concepts — Lesson 6
Working with Applications

Q&A

Multiple Choice

1. A row of buttons that provides quick access to frequently used commands:
   a. Spacebar
   b. Status bar
   c. Menu bar
   d. Toolbar

2. The list of jobs about to be printed is called the:
   a. Print line
   b. Print segment
   c. Print queue
   d. Picket line

3. To insert a page break, you can use this keyboard shortcut:
   a. Ctrl+Enter
   b. Enter
   c. Shift+Enter
   d. ShiftLock

4. Which command do you use to move text?
   a. Edit, Move
   b. Edit, Copy
   c. Edit, Rearrange
   d. Edit, Cut

Fill in the Blank

1. To choose a command, click its name in the _____.

2. In addition to starting a program from the Start menu, you can also double-click its _____ icon on the desktop.

3. To redisplay a saved document so that you can work on it again, use the File _____ command.

4. The two keys for deleting data character by character are the _____ key and the _____ key.

Short Essay

1. Describe why it's important to save your work.

2. Name some things to check if your printer isn't working.

LESSON 7: FORMATTING DOCUMENTS

Objectives:

- Format text
- Format paragraphs
- Format pages
- Add graphics and tables
- Work with multiple collaborators

Formatting Text

The content of any document is the most important part of the document, but the content may be ignored if the document's appearance isn't presentable. To make sure your document is attractive and readable, you can make enhancements to the text. Changing the appearance of something is called *formatting*. This lesson focuses on the main formatting changes you can make to a document, starting with formatting the text or data.

DEFINING FONTS

A typeface is a set of characters (letters and numbers) in a particular style. A font is a specific combination of the size, style, and weight of a particular typeface. That concept can be confusing. Times New Roman is a typeface. Times New Roman 12-Point Bold is a font. For the most part, the terms "typeface" and "font" are used interchangeably.

You can use any of the fonts on your system and printer. Each printer has its own set of internal fonts; these are indicated with a printer icon in the font list. Windows also can use TrueType fonts (fonts stored as files on your drive) and comes with several fonts. Your programs may also add new fonts to the Windows font folder. You can use any of these fonts.

Fonts are measured in points, with 72 points to an inch. To make text smaller, use a smaller point size. To make text larger, use a larger point size. The body text of a document is usually 10 to 12 points. For instance, this text is 11 points.

In addition to the typeface and size, you can also use styles. The three most common include bold, italic, and underline. Depending on the font and the program, you may also have special effects available, such as shadow and emboss.

CHANGING THE FONT

Most programs provide toolbar buttons for changing the font. For instance, Microsoft Office Word, Excel, and PowerPoint all have toolbars for changing the font. You can use

Learning Computer Concepts
Lesson 7
Formatting Documents

these buttons to select a typeface, a point size, and a style. Figure 7.1 identifies the toolbar buttons for each of these changes. The document shows you some examples of changes.

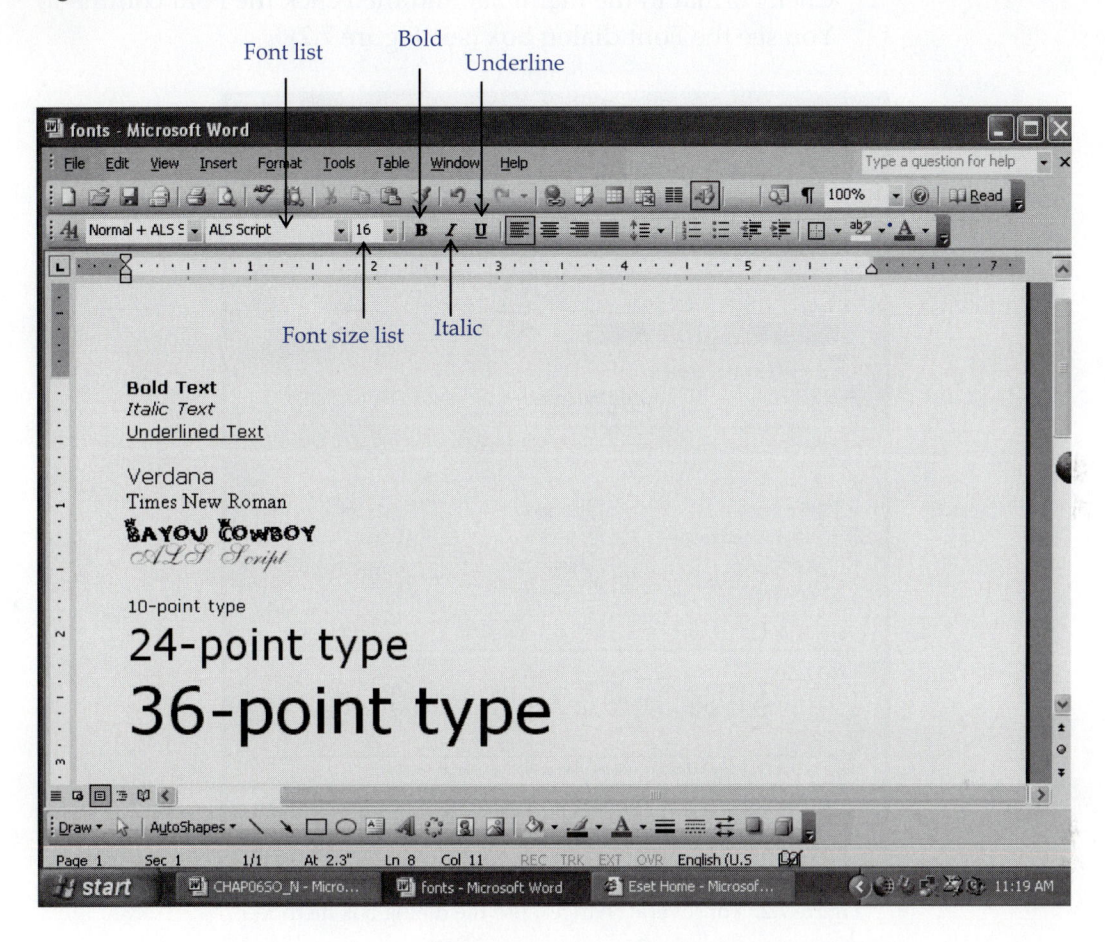

Figure 7.1. You can use the toolbar buttons to change the font.

You can use one of two methods to change the font: the toolbar method or the command method. The toolbar method is the fastest method, but if you have several changes to make at once or you want to try some special effects, use the command method.

Follow these steps to change the font with the toolbar:

1. Select the text you want to change.
2. To change the emphasis of the text, do any of the following:
   To make text bold, click the Bold button.
   To make text italic, click the Italic button.
   To underline text, click the Underline button.
3. To change the font, click the down arrow next to the Font list and then select the font you want to use.
4. To change the size of the font, click the down arrow next to the Font Size list and then click the font size you want to use.

Follow these steps to change the font with the Font command:

1. Select the text you want to change.

2. Click Format in the menu bar and then click the Font command. You see the Font dialog box (see Figure 7.2).

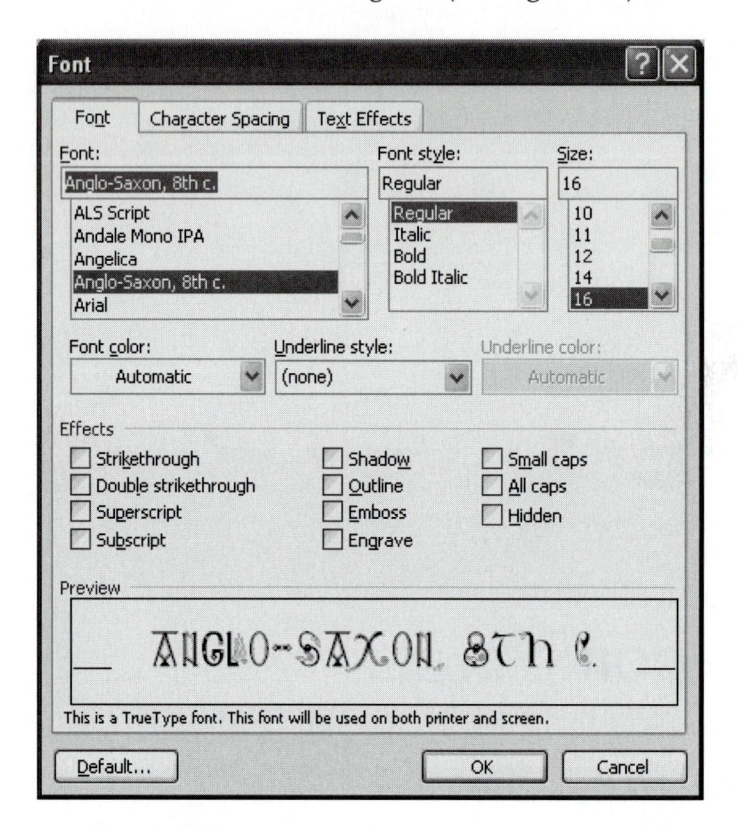

Figure 7.2. For several changes, use the dialog box method.

3. To change the font, select it from the Font list.

4. To change the font size, select the size you want from the Size list.

5. To change the font style (make text bold or italic), select your choice from the Font Style list. You can see a preview of how your selections will look.

6. Click OK.

Notice that you can not only select the font, size, and style, but also try some special effects, including changing the color of text or adding a shadow or strikethrough. The preview shows a sample of the text with these formats.

TIP: Don't go overboard! Too many fonts, sizes, and styles in a single document are distracting. Keep your formatting simple.

Formatting text is especially important in "fun" documents, such as invitations to a party or a flyer describing a sale. You can experiment, mixing fonts and sizes, until the look of the document is perfect.

Formatting Paragraphs

In addition to changing the look of the text, you may also want to format the paragraphs. Common changes include changing the alignment, indenting text, double-spacing lines, and adding bullets or numbers. Most word processing programs provide these features. You can also make these same changes in other programs. For instance, in a worksheet, you can center an entry in its cell, indent an entry, right-align entries, and more. You can also format paragraphs in presentation programs. In fact, most formatting features work the same in most programs, although there are some variations. For instance, in a worksheet, the data is in a cell, so the alignment affects only the cell, not the entire row of entries. This section describes common formatting changes to lines of text.

CHANGING THE ALIGNMENT

When you type text in most programs, it is left-aligned. That means the text aligns with the left margin. For document headings in a word processing program, you might prefer a different alignment—for instance, centering. You can center a line or an entire paragraph. You can also right-align a paragraph. Some programs offer another alignment choice: justified text. In justified text, the left and right margins are flush (even). Figure 7.3 shows an example of four alignments.

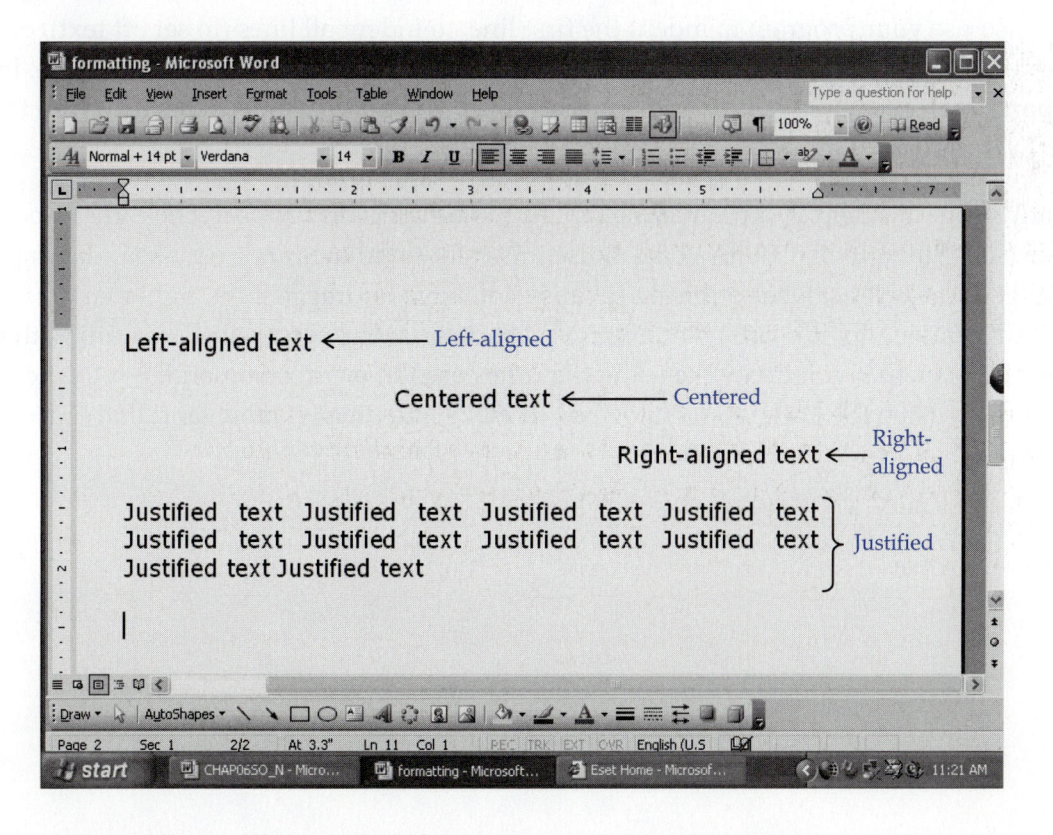

Figure 7.3. You can use different alignments for the paragraphs in a document.

As with formatting text, you can use the toolbar buttons or a menu command. The fastest way is to use the toolbar button, but the menu command provides more options. (The steps for using the Paragraph formatting options is covered later since you can use this dialog box to indent, change line spacing as well as change the alignment.)

Follow these steps to align text using toolbar buttons:

1. Select the paragraph you want to change. If you want to change just one paragraph, you can click in it. To change several paragraphs, select them.

2. To change the alignment, do any of the following:

    To left-align text, click the Align Left button.

    To center text, click the Center button.

    To align text with the right margin, click the Align Right button.

    To justify the text, click the Justify button.

Undo a change: To undo a change, you can click the Undo button. Or select the text again and then click another alignment button.

INDENTING TEXT

To make the first line of a paragraph stand out, you can press Tab to indent the text. You can also use your program to indent the first line, to indent all lines (to set off text), or to create a hanging indent, where all lines but the first line is indented. As an example, in a report if you cite text that is longer than five lines, you usually indent this text from the left and right margin.

Many programs display a ruler at the top. (If the ruler doesn't appear, click View and then click Ruler to display it.) You can use this ruler to set tabs and to make indenting changes. The ruler can be confusing because you have to drag just the right marker to make a change. Try it if you want. Figure 7.4 shows a word processing program with the ruler displayed. If you don't like using the ruler, use the menu command. See the next section on using the Paragraph dialog box to make indent, alignment, and line spacing changes.

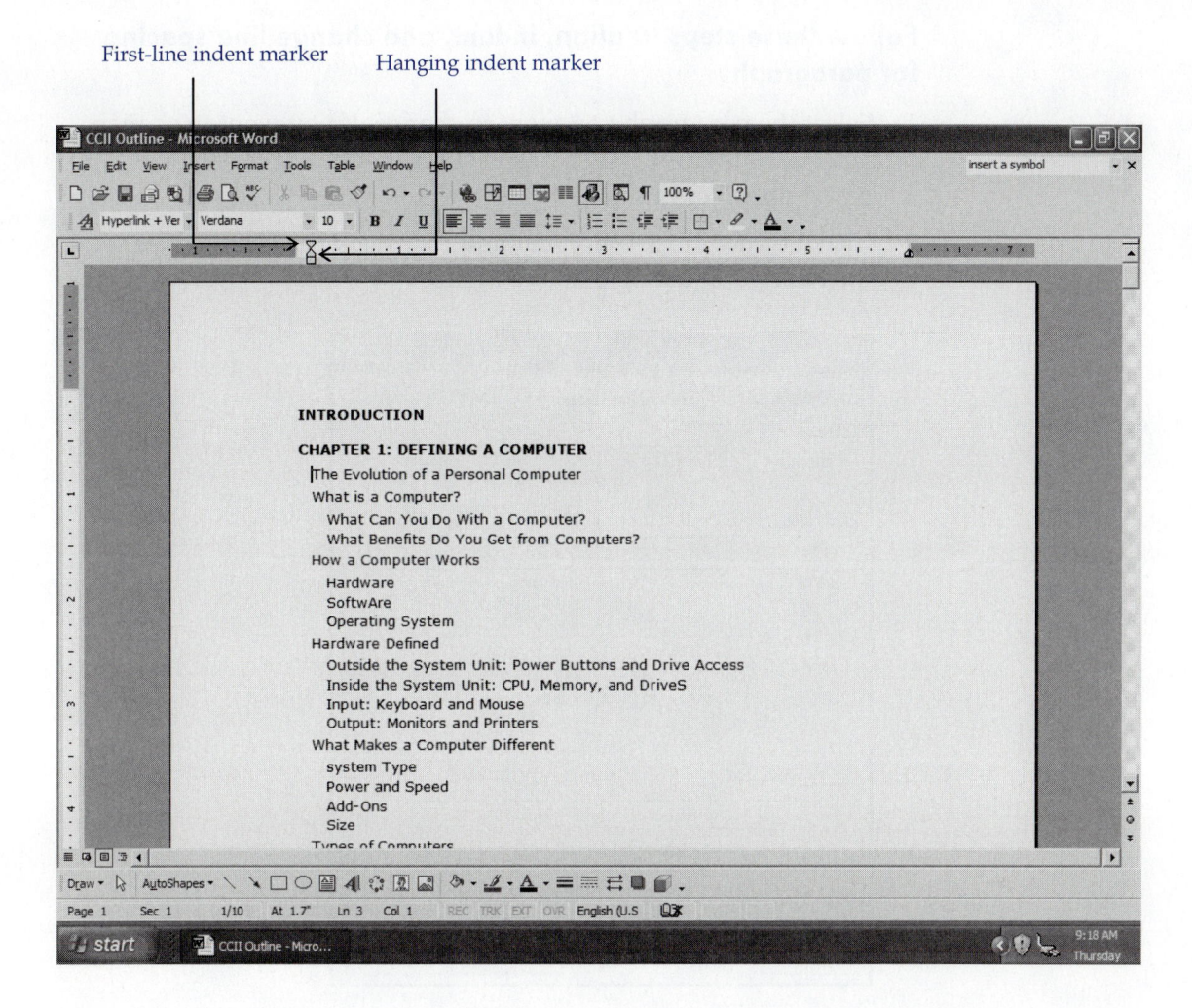

Figure 7.4. You can use the ruler to indent text (as well as set tabs, covered later).

Keep in mind that when you set indents, you do so for the selected paragraphs only. This does not change the margins. If you want to move all of the text over, you can change the margins of the page.

CHANGING LINE SPACING

If you need to alter the spacing of the paragraph, don't manually insert blank lines. Instead, you can use the program to add space. Most term papers and other manuscripts are double-spaced. You may also be able to use other intervals (1.5 spacing, for instance) or add space above or below a paragraph.

> **TIP:** You can use keyboard shortcuts for line spacing. Press Ctrl+1 for single-spacing or Ctrl+2 for double-spacing.

Follow these steps to align, indent, and change line spacing for paragraphs:

1. Select the paragraph you want to change. If you want to change just one paragraph, you can click in it. To change several paragraphs, select them.

2. Click Format in the menu bar and then click Paragraph. You see the Paragraph dialog box (see Figure 7.5).

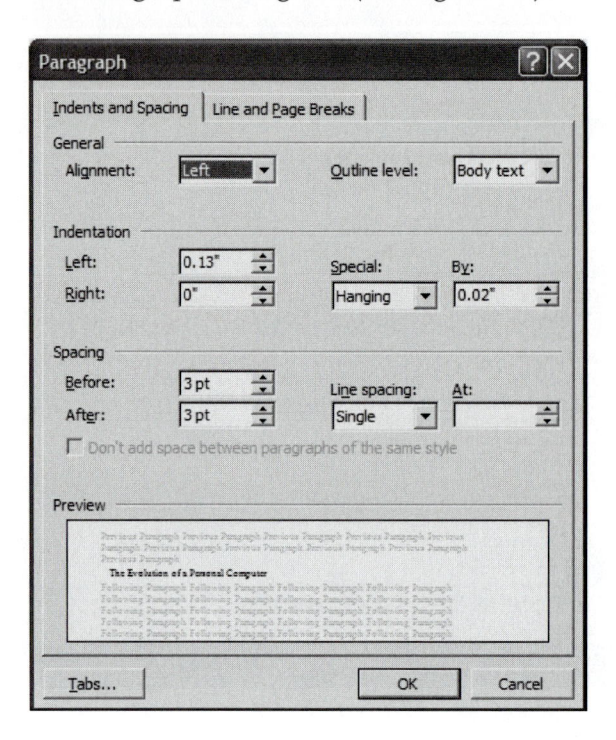

Figure 7.5. You can make several changes to paragraph spacing and alignment using the options in this dialog box.

3. To change the alignment, display the Alignment drop-down list and select the alignment you want.

4. To indent text, enter a value in the text boxes or use the spin boxes to set the value for you. You can set both left and right indents.

5. To create a hanging or first line indent, display the Special drop-down list box and select the type of indent. Then select the amount to indent from the By spin box.

6. To change the line spacing, display the Line spacing drop-down list and then select a spacing (double, 1.5 lines, or others).

7. To add space above or below a paragraph, enter a value in the Before and/or After spin boxes or use the spin arrows to increment the value for you. Check the preview to see how these changes affect the paragraph.

8. Click OK when you are finished.

CREATING CUSTOM TABS

Most programs come with some preset tabs. For instance, if you press Tab in Word, the first line of the paragraph is indented .25 inches. You can use these preset tabs, or you can set up your own tabs, including different types of tabs. For instance, you can create center tabs, tabs that align on a decimal point (handy for numbered lists), right tabs (useful for table of contents with page numbers), and so on. You can also add leaders. Again, a table of contents is a good example. You can set a right tab with dotted leaders that connect the text to the page number at the right of the paper.

You have two methods for setting tabs: you can use the ruler or you can use the Format, Tabs command. First, move to the paragraph you want to change. Then to use the ruler, click the tab icon at the far left of the ruler until you see the tab type you want. Then simply click on the ruler at the place you want to set the tab.

To use the Tabs command, you can select a tab type by name (if the icons are hard for you to figure out), and you can type in an exact location. You can also select different leader styles such as dashed lines, dotted lines, and others.

View formatting marks: If you want, you can display characters that represent paragraph breaks, tabs, and spaces on-screen. Displaying these marks can help you troubleshoot any spacing problems such as extra paragraphs (blank lines) or extra spaces. Click the Show/Hide [insert paragraph mark here} button to display these items. Click the button again to hide them.

ADDING BULLETS AND NUMBERS

To set off ideas, you can use a bulleted list. Don't type an asterisk before each line. Instead, let your program add a bullet. For instance, you can create a bulleted list in memo agenda in a word processing document. If you want to list the steps to follow for a procedure, you can create a numbered list. Presentations also often use bulleted or numbered lists. You can create these by using the buttons in the Formatting toolbar or by using a menu command. To use the toolbar button, select the text to which you want to add bullets or numbers and then click the Bullets or Numbering button. If you want more control, use the menu command. With this command, you have more control over the character used for the bullet and the indent spacing.

Follow these steps to add bullets or numbers to a list:

1. Select the paragraphs to which you want to add numbers or bullets.
2. Open the Format menu and select Bullets and Numbering.
3. To add bullets, click the Bulleted tab and select from one of the preset bullets (see Figure 7.6). Then click OK.

Lesson 7
Formatting Documents

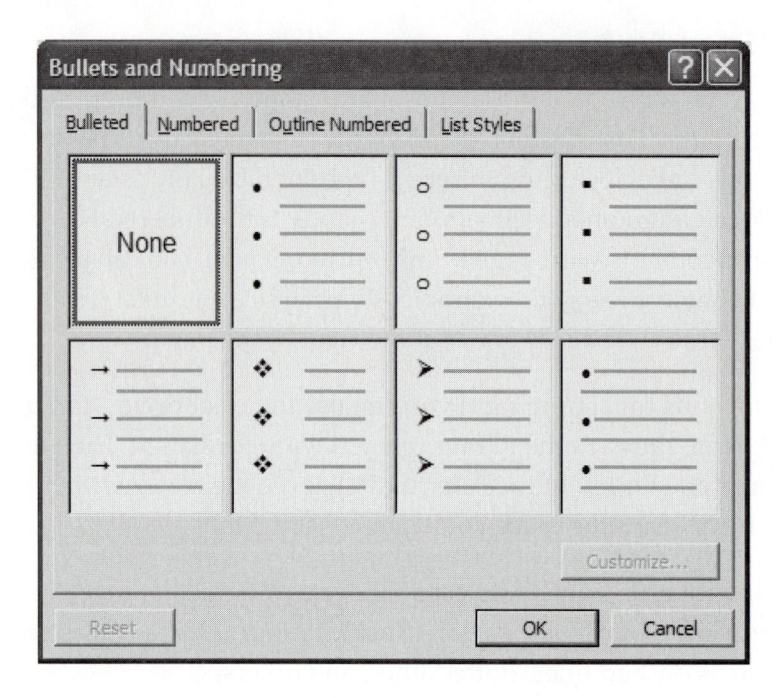

Figure 7.6. You can select from several different bullet styles.

4. To add numbers, click the Numbered tab and then select a numbering style (see Figure 7.7). Click OK.

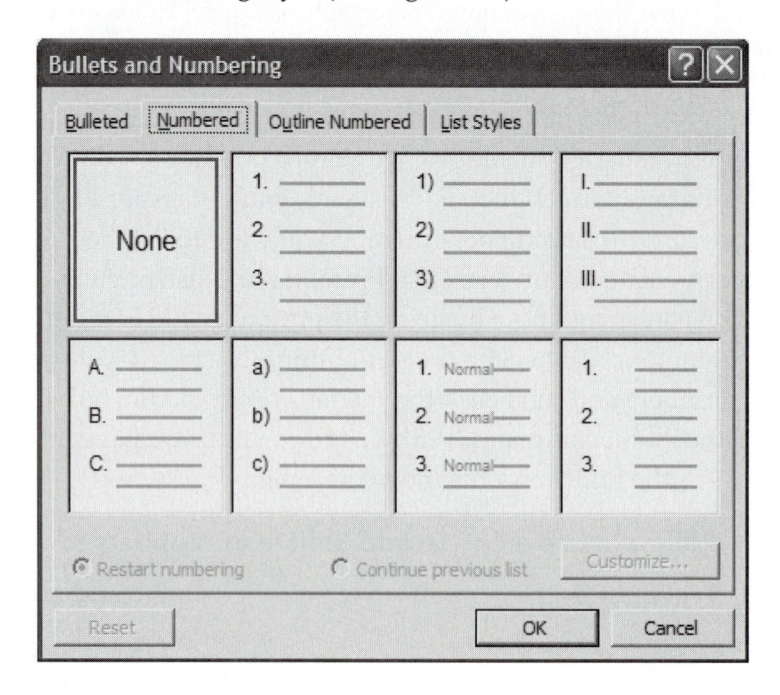

Figure 7.7. You can select from several different numbering styles.

> **Outlines.** Both Word and PowerPoint (a presentation program) include features for creating outlines. You can choose the numbering style and other options. In both programs, you can change to Outline view to create outlines.

ADDING BORDERS AND SHADING

Another way to make text stand out is to add an outline either around the entire text or underneath it or any combination. For instance, you may want to use an underlined border for your headings to separate a document. You may want to shade every other line in a worksheet so that it's easier to stay in the same row when reading across the worksheet.

Most programs enable you to select from preset borders as well as to create custom borders. You can also shade paragraphs, worksheet cells, or text boxes in a presentation. You can find these commands in the Borders and Shading dialog box.

Follow these steps to add borders or shading:

1. Select the text you want to change.
2. Open the Format menu and select the Borders and Shading command.
3. To add a border, select one of the preset options under Setting (see Figure 7.8). Or select a line style, color, and width from the drop-down lists and then click in the preview area where you want the border to appear. (You can also change the lines used for the preset borders using the Style, Color, and Width drop-down lists.)

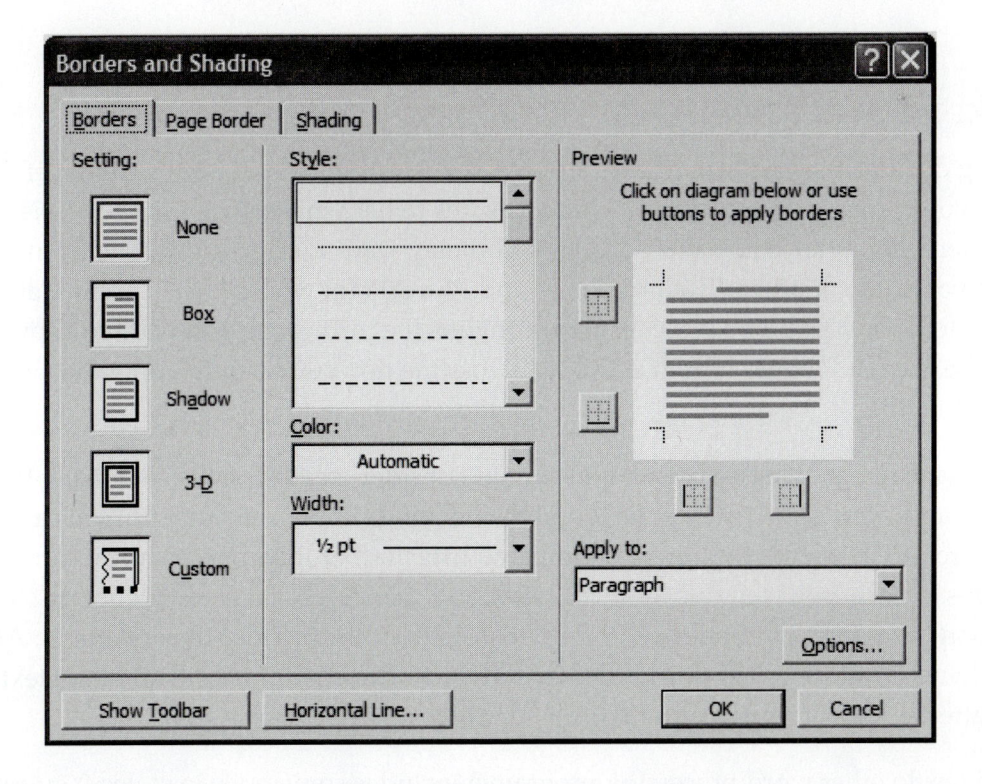

Figure 7.8. Use this tab to add a border to any of the edges of your paragraph (or cells in a worksheet).

4. To add shading to a paragraph (or worksheet cell or text box), click the Shading tab (see Figure 7.9). Then select a fill and pattern and click OK.

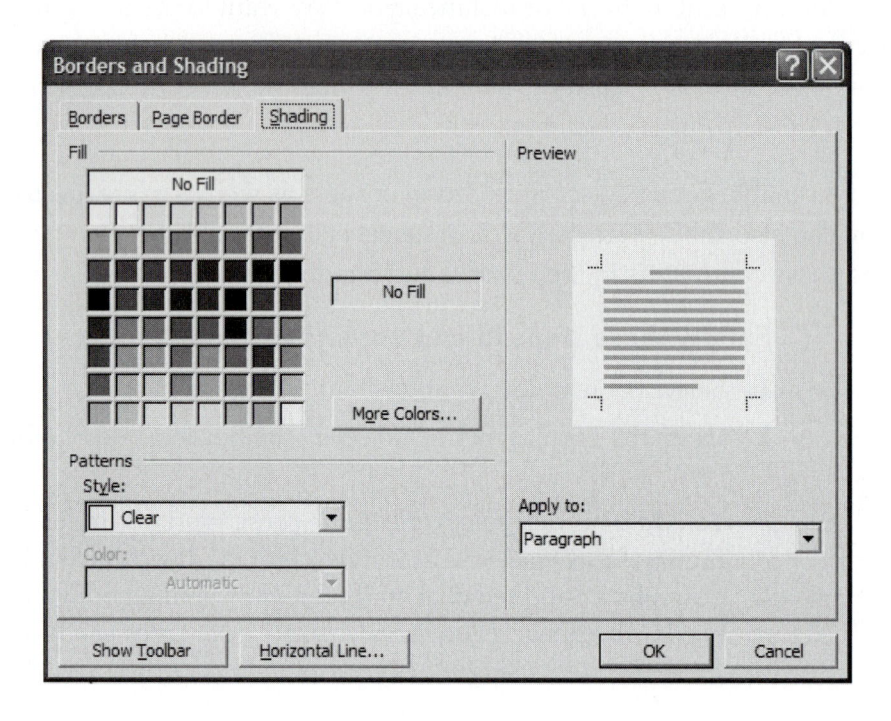

Figure 7.9. You can apply shading to text or cells in a worksheet or database.

USING THE SAME FORMATTING

In long documents, you want the look of the document to be consistent. To that effect, most word processing programs include features to help make style changes easier and consistent. If you have just a few changes, you may want to copy formatting from one section of text to another. In Word, Excel, and PowerPoint, you use the Format Painter button to do so. Drag across the text that contains the formatting you want to copy. Then click the Format Painter button and drag across the text you want to apply the formatting to.

If you have many items to format, you should consider creating styles and using them. For instance, you can create a style for all the headings in your document. You can create a style for all the figure captions or numbered lists. Rather than make several formatting changes at once, you can save them in a style and then apply them all at once. In addition to saving time, styles also ensure consistency throughout the document. Also, if you change your mind about a particular style, you can change it, and all of the text formatted with that style is automatically updated.

Word (as do other word processing programs) includes some built-in styles. You can also create your own custom styles. Look in the Format menu for the Styles and Formatting command. Also, use online help to describe exactly how style features work in your program.

Formatting Pages

For one-page documents, you probably won't need to make changes to the page. For longer documents, use your program to make appropriate changes, such as changing the margins, adding page numbers, including headers and footers, and more.

CHANGING THE MARGINS

Most programs have default margins that work well. (They usually are set to 1" for the top and bottom margins and 1 ¼ " for the left and right margins.) To fit more on a page, you might want to make the margins smaller. To fit less on a page (and make the document fill more pages), use bigger margins. As another example, if you use letterhead, you may want to adjust the top margin to accommodate the letterhead.

To make these types of changes, use the File, Page Setup command. (This command can be hard to find because you would think the command would be within the Format menu. Look under File.) As you can see from Figure 7.10, most Page Setup dialog boxes have options for changing the margins. Make your selections and then click OK.

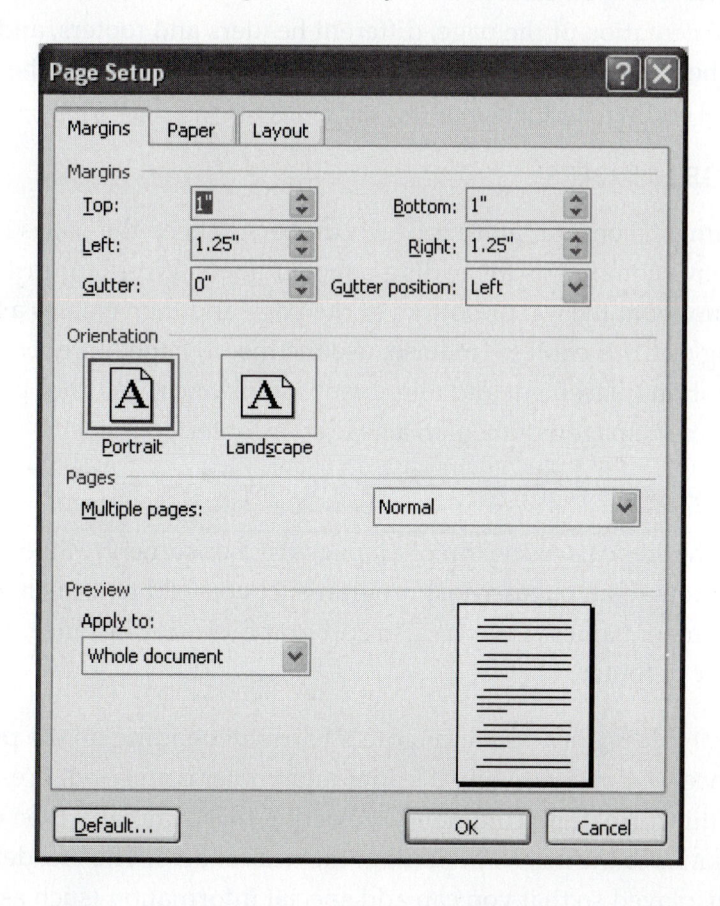

Figure 7.10. Make changes to the page formatting in the Page Setup dialog box.

Lesson 7
Formatting Documents

INSERTING PAGES AND SECTIONS

When you get to the end of the page, Word will automatically create a new page for you. In some cases, you may want to insert a manual page break. For instance, you may want to create a title page. You can do so using a keyboard shortcut (press Ctrl+Enter) or a menu command.

Follow these steps to use the menu command:

1. Click the Insert menu, and click the Break command.
2. In the Break dialog box, the default Page Break is selected, so simply click OK.

You can also use the Break dialog box to insert section breaks. You may want to divide a document into sections if you want to vary the formatting in the document. For instance, you may want some pages to be in a two-column format and others in a one-column format. As a simpler example, you may not want to include page numbers or a header or footer on the first page of a document. For these types of document formatting, you set up sections and then you can set up each section as you choose—setting the number of columns, the orientation of the page, different headers and footers, and so on. As mentioned use the Insert, Break command to insert section breaks (at the start of the section and at the end where the next new section starts).

INSERTING PAGE NUMBERS

In a longer document, consider adding page numbers to keep the pages in order. Some programs may have commands for adding page numbers. Word, for instance, lets you set up a page number at the top or bottom of the page and then creates a header or footer depending on your choice. To do so, use the Insert, Page Numbers command and then select the option (placement and alignment for instance). In other programs, you may have to set up the page numbers in a header or footer.

ADDING HEADERS AND FOOTERS

A header is text that repeats at the top of all pages in a document. A footer is text that repeats at the bottom of all pages. Most programs let you add text, such as page numbers or document names. You can also add graphics—for instance, a company logo—in a header or footer.

The procedure for adding headers and footers varies depending on the program. In Word, for instance, you use the View, Header and Footer command. (Yes, it seems a weird place for this formatting command.) Selecting this command then opens the header area and moves the insertion point in the header area. The Header and Footer toolbar is also displayed so that you can add special information (such as the date and page numbers). You can type the information in the Header. (To switch to the footer, click the Switch to Footer button in the toolbar.) Click Close when you are done to close the Header and Footer toolbar and return to the main document area.

TIP: Get fancy! Some programs let you turn off headers and footers on the first page or use different headers or footers in sections or for odd and even pages. Check your program documentation.

Adding Graphics and Tables

To jazz up a document, you can add graphical elements. These may include simple drawings, a picture, a clip art image, tables, or others. This section focuses on the graphical changes you can make to your document.

DRAWING IN A DOCUMENT

If you want to add illustrations, you may be able to use simple drawing tools included with your program. For instance, in Word, you can draw shapes, such as a circle, arrow, and square. To do so, click the Drawing button to display the Drawing toolbar (see Figure 7.11).

Figure 7.11. Use this toolbar to draw simple illustrations.

You can use the tools in this toolbar to draw circles, rectangles, squares, and lines. You can also insert a text box and then type text and move it around in the document. You also have a lot of options for modifying the drawings including changing the line thickness, color, filling the object, adding arrows, making the object 3D, and more. The best way to learn how to use these tools is to experiment!

INSERTING A CLIP ART IMAGE AND PICTURES

You also can insert graphics using the Insert command. You may insert predrawn images called *clip art*. The program may come with a set of clip-art images, which you can use freely. You can also find clip art on the Web or sold as collections in the software section of retail stores. You can use clip art to create your own special stationery.

As an alternative, you can scan in images using a scanner and insert these in a word processing document. Or you might have a digital camera and insert these photographs in a document (see Figure 7.12).

Lesson 7
Formatting Documents

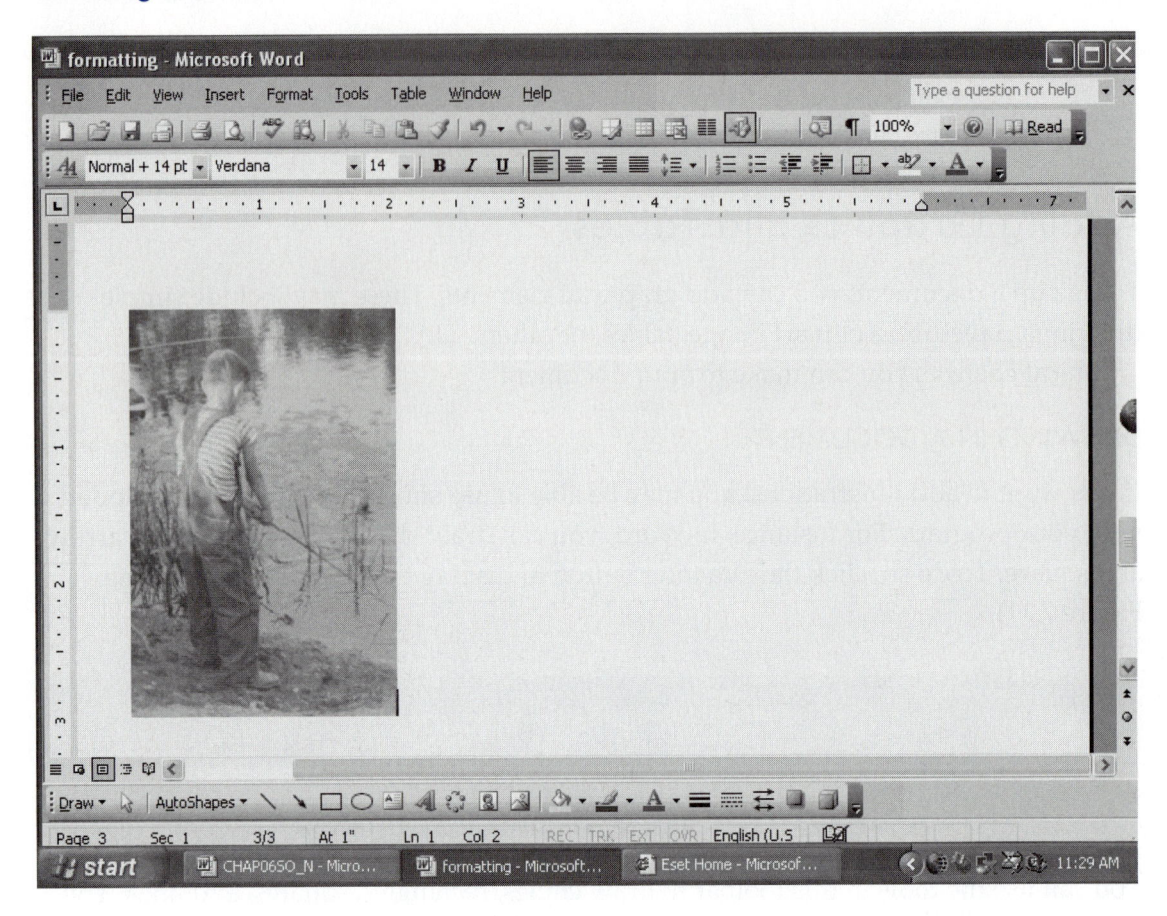

Figure 7.12. You can insert clip art, scanned images, or digital images from a camera into your document.

Be aware that adding graphics is a simple way to enliven a document, but keep these pointers in mind:

- The quality of the printout will depend on your printer. Also, the more complex the graphic, the longer the printing time.
- You may need to spend some time adjusting the graphic — getting the text and the graphic to flow just how you want and resizing or cropping the image.
- If you plan to publish the document on the Internet, use a file format that most browsers can display (JPEG and GIF are common Web graphic file formats).
- You cannot use copyrighted graphics without permission.

ADDING TABLES

If you have to type a list, don't use tabs. Instead look for a Table command. Programs such as Word let you create a table, selecting the number of columns. When you use a table, you can easily keep the entries aligned because each entry will be in its own cell. You can also add columns and rows and sort entries.

Follow these steps to insert a table:

1. In Word, to insert a table, click the Insert Table button. You see a drop-down palette that lets you select the number of rows and columns. (You can always add rows and even columns if needed.)

2. Click the number of rows and columns you need. The table is inserted into your document.

3. To type in a table, click in the cell and type. The text will wrap within the borders of the cell. To move to the next cell, press Tab.

4. To format text in the cell, follow the same steps as you do to format "regular" text. Select the text you want to format and then execute the command. For instance, to make text bold, click the Bold button.

5. When you get to the last cell in the last row, click Tab to add a new row. You can continue adding rows until your table is complete.

You can do a lot more with tables. For instance, you can use the Table, Sort command to sort entries based on a column. You can add borders and shading to the table either using custom borders and shading or using Table AutoFormats (a set of formatting options such as borders, shading, alignment, and others). If you have unneeded rows or columns, you can delete them. Use the Table, Delete command. On the other hand, to insert new rows or columns, use the Table, Insert command.

In Word and WordPerfect, you can also insert worksheets (data from a spreadsheet program). This type of format is also handy for tabular data. You can divide a document into columns, another way to enliven the presentation and create special documents, such as newsletters or brochures.

Working with Multiple Contributors

Often a document goes through many changes, with others contributing comments or changes. Most programs, especially word processing programs, include features for inserting comments, tracking changes, counting words, and more. Here's a quick summary of some of these features:

- In Word, you can insert comments into a document; these are hidden, but you can choose to display them when you want to review them. In Excel, you can also attach a comment to a cell. You might for instance, include any assumptions that the formula was based on or add a note to check some part of the equation. In both programs, use the Insert, Comment command to insert a comment.

- For some documents, you may need to include footnotes or endnotes to provide a citation for your source. Word provides options for both. To insert a footnote, open the Insert menu and then select Reference and Footnote. The dialog box that appears enables you to select whether to include the references as footnotes (at the bottom of the page) or endnotes (at the end of the document). You also can select the style of the footnote or endnote marker.

- If you want to see changes made to a document, you can turn on revision marking. For instance, editors often use this so that the author can review the changes made to the text. Not only does revision marking mark the changes, but you can also choose to accept or reject the changes. To use this feature, click Tools and then Track Changes. Word includes a toolbar to help manage the review of a marked up manuscript.

- If you write for a magazine and need to keep your text to a precise word count, you can have Word count the words in your document (as well as display other statistics). Open the Tools menu and select the Word Count command.

Other programs: This lesson uses Word for the examples, but most word processing programs provide similar tools and features.

Summary

- Formatting means to change the appearance of a document. The most common formatting change is to format the text (change the font, make text bold, etc.).
- You can also format lines or paragraphs in your document. For instance, you can indent a line, add tabs, create a bulleted or numbered list, change the line spacing, and more.
- The next level of formatting involves the whole page. For this, you can change the page margins and add headers and footers.
- Inserting tables and adding graphics are some special ways you can add graphical elements to a document.
- Most programs also include features that help you collaborate on a document. You can insert comments, track changes, count the number of words, and more.

Q&A

Multiple Choice

1. Fonts are measured in:
    a. Points
    b. Hexadecimals
    c. Centimeters
    d. Liters

2. Which feature enables you to set indents and tabs without using a dialog box:
    a. Toolbar
    b. Ruler
    c. Menu bar
    d. Status bar

3. This line of text or graphics appears at the top of every page in a document:
    a. Word count
    b. Header
    c. Footer
    d. Fax number

4. When you get to the last row in a table, you can press what key to create a new row?
    a. Insert
    b. Delete
    c. Tab
    d. New Row

Fill in the Blank

1. A _____ is a set of characters (letters and numbers) in a particular style.
2. With _____ text both the right and left margins are even.
3. Predrawn images are called _____.
4. To access the drawing tools for a program, click the _____ button.

Short Essay

1. Describe some design rules for keeping your document inviting, yet readable.
2. Name some of the benefits of using a command to make a formatting change vs. using the formatting button.

LESSON 8: CREATING WORKSHEETS

Objectives

- Enter data
- Create formulas
- Format data
- Create charts
- Use your spreadsheet as a database
- Use other financial programs

Entering Data

The hardest part of creating any document is entering the data. Once you've done this task, you'll find you have a great deal of flexibility in working with that data. In this section, take a look at the layout of a typical worksheet and also read about some shortcuts for entering data and formulas.

UNDERSTANDING THE PROGRAM TOOLS

You start a spreadsheet program in Windows the way you start most programs: click the Start button, select All Programs, and then click the icon for the program. You then see the program window.

> **Create a shortcut icon:** If you use a program often, create a shortcut to that icon on your Windows desktop. To do so click Start and then All Programs. Using the *right* mouse button, drag the program icon to the desktop. From the menu that appears, click Create Shortcuts Here.

Most spreadsheet programs look similar, work similarly, and include similar features. Figure 8.1 shows the program window for Excel. If you use another program, your window will look different, but it probably contains the same features:

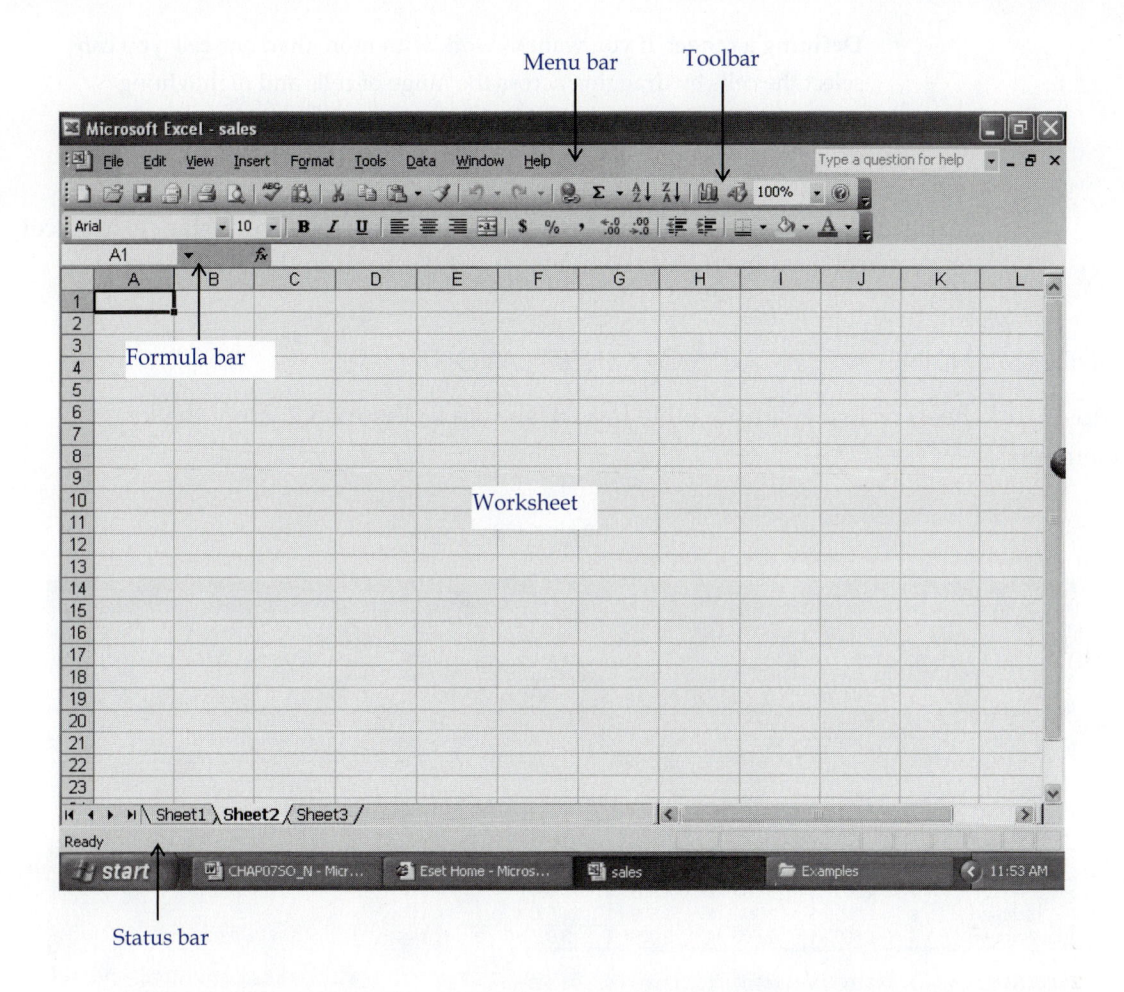

Figure 8.1. Like most programs, a spreadsheet program includes a menu bar and toolbars.

- *Menu bar*. The menu bar lists the names of the menu. To open a menu, click its name. You see a list of commands. To select a command, click that command.

- *Toolbars*. Most programs include toolbars with buttons for frequently used commands. In Excel, you'll find buttons for working with files (Open, Save, and Print, for instance), buttons for copying and pasting data, buttons for creating formulas, and buttons for sorting data. The second toolbar row in this program (called the Formatting toolbar) includes buttons for changing the appearance of the worksheet entries.

- *Worksheet*. The worksheet is the area where you enter data. A worksheet is a grid of columns and rows, and the intersection of a column and row is called a cell. Each cell has a reference or name, and the reference is composed of the column letter followed by the row number. For instance, A1 is the first cell in the worksheet (column A, row 1).

- *Formula bar*. The formula bar contains the entry of the current cell and the cell reference. When you are creating or editing an entry, this formula bar also includes buttons for making or canceling the entry.

Lesson 8
Creating Worksheets

> **Defining a range:** If you want to work with more than one cell, you can select the cells by dragging across the range of cells and highlighting them. A group of cells is called a range and is referenced by the cell in the upper-left corner, a colon, and the cell in the lower-right corner.

- *Status bar.* The status bar displays handy information. For instance, in Excel if you select a range of numbers, you'll see the total in the AutoCalculate area.

UNDERSTANDING A TYPICAL WORKSHEET LAYOUT

Most worksheets follow a simple table layout, shown in Figure 8.2. Note the key elements:

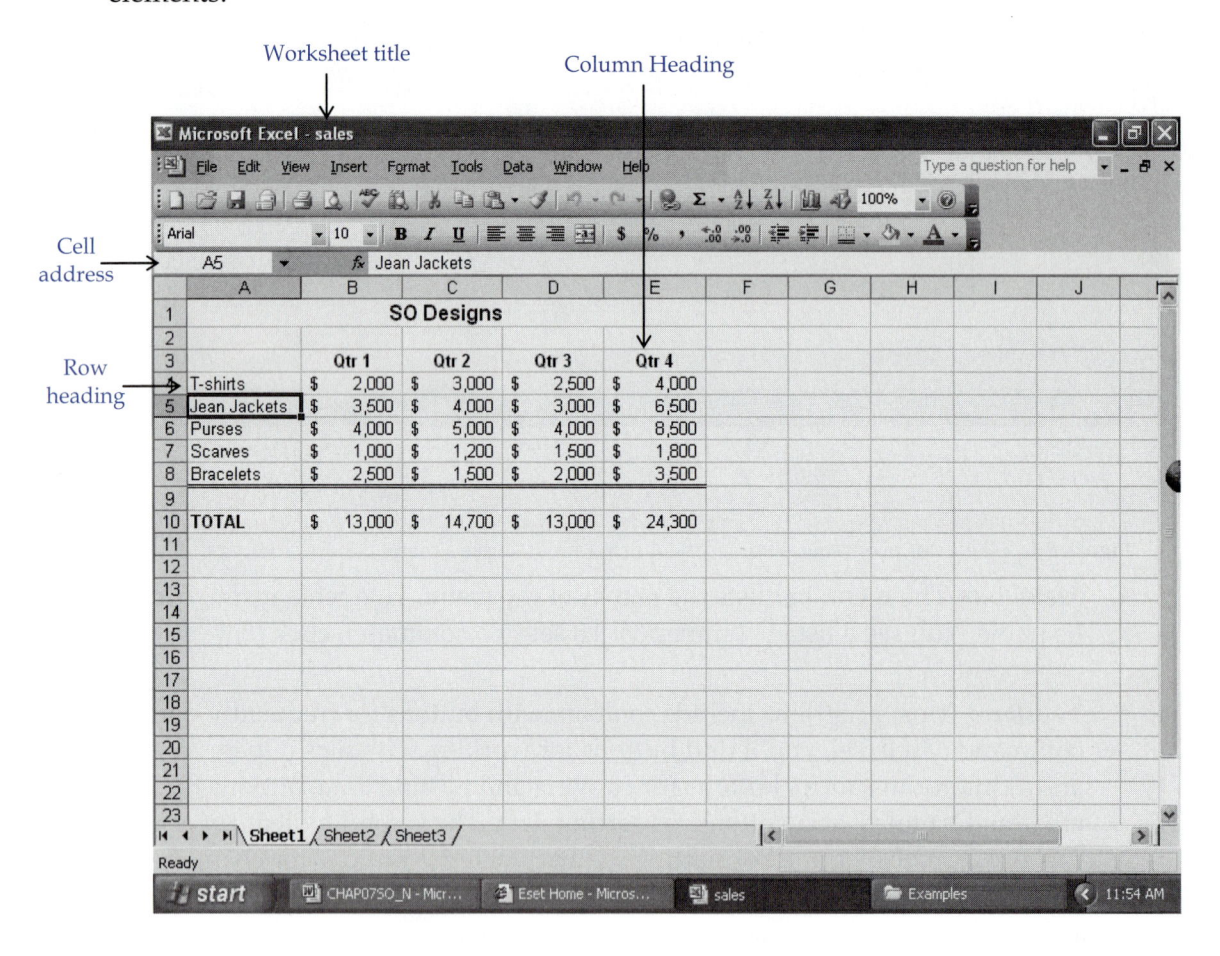

Figure 8.2. Most worksheets are set up in this table format.

- *Worksheet title.* To identify the contents of the worksheet, you might include a title at the top. You can also include other information, such as the date or the creator of the worksheet.
- *Column and row headings.* The column headings identify the contents of the columns and are usually categories (quarters, months, divisions, years, for instance). The row headings identify the contents of the rows and are usually

specific items. For example, in this worksheet, the columns list the quarters, and the rows list the specific product.

- *Cell address.* The current cell is indicated with a black box. The address for this cell appears in the formula bar. The cell address consists of the column letter and row number.
- *Values*. The values are the numeric entries.
- *Formulas*. The last row of the worksheets on the previous page includes formulas. In this example, these formulas total the entries in that column using the SUM function.

Keep in mind that this is a typical layout, but you aren't limited to this structure. You can set up rows and columns and formulas in any pattern that suits your purpose.

ENTERING TEXT AND NUMBERS

To make an entry in a worksheet, you select the cell by clicking it. You then type the entry and press Enter. If the entry contains any letters, it is considered a text entry or label. If the entry is all numbers, it is treated as a number. To type a negative number, type a minus sign before the number or type the number in parentheses.

Some numbers are not really numbers; for instance, your Social Security number or address. When entering a number that is not a value, type an apostrophe before the entry to indicate it is a label.

When you want to edit an entry, you move to the cell that contains the entry. You can move around the worksheet by using the cursor movement keys or by clicking the cell where you want to make an entry. You can then type a new entry and press Enter to replace the original entry. Of if you want to edit part of the entry, you can double-click the entry and then move the insertion point to where you want to make a change. Press Enter when you are done editing the entry.

> **Look for shortcuts:** If you have to set up a worksheet, look for program shortcuts. For instance, in Excel you can use the fill feature to fill in data, such as the months of the year, days of the week, or some other sequence you set up. You can also copy cells.

SELECTING DATA

Like in word processing programs, a common first-step in making changes is to select the cell, range, row, column, or even the entire worksheet. You can make these selections by doing the following:

- To select a single cell, click it.
- To select several cells, click the first cell, hold down the mouse button, and drag across the other cells you want to select. You can also click the first cell, hold down the Shift key, and use the movement keys to select the cells. The range appears highlighted.

- To select cells that are not next to each other, hold down the Ctrl key and click each cell you want to select.
- To select an entire column, click the column letter.
- To select an entire row, click the row number.
- To select the entire worksheet, click the selection box to the left of the column letters and above the row numbers (see Figure 8.3).

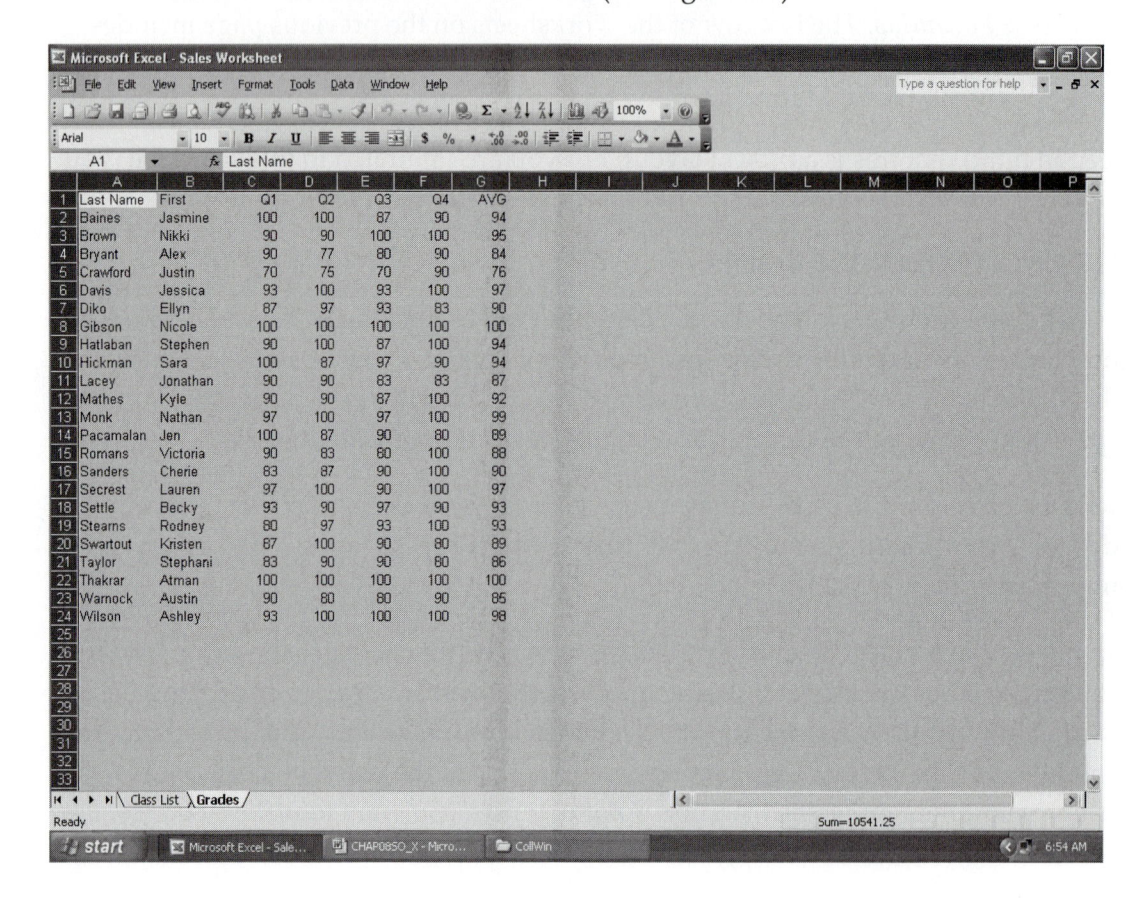

Figure 8.3. You can select a group of cells, a single cell, an entire row or column, or the entire worksheet.

FILLING DATA

Excel provides some shortcuts for entering data. These include:

- Copying and pasting data. Just like in a word processing program, you can copy text and paste it in another spot in the worksheet or in a different worksheet entirely. The process works the same: Select the data you want to copy, click Edit and then Copy, select the first cell where you want the data to appear, and then click Edit and then Paste. The pasted data will fill the same cells in the same pattern as the original.
- You can also move data. This is similar to copying, only you use the Edit, Cut command and the data is removed from its original location and appears only in the new location.

Learning Computer Concepts

**Lesson 8
Creating Worksheets**

- Excel also enables you to fill in patterns of numbers, dates, quarters, or other common worksheet headings and entries. See the following set of steps for filling data.

- As another bonus, Excel automatically adjusts cell references (used in formulas) when you copy or move a formula. This means you can create one formula and copy it down a row, for instance, without having to reenter the formula. See the section "Creating Formulas" for more information.

Follow these steps to fill data in a worksheet:

1 If you want to fill in a patterned series of data, such as months or quarters or even numbers, enter the first two entries and have Excel fill the rest. For instance, you can enter Jan in one cell and Feb in the cell next to it. For numbers, you can enter 100 in one cell and 200 in the cell next to it. Excel will recognize the pattern and use these entries as the basis for the fill.

2 Select the two cells that define the fill. You should see a small black handle at the bottom right corner of the selection marker.

3 Drag this handle to fill data across the rows or columns you want to fill (see Figure 8.4).

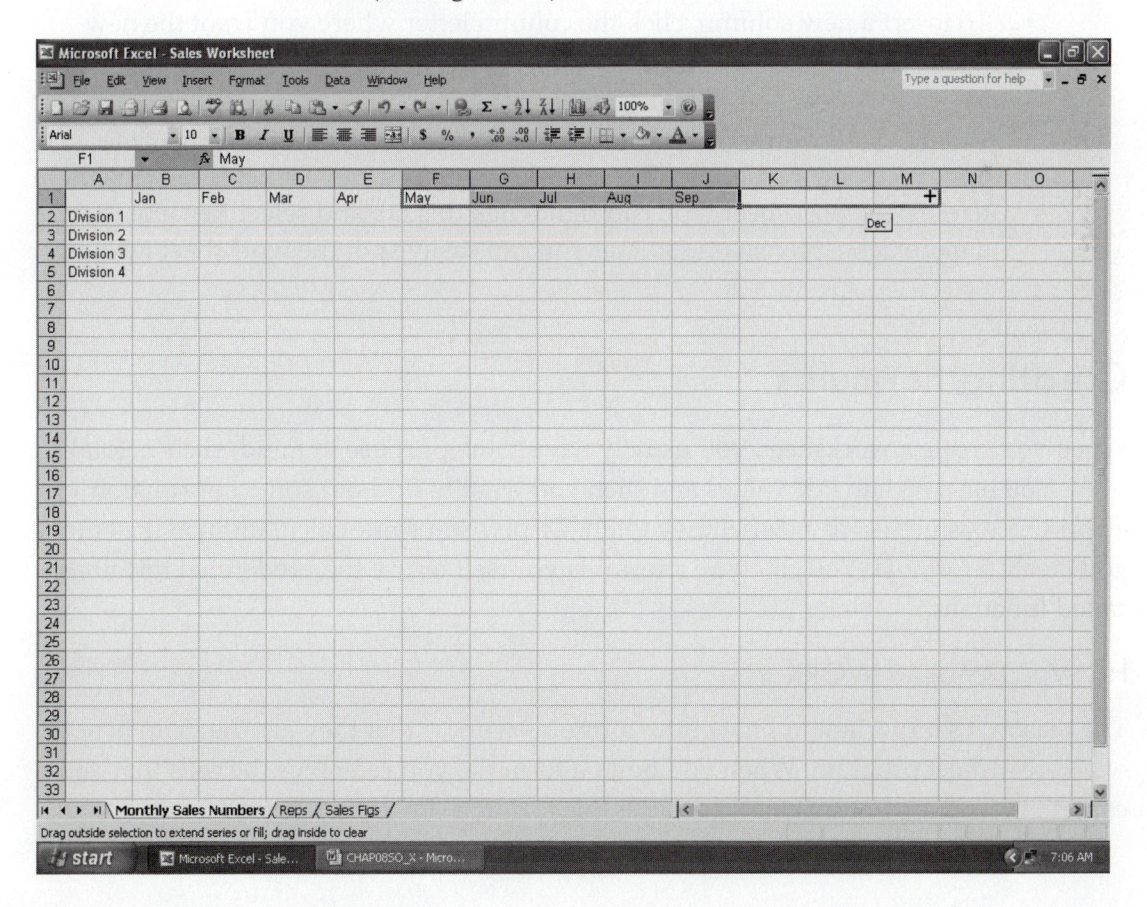

Figure 8.4. You can fill in a series of data using Excel.

INSERTING AND DELETING ROWS AND COLUMNS

Excel worksheets include many rows and columns; they also start with new worksheets stored in the workbook. You can add (or delete) rows, columns, or worksheets as needed. For instance, you may need to add a new column in the middle of existing columns. Or you may delete a row that includes a product that is no longer sold. You may add new worksheets to your workbook to store data for each of the four quarters of the year.

One caution when deleting worksheets. While you can undo deleting a row or column, you cannot undo deleting a worksheet. So be sure you want to delete it. Excel will prompt you to confirm the deletion.

Excel provides commands for deleting and inserting rows, columns, and worksheets:

- To delete a row, click the row number and then click the Edit, Delete command. To delete a column, click the column letter and then click the Edit, Delete command.
- To insert a row, click a row below where you want the new row. Then click the Insert, Rows command. A new row is added above the selected row.
- To insert a new column, click the column letter where you want the new column. New columns are inserted to the left of the selected column. Click Insert, Columns to add the new column.
- To add a new worksheet, click Insert, Worksheet. A new worksheet tab appears along the bottom of the worksheets. You can click this tab to switch to the new worksheet. You can right-click this tab and select Rename to type a more descriptive name so that you can easily spot the worksheet tab you need.

Creating Formulas

When you create a worksheet, you usually have some purpose in mind, such as totaling sales. You have certain key values and then you want to find out some information about those values (such as what they total). To perform some calculation on the entries, you create a formula. You can type a formula yourself or use the predefined formulas, called functions.

HOW FORMULAS WORK

The reason it's important to know how formulas work is that they are the main benefit of a spreadsheet program. When you build a formula, you reference the cells that contain the values. For instance, consider this formula shown in Figure 8.5:

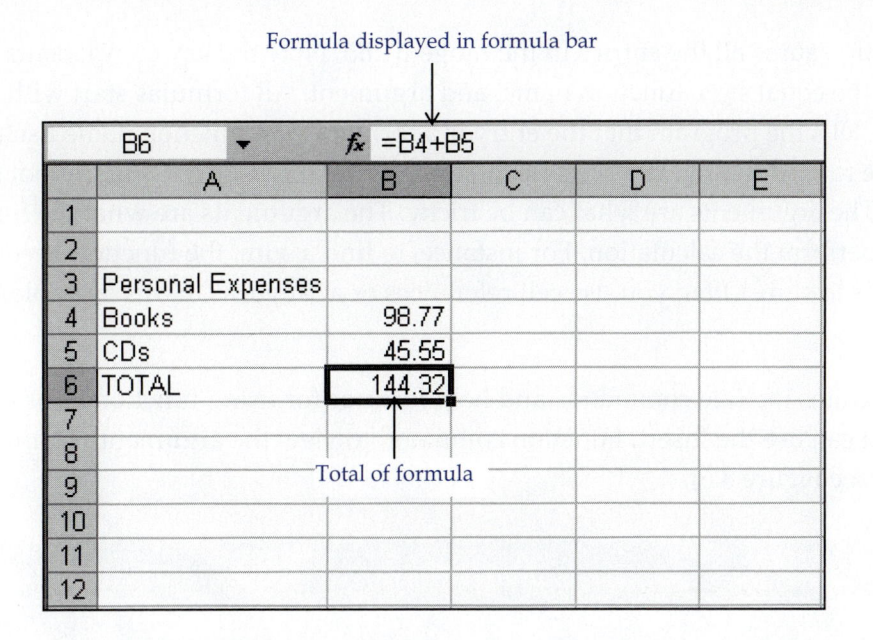

Figure 8.5. Most formulas reference cells.

= B4 + B5

This formula takes the value in B4 and adds it to B5. How is this different than simply adding these two values? It's different because you can change B4, B5, or both B4 and B5, and the formula will be recalculated automatically. This enables you to perform "what-if" analysis.

Excel also automatically adjusts the cell reference when you move or copy a cell so that the formula still references the correct entries. This is called relative references. You can also tell Excel to always refer to a particular cell (for instance, a rate increase of 10% that appears in one cell and should be used in all calculations). In this case, you use an absolute reference. You can create an absolute reference by typing $ signs before the row or column letter. $A1 would always refer to column A, but the row would vary. A$1 would always refer to row 1, but the column reference would vary. A1 would refer to cell A1 and would not vary.

WHAT ARE FUNCTIONS?

You can type formulas, using any of the typical mathematical operators: + for addition, − for subtraction, * for multiplication, and / for division. You can also use predefined formulas called functions. These take some of the tedium out of building formulas. For instance, rather than use this formula:

=B1+B2+B3+B4+B5

You can use this one:

=SUM(B1:B5)

Lesson 8
Creating Worksheets

This function sums all the entries in the range B1:B5. Note the key components of a function: the equal sign, function name, and argument. All formulas start with an equal sign. This tells the program that the entry is a formula. The function name usually gives you a clue to the function purpose. SUM sums entries. SQRT finds square root for a number. The arguments are what can be tricky. The arguments are what the function needs to perform the calculation. For instance, to find a sum, the function needs to know which cells to sum. Often you use cell references or a range, as in this example, for the argument.

Most programs include commands and help features for using functions. For instance, in Excel, you can use the Insert, Function command to view the arguments required for the function (see Figure 8.6).

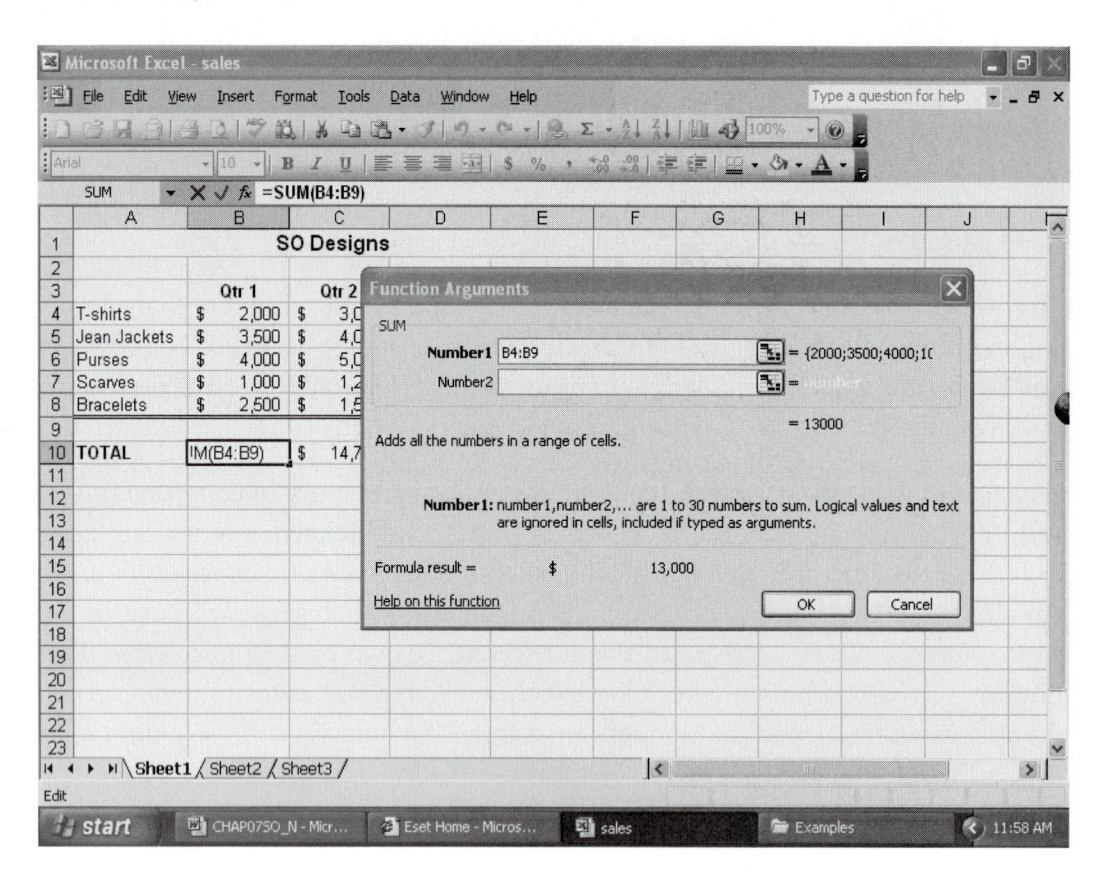

Figure 8.6. You can get help creating functions.

Use AutoSum: In Excel, you can quickly sum a range using the AutoSum button. Click where you want the function, click the AutoSum button, select what you want to add, and press Enter.

USING AUTOSUM AND OTHER COMMON FUNCTIONS

Some of the most common functions include:

- SUM which automatically sums a selection of numbers. (In Excel the toolbar button to use this function is called AutoSum.)
- AVERAGE which averages the numbers selected in a range.
- COUNT which counts the entries in a range.
- MAX which finds the maximum value in a range.
- MIN which finds the minimum value in a range.

Figure 8.7 shows examples of these common functions. The actual formula is displayed in the column next to the results so that you can see how these formulas are created.

	A	B	C	D	E	F	G
1		Qtr 1	Qtr 2	Qtr 3	Qtr 4	Result	
2	Sum	1200	1300	1600	2100	6200	=SUM(B2:E2)
3	Average	1200	1300	1600	2100	1550	=AVERAGE(B3:E3)
4	Count	1200	1300	1600	2100	4	=COUNT(B4:E4)
5	Max	1200	1300	1600	2100	2100	=MAX(B5:E5)
6	Min	1200	1300	1600	2100	1200	=MIN(B6:E6)

Figure 8.7. Excel includes a wide range of functions for many purposes; this worksheet shows examples of some of the most common ones.

DRAWING CONCLUSIONS FROM WORKSHEET DATA

By using formulas and just looking at the data in a worksheet, you can draw some conclusions. You can look at the results of formulas in other columns or rows to see how they compare. For instance, suppose that you totaled your product sales. You could easily see which was your best-selling product (same thing if you totaled sales by region, sales representative, quarter, or other division).

Straightforward simple formulas are useful for drawing conclusions. For more detailed conclusions or decisions, you can't rely on the data alone. For instance, if you raised prices and sales dropped, it might seem there's a correlation, but the decrease may in fact be due to other factors. You need to consider carefully what data was input and what assumptions were made and then be sure to take into account the entire picture.

AVOIDING COMMON FORMULA AND FUNCTION ERRORS

Excel won't make a mistake when calculating a formula, but you might when you create it. You may, for instance, refer to a wrong cell or type the wrong mathematical operator. You should check your formulas. One way to do this is to display the formulas in a worksheet by clicking Tools and then Options. Check the Formulas check box. You can then view and audit your formulas.

You can also use Excel's auditing tool which enables you to do several things. You can select a formula and then view all the cells referenced in that formula. On the flip side, you can select a cell and see which formulas reference that cell. You can also check for circular errors (when you include the total or result in the calculation, for instance). To display the auditing toolbar, click Tools, Formula Auditing and then use the commands on this submenu. You can use Excel's new error checking feature. Click Tools and then Error Checking.

Finally, if you make a mistake, Excel will often display an error message in the cell. These start with a number sign—#NAME, for instance. Use Excel's online help to get complete descriptions of common errors as well as how to fix them.

Formatting the Worksheet

Like a word processing document, the content of any document is the most important part of the document. But is appearance important? Compare the two worksheets in Figures 8.8 and 8.9. Which is easier to understand? In Figure 8.8, you don't know if the numbers represent units or money amounts. Figure 8.9 makes this clear by formatting the numbers. Also, lines and boldface are added to make the column headings stand out and to emphasize the totals.

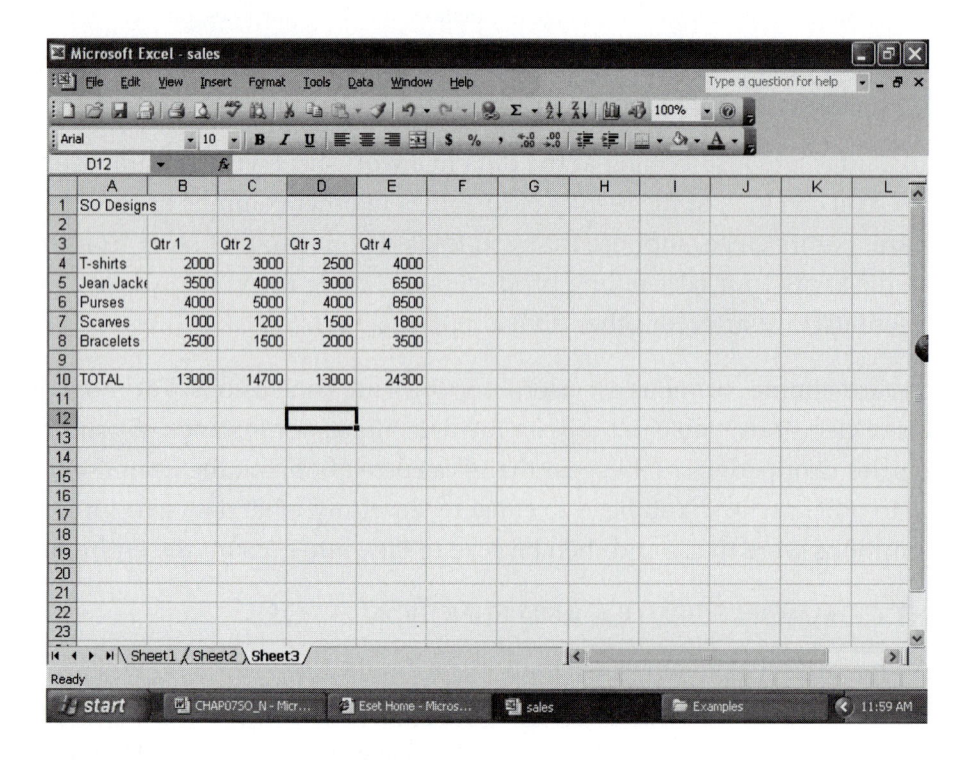

Figure 8.8. A worksheet before formatting.

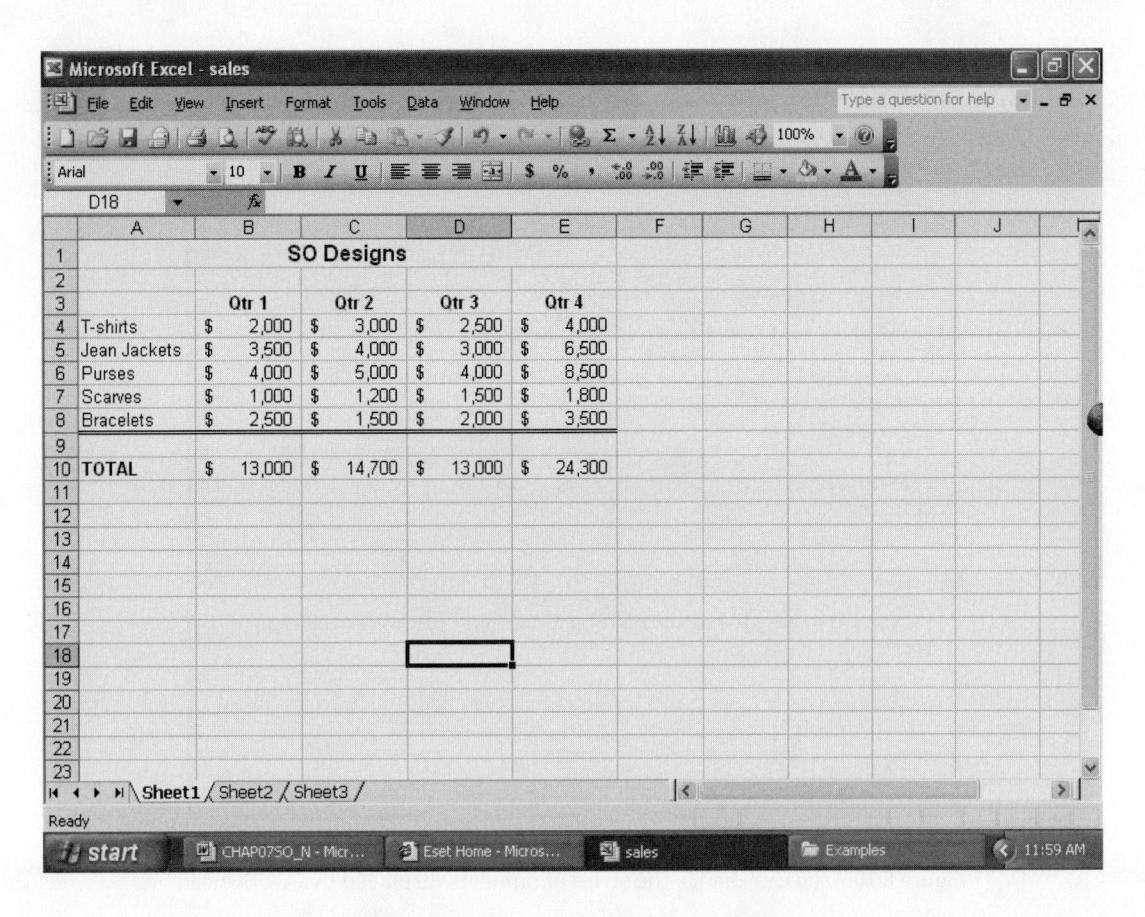

Figure 8.9. A worksheet after formatting.

Remember that changing the appearance of data is called formatting. The features you can use to format a worksheet are similar to those for formatting word processing documents. Here are some changes you might consider:

- *Change the font*. You might want to use a different font or font size. A common change is to make the worksheet title bigger or to use bold or underline for the column headings so that they stand out.

- *Change the look of the numbers*. Numbers can mean different things. For instance, 100% and $100 are not the same. To make the meaning clear, you can select an appropriate number format for your entries. You can select from several styles. The most common styles are listed on the toolbar; click the style you want (currency, percent, and comma). You can also use the Increase Decimal and Decrease Decimal buttons to change the number of decimal places used in the numbers. If you want to view more number styles, use the Format, Cells command. Then click the Number tab and select the style and number of decimal places (see Figure 8.10).

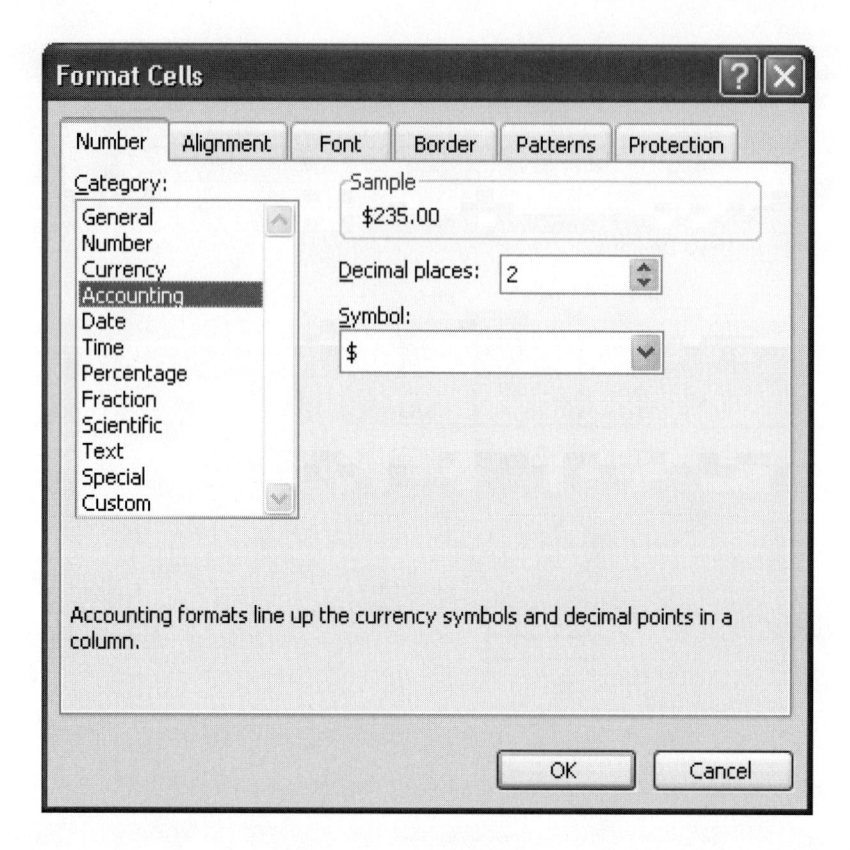

Figure 8.10. You can change the styles of numbers displayed in a worksheet.

- *Change the alignment.* By default, text entries are aligned with the left edge of the cell and numeric entries with the right. To keep your data aligned, you can make changes, selecting left, center, or right alignment for entries. You can also center a title or heading over several columns by using the Merge and Center alignment button.

- *Shade or add borders.* You can also shade a range to call attention to it. As another choice, you might add borders; for instance, a double underline below the totals. To do so, use the Format, Cells command and then click on the Borders tab (see Figure 8.11). You can select which sides of the cell to border, select a line style, and choose a color. For adding shading, click the Patterns tab and select from colors or black-and-white patterns.

Learning Computer Concepts

**Lesson 8
Creating Worksheets**

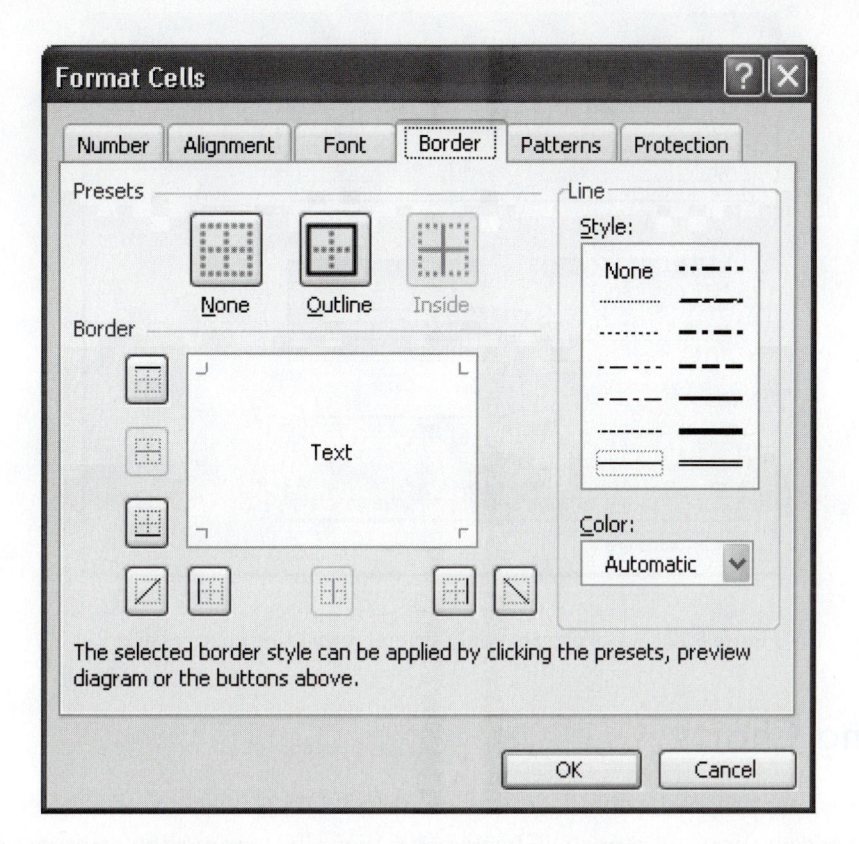

Figure 8.11. You can borders around the edges of the cells..

- *Add headers and footers*. Like a word processing document, you can insert page numbers, the worksheet name, the worksheet date, or other information on each page. To do so, set up a header or footer.

    Date stamp: Worksheets are usually updated over a period of time. To keep track of when changes were made, add a date to the header or footer.

- *Change the page setup*. You can make changes to the margin of the page. Another common change is to use landscape orientation (rather than portrait). With this paper orientation, the text prints across the page rather than down. Use this for a worksheet with lots of columns.

- *Use an AutoFormat*. Excel also includes some predesigned styles for common worksheet table types. You can display and select from these by clicking Format, AutoFormat and then choosing the style you like (see Figure 8.12).

Lesson 8
Creating Worksheets

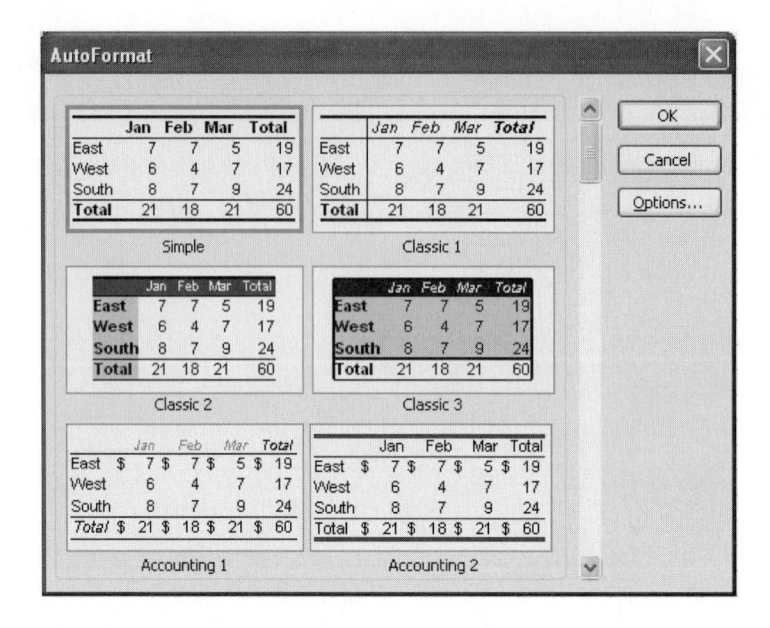

Figure 8.12. AutoFormats apply several formatting changes at once.

Creating Charts

Most spreadsheet programs enable you to chart the data. This charted data comes in handy for presentations or reports. Charts often visually summarize numbers at a glance. For instance, look at the pie chart in Figure 8.13. What can you quickly see from this chart? What is the best-selling product from this quarter?

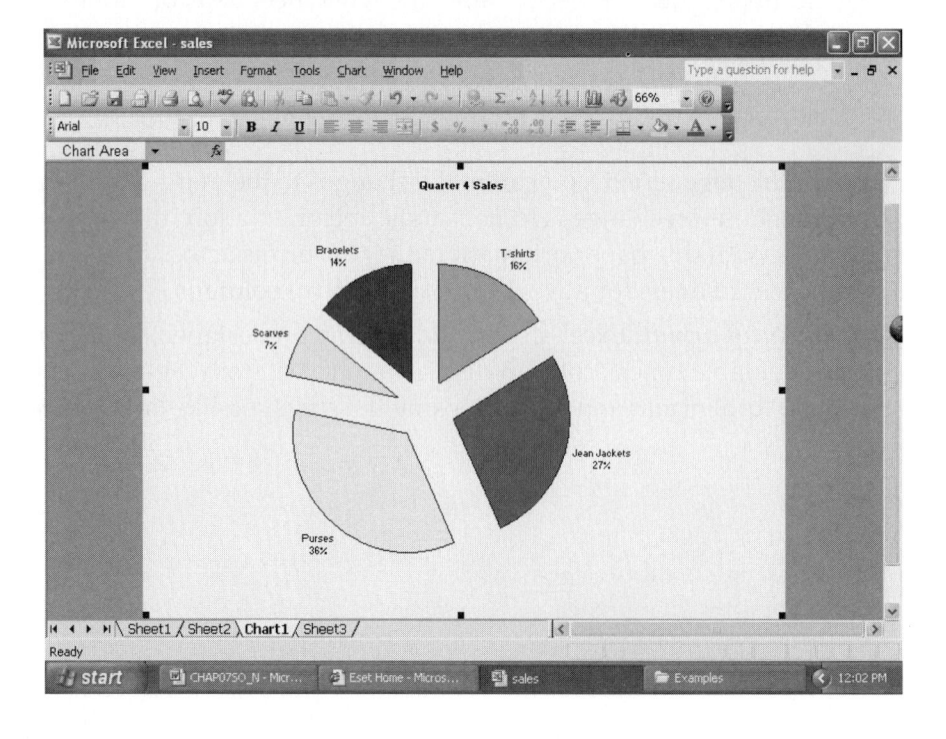

Figure 8.13. You can chart data from a worksheet.

You'll find lots of different chart types, including bar, line, column, pie, 3D charts, and others. Each chart is suited for a particular message. For instance, line charts often show changes over time. Pie charts show how the parts add up to the whole. You can include a chart on the worksheet itself or as a separate page in the workbook. The great thing about creating a chart is that if you change the data, the chart is updated automatically.

Follow these steps to create a chart with the Chart Wizard:

1. Select data to chart.
2. Start the Chart Wizard by clicking on the Chart Wizard button.
3. Select a standard or custom chart type.
4. If desired, change data range options.
5. In step 3 of the Chart Wizard, select desired chart options.
6. In step 4 of the Chart Wizard choose the chart location.
7. Click Finish.

Using a Worksheet as a Database

As a last example of a spreadsheet's usefulness, consider using a worksheet as a simple database. Most programs include features for managing simple data lists. For instance, consider the worksheet in Figure 8.14. This worksheet keeps track of product inventory. You can perform lots of tasks with this list. You can sort in alphabetical (ascending) order or by product number. You can sort by price. You can use a function to calculate the average price. You can create a function to return the highest (MAX) and lowest prices (MIN). You can filter the list to show just the top entries.

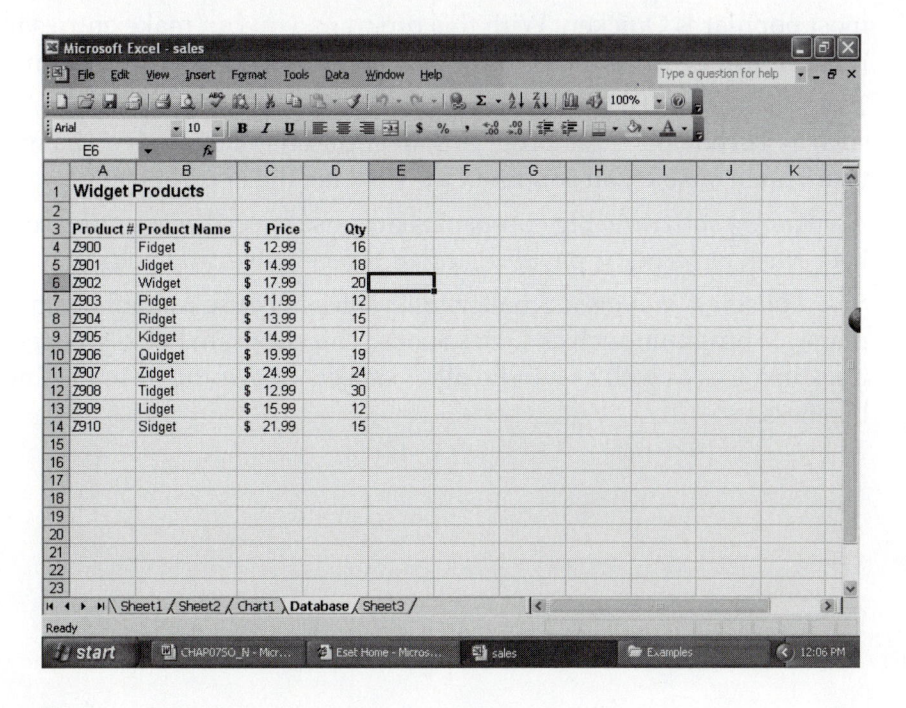

Figure 8.14. Set up a simple database as a worksheet.

When you use the worksheet to track data lists, note that the column headings identify the contents of that column or field. (Field is a database term used to define a single piece of data, such as a product name.) The rows contain the specific information or records. (Again, if you are not familiar with databases, a record is one set of data; for instance, the information about one product.)

Follow these steps to sort data:

1 If the worksheet is in a table format, you can click within it and Excel will recognize it as a data table. If not, you can select the data you want to sort.

2 Open the Data menu and select the Sort command.

3 Select the column to sort on and the sort order.

4 Click OK. The data is sorted.

Save your work: You can have several worksheets, all saved together as one workbook file. Each page or sheet in the workbook can contain data, charts, any type of entry. You can also create formulas that refer to other cells on other pages in the workbook. All of the sheets are saved together with one name as a workbook file.

Using Other Financial Programs

In addition to spreadsheet programs, you can find other special-purpose programs for dealing with financial data. Here are some of the most common:

- *Checkbook manager.* You can buy programs to manage your checkbook. The most popular is Quicken. With this program, you can make entries in the register, print checks, balance your account, set up a budget, and more.

- *Tax preparation.* To help prepare your taxes, you can purchase tax programs, such as TurboTax. These programs, in addition to helping you complete your taxes, often enable you to submit the final tax file electronically.

- *Accounting software.* Big companies may use special accounting software to keep track of accounts payable, accounts receivable, and payroll.

- *Small business manager.* Smaller companies may use a small business manager program, such as QuickBooks. This program helps you create and track invoices as well as handle other aspects of owning or managing a small business.

Summary

- A spreadsheet program not only performs calculations without error, but also enables you to make changes to entries and have the formulas that reference those entries be recalculated automatically.

- You can use predefined formulas called functions.

- You can change the appearance of the entries to make the worksheet easy for your audience to understand. You can make text bold or italic or change to a different font or font size. You can also add borders or shading to make certain parts of a worksheet stand out, such as the grand totals.

- You have a great deal of ways to change the worksheet including adding new rows, deleting rows, adding columns, deleting columns, and adding and deleting worksheets.

- Create charts to visually show data. You can select from several chart types, each appropriate to illustrate a key trend or idea. For instance, line charts show growth over time. Pie charts break down data into pie sections so that you can see how each section contributes to the overall pie.

- You can use a spreadsheet program to manage simple data lists. You can sort data in different orders. For instance, for a mailing list, you may sort by city or state. For a phone list of people, you may sort by last name.

Lesson 8
Creating Worksheets

Q&A

Multiple Choice

1. In a formula, a reference that does not adapt if you move or copy it is called:
    a. A static reference
    b. A relative reference
    c. An absolute reference
    d. A stable reference

2. The function that automatically sums a row or column of numbers is called:
    a. AutoCalculate
    b. SumUp
    c. Express Calc
    d. AutoSum

3. To select the entire worksheet:
    a. Click the selection box to the left of the column letters and above the row numbers
    b. Click any column
    c. Click row 1
    d. Drag across rows 1-3

4. You can select the following numeric styles from the Formatting toolbar:
    a. Currency
    b. Percent
    c. Comma
    d. All of the above

Fill in the Blank

1. The _____ bar is where formulas appear when you edit a cell that contains a formula.

2. _____ are used to designate columns. _____ are used to designate rows.

3. _____ is a popular checkbook manager program. You can keep track of checks you've written, balance your checkbook, and print detailed accounts of your spending.

4. The numeric entries in a worksheet are called _____.

Short Essay

1. List some ways you can use a spreadsheet

2. Name some of the tools you can use to check formulas.

LESSON 9: PRESENTATIONS

Objectives

- ➢ **Design presentations**
- ➢ **Create presentations**
- ➢ **Create slides**
- ➢ **Edit and reorder slides**
- ➢ **Format slides**
- ➢ **Preview the slide show presentation**
- ➢ **Print speaker notes and handouts**

Designing Presentations

An effective presentation requires some planning, and often the people responsible for creating presentations aren't design experts. Still, you can follow a few simple guidelines for making sure your presentation has an appropriate impact. Consider these suggestions:

- To help your audience quickly review the main points, consider using a bulleted list. Use bullets when items have the same importance. You can also create a numbered list. This type of list works best when steps are followed in sequence such as the steps for an upcoming marketing plan.

- Be sure that the text is readable on the slide. You can do this by adjusting the font size. Also, be sure not to include too much text on a slide. You may edit the material so that your ideas are more concise, or you may break up a slide with a lot of text into two ore more slides.

- Graphics and charts are excellent visual elements—when they have a purpose. Don't throw them in just to jazz up the presentation; your audience wants to see information that is important to the goal of the presentation so stick to visuals that relate to what you want to say.

- Make sure you use a consistent style throughout the presentation. This means using the same color scheme, transitions, and other elements. It's also a good idea to include identifying information on each slide (such as the company name, date).

- When formatting text, don't go overboard with too many font or color changes. Readability is the most important factor, not the number of fonts you can include on a slide. Also choose fonts that are appropriate. For instance, you wouldn't want to use the Mobster font (which includes weapons for some characters) in a business presentation.

- Practice going through your presentation, checking the timing, the amount of material, the level of interest (are there parts that lag, for instance).

- Remember that simple is best: you want your audience to remember your message not the 12 different slide transitions you used.

Lesson 9
Presentations

Learning Computer Concepts

Creating Presentations

If you are a speaker or need to make any kind of presentation, you'll find another category of software designed to meet this type of publishing—a presentation program. Traditionally, a presentation is done with a slide show and screen. Presentation software has simplified the creation of slide shows and expanded the way presentations can be given. You can create presentations designed for the computer or the Web.

UNDERSTANDING PRESENTATION PROGRAM TOOLS

Like other Windows programs, PowerPoint includes standard elements such as a menu bar and toolbar. You can get a good idea of the other on-screen features that help you create slides and presentations (see Figure 9.1). Note these key features:

Create presentations from an outline: Some presenters prefer to work from an outline. You can create a presentation from a word processing outline. You may also be able to create a presentation in different views. For instance, in PowerPoint you can create a presentation in Outline view.

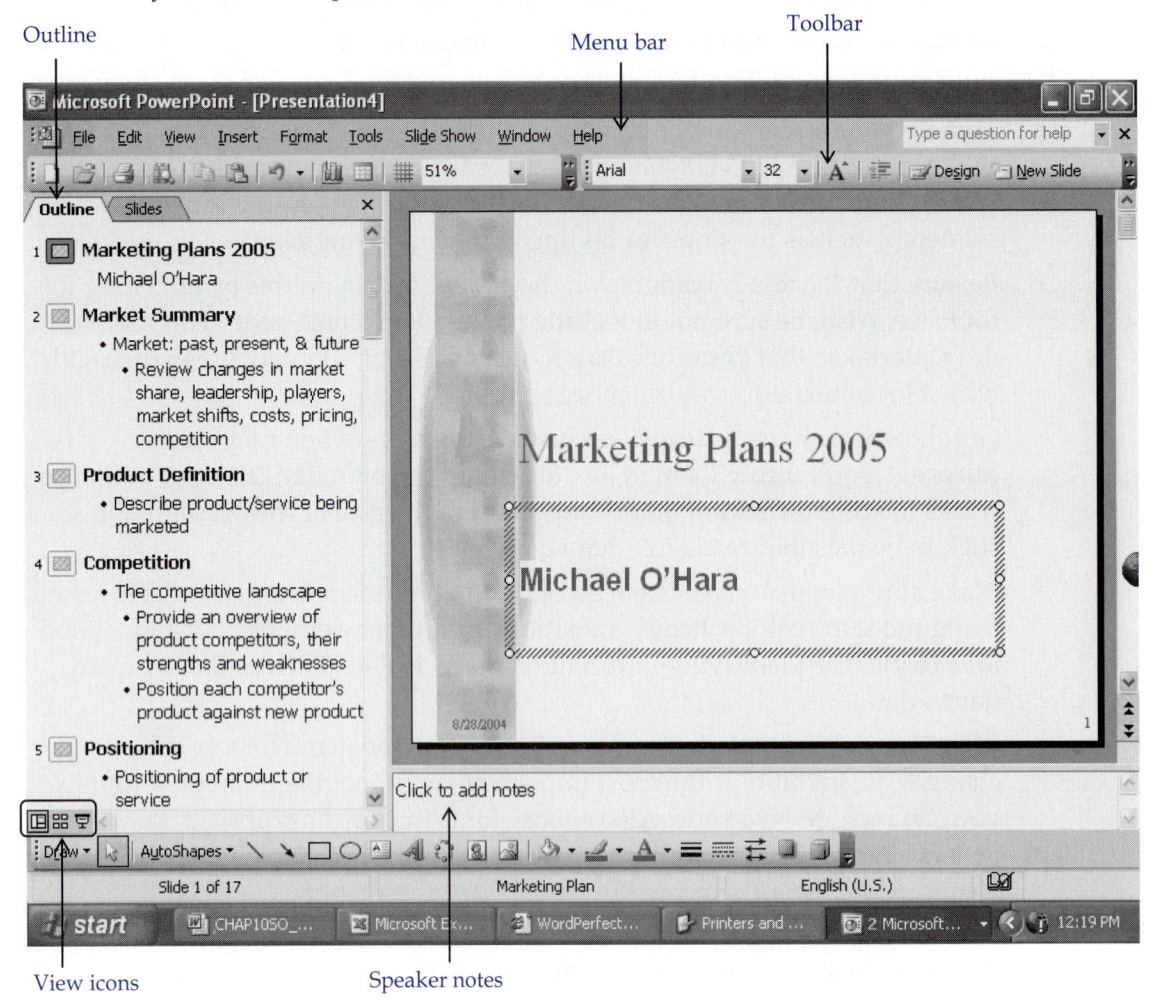

Figure 9.1. Presentation programs include tools for adding and viewing the slides in a presentation.

- *Menu bar and toolbars*. Like other programs you've come across, the menu bar contains the names of the menus, and the toolbars provide quick access to frequently used commands. Note that a lot of the buttons in a toolbar are the same from program to program (for instance, the buttons for copying, cutting, and pasting text). The buttons that are different are those that are pertinent to that particular program. For instance, in PowerPoint you use a button to add a New Slide.

- *Outline and Slides tabs*. The left side of the screen in Normal view has an area that displays different information about the presentation. You can click the different tabs to change what's displayed. For instance, click the Outline tab to view an outline of the slides in the presentation. To view the individual slides, click the Slides tab.

- *View icons*. While working on a presentation, you want to see the slide and perhaps the outline. To check the flow and special effects, you will want to view the slide show. If you are changing the order of the slides, you may want to see a thumbnail view (called Slide Sorter view). To make formatting changes to all slides, such as inserting page numbers, use the Slide Master view. You can change to various views using the view icons in the status bar (or look for commands in the View menu).

- *Notes area*. You can add speaker notes to a slide. These will not be displayed as part of the presentation, but can be used by the presenter for notes, comments, points, and other hints for discussing any particular slide.

CREATING PRESENTATIONS

Presentation programs naturally include features that help you in creating a presentation. But they go beyond that to add other elements:

- *Wizards.* Giving presentations is usually part of a job, not the entire job. Therefore, most people do not spend day in and day out creating presentations. Thus, the creators of this type of program provide wizards to help get you started. PowerPoint, for instance, includes wizards for popular presentation types (see Figure 9.2).

Lesson 9
Presentations

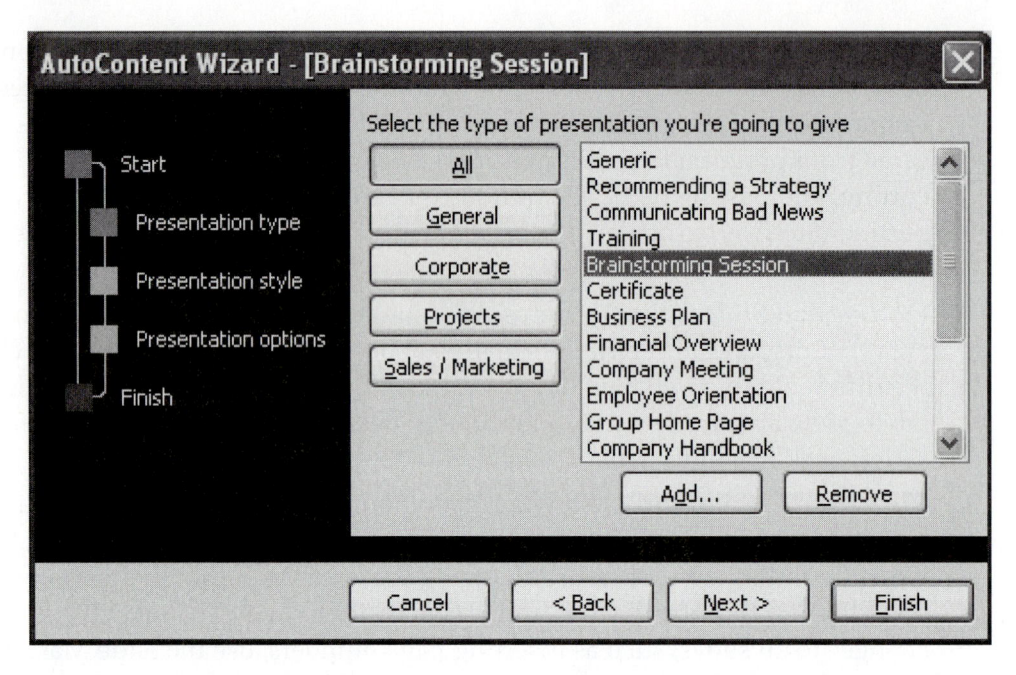

Figure 9.2. You can use the AutoContent Wizard in Microsoft Office PowerPoint to create common presentation types.

- **Templates.** You can also select design themes to apply consistent formatting (background, headers and footers, logos, and so on) to your presentation. Figure 9.3 shows some of the design templates in Microsoft Office PowerPoint in the task pane.

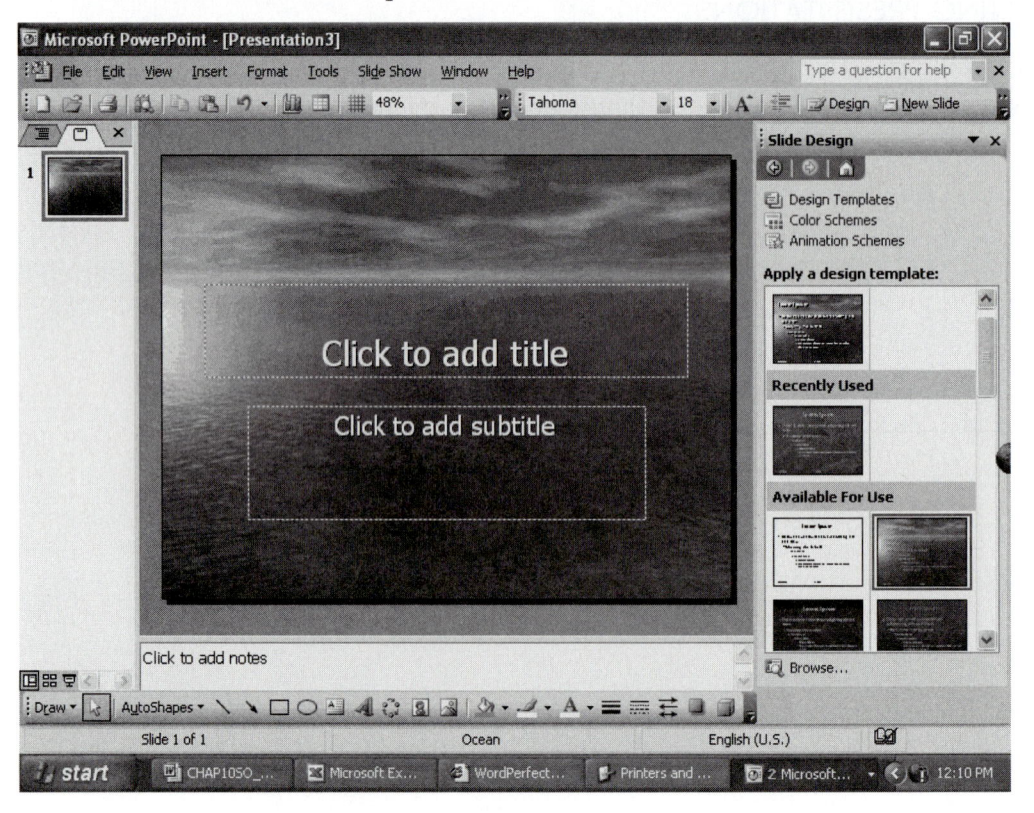

Figure 9.3 In addition to templates, you can select from some predefined slide types.

Learning Computer Concepts

**Lesson 9
Presentations**

Follow these steps to create a presentation:

1. Click File in the menu bar and then click New. You see the New Presentation task pane.

2. Do any of the following:

   To create a blank presentation without any formatting, click Blank Presentation.

   To create a presentation based on a design template, click From design template. Scroll through the list of design templates. When you see one you like, click the arrow next to it and then select to apply the design template to all slides in the presentation or just the selected slide(s). Figure 9.4 shows a design template added to all slides.

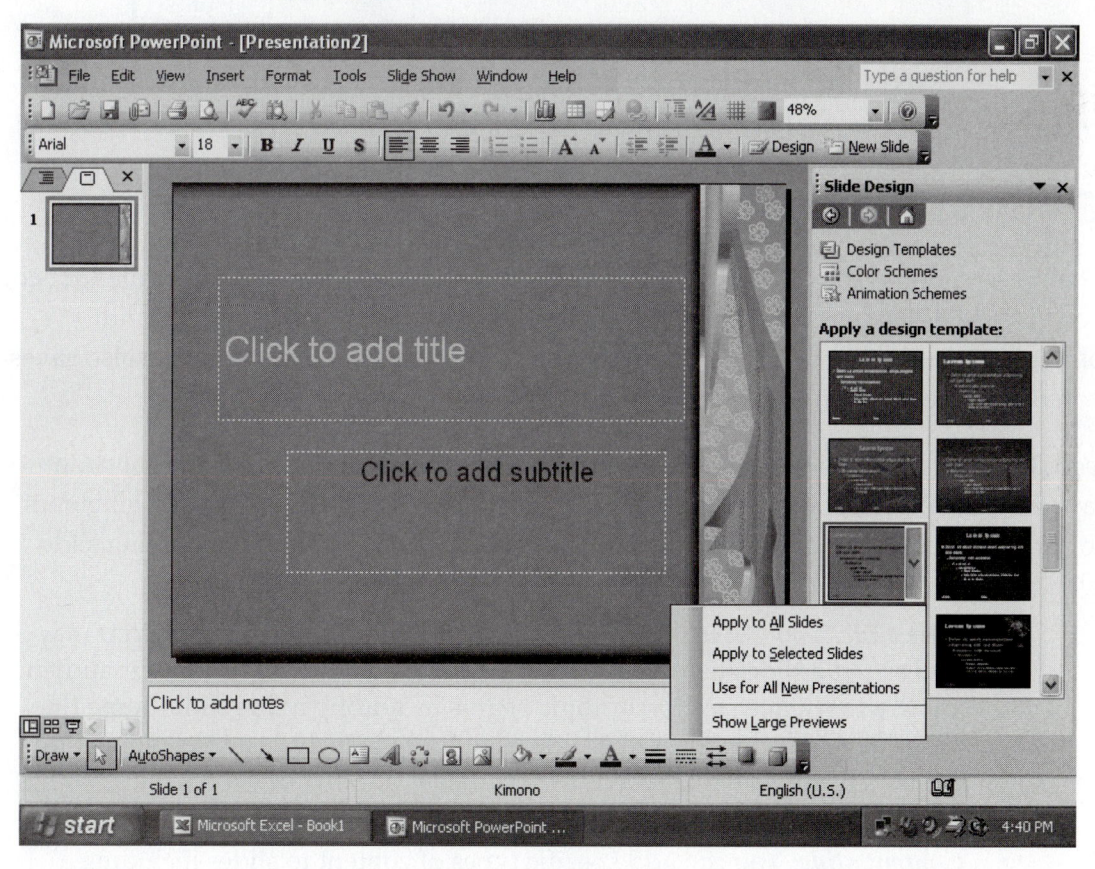

Figure 9.4. You can apply a design to all slides or just certain slides in a presentation.

To create a presentation based on a wizard, click From AutoContent wizard. Then make your choices in the AutoContent Wizard, clicking Next to move from screen to screen. Figure 9.5, for instance, shows some of the common types of presentations.

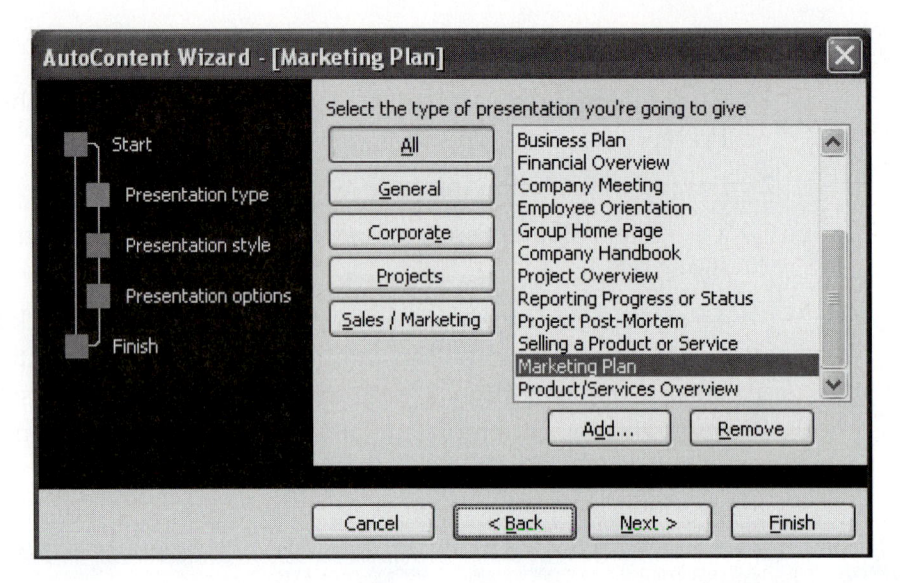

Figure 9.5. Use the AutoContent Wizard to lead you step-by-step through the process of creating common presentation types.

Creating Slides

The presentation is the container for all the slides in the presentation, and as mentioned, you can use design templates to format the slide background and text styles and placement so that the slides are consistent in design. Using a design template also saves you time since you don't have to individually format each slide.

You do though have to create the slides, but PowerPoint includes some typical slide layouts that you can choose from. For instance, you can select slides with placeholders for graphics, tables, bulleted lists, and so on. You can choose from the following slide types:

- *Title slide*. You can use this slide to introduce your presentation. You may also use title slides if you have several sections and want to let your audience know when a new section or topic begins by adding a title slide. Some title slides have just the title. Other title slide formats include a title and text (a bulleted list or a table). You can select the layout that best suits the information you need to present.
- *Content slide*. You can add specific types of content to slides including a picture, a worksheet, a chart, a diagram or organizational chart. Figure 9.6 shows an organization chart from a PowerPoint presentation.

Learning Computer Concepts

Lesson 9
Presentations

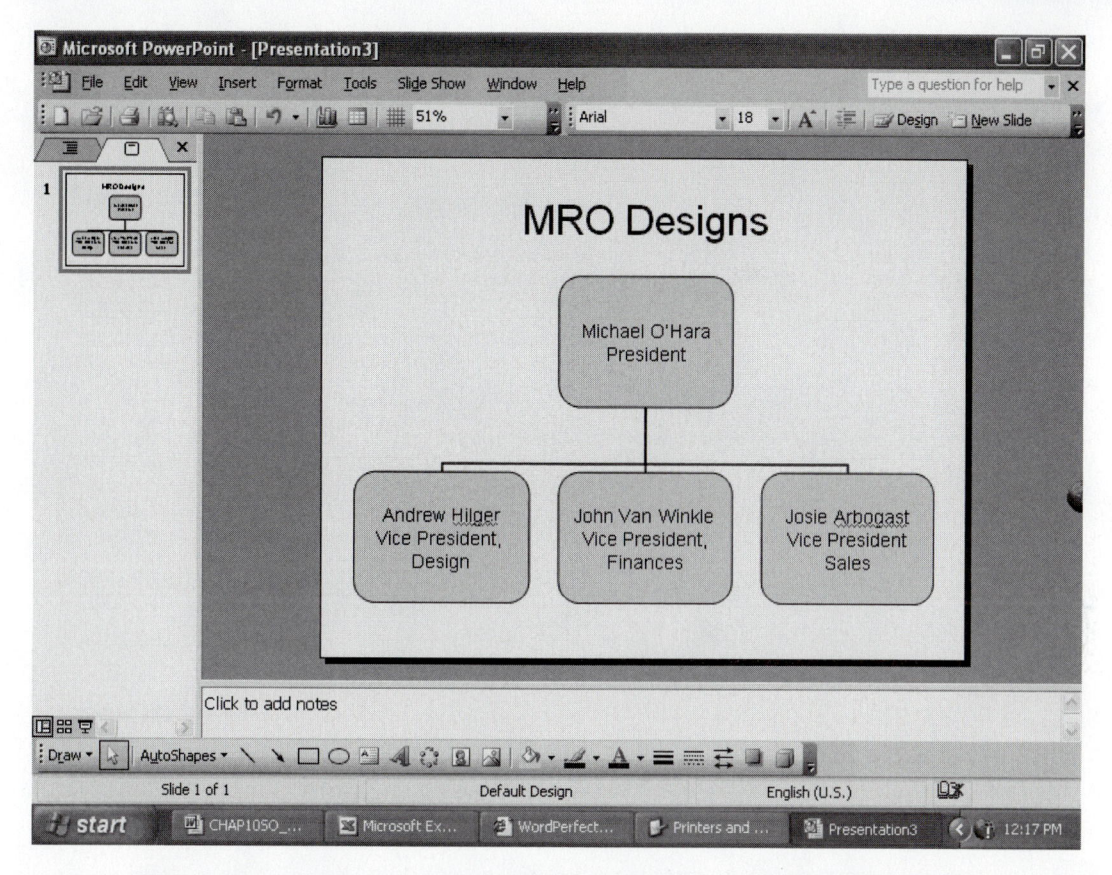

Figure 9.6. You can add special elements like an organization chart, shown here.

- *Combination slide*. You can include text as well as a special content item. For instance, you might include a worksheet with a bulleted list with key data you want to stress.
- *Media slides*. You can also include media slides such as animations or video clips on a slide. These may just contain this special content or text, title, or a bulleted list.

Follow these steps to insert a new slide:

1. To insert a new slide, click Insert and then New Slide.
2. From the task pane, select the type of slide you want to insert (see Figure 9.7).

Lesson 9
Presentations

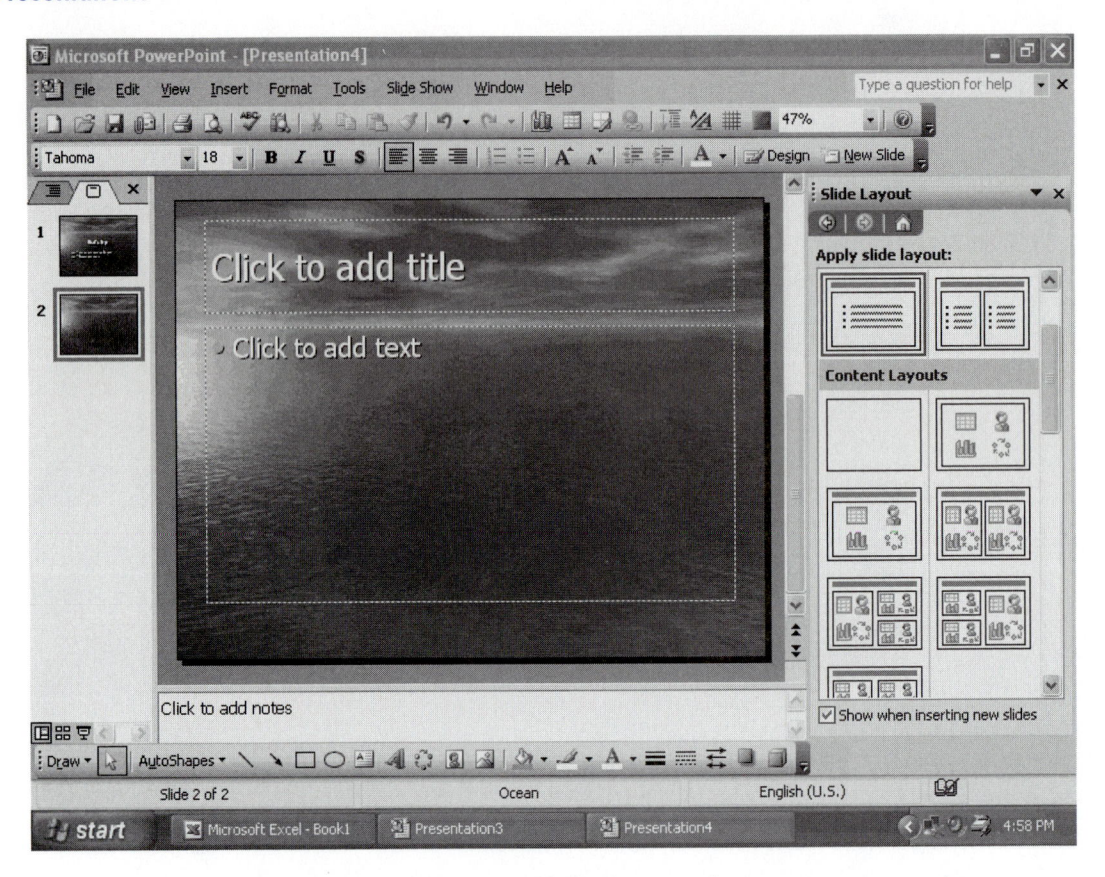

Figure 9.7. You can insert slides with different layout styles into your presentation.

3   Add the text or other content items to the slide.

ADDING TEXT TO SLIDES

To add text to slides, click the text placeholder and then type the text. The font, font size, and color are determined by the slide layout and design, but you can change these. The next section covers making formatting changes. You can also edit the text, just as you do in a word processing document. You can select text, delete text, move or copy text, and so on. You also can use the Edit, Undo command if you want to undo a change you've made.

FORMATTING SLIDES

Just as you can format text and paragraphs in a word processing program, you can also make formatting changes to the text in a presentation. You can do any of the following:

- To make text bold, italic, or underline, click the Bold, Italic, or Underline button. You can also add a shadow effect by clicking the Shadow button.
- Use the Font drop-down list to change the font. You can also change the font size using the Font Size drop-down list. You can also use the Increase Font Size and Decrease Font Size buttons to change the font size.
- To change the font color, display the Font Color palette and select the color you want to use.

- To change the alignment, click the Align Left, Center, or Align Right buttons. Or use the Format, Alignment command. To indent text, click the Increase Indent or Decrease Indent button.

- To change the line spacing, click Format in the menu bar and then click Line Spacing. You can then select a line spacing interval (single, double, for instance), as well as space above or below a paragraph.

- To add bullets or numbers, click the Bullets or Numbering button.

- If you want to change the layout for a slide, select the slide you want to change. Then click Format, Slide Layout. You see the Slide Layout task pane. Click the arrow next to the new slide layout and then click Apply to Selected Slides.

- The slide uses the colors from the slide template for the items on the slide (text, charts, and so on). You can change these colors if you want. You can select from the set of colors used for this particular template, or you can select from any color in the color wheel. To make a change, select the slide and then click Format, Background. Display the color-drop down list and select a color. (Note for the most part it's best to stick to the complementary color schemes used in the slide templates.)

Viewing and Editing a Presentation

To check the flow of the slides in your presentation, you can display it on-screen. You can also manage the slides by deleting slides you no longer need, moving slides to a different order, or copying slides. PowerPoint provides these view options:

- Use Slide Sorter view to display a miniature thumbnail of each slide. You can use this view to rearrange the slide order or delete slides. To delete a slide, click it to select it and then press the Delete key. If you delete a slide by mistake, you can undo the deletion by clicking Edit, Undo.

- To change the order of a slide, select it and then drag it to the new location. A vertical line indicates where the new slide will be placed as you drag.

- To view the slide show as a presentation, click the Slide Show button. You can also click Slide Show in the menu bar and then View Show. To view the next slide in the presentation, click the mouse button or press the spacebar. To quit viewing the slide show in the middle of the presentation, press the Esc key.

- You can also add a transition which controls how the next slide in the presentation appears, selecting from a variety of different styles from blinds to checkerboards to fades and more. Select the slide to which you want to apply the transition. Then click Slide Show in the menu bar and click Slide Transition. You see the Slide Transition task pane. Scroll through the list of available transitions and select the one you want (see Figure 9.8). You can also select the speed, whether a sound is played, and if the slide is advanced on a mouse click or after a certain time interval. You can also choose to apply this transition to just this slide or to all slides.

Lesson 9
Presentations

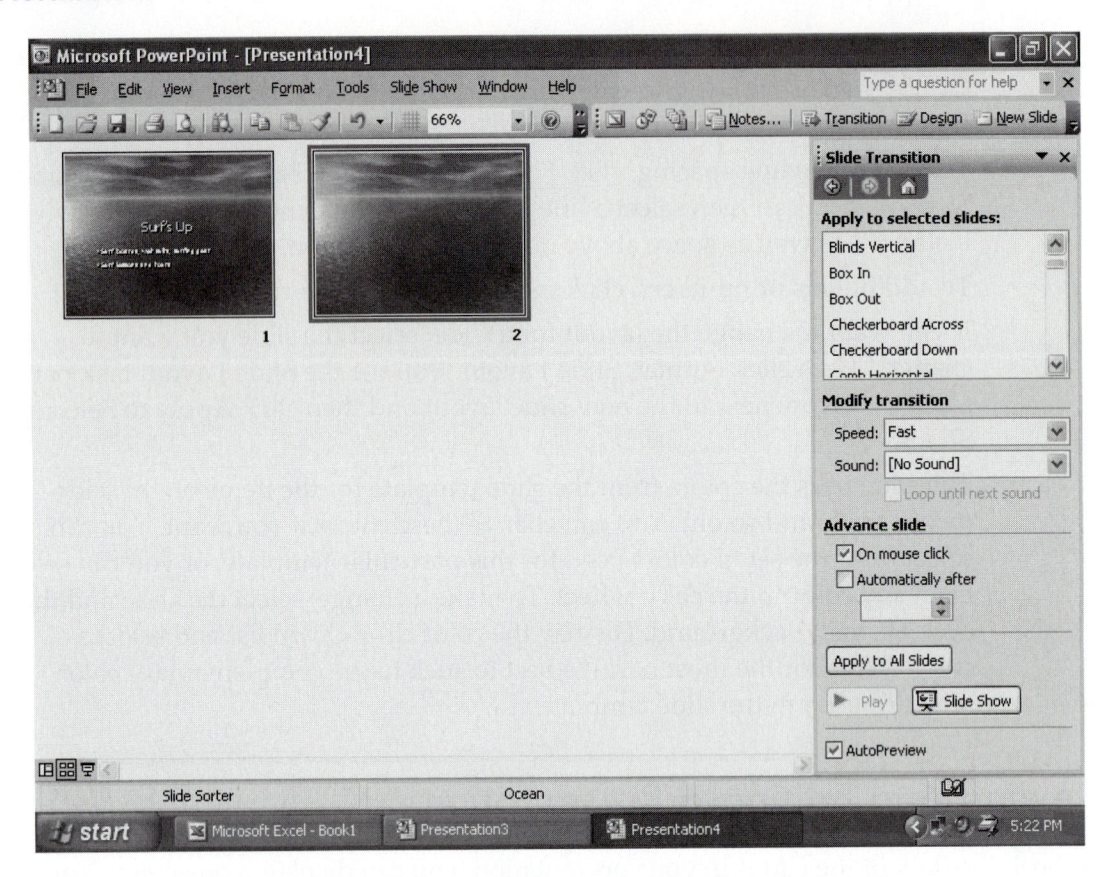

Learning Computer Concepts

Figure 9.8. You can add transitions to the slides in your presentation.

Printing Speaker Notes and Handouts

To make giving a presentation easier, most presentation programs enable you to printout:

- *Speaker notes.* To help the presenter, most programs enable you to create speaker notes. The note includes the slide as well as comments or points you may want to remember. To add notes, select the slide for which you want to add a note and then click View, Notes Page. You can then click in the notes area to type your notes.

- *Audience handouts.* These are most often the actual slides from the presentation. Your audience can use these handouts to follow along and to take notes. You don't need to do anything special, other than print handouts. You can choose to print several handouts per page.

Follow these steps to print audience handouts:

1. Click File in the menu bar and then click Print.
2. Display the Print what drop-down list and select Handouts.
3. Select the number of handouts to print per page as well as the print order (horizontal or vertical), as shown in Figure 9.9.

Learning Computer Concepts

**Lesson 9
Presentations**

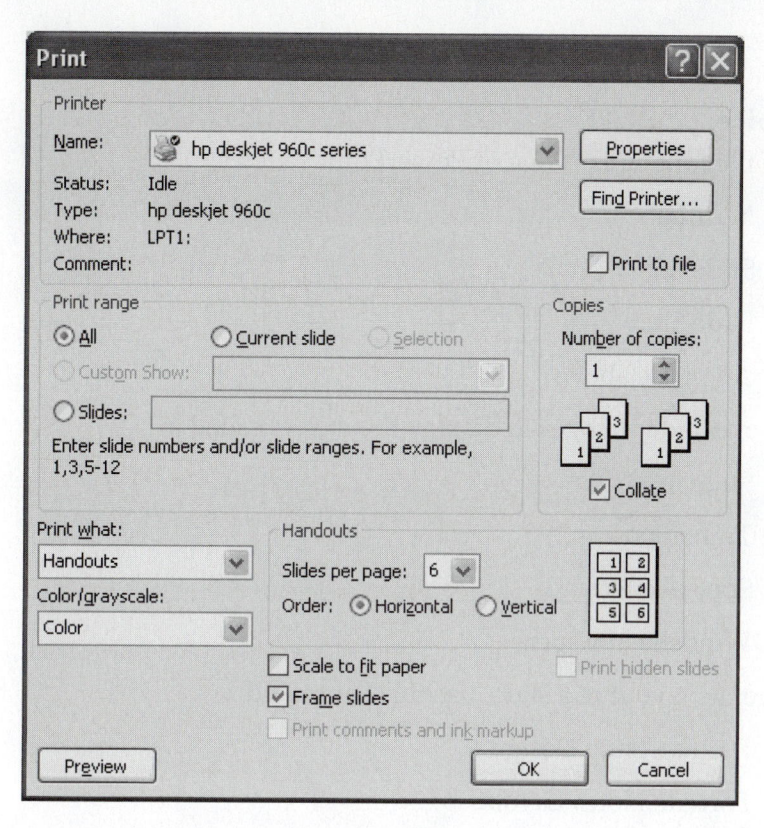

Figure 9.9. You can print slides and handouts using the options in the Print dialog box.

4   Click OK.

Summary

- Sales representatives, trainers, teachers, managers, and many other professionals need to make presentations to a group. To do so, they can use a special type of program called a presentation program. PowerPoint is the most popular presentation program.
- You can display a presentation as a series of slides, from a computer displayed on a screen, or broadcast over the Web. Other ways to display presentations include in special kiosks.
- You can use a template or wizard to help you get started creating a presentation.
- A presentation is made up of slides, and you can include a variety of slide types including title slides, bulleted lists, tables, pictures, worksheets, animations, organizational charts, diagrams, and more. Most programs like PowerPoint include predesigned slide layouts for common slide types.
- You can format the text and objects on a slide, changing the font, resizing pictures, adding transitions, and more.
- To help give a presentation, you can create speaker notes that remind you of key points you want to make or things you want to highlight. For your audience, you can create handouts.

Lesson 9
Presentations

Q&A

Multiple Choice

1. Which of the following is one of PowerPoint's views:
    a. Normal
    b. Slide Sorter
    c. Slide Show
    d. All of the above

2. The way one slide changes to display the next is called a:
    a. Slide in
    b. Transition
    c. Special effect
    d. Windshield wiper

3. To change the layout of a slide, use this command:
    a. Format, Slide Design
    b. Format, Notes Layout
    c. Format, Font
    d. Format, Slide Layout

4. When displaying a slide show, you can move to the next slide by clicking the mouse or pressing:
    a. Spacebar
    b. Esc
    c. NumLock
    d. CapsLock

Fill in the Blank

1. Presentation programs enable you to print _____ to go along with the slides; you can include reminders of things you want to say or point out in these notes.

2. To view all of the slides in miniature format for deleting or rearranging, change to _____ view.

3. _____ leads you step-by-step through the process of creating a presentation, allowing you to select from common presentation types.

4. To stop the display of a slide show, press the _____ key.

Short Essay

1. Describe some of the different content items you can add to a slide.

2. Name some ways you can change the text in a presentation.

LESSON 10: NETWORKING

Objectives

- Understand the concepts and terminology of networking
- Become familiar with types of networks
- Learn the benefits and risks of networking
- Understand the fundamental principles of network security
- Understand the similarities and relationships among different telecommunications networks
- Learn about networking hardware and software
- Understand different Internet connection methods and transmision rates
- Become familiar with the responsibilities of an Internet Service Provider (ISP)
- Learn how computers and the Internet are used to collect, organize, evaluate, and share information
- Understand how computer technology works behind the scenes in everyday activities
- Learn about the impact of electronic commerce (e-commerce) on business, individuals and governments

What is a Network?

A *network* is a group of computers connected by cables or wireless transmitters and receivers so that they can communicate with one another and share computing resources.

When computers first came into common use in large organizations, users operated "dumb" terminals that connected directly to a central mainframe computer. The terminals had no computing capabilities of their own. The term "dumb" was applied to them only after PCs began to replace them. When personal computers became common in businesses, managers and users began to look for ways to make it possible for personal computers to share data and programs with one another.

The first solution was *sneaker net*, so named because of the casual footwear worn by many computer users. Users copied files from one computer and carried them to another. That method, however useful, had limits. If the receiving computer was across town, it took a while for the communication to be completed. In addition, businesses have large amounts of data residing under the control of their mainframe computers, but the personal computers on desktops at first couldn't make use of that data. Communication was a problem that needed to be solved.

Today, PC users can share data and programs over networks; they can use the facilities of the company's mainframe computers using terminal emulation software and hardware. They can communicate with colleagues in remote locations through networks, electronic mail, and the Internet and World Wide Web—all because the communications problem was solved by connecting personal and other computer types into networks.

There are two common networking methods :

- *File server* local area networks (described below).
- *Peer-to-peer* local area networks (described in the next section).

File Server Local Area Networks (LANs)[1]

In a *file-server* network, also called *client-server* network, data or programs are stored on the server and the other machines retrieve data from and save data to the server. To share data with another network user, you have to find a way to copy or save the data to a server location that is accessible to the other user. For example, a teacher at a community college may make files available to students by copying the files to a specific location on the server to which the network's administrator has given the students rights.

If you use a personal computer in a reasonably large organization—school, university, or company—you probably work on a file server Local Area Network or LAN. Your computer can work *locally*, using the programs and drives that are installed on it. Your computer, however, is also a *client workstation*, a machine that can use the drives, folders, files, and programs on the network.

On file server networks, one or more computers act as the central filing system for the clients on the network. Data and programs that are to be shared reside on the disk drives controlled by the servers. Smaller organizations (up to 100 workstations) may have only one server; larger organizations may have dozens.

File server LANs usually involve workstations in the same building or group of neighboring buildings that can be connected directly by cables. The following illustration gives a generalized picture of a file server network. The network has two servers and is connected to the *Internet* through a *firewall*.

---

[1] The Web site of the networking equipment manufacturer Cisco has excellent, technical information about the components and architecture of file server and other networks:
http://www.cisco.com/univercd/cc/td/doc/cisintwk/idg4/index.htm

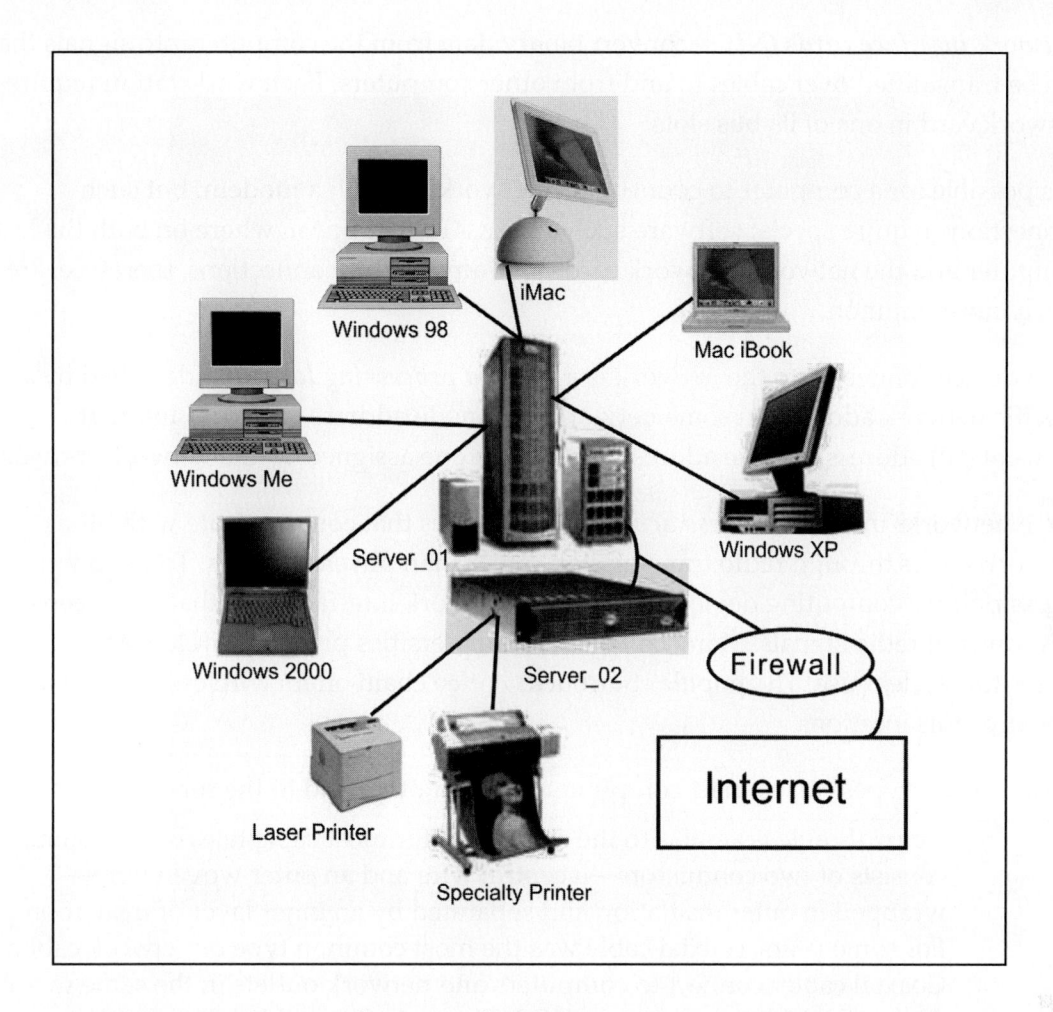

Figure 10.1. This is an illustration of a generalized file server local area network[2].

The *server* is a computer that provides files or services to another computer. The server has hard drives and programs that let it communicate with other computers and provide services to them. Some servers are dedicated (they function only as servers) and are used to manage the network and its facilities.

Client workstations are computers that request files or services from servers. Most modern networks can mix computers of different types and capabilities, including Apple machines running MacOS, PCs running Windows or DOS, and computers running the Unix operating system.

Printers can be shared across the network. Each printer is identified by a name or number. When users want to print, they choose a printer through the application they are using. Other peripherals, such as scanners, are managed in the same way as printers.

---

[2] Not shown in the diagram but defined later in this section, are patch panels, bridges, switches and hubs used to connect portions of the network together.

Network interface cards (NICs) convert binary data from the computer into signals that can be transmitted over cables to and from other computers. Each workstation requires a network card in one of its bus slots.

It is possible for a computer to connect to a network through a modem, but such connections require special software such as CrossTalk or pcAnywhere on both the local computer and the network. Network cards and direct cable connections, therefore, are much more common.

Each device connected to the network is a *node* or *processing location* identified by a specific network address. In some networks, the node address is also an Internet Protocol (IP) address, but the address can also be one assigned by the network software.

Some networks include *wireless access points*, nodes that communicate with other network nodes through radio transmission rather than physical cables. To use a wireless access point, a computing device must have a network interface card that can receive and transmit radio signals. Many colleges and universities provide wireless access points for student use. The popular Starbucks coffee chain offers wireless Internet access at many of its locations.

Various *cable* types can connect computers to one another and to the server.

- *Coaxial* cable is similar to the cable used for most cable television systems. It consists of two conductors—a central wire and an outer woven wire—wrapped in outer insulation and separated by an inner layer of insulation. For some years, coaxial cable was the most common type of network cabling. Coaxial cables connect to computers and network outlets in the same way that a television connects to a VCR. The end of the cable has a cap that screws on to the outlet and secures the conductor in the center of the outlet.

- *Twin twisted pair* or *Category 5* or *Category 6*[3] cable consists of pairs of wires twisted together. The twisting improves resistance to interference. In the past few years, this method of cabling has overtaken coaxial cable as the most common for new network installations. Connections are made with snap-in connectors that are similar to, but larger than, normal telephone connections to prevent confusing the two. (Telephone connections usually have two pairs of twisted wire, while network cables have four pairs.)

- *Fiber optic cable*, which uses light to communicate, consists of a glass filament encased in a plastic coating. The light travels along the filament and reflects off the coating material.

---

3 For more information on Category 5 and Category 6 cable specifications, see, http://www.blackbox.com/tech_docs/tech_overviews/cat5_beyond.html and http://www.tiaonline.org/standards/category6/.

When network wiring stretches over long distances, a series of switches or other signal repeating devices may be used to increase the signals transmitted across the cables. The distance from one switch to another depends on the cable type, with fiber optic cables allowing the longest runs without a device to boost the signal.

Several components help keep traffic flowing on the network:

- A *patch panel* contains the network ports and connects the network devices to each other and to outside lines that connect to the Internet or other networks.
- A *bridge* is a device that connects two LANs or two parts of a LAN.
- A *switch* forwards network traffic from one segment of a LAN to another.
- A *hub* provides a common connection point for several devices on the network.

A network may connect to the Internet using one or more of the following pieces of software and hardware:

- A *proxy server* is a computer program running on a server that acts as an intermediary between a Web browser (for example, Microsoft Internet Explorer) and the World Wide Web. Proxy servers give users rapid access to popular Web destinations by storing frequently requested pages. Storing pages in this way reduces the number of times the browser must link to the Web and permits more control over the Web sites that users can visit.
- A *firewall*, which can be a software program or programmable hardware, prevents unauthorized intrusions into the local network. The software or device is configured to allow only authorized transmissions in and out of the network's computers.
- A *router* is a device that connects a network to the Internet or to another network; it helps manage the traffic between networks. For example, a router can be used to connect two LANs or a LAN and the Internet.

How File Server Networks are Organized

To make management and use of the network as easy as possible, the components of a file server network are organized into *physical* and *logical* units. Physical units are servers and the actual hard drives that are connected together to form the network. Logical units are *volumes*, *drives*, and *folders* (or *directories*) that allow users to locate and manage the data they need.

Lesson 10
Networking

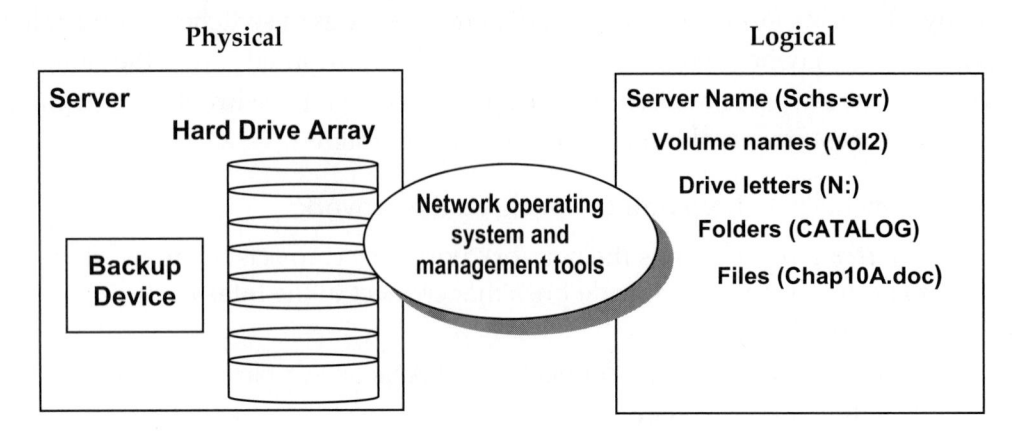

Figure 10.2. A network organization.

Server. Servers are computers especially designed for running networks. Each server is identified by a name, and each has one or more hard drives attached. Like a workstation computer, the server has a CD-ROM drive for use in updating its software. A server usually also has a tape drive or removable disk drive for creating backups.

The server has an operating system such as Novell Netware or Windows 2003 Server. The operating system and its management functions provide network administrators with the tools they need to keep the network running.

Hard Drives. The hard drives are usually linked together into a group called an *array*. For example, a server may control an array of 16 hard drives, each of which has a storage capacity of 18 gigabytes (GB) for a total storage capacity of close to 290 GB. (The actual number is less because of the way drive arrays operate.)

Volume. A volume is a name assigned to organize a portion of the hard drive array attached to a server. The volume name does not correspond to a specific physical area of the array. It is a logical organizing principle for managing storage space. For example, the array of sixteen hard drives attached to Schs-svr is organized into five volumes: NSS_ADMIN, SYS, VOL1, VOL2, and VOL3. NSS_ADMIN and SYS are used by the network's administrators; the other three volumes contain data used by Schs departments.

Drive. A drive is a letter assigned to organize a portion of a volume for one or more users. Like the volume name, the drive letter is a logical organizing principle that lets users store their data and network administrators manage storage space. Drive letters are said to be *mapped* to a particular unit of storage. A drive letter can be mapped to a volume, a folder, or a sub-folder.

NETWORK USE

When you turn on a computer attached to a network, it boots up, but before you actually start using it, you are requested for a *login name* or *user name* and *password*. The login name identifies you to the network and the password ensures that you are the person who is identified. If you do not have a valid login name or you don't remember your password, you are not allowed to use the network.

Some networks call the process of connecting and identifying users as a *login procedure;* you log in to the network. Others use the term *sign on* to mean the same thing; still others use *log on* and you have a *logon name* or *ID*. All these terms mean the same thing: Identify yourself and provide the password to determine what drives, folders, files, programs, and peripherals you can use.

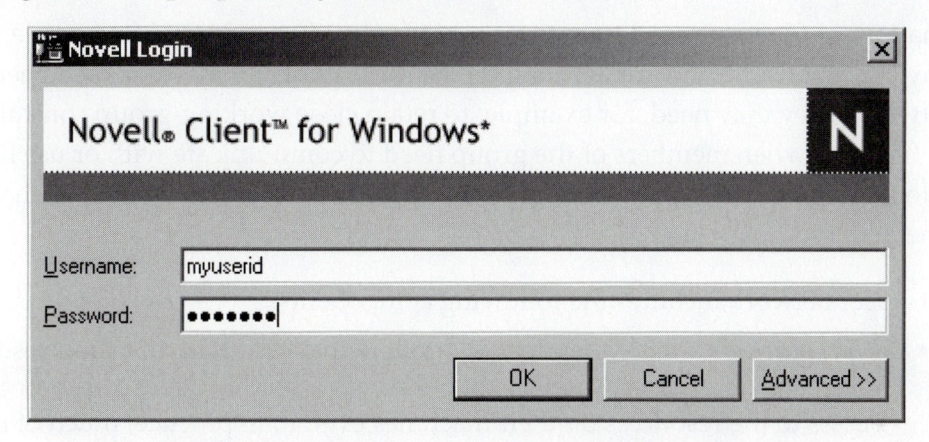

Figure 10.3. Login screen for Novell NetWare™ network.

The login or user name is a string of characters assigned by network administration that identifies you as a network user. Your rights to use network folders and files are defined to the login name.

Users *log in* to the network for two complementary purposes:
- Access data and programs that you have rights to use.
- Ensure that unauthorized users do not gain access.

Many networks maintain a login ID, usually *guest,* that does not require a password but has limited rights to a network's drives and folders. Guest IDs are maintained for the convenience of visitors who may need to use a computer temporarily.

On LANs your access is usually restricted to certain drives, folders, and files. On a file server network, maintaining access rights is the job of the *network administrator*. The network administrator assigns login IDs, defines and maintains access rights, ensures that backups are performed regularly, and works to keep the network operating smoothly.

Peer-to-Peer LANs

On *peer-to-peer* networks, each workstation can have disk areas that are accessible to other users. In such a network, no machine acts solely as a server. If you want a file from another workstation, you act as a client and the other machine is the server; if someone retrieves files from your machine, your workstation is the server and the other is the client.

Peer-to-peer networks usually work best when only a few users are involved, as in a home or small office. Microsoft Windows 98, 2000, NT, and XP all have built-in support for peer-to-peer networks. Apple's Mac OS operating systems also have built-in support for peer-to-peer networking called AppleTalk.

Combinations of file server and peer-to-peer networks often exist within a single company. Several users who are working on the same project may work on a peer-to-peer network. They may need, for example, to retain close working-group control of specific files. But when members of the group need to communicate with or use files that belong to the organization as a whole, they may access the file server network that everyone in the company uses.

A peer-to-peer network includes the following components:

- *Workstations* are independent computers that can share data and resources with each other directly rather than through a server. Users can control access to the resources on their machines even if, in practice, much of the administration of the network is handled by one user.
- *Printers* are shared across the network. Each printer is identified by a name. When users want to print, they choose a printer through the application they are using. Other peripherals are managed in the same way as printers.
- *Network interface cards* (*NICs*) convert binary data from the computer into signals that can be transmitted over cables to and from other computers.
- *Cables* or wireless transmitters connect computers to a router or hub or directly to one another.

The following illustration shows a four-station peer-to-peer network and its connection through a router or hub to the Internet.

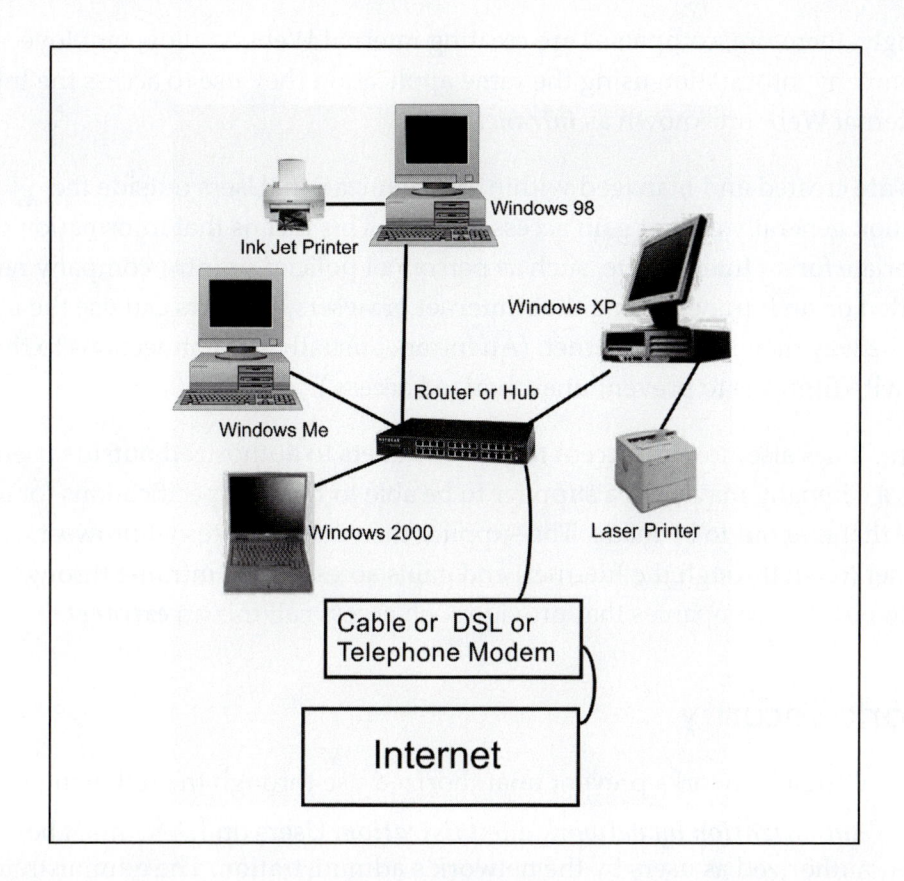

Figure 10.4. Four-station peer-to-peer network.

Wide Area Networks (WANs)

Another kind of network is called a Wide Area Network (WAN). In some companies, a WAN is used to connect workers in different geographic locations. In the central location, the network operates like a LAN. Workers outside the central location communicate with the network via modem, satellite, or leased telephone lines through hardware and software facilities called *gateways*. The gateways give distant users access to the services of the central location.

Most people reserve the term WAN for networks that serve only members of the same company or organization. Others consider AOL, Prodigy, and the World Wide Web as WANs.

Intranets and Extranets

Many users within an organization may have access to the Internet, using their Internet browsers to find information, send e-mail, and exchange files with coworkers. But when they leave the Internet, many of them have to use other applications to review information and exchange files.

Increasingly, therefore, companies are creating internal Webs to allow employees to access company information using the same application they use to access the Internet. These internal Webs are known as *intranets*.

Intranets are created and managed within an organization. Users outside the organization generally cannot gain access to them. This means that information that is inappropriate for an Internet site, such as personnel policies or intra-company news, can be provided on an intranet. Using their Internet browsers, workers can use the intranet in the same way they use the Internet. (An intranet usually has connections to the Internet with firewalls to prevent unauthorized access.)

Some companies also provide access to their intranets to authorized outside users. For example, a company may wish a supplier to be able to review specifications for a purchase that is about to be made. The supplier then uses an Internet browser, contacts the intranet (often through the Internet) and gains access to the intranet through an ID and password. The companies that provide such access call this an *extranet*.

Network Security

Secure Local Area Networks prevent unauthorized use through the following methods:

- *Authorization by network administration.* Users on LANs must be authorized as users by the network's administration. The administrators establish a record in the network's administrative database that identifies the user and the user's rights to various network resources. This record, often known as the user's network account, includes the user identifier (user ID) and a beginning password.

- *User ID and password authentication.* Initially provided by the network's administration, a user ID, for example, might be a combination of characters such as *pjw2*. The initial password usually must be changed the first time a user logs on (connects) to the network. The process of entering the user ID and password is called *authentication*. As the word implies, authentication is the way the network can be certain that the user is authentic, and really is the person who is associated with the user ID.

    Network administrators generally insist that passwords be changed at regular intervals and that they not be easy to guess by outsiders. Users also are discouraged from sharing their passwords with others.

- *Firewalls, proxy servers, virus scanning software and other security measures.* Prevent unauthorized users from gaining access to the network's resources.

- *Network administrators manage the network.* They monitor network usage to ensure that users have enough network space for their data, that the network's resources—servers, printers, and Internet connections—are available and secure. They also monitor network activity to detect unauthorized attempts to use the network.

Telecommuting

More and more workers are working away from the office. Some of them simply use their PCs as local machines and communicate with the office only when they have files they want to send or receive. Such users may use the Internet or e-mail service as their way to communicate with the office and never actually log in to the office's computers.

Other workers, however, connect via telephone lines and work directly on the office network. Telecommuting of this type requires hardware and software on both the workstation and the server. Usually the telecommuter starts the communications software on the workstation, dials up the office computer, and logs in as a network user. The full facilities of the company's network are then available to the workstation.

For example, employees may use a popular telecommunications program called Symantec® pcAnywhere™, a product of the same company that offers Norton AntiVirus™ software.

Another popular telecommuting method is *virtual private networking* (VPN). A user starts the VPN software on a local machine and connects to the Internet. VPN requires that the user log in to the VPN server of the organization. Once the user is logged in, such services as e-mail and access to server drives may be available.

Benefits and Risks of Networking

The most obvious benefit to networking is that you can share resources. Several users can use the same printer, resulting in savings on hardware costs. Files can easily be shared among a number of users. In a law firm, for example, all the attorneys, paralegals, and legal secretaries can share the draft of a document, editing and rearranging as necessary until the document is finished.

A customer database can be available to all those responsible for processing orders, managing inventory, and collecting payments. In addition, a network allows for centralized backup of an organization's data.

With corporate-edition virus software and firewalls to prevent unauthorized access networks can be made secure. Networks may be vulnerable to virus and hacker attacks unless they're well defended. And, if a virus gets through, it can spread to a great many computers.

With a network, sometimes catastrophe can strike. A server can crash, causing loss of some data, or the response time can be slow when network traffic is heavy. Such network problems can be overcome with backups, and these problems are not unique to networks. Standalone computers are also vulnerable to crashes and data loss.

Standalone systems offer more privacy and independence of use, but they can be more expensive if you have to have a printer and a scanner for each machine. Organizations that need workers to cooperate on projects using shared files and resources will continue to use networking; individual users may opt for the independence and privacy of standalone systems.

The Internet

The Internet is a network of computers and computer networks. It combines client-server and peer-to-peer networking to make it possible for users all over the globe to share the network's facilities and to communicate with other users.

In this way, it is like the worldwide telephone network that allows someone with a telephone to connect to anyone else with a telephone, whether wired or cellular, to transmit voice, facsimile documents and images (faxes), and data. When you make a local telephone call, your call may be handled by the telephone company that provides your service. If you call over any distance, however, your telephone call may be handled by several different telephone companies. The companies, both foreign and domestic, pass signals along over telephone networks. Together the individual telephone networks create an international network.

The Internet resulted from the desire to have computers talk to one another so that users could share information, data, and ideas. It originated as a way for researchers, especially in defense industries and universities, to share their knowledge. With the introduction of the *World Wide Web* in 1989, businesses, schools, governments, and nonprofit organizations realized that it would be a valuable tool to communicate with customers and clients and to provide information and services.

Although it is the most familiar part of the Internet, so much so that Web and the Internet are often used interchangeably, the World Wide Web is just one segment of the Internet: e-mail servers, file transfer protocol servers, newsgroup servers, and telnet are other important components of the Internet.

The Internet's computers and networks are linked by a variety of connections—cables, telephone lines, and satellite. They pass information back and forth using the communications protocol called *TCP/IP*.

TCP/IP (Transmission Control Protocol/Internet Protocol) is actually a suite of protocols that make the Internet work. It performs the following communications functions:

- Permits login from remote computers.
- Routes data between Internet servers.
- Makes sure that data packets are error-free and assembled in the right sequence.
- Converts text-based domain names into numerical IP addresses.

The computers that form the Internet can be divided into the following groups:

- *Clients*. These are computers that connect to the Internet to do research and send e-mail. Most personal computers that access the Internet are in this category. A wide variety of personal computing devices can use the Internet. Personal computers (desktop PCs and laptops), Personal Digital Assistants (PDAs), and cellular telephones can all be client computers connecting to the Internet.

    Client computers access the Internet in one of two major ways:

    - *Internet Service Provider (ISP)*. ISPs are computers that provide other computers with access to the Internet. Networks such as Earthlink, NetCom, and AT&T Worldnet are ISPs. An ISP maintains hardware and software that give you access to the Internet. The ISP also provides support and protects its service from outside threats and illegal use. Many ISPs provide e-mail accounts, space for Web pages, and other services.

        Internet access at schools and businesses is often provided via high-speed connections (DSL, cable modems, T1, T3). Although users seem to access the Internet directly through these connections, the high-speed services are provided by an ISP.

    - *Online services, such as America Online (AOL), Prodigy, and Microsoft Network (MSN)*. Online services provide a variety of shopping, research, and e-mail services and also provide access to the Internet. America Online (AOL), Microsoft Network (MSN), and Prodigy are examples of online services. Such services are not actually part of the Internet, but they give access to the Internet, so to most users there is little distinction.

- *Internet servers (sometimes called hosts)*. These are computers that provide access to information. When an Internet user contacts an Internet site, the computer that contains the site is a server. Internet servers may also act as clients when they request a link to another site. Some servers offer specialized services, such as e-mail and file transfer.

- *Search engines or sites*. Internet computers dedicated to providing information about other Internet sites. Yahoo!, Google, HotBot, Lycos, and AltaVista are examples of search sites although most of these provide many services in addition to search capabilities.

- *E-mail servers*. Computers that provide electronic mail boxes and services.

- *File transfer protocol (FTP) servers*. Computers dedicated to allowing the transfer of files from one computer to another.

- *Usenet*. A global system of discussion groups called *newsgroups*. Many Internet browsers include a newsreader program to access the newsgroups.

- *Telnet*. A program that lets one computer log on to a remote computer. Telnet is often used to search libraries and databases.

INTERNET ADDRESSES—URLS (UNIFORM RESOURCE LOCATORS)

Because the Internet is not a single network but a collection of networks, the ***domain*** name system is used to identify the exact location of Internet servers and their primary Internet activity. It's something like the telephone numbering system that includes country codes, area codes, and individual phone numbers.

An Internet address (IP address) is made up of a four-part series of numbers. The domain-name system translates the numbers into a user-friendly system of text-based names. So instead of typing in http://4.18.84.83/ to order a pizza online, you can type in "www.pizzahut.com." Text is easier to remember.

INTERNET USE

Your computer requires the following if you want to connect to the Internet:

Hardware Requirements. You must have a dial-up modem, DSL modem, cable modem, or a connection through a local area network as at a company or school. The term *modem* is derived from *modulator-demodulator*, a device that converts one type of signal into another. For example, both dial-up and DSL modems convert analog[4] telephone signals into digital signals. Cable modems convert TV frequencies into digital signals.

- A ***dial-up modem*** uses a voice telephone line to connect. Dial-up modems are usually rated at 56K ***bits per second (bps)***—a maximum of 56,000 bits every second. They often do not actually communicate at 56K bps because of variations in the quality of the telephone connection.

- The original ***Integrated Services Digital Network (ISDN)*** offers transmission rates up to 64 Kbps.

- A ***DSL (Direct Subscriber Line) modem*** uses a voice line but at a different frequency from the voice transmissions.

- A ***cable modem*** uses the same connection as cable television. Cable connections are known as ***broadband*** connections because they can carry multiple signals at once. In general usage, the term ***broadband*** often refers to all higher-speed connections such as DSL, cable modem, T1 and T3 lines, and satellite connections.

- Cable and DSL connections are generally significantly faster than dial-up modems. Cable and DSL modems can be twenty times the speed of dial-up modems.

---

4 *Analog* means that the message is transmitted by a method that is "like"—analogous to—the original message. For example, when you speak into a telephone, the sounds of your voice are converted into electrical pulses by the microphone in the telephone's mouthpiece. These pulses change with each change in your voice; they are the electrical equivalent or analog of the sound vibrations of your voice. The pulses are re-converted into sound by the receiver of the person you are talking to.

Digital signals encode information as a series of 1s and 0s. When digital signals are sent over telephone lines, they must be converted into analog signals (electrical pulses). The modem on the sending end converts digital signals to analog: it *modulates* the digital signals. The modem on the receiving end converts the analog signals back to digital signals: it *demodulates* the analog signals.

- Even higher data transfer speeds are achieved with such direct connections as T1 and T3 lines and *B-ISDN*. *B-ISDN* uses broadband transmission but requires fiber optic cable. B-ISDN can support rates of 1.5 Mbps (megabits per second).
- A *network interface card (NIC)* is required if you are connecting through a DSL or cable modem or though a LAN.

Software Requirements. Besides the software drivers that make your hardware work with your computer, you need the following software:

- *Internet browser*, such as Microsoft Internet Explorer, Netscape Navigator, or Mozilla Firefox. A browser is an application that:
  - Lets you connect to the Internet either directly or through a modem and a telephone line using an ISP or online service.
  - Lets you enter URLs.
  - Displays information provided by an Internet site.
  - Lets you save or print displayed information so it can be reviewed later.
  - Recognizes and lets you activate connections (called *hyperlinks*) to other addresses.
  - Lets you save addresses that you'd like to visit again using *Favorites* (Internet Explorer) or *Bookmarks* (Netscape Navigator).
- *Software from your Internet Service Provider (ISP) or online service (such as AOL)*. Some ISPs require that you log in to their server (authenticate), especially if you are using dial-up. Online services require logins so that the use of their services is restricted to subscribers.

Internet Service Provider (ISP)

An *Internet Service Provider* (*ISP*) is a company that offers connection to the Internet.[5] The primary job of an ISP is to provide a constant connection to the World Wide Web and Internet. To do so, the ISP must maintain software and hardware that let you connect using your modem (dial-up, cable, DSL).

In the days when the term was popular, ISPs were said to provide an "onramp" to the *information superhighway*. Still, ISPs provide customer support to help subscribers with problems, and they maintain software that protects their hardware and software from virus threats, unauthorized access, and illegal activities.

Most ISPs also provide e-mail services. For example, Time-Warner's cable service, RoadRunner, provides connection to the Internet and e-mail accounts to its users. Verizon, Earthlink, Cablevision's Optimum Online, and a host of other ISPs provide similar services.

---

[5] Online services, such as AOL, MSN, and Prodigy serve as ISPs, but they offer additional services that other ISPs may not.

Lesson 10   Learning Computer Concepts
Networking

Computers and Our Lives

You probably can think of a number of ways that computers are used at home, at school, and at work. But computers are used in areas that you might not ordinarily think of. And they are used for a wide variety of purposes.

It is almost a cliché to speak of how much information is available on the World Wide Web. As a research tool, it has no historical parallel because it brings together in one, easy-to-access way, an enormous number of information sources—databases, dictionaries, individual Web pages, company and organization Web sites, library card catalogs, and many others.

Much of the work of collecting this and other information and organizing it is done by computers. If you go to the library, chances are you'll use an online card catalog to search for books and periodicals that the library contains. For example, the libraries at many state colleges and universities in New York use Aleph, a software product from a company called Ex Libris to manage their library collections.

Computers are often used in evaluating information. For example, you might collect—either via the Web or from newspapers and magazines—prices and specifications for a variety of digital cameras and put them in a spreadsheet so you can compare prices, mega pixel ratings, speeds, storage capacities, zoom features, and other characteristics.

Computers are used to communicate information. E-mail messages and instant messaging represent two well-known means of communication. But many people use Web logs or *blogs* to deliver their opinions on a variety of topics. Some people have individual or family Web pages where notices and messages can be left, and many sites support bulletin-board services for users who want to post messages and questions. A Web site such as snapfish.com or Yahoo!'s photo posting area lets people post their photos on the Web and then send links to those interested in viewing the pictures.

Computers are behind the scenes in almost every daily activity. Supermarket and retail store scanners—called *point of sale systems*—rely on computers. Computers control machine tools, manufacturing robots, and other industrial processes.

Automated Teller Machines (ATMs) can read the magnetic strips on bank cards and verify personal identification numbers (PINs) because of the computers built into them. ATMs connect to other computers to verify account information and provide access to banking services. Credit card transactions start with small computers that read a card's magnetic strip that then communicate to the card company's computers for authorization of the transaction.

Automobiles, household appliances, modern thermostats, and many other mechanical devices have computer chips embedded in them for storing information and controlling how the device works.

Learning Computer Concepts — Lesson 10 Networking

ELECTRONIC COMMERCE OR E-COMMERCE

The terms *electronic commerce* and *e-commerce* are used to describe the use of the Internet for buying and selling stuff. E-commerce may take the form of a purchase from a company such as Barnes & Noble that also has retail outlets known as "bricks and mortar" stores. Or it may involve a transaction with a company that has only a Web outlet, such as Amazon.com. E-bay, the auction site, is one of, if not the largest e-commerce site.

Those people who shop online can compare prices and selection from a number of sites. E-commerce provides a way to reach a wider range of customers than might be possible using only stores or catalogs. Web sites and e-commerce security are efficient and cost-effective tools for companies and organizations that have products to sell.

TECHNOLOGIES THAT HELP PEOPLE

Computers offer a variety of tools that can help people who have a variety of problems. Voice-recognition software can help those who have trouble using a keyboard. A wide range of software and hardware devices provide a way for the visually impaired to read information from the computer screen or from a book page. Some methods, such as Microsoft Reader® or JAWS®, use synthesized sound. Screen readers that turn text into sound are useful not only to those who cannot see well, but children learning to read can also benefit from using such software. Other software for the visually impaired, such as ZoomText®, enlarge text to make it readable on the screen.

Computer-based training can be made available on computers, like those in public libraries, accessible to people who cannot afford their own computers. Such users can also use libraries to research job possibilities, prepare résumés, and participate in online training.

Summary

- A *network* is a group of computers connected by cables or wireless transmitters and receivers so that they can communicate with one another and share computing resources.
- In a *file-server* network or *client-server* network, one or more computers act as the central filing system for the *clients* on the network. *Client workstations* request files or services from the servers.
- Some important devices keep network traffic flowing including patch panels, switches, bridges, routers, and hubs. Proxy servers and firewalls help protect the network from unauthorized access.
- Servers are identified by names, and have one or more hard drives attached, usually in a group called an *array*. A volume name is assigned to organize a portion of the hard drive array and a drive is a letter *mapped* to a particular unit of storage.

Lesson 10
Networking

- To use a network you authenticate yourself as an authorized user. Network administrators assigning network IDs and initial passwords and give user rights to network drives and printers.

- In peer-to-peer networks, each workstation can act as a client and server.

- A Wide Area Network (WAN) connects workers in different geographic locations through hardware and software facilities called *gateways*.

- A group of Web pages accessible only to the members of an organization is called an intranet.

- Network security is maintained through user authorization by network administration, user authentication, firewalls, proxy servers, virus scanning software, and by network administrators who manage the network and monitor its use.

- Telecommuting is the means by which workers who are not in the central office can connect to the organization's network and use its facilities.

- An obvious benefit of networking is the ability to share resources—drives, printers, and other peripheral devices. A risk of networking is lost productivity that can occur when a network server is out of service.

- The Internet is a network of computers and computer networks that combines client-server and peer-to-peer networking having a global reach. The World Wide Web is the most familiar part of the Internet; other parts include FTP sites, e-mail servers, newsgroup servers, and telnet. The Internet generally relies on the TCP/IP communications protocol.

- Client users connect to the Internet through an ISP or online service. Search engines are dedicated to providing information about other Internet sites. E-mail servers provide messaging services, and FTP servers facilitate file transfer.

- Computers on the Internet are identified by an IP address. The domain name system (DNS) associates these numbers with their text counterparts.

- Computers in everyday life are found in ATMs, automobiles, point-of-sale scanners, household appliances, and many other devices.

- The terms *electronic commerce* and *e-commerce* describe the use of the Internet for buying and selling stuff.

- Technologies such as voice synthesis and text enlargement, aid those with disabilities.

Learning Computer Concepts — Lesson 10: Networking

Q&A

Multiple Choice

1. Which of the following can be shared on a network?

    a. hard drive

    b. printer

    c. Internet connection

    d. scanner

    e. All of the above

2. Which communications protocol is the most used on the Internet?

    a. FTP

    b. Xon/Xoff

    c. TCP/IP

    d. Z-modem

3. The hardware or software that protects a network from unauthorized access from outside the organization is called a:

    a. router

    b. switch

    c. bridge

    d. firewall

4. Which of the following is an ISP?

    a. Earthlink.net

    b. Verizon.net

    c. Optimum Online

    d. RoadRunner

    e. All of the above

Lesson 10
Networking

Learning Computer Concepts

Fill in the Blank

1. A(n) _____ is a group of computers connected by cables or wireless communications so they can share resources.

2. A(n) _____ usually includes machines in the same geographic location.

3. The software application that lets you use the Internet is called a _____.

4. Screen readers, such as Microsoft Reader, use synthesized voices to help the _____ take advantage of computing resources.

Short Essay

1. Describe what a LAN and a WAN are.

2. What are some of the benefits of networking?

LESSON 11: E-MAIL

Objectives

- Define e-mail
- Send and receive messages
- Handle e-mail
- Work with attachments
- Create an Address Book
- Set up mail options
- Troubleshoot e-mail problems
- Follow e-mail etiquette rules
- Use other Internet communication methods

What Is E-mail?

E-mail is the most common activity on the Internet. You can send a message to anyone else with an e-mail address. E-mail has several benefits. First, it's quick. Once you send the message, it is available to the recipient pretty much instantaneously. Second, it's inexpensive. You do not have to pay for your e-mail messages. Third, it's convenient. You can send messages at any time. Fourth, it's versatile. You can include more than just messages. You can attach documents, photos, or send Web pages with your message. Fifth, it provides a trail of communication that you can follow to resolve problems or keep for legal reasons.

DECODING YOUR E-MAIL ADDRESS

When you sign up for Internet access, you receive an e-mail account and an e-mail address. This address is in the following format:

sohara@aol.com

The first part of the address is the username. You can usually select your e-mail username (unless it's taken by someone else). The two parts of the address are separated by an at sign (@). The second part of the address is the domain name, the name of your Internet provider. In this example, aol.com is the ISP, or Internet network.

When someone wants to send you a message, they type in your e-mail address. As a shortcut, you can save frequently used addresses in an Address Book. This topic is covered later in this lesson.

Lesson 11
E-mail

UNDERSTANDING HOW E-MAIL WORKS

When someone sends a message to you, basically, the message is sent to your Internet provider's network. When you log on to your e-mail account using a mail program, your mail program retrieves all of the messages from your ISP's server and copies them to your computer.

You can use any number of e-mail programs for accessing your e-mail. Windows includes Outlook Express, which is a popular free program. Microsoft Office also comes with a version of Outlook with additional features (such as a calendar, a task scheduler, and more). If your Internet Service Provider is America Online (AOL), you can access your e-mail when you log on to AOL. Some e-mail programs, like Hotmail!, let you access your mail through the Internet at any site (rather than from your own personal computer).

Another form of access to the Internet is through a Personal Digital Assistant (PDA) or a cellular phone. Both of these connect wirelessly through wireless hubs. Some homes and many offices have wireless networks. You can also find wireless access at restaurants, hotels, airports, and other public places. You have to be close to a hotspot to get connected. You can then use your mail program to check and review your mail.

Keep in mind because of the size of cell phones, Internet access is predominantly text-based. Also, typing messages using the cell phone keypad is cumbersome. Cell phones are most effectively used to check quick messages or current information such as stock quotes or the score of a sporting event.

THE COMPONENTS OF AN E-MAIL MESSAGE

A typical e-mail message contains the following:

- The recipient's e-mail address. See the section on e-mail addresses earlier in this lesson.
- The sender's name and e-mail address.
- A subject line to identify the content or purpose of the message.
- The message itself.
- Any attachments.

Later sections in this lesson cover how to create and send e-mail messages as well as how to handle attachments.

Sending and Receiving E-mail

To read mail, you need a mail program (see Figure 11.1). Windows, for instance, includes Outlook Express, a program for sending and receiving e-mail. You can also find and use other mail programs. Most mail programs include similar features.

Learning Computer Concepts   **Lesson 11**
E-mail

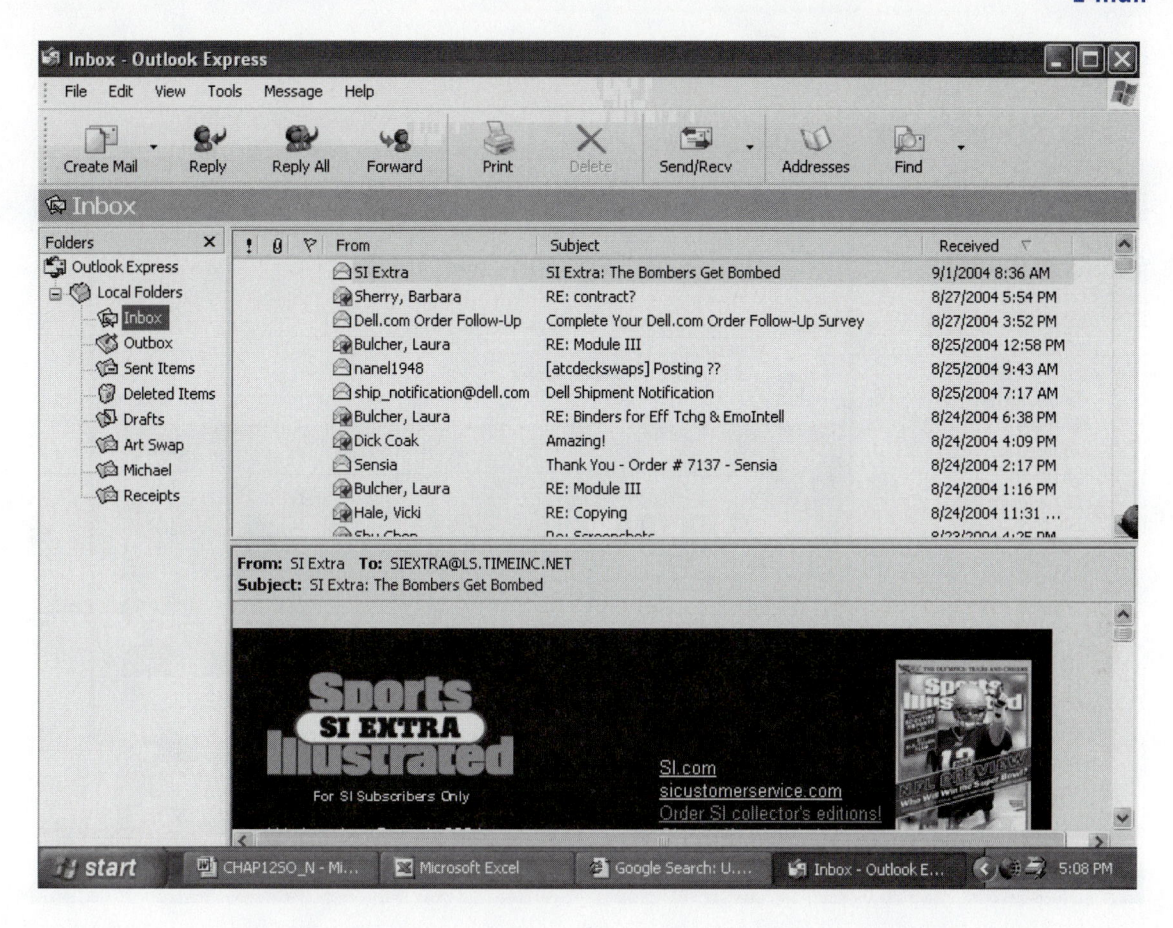

Figure 11.1. You can check and read your mail using your mail program.

You can check your mail and download messages from your mail server to your system. New messages are displayed in your Inbox, marked in bold. The number of new messages may also appear.

READING AND RESPONDING TO E-MAIL

From the list of messages, you can click the message you want. In Outlook Express, you can view part of the message in the preview pane (the lower half of the window). To open a message in its own window, double-click the message (see Figure 11.2). You can review the message and then decide how to handle it.

Lesson 11
E-mail

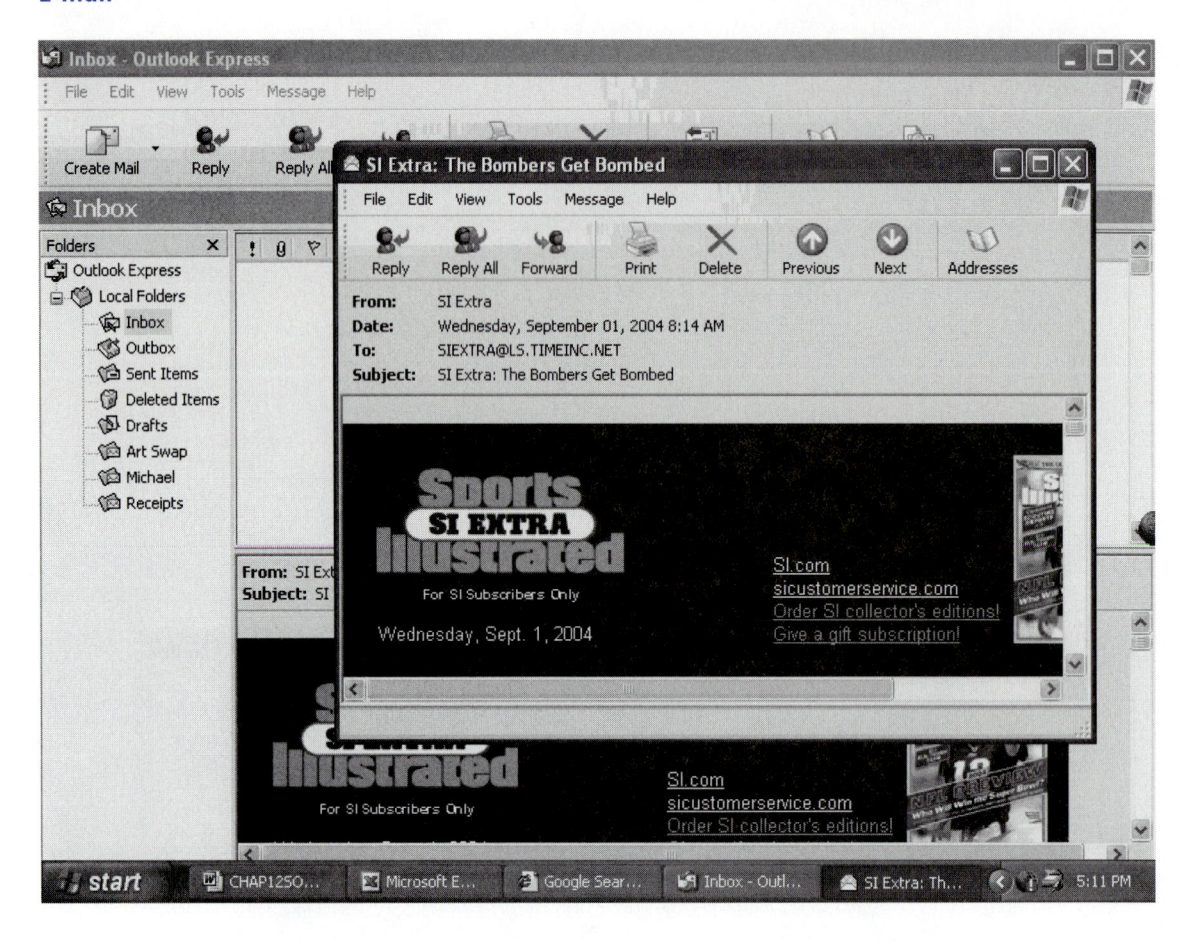

Figure 11.2. You can open and read the messages you receive.

When you receive a message, you can choose to do the following:

- To reply to the sender, click the Reply button. Doing so creates a new mail message with the address and subject line complete. Depending on your mail settings and program, the new message may contain the text of the original message. You can type your reply and then send the message with the original message. Or you can delete it if it's not necessary. (Sometimes it helps the reader follow along with the conversation, reminding the recipient what's been said and what issues are still outstanding.)

- If the message was sent to several people and you want to reply to all recipients, click the Reply All button. Type your response and then send the message.

   Replying to All: If you intend for the message you are sending to go only to the individual that sent it (not the entire group), don't click the Replay All button. Doing so can send unnecessary (and sometimes inappropriate) information to others.

- If you want to forward the message (jokes and inspirational stories are the most commonly forwarded items), click the Forward button. You can then type the address of the person(s) to whom you want to forward the message.

Or you can select the recipients from your address book. See the next section on creating and sending messages.

- To delete the message, click the Delete button. You can also select messages from the Inbox and click Delete to delete them. Note that, in Outlook Express, deleted messages are moved from your Inbox to the Deleted Items folder (unless you have made a change to the default settings). You can click the Deleted Items folder to recover any messages you have deleted by mistake.

- To view other messages in your Inbox, click the Next or Previous buttons. To close the message window and return to the mail program, click the Close button in the message window.

- If the message has an attachment, you can double-click the attachment. You can then choose to save the attachment to your computer or open it. Be very careful with e-mail attachments as they are one way that viruses are spread. The message may contain a program that can destroy files, for instance. See Lesson 13 for more information on checking for viruses.

CREATING AND SENDING NEW E-MAIL

In addition to receiving and responding to e-mail messages, you can create new messages and send them. When you create a new message, you need to type the address, subject, and content. Because it's easy to make a mistake when typing an e-mail address, you can set up an address book. You can then select names from this list when you create a new message. When the message is complete, you can then click the Send button to send the message (see Figure 11.3). Depending on your setup, the message is either sent immediately or placed in your Outbox and sent when you click the button for sending and receiving messages.

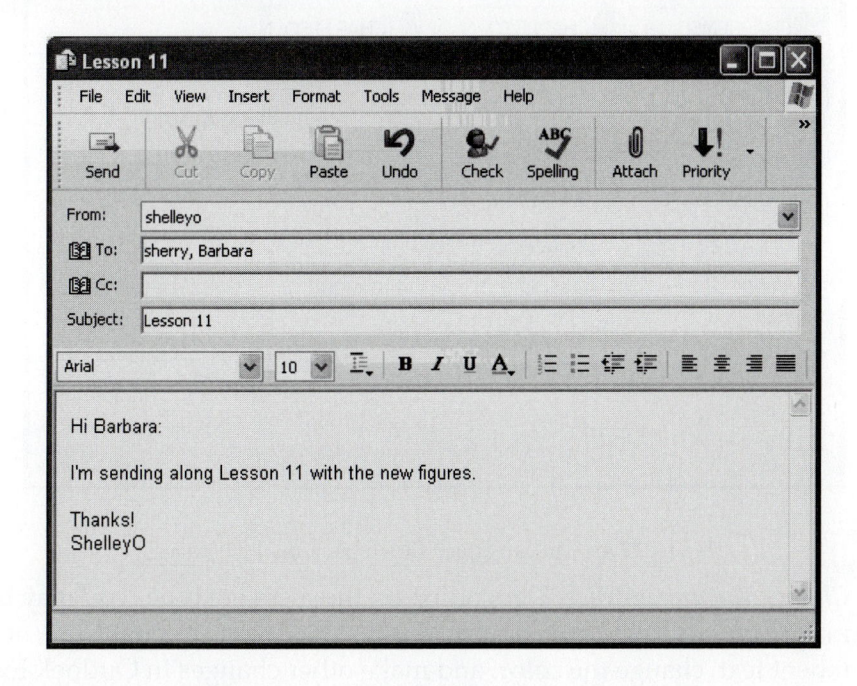

Figure 11.3. You can create and send new messages.

When you create messages, you also can do the following:

- *Attach files.* Most programs enable you to attach files and photos to a message. This enables you to share the document immediately with others. For example, when authors submit chapters of a book to the editor, some send a message and attach the document file. To attach a file in Outlook Express, click the Attach button and then select the file to attach (see Figure 11.4). Note the recipient needs the appropriate software to open the attachment. For instance, if you send a Word document, the recipient needs either Word or another word processing program that can open Word documents.

  Attachment size: Keep in mind that messages with large attachments take awhile to download, which is especially irksome for those without fast connections. Also, some e-mail providers have a limit on the size of attachments. It is, therefore, best to try to decrease the size when possible. For instance, you may compress files so that they are smaller. Or you may send multiple messages with file attachments rather than one message with several attachments.

- *Insert a Web link.* You can insert a link to a particular Web site or page; the recipient can then click the link to go to that site. You may want to do this for pages that contain information that is updated frequently (like stock quotes, for instance). You can also insert the Web page as a graphic. In this case, it's just a picture of the page, and the recipient can't interact with it (use its links).

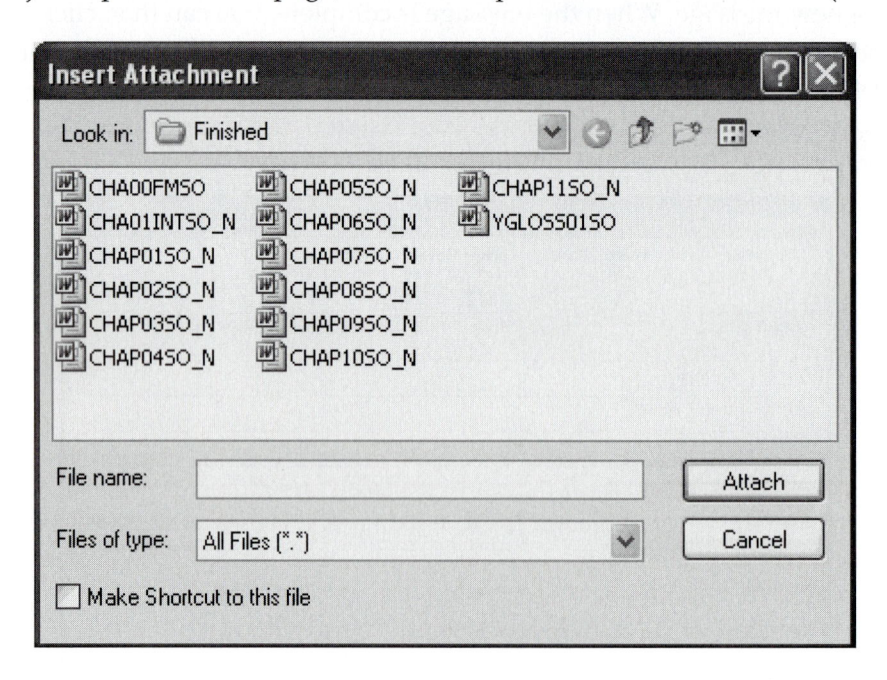

Figure 11.4. You can attach files to an e-mail message.

- *Change the appearance.* Depending on the message type, you may be able to make changes to the appearance. For instance, you can make text bold, indent text, change the color, and make other changes in Outlook Express for Rich Text (HTML) messages. Keep in mind that your recipient's mail program may not be able to display (or display properly) your formatting changes. Also, formatting makes the message larger (and therefore it takes more time to send/receive). Keep your formatting to a minimum.

- *Check your spelling*. Even though e-mail is an informal communication, it's still a good idea to check your spelling and grammar. You'll find in very informal communications people often use abbreviations such as LOL (laughing out loud) and BTW (by the way). That's fine for communications with friends, but probably not a good idea for business communications.

Junk mail: Junk mail is called Spam. Some mail programs help you filter out this type of message. See the section "Handling Spam" later in this chapter. Also, Lesson 13 covers more about handling junk mail and dealing with privacy issues.

Handling E-mail

Your Inbox will quickly fill up with messages, so it's imperative that you keep your messages organized. Just like "regular" mail, you need to adopt a "handle once" method of dealing with mail. You can delete it, respond to it, or save it. E-mail messages provide a few additional options:

- For some messages, you may want to print them. For instance, if someone sends you info on a book you want to look for in your library, you may print the book information (title, publisher, author name, and so on). If you receive directions to a party, you may want to print a hard copy to take with you. To print a message, click the Print button. When the Print dialog box appears, click Print.
- For messages you no longer need, delete them by clicking the Delete button. Messages are not really deleted, but moved to the Deleted Items folder. You can retrieve messages if needed. You can also permanently delete the message by selecting it, clicking the Delete button, and then clicking Yes to confirm that you do want to permanently delete the message.

Empty Deleted Items Folder: If you want to get rid of all the deleted messages in your Deleted Items folder, click Edit and then click Empty 'Deleted Items' Folder. Click Yes to confirm the deletion.

- If you don't have time to respond to a message but want to remind yourself, you can flag the message. To do so, click Message, Flag Message. Outlook Express adds a little flag icon to the message. You can unflag the message by clicking Message, Unflag Message. (The command is a toggle.)
- You can also mark a message as read (or unread). For instance, if you get spam, you can mark it as read and delete it. If you don't mark it as read, it appears in bold and may make you think you have a message you need to read. If you read a message but need to reread it, you can mark a read message as unread. To do so, right-click the message and then click Mark as Unread (for read messages) or Mark as Read (for unread messages).

- You can create folders to store and organize your messages. For instance, you might create a folder for a project and then store all messages relating to that project in that folder. Usually, you use the File, New, Folder command to create a new folder. You can also move or copy messages to other folders. Look for Move and Copy commands in the Edit menu. Your program may also include toolbar buttons for these tasks. (The actual procedures vary depending on the mail program you use.)
- You should archive your e-mail on a regular basis so that your Inbox and other e-mail folders aren't cluttered. Check with your particular e-mail program for instructions on how to archive or back up messages. Usually you do so by date. For instance, all messages before a certain date are saved in an archive file.

Creating an Address Book

It's easy to make errors when entering e-mail addresses. You need to type the characters in the exact order and be sure to include the at (@) sign and the correct domain name. To help you with addresses, you can create an Address Book. Then, rather than type an address, you can select it from a list. To add a person to the Address Book, you can type the address manually or pick it up from an existing message and add it. You can also select the display name used in the Address Book list.

Follow these steps to add a name and e-mail address to your Address Book:

1. Open a message from the person you want to add to your address book.

2. Right-click the name and select Add to Address Book (see Figure 11.5). You see the Properties dialog box.

Learning Computer Concepts   Lesson 11
                                                              E-mail

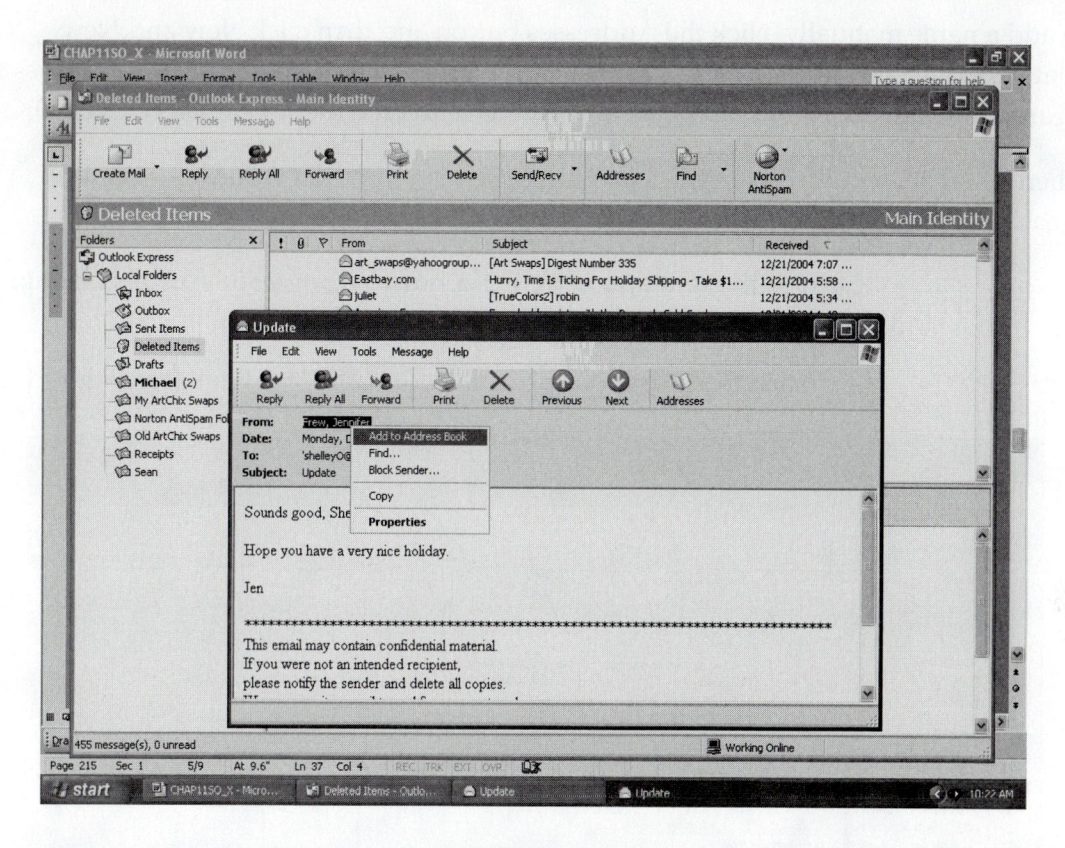

Figure 11.5. You can pick up an address from an existing message and add that contact to your address book.

3 Click the Name tab and make any changes to the name (see Figure 11.6). For instance, some e-mail addresses are a combination of all or partial first and last names. You may want to change to the actual name. Click OK to add the person to the Address Book.

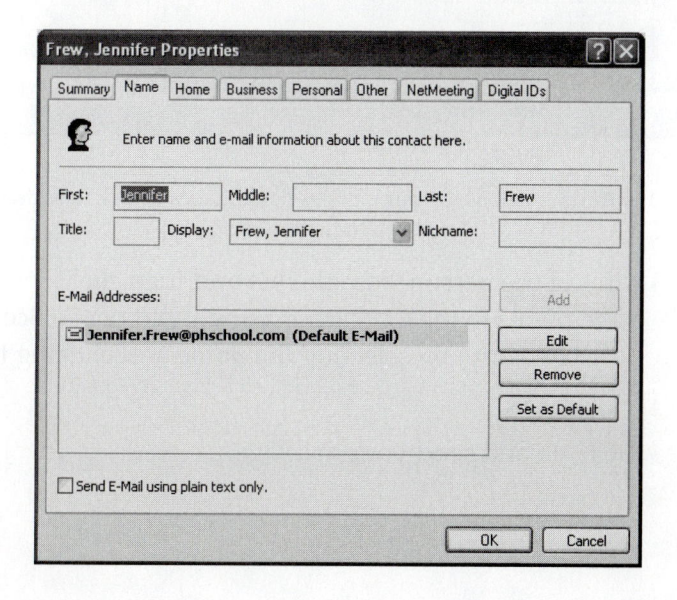

Figure 11.6. You can edit the name used in the Address Book list.

Lesson 11
E-mail

To add a name manually, click the Addresses button and then click New and New Contact. Complete entries in the Name tab of the Properties dialog box (the same ones in Figure 11.6, only the entries are blank and you have to type them manually). Click OK.

When you want to address a message to someone in your address book, you can do so easily.

Follow these steps to select a name from your Address Book:

1. Create a new mail message.
2. Click the To button to display your Address Book (see Figure 11.7).

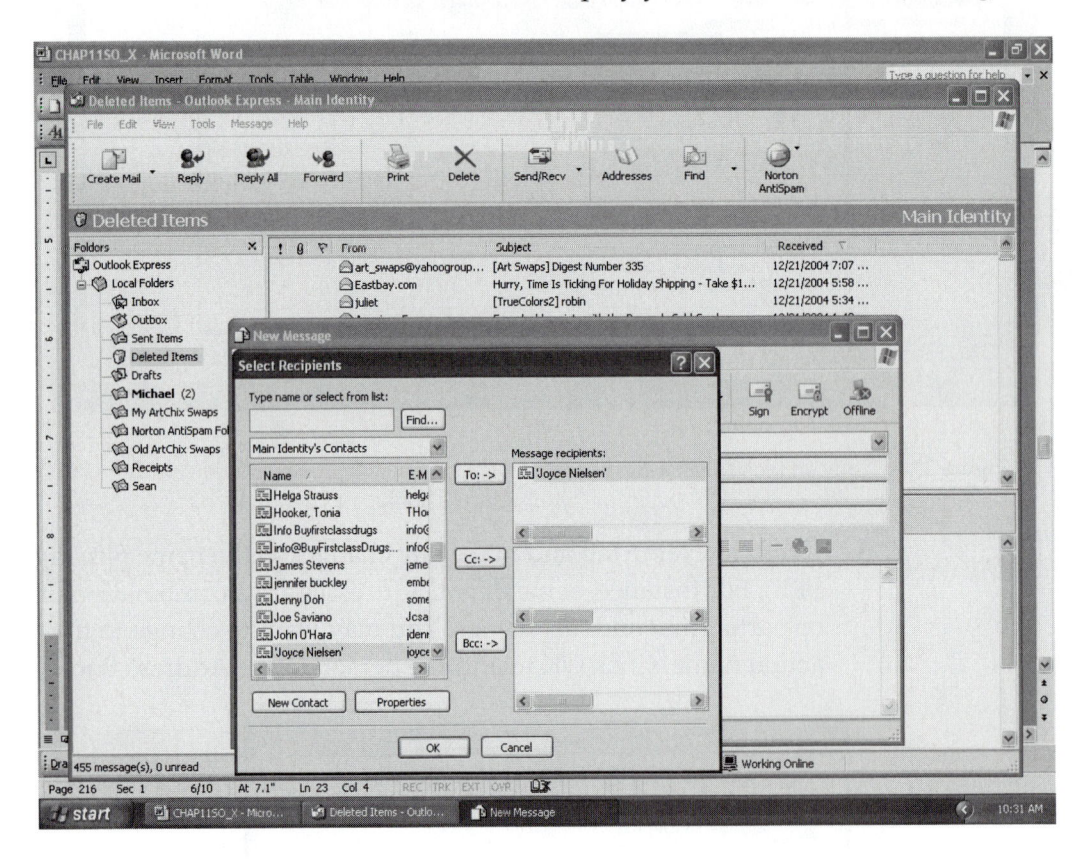

Figure 11.7. Adding names to your address book makes it easy to address new e-mail messages.

3. Select the person from the list and then click To. You can also add recipients to the Cc (carbon copy) field or the Bcc field (blind carbon copy) by selecting the name and clicking these buttons.
4. Click OK.
5. Create and send your message.

Setting Up E-mail Options

To keep your e-mail streamlined, you can set mail configuration options. Doing so makes e-mail more effective and efficient. You can add your signature, send a message if you are out of the office, block messages from certain senders, and set a default mail format. The steps you follow (and the available features) depend on your specific e-mail program. The following gives you a good idea of the features (as well as where to find them in Outlook Express):

- You can set up an automatic signature that includes not only your name, but also your title, contact information, and any other information (such as a company motto or marketing message) you want to include. In Outlook Express, for instance, click Tools and then Options. In the Options dialog box, click the Signature tab and then complete the information to set up your signature (see Figure 11.8).

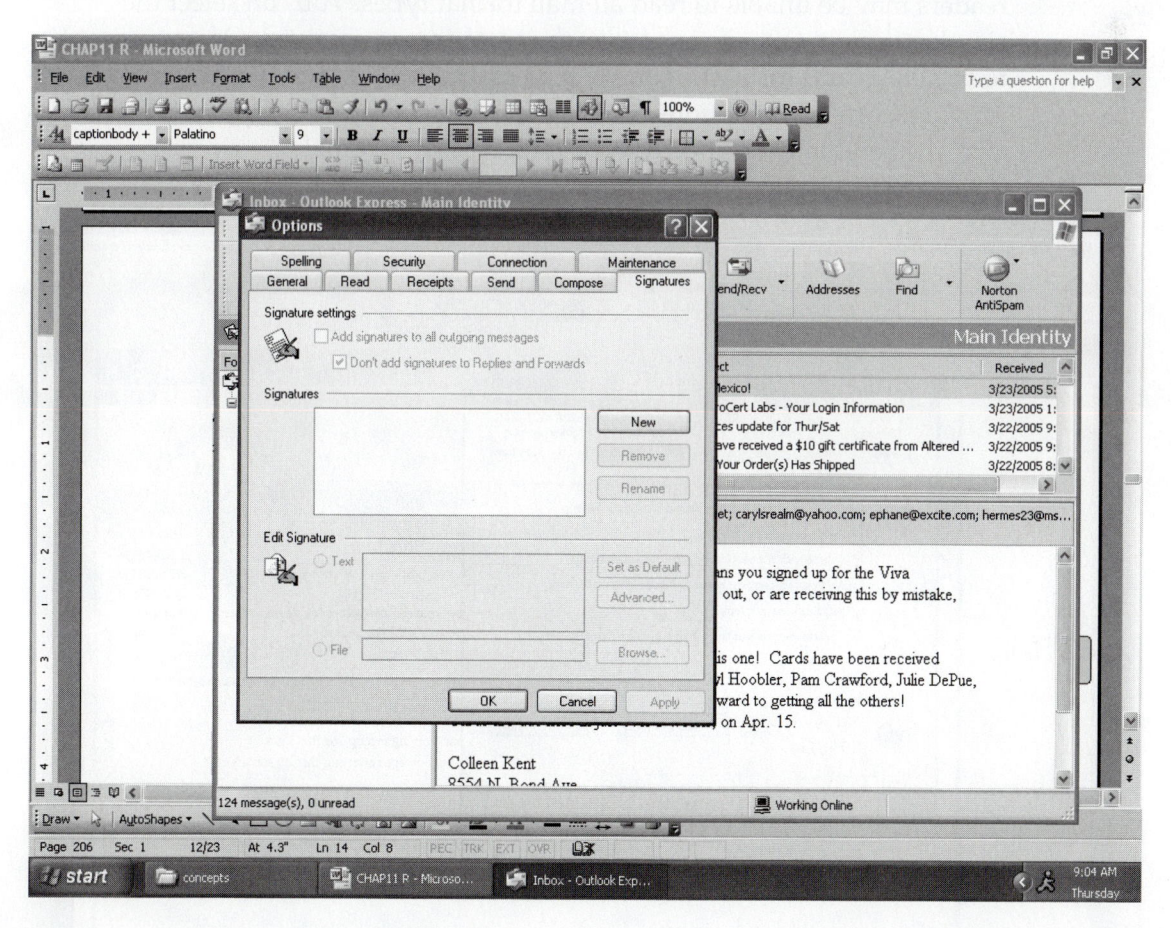

Figure 11.8. You can set up a signature that is automatically added to messages you create.

- If you are going to be out of the office, you can set up a message that is automatically sent in reply to messages you receive. You can let the sender know when you will return, whether you will be checking e-mail, whether you can be reached by telephone, whom to contact for problems, as well as any other pertinent information. To do so, you set up a message rules. Use the Tools, Message Rules, Mail command in Outlook. Because you can create rules for many different situations, and you need to set up specific criteria, check online help for specific information.

- You can also set up message rules to forward messages you receive in one account to another. Again, check online help for instructions on setting up mail rules for forwarding mail.

- If you receive e-mail from an unwanted sender, you can block that sender. When you do so in Outlook Express, the message is automatically deleted. To block a sender in Outlook Express, select a message from that sender and then click Tools, Block Sender. Select whether to delete the message. You can view blocked senders (and remove them from the list) by clicking Tools, Message Rules, Blocked Senders List.

- You can set the default format used for messages. (As mentioned, some mail readers may be unable to read all mail format types. You can select the simplest—plain text—to ensure your messages are received. Or if you want to be able to add formatting to your message, you can select a format that provides formatting options (such as HTML). Click Tools, Options. Then click the Send tab and specify your mail message format.

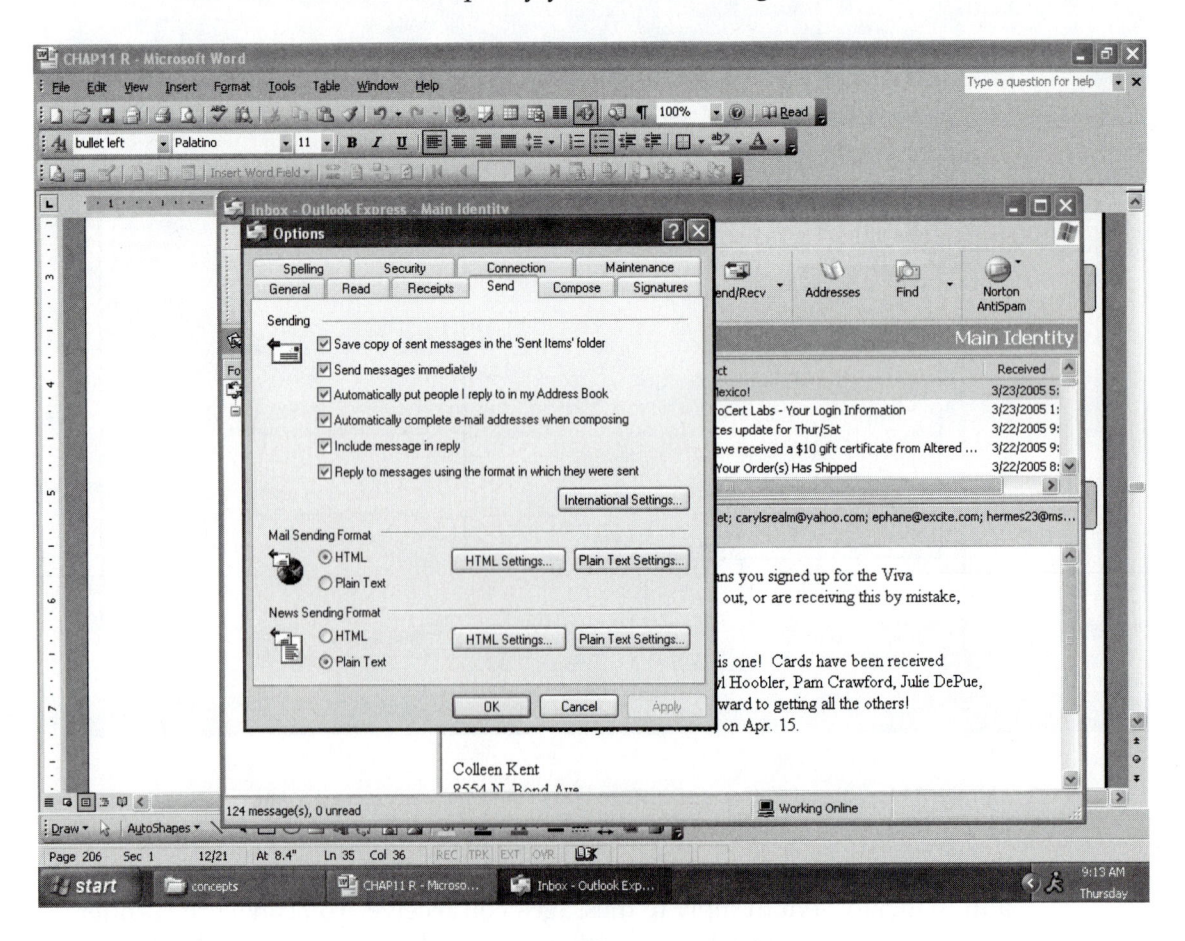

Figure 11.9. You can select the mail message format.

Troubleshooting E-Mail Problems

When you send and receive messages, you can expect some problems, such as handling message problems, receiving unwanted e-mail (called spam), and keeping messages secure. This section focuses on handling these e-mail issues.

DEALING WITH MESSAGE PROBLEMS

When dealing with messages, you may find that messages aren't received, you can't open attachments, the message is full of garbage, you receive a load of forwarded e-mail, and other issues. Most of these problems can be solved by following appropriate e-mail etiquette. For instance, don't forward a joke to everyone on your mailing list. And if you receive jokes or other chain-mail type messages from others, ask them to please not send this type of message. You can lose productivity if your Inbox is constantly full of messages that are unrelated to work or issues you need to handle.

Proper etiquette also ensures that you communicate professionally and with consideration (rather than in hastiness). Just because e-mail messages are quick doesn't mean you should fire off a message without giving proper thought to its content, approach, and any areas open for misinterpretation.

You should also make sure that your messages are in a format your recipient can handle, and that you don't include unnecessary formatting, animation, graphics, and other elements that not only slow the message but also distract from the content of the message.

For other problems, you may need to contact your e-mail provider or the sender. For instance, if you get garbled messages, is it the message format? If so, ask the sender to use a simpler format? Or is it a problem with the mail server? In that case, report the problem to your e-mail provider.

If messages aren't delivered, you most often receive a "failure to deliver" notice. In this case, check that you have entered the address correctly. You may also check to be sure your message format can be handled by the recipient. Also, make sure you don't include attachments that are too large (or that contain viruses).

If you don't receive messages, check with your provider to inquire about any problems. Is the message too large? Is there a problem with the mail message itself? Is there a problem with the server? Also check with the sender to make sure the format works for your e-mail program and that they have typed the correct address. Do the same for attachments. Make sure the sender includes attachments in a file type you can open and work with. Also, if your e-mail provider has limits on the attachment size, make sure the sender strives to keep the attachment size manageable.

HANDLING SPAM

Junk e-mail, as mentioned, is called *spam*. Spam mailers send messages to sell products, offer ways to make fortunes, and other typical junk mail contents. Not all spam is a scam, but you should approach any offers that sound too good to be true with skepticism.

You can cut down on the amount of spam you receive in several ways. First, your e-mail provider may look for and filter spam. You may see this feature advertised as one of the benefits of an Internet and e-mail providers. Check with your particular provider to see what spam filtering features they provide.

Second, your e-mail program may include features for blocking spam. In Outlook Express, for instance, you can block certain senders so that the mail they send is automatically sent to the Deleted Items folder.

Third, you may want to purchase and use an anti-spam program. These programs provide much more control over dealing with spam. You can also find spam blocking features in security suites such as Norton Internet Security. Or, you can purchase or download software designed specifically for dealing with spam, such as Spam Inspector and Spam Catcher.

Fourth, you can also cut down on spam by keeping your online information to a minimum. That is, don't give out your personal information at public sites. Don't fill in survey forms or participate in contests. And if you order something online, be sure to turn off the automatic e-mail solicitations. You should also follow legislation as it relates to spam. Marketers want to keep the right to send advertising; users want to protect privacy. Expect legislation to provide some guidelines on what is acceptable practice in this area.

If you receive spam, you can delete the messages. You should also look for a way to get off the mailing list. Usually you respond to a certain e-mail address and unsubscribe.

KEEPING E-MAIL SECURE

E-mail travels through a lot of different sources before arriving at your recipient's Inbox (or from a sender's to your Inbox). Therefore, e-mail is often not the best method for private, sensitive, or confidential messages. However, you can use encryption software so that only the person with the encryption key can read the message. Your e-mail program may provide encryption features, or you may purchase and use security programs that provide a more advanced encryption procedure.

As mentioned, you should also check e-mail for viruses and other security threats. Use a virus protection program to scan messages and attachments for problems. (You can find out more information about virus protection in Lesson 13.) Also be aware that some e-mail messages report a virus scare as a hoax. Check Internet sources to be sure the threat is real. Norton (www.norton.com) and McAfee (www.mcafee.com) sites are good places to get information about any new viruses.

Following E-mail Etiquette

E-mail has become a unique communication problem, full of advantages and some possible problems. One of the problems is ensuring your message is professional. E-mail is not as formal as a written letter, but that doesn't mean you can ignore certain communication rules. For instance, because an e-mail message can't convey your tone of voice or facial expressions, you need to reread your message, checking the tone. Is it too short? Does it come across snitty? Or disrespectful? Is it condescending? Because of its informal nature, e-mail can come across as sarcasm or be misinterpreted. It's best to err on the side of caution when conveying information in an e-mail message. Be sure to review e-mail carefully before sending.

Because it is an informal communication medium, some people make the mistake of being too flip and this can cause problems. There are some fun ways, though, to keep an e-mail light. You'll also find many shorthand expressions for stating common phrases (for instance, BTW means By the way). You should match the level of formality of your language to the recipient and the purpose. An e-mail to a friend doesn't require the same level of formality as does a letter to a teacher asking for a recommendation or to a boss proposing a new project.

GENERAL E-MAIL GUIDELINES

When creating e-mail, keep the following communication etiquette and guidelines in mind:

- Be concise and to the point. People get a lot of e-mail, and you want your reader to get your point without having to struggle through wordiness or extraneous information.
- Check your spelling and grammar. Most programs include a program for checking spelling, but you should also proofread since a spelling program cannot catch words used incorrectly (yet spelled correctly). Proofread your message and correct any mistakes. Even though e-mail is less formal than written communication, you need to be sure that your writing is professional and error-free.
- Identify the purpose or content of the e-mail in the subject line. Doing so helps the recipient see immediately the main purpose of the e-mail and can then prioritize reading the messages in his or her Inbox.
- Don't type in all uppercase letters. Doing so is the equivalent of screaming, and reading all uppercase letters is difficult.

- Don't go overboard on the formatting, adding color, font changes, pictures, animations, and other visual elements. Doing so can slow the time it takes to download the message. Also, some readers will not be able to view these formatting changes depending on their e-mail program.
- You can choose different formats for the mail message. Some formats (such as HTML support formatting). You want to be sure that your recipient can read your message, so you may want to choose a different format (such as plain text which all mail programs should be able to handle).
- Keep in mind that e-mail isn't the proper format for some messages. For instance, legal documents, documents with sensitive confidential information, or documents that require signatures may be more appropriate sent as written documents. (Although in some cases, you can send the document and ask the recipient to print, sign, and return the printed copy.)
- You may want to include information from another person's message. When you do so, use some method to indicate you are citing another's message. For instance, it's common to use brackets to indicate text from another source. (Note that when you reply to a message, the text is often included and formatted in a way to indicate it is part of the original message.)

EXPRESSING EMOTIONS IN E-MAIL

To help express emotions, someone came up with a way to use special symbols, called "emoticons," to indicate expressions. Never use emotions in business or formal e-mail. The basic smiley face is:

:)

(Turn the page sideways to see the face.) You'll find an entire gallery of faces you can use in your message. This table highlights some popular, some weird, and some creative emoticons for your e-mail messages.

Symbol	Meaning
: (	Sad
;)	Winking
B -)	Person wearing glasses
8 -)	Excited (bug-eyed)
: - D	Laughing
: - O	Oh No!
: - P	Sticking tongue out
: - J	Tongue in cheek
: - #	Censored

Learning Computer Concepts

Lesson 11
E-mail

Symbol	Meaning
:-&	Tongue-tied
:-*	Kiss
:-x	My lips are sealed
<:-)	Dunce
|-(	Late night
:^)	Big nose
:-(=)	Big teeth
:-{#}	Braces
O:-)	Angel
C=:-)	Chef
=|:-)=	Uncle Sam
[:-)	Wearing a Walkman (or Frankenstein)
%-^	Picasso
*****:-)	Marge Simpson

SHORTHAND EXPRESSIONS

Here are just a few of the many, many shorthand expressions used in e-mail. Keep in mind when e-mailing a friend, these shorthand expressions are probably fine. With a boss or a potential employer, though, you should probably stick to actually writing out the message.

Shorthand	Means
LOL	Laughing out loud
ROFLOL	Rolling on floor laughing out loud
BTW	By the way
IMHO	In my humble opinion
FYI	For your information
OTOH	On the other hand
AKA	Also known as
CU	See you

Lesson 11
E-mail

Other Internet Communication Methods

In addition to e-mail, you can send and receive instant messages (covered in more detail later in this lesson). You can also participate in chats (online discussion groups). Chats are like a party or meeting, only you aren't physically present. Instead, you type your comments. You can connect with people across the world.

As another example, you can participate in newsgroup discussions. A newsgroup is a message board. You post comments, and others respond, creating a conversation through these messages. Newsgroups are different than chats; chats are "live," or real-time, communication, newsgroups are not. You can find everything from groups about biochemical engineering to Elvis sightings. Both chats and newsgroups enable you to find other Internet users with your same interests.

Internet phones are also becoming popular. In the past, the sound quality was not good, but it has improved, and you can find telephones and programs that let you use the Internet to make long distance calls.

INSTANT MESSAGES

With instant messaging, you set up a list of your friends and family and when someone from your list is online at the same time you are, you are notified. You can then type and send messages instantly using instant messaging programs. Instant messaging is like a phone conversation, only you type your comments.

One popular instant messaging program is AOL's Instant Messenger (AIM). Windows also includes Windows Messenger. Note that these two are not compatible; you cannot send messages to AOL members via Windows Messenger unless the recipients also have signed up with Windows Messenger. Expect this to change as new instant messaging programs let you instant message anyone, regardless of the program they use.

CHATS

Like instant messages, chats are a form of live conversations, and to participate, you type comments. You can visit general chat rooms or chat rooms devoted to special topics. You can also participate in private chats in private chat rooms.

Be safe: You should never give out personal information in a message or chat. Don't tell your real name, address, or other personal information.

Modulated or monitored chats have a person that monitors and feeds questions, usually to a guest speaker. For instance, you can find celebrity chats where you can submit questions to the celebrity and if your question is chosen by the modulator, the celebrity will respond. Some forums have moderators that determine what can and cannot be posted to the list or group (such as removing messages that are irrelevant to the discussion).

ONLINE CONFERENCING

You can also use the Internet to host online conferences. With video equipment, you can both talk and see other meeting participants in locations around the world. Online conferencing helps cut back on travel and adds convenience for more frequent meetings. To do this type of conferencing, you need the appropriate hardware (cameras and microphones). You also need an Internet connection (naturally) and a conferencing program to handle the details of scheduling the meeting and getting connected (for instance, NetMeeting).

NEWSGROUPS

Still another form of communication is newsgroups. These are not live, but they are online discussion groups. Anyone can post a message to a particular newsgroup, and anyone that reviews that message can respond. You can reply to existing messages or start your own "conversation" with a new message.

The collection of newsgroups is called USENET, and you can find literally thousands of newsgroups devoted to a range of topics. Each newsgroup has a unique name, and you can get a pretty good idea of the content of the newsgroup by its name. The first part of the name is the domain name, and each domain is divided into subcategories. For instance, here's one newsgroup devoted to tennis:

Rec.sports.tennis

Netiquette: When you communicate online, you are expected to follow certain etiquette rules. For instance, it's rude to type in all capital letters because that is similar to screaming. In newsgroups, look for a FAQ (frequently asked questions) list to get an idea of any conventions.

Here is a list of common domain names:

- Rec   Recreation
- Sci   Science
- Alt   Alternative
- News   Relating to newsgroups (not news)
- Soc   Social and society
- Misc   Miscellaneous

To participate in newsgroups, you need a newsreader. Most mail programs also serve as a newsreader. You also need to set up your news server; you get access to a particular set of newsgroups from your Internet provider. To participate, you subscribe to the newsgroups of interest (you don't have to pay a fee). Then you post messages, much like creating and sending e-mail.

Lesson 11
E-mail

Summary

- You'll most likely use e-mail as the most common activity with the Internet. You can send messages to friends, family, co-workers, and so on. E-mail is quick, inexpensive, convenient, and versatile.

- To send e-mail, you need an e-mail provider (usually your Internet provider) and an e-mail address. Your e-mail address consists of your username, an at sign (@), and the name of your network or Internet provider (for example, ladygodiva@msn.com).

- To send and receive mail, you use a mail program. Popular programs include Outlook Express (included with Windows), Outlook (included with Microsoft Office), America Online (AOL), and MSN.

- To receive mail, you connect to your mail server and then your mail is downloaded automatically from that mail server to your computer. You can then open and read any messages you've received.

- You can reply to messages you've received as well as create new messages. To make it easier to address messages, you can create an Address Book with e-mail addresses of those that you frequently communicate with.

- To keep your Inbox uncluttered with old messages, you should delete messages you no longer need. You can also print messages so that you have a hard copy version. As another alternative, you can set up folders to save and organize messages you want to keep.

- In addition to e-mail, you can send and receive instant messages. You can participate in chats, you can post messages to called newsgroups, and you can make phone calls over the Internet.

Learning Computer Concepts — Lesson 11 — E-mail

Q&A

Multiple Choice

1. An e-mail message usually contains the following components:
    a. Sender's address
    b. Recipient's address
    c. Subject line
    d. All of the above

2. In what newsgroup category would you find sports?
    a. sports
    b. rec
    c. sci
    d. comp

3. When joining a newsgroup, look for a document that provides information about the group and common questions; this document is known as a:
    a. Q&A List
    b. FAQ
    c. What's Up
    d. Rules and Regulations

4. If you want to reply to all the recipients of a message, you can do the following:
    a. Type in all the addresses
    b. Click the Reply button
    c. Click the Reply All button
    d. None of the above

Fill in the Blank

1. A(n) _____ is a way of showing emotion in an e-mail. Examples include smiley faces.

2. Deleted messages aren't really deleted but instead are stored in the _____ folder.

3. New messages are stored in your _____.

4. Junk mail is called _____.

Short Essay

1. List some of the advantages of e-mail.

2. List some other ways you can use the Internet to communicate.

LESSON 12: THE INTERNET

Objectives

- Define the Internet
- Get connected
- Browse Web pages
- Work with Web Pages
- Search the Internet
- Internet Communications

What is the Internet?

The Internet is a network of networks, literally thousands and thousands of networks connected to thousands and thousands of computers. By accessing one network on the Internet, you gain access to all of the other networks and all of the information and services provided on that network. The Internet has revolutionized the way we get and provide information. The Internet can provide a wide source of information, all from the convenience of your home. For instance, suppose that you were interested in Leonardo da Vinci. You could go to the library to look for books or articles on him. Or you can go online and take a look at some of da Vinci's most famous artwork, find books relating to your topic, get biographical information, research related topics, such as the Renaissance period, find articles about current showings or studies of da Vinci's work, and more.

As another example, maybe you are thinking of purchasing a car. Before the Internet, you had limited access to information about cars, mostly provided in publications like *Consumer Reports* and by the dealer or salesperson. Now you can look up a blue book value for a car, get information about different loan rates, check the safety rating for a vehicle, research the list and invoice prices, review a list of options for particular car models, and perhaps even find a car online.

The Internet is a grand resource that is exploding. More and more people are getting connected each day. With the Internet, you literally have the world at your fingertips.

HISTORY OF THE INTERNET

Here's a brief history of the Internet:

1968	Defense Department contracts with a computer design company to build ARPAnet, a network to link research computers
1985(86)	National Science Foundation formed the NSFNET, linking five supercomputer centers
1985	America Online founded

1989(90)	Tim Berners-Lee, a researcher at CERN, developed HyperText Markup Language (HTML), the language used to create the World Wide Web
1990	World is the first commercial provider of Internet dial-up access
1991	Gopher (menu-driven search tool for Internet) developed
1993	First Web browser (Mosaic) developed
1993	50 World Wide Web servers
1993	White House has a Web page and e-mail address
1994	Netscape launched
1994	Yahoo! was launched as an Internet directory
1995	AT&T introduces WorldNet, providing Internet access to its AT&T customers
1998	30 million households purchase goods over the Internet
2000	150 million to 200 million people worldwide use the Internet
2001	A survey estimated the size of the Internet at 2.5 billion documents and growing by a rate of 7.5 million documents per day
2004	Estimates put the number of people connected to the Internet (and this is just a guess) at 605+ million people

Check latest statistics: For the latest information about the Internet's demographics, visit Nua Internet Surveys (www.nua.org or http://www.clickz.com/stats/).

WHAT IS THE WORLD WIDE WEB

When you hear the Internet discussed, you may also hear the term "World Wide Web." The Internet encompasses all the various types of information and activities you can do. The World Wide Web isn't a physical part of the Internet, but more the way the information is presented. On the Web, information is presented in a graphical hypermedia format. What's that mean? It means a Web site will contain text, pictures, video clips, sounds, animation, and other multimedia elements.

A Web site also includes links (also called hyperlinks). These links are connections to other sites, to other pages at the current site, or to other places in the current document. With links you can explore related information by simply clicking the link. Figure 12.1 shows MSN's home page. You can click any of the links in the left column to view that information. For instance, click Travel to view travel articles as well as links to other travel-related information.

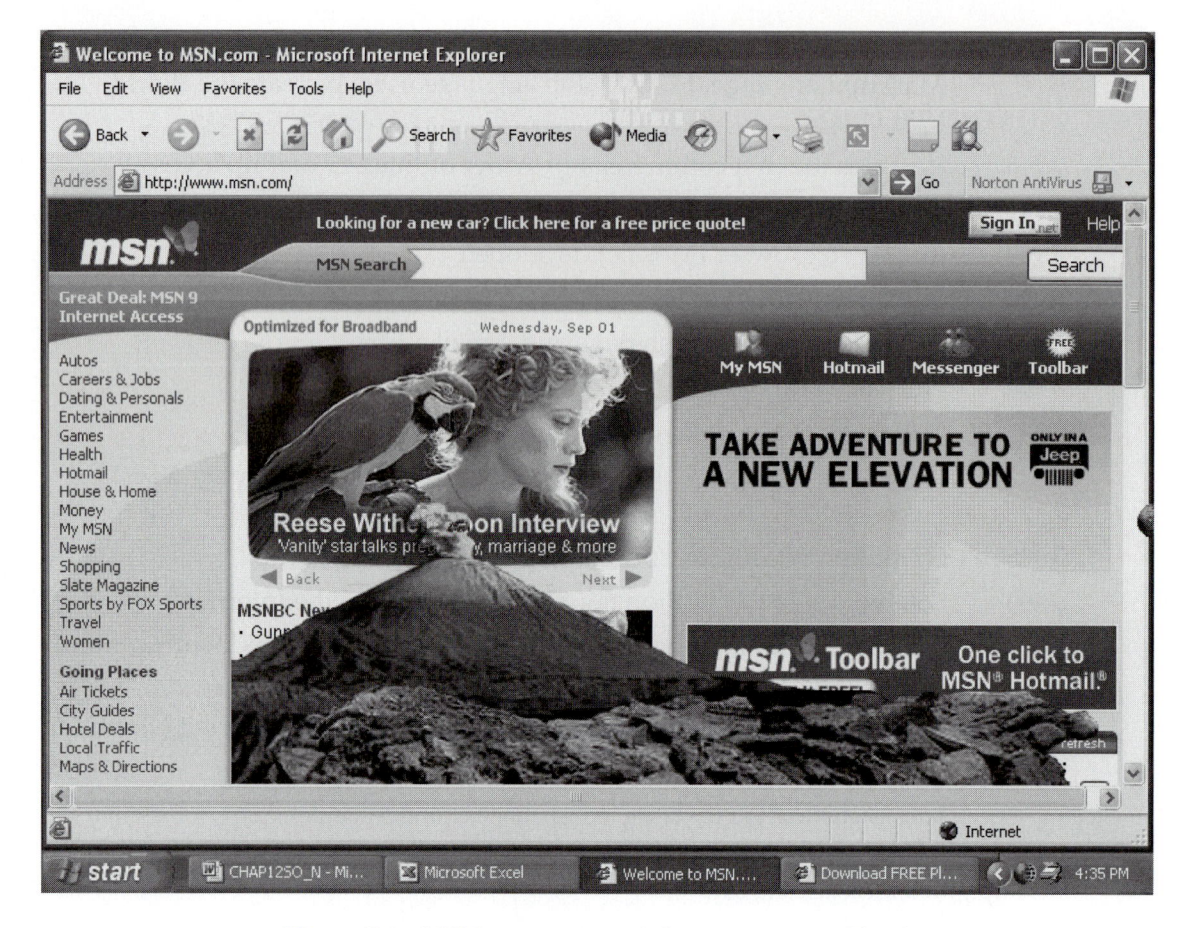

Lesson 12   **Learning Computer Concepts**
The Internet

Figure 12.1. A Web page presents information in a graphical format and includes links to other sites.

WHAT YOU CAN DO ON THE INTERNET

The reason the Internet is so popular is that you can do so much, including sending electronic messages (called *e-mail*), browsing for content, and connecting with other users either live (via a chat) or by posting messages on an electronic message board (called newsgroups). These features were covered in Lesson 11.

In addition to the various ways to connect with others, the Internet is also a rich resource for all kinds of information. Not only can you find information on almost any topic, written by authorities from all over the world, but the information is updated and you can find the most current data that is available. You can read the latest news, listen to new CDs, or purchase anything from an autographed football from Brett Favre to textbooks. You can research papers, search for a job, get advice for computer problems, find apartments for rent, look up current stock quotes, or listen to a live radio broadcast. The possibilities are endless. You'll read more about some of the things you can do on the Internet later in this lesson.

Check your source: A word to the wise: it is important to check your sources. Not everything you read on the Internet is correct or accurate.

The Internet is an excellent publishing tool. You have the ability to share your ideas, work, and opinions with the world. Lesson 4 covered some of the various programs for creating and managing Web pages.

HOW THE INTERNET HAS CHANGED OUR LIVES

The Internet has affected many aspects of our lives including some of the things mentioned in the preceding sections (e-mail, researching information on the Internet, and so on). It's not just individual users that are affected, but companies, the government, news organizations, and more that are affected by the ways the Internet can help find and share information. Consider just a few of the following scenarios:

- The Internet is a great source for information on a wide range of topics, sometimes topics that the average person might have trouble finding. Because the Internet can collect, organize, and evaluate information, it's a great tool for promoting learning.
- The Internet is used in many "behind-the-scenes" ways such as conducting medical research, tracking and evaluating weather trends, and more. It's an invaluable source of information that can help journalists, scientists, doctors, lawyers, and other professionals remain up-to-date on current news, case studies, research, and new techniques.
- Businesses greatly benefit from the Internet, not only in selling and promoting their products or services, but also in tracking customer information and creating customized mailing lists so that customers get information about their specific hobbies or interests.
- The government is another source of information that is now made more accessible to people. For instance, you can look up job outlooks, salary information, and more at the Bureau of Labor and Statistics (www.bls.gov). You'll find many other government sites with helpful information. A good site for finding what sites are available is www.fedworld.gov.
- The Internet as well as many computer programs are including features that make it easier for the disabled or disadvantaged to use computers. Windows, for instance, includes a Narrator feature that reads dialog box messages. You can also magnify parts of the screen if your eyesight is bad. Other features help make typing or moving the mouse easier. Look for Accessibility Options in the Control Panel. You can also use voice recognition software to give commands (open file) and enter text. This type of input device was covered in Lesson 3.

Getting Connected

To do any of the Internet activities described here (send mail, browse the Web), you need to get connected. Getting connected requires these things:

- A modem or network connection
- An Internet provider
- Programs for reading mail and browsing the Web

Lesson 12   **Learning Computer Concepts**
The Internet

MODEMS: CONNECTING TO THE INTERNET

Many users connect to the Internet with a special hardware device called a modem. Modem stands for MOdulator-DEModulator and is a device used for connecting to other computers via the phone lines (see Figure 12.2). Phone lines transmit data using an analog signal; computers transmit and store digital data. Therefore, to use the phone lines to transmit data, you need a device to translate the digital data (from the PC) to an analog format (which the phone lines can handle and transmit) and then back to digital format (on the receiving PC). This device is the modem.

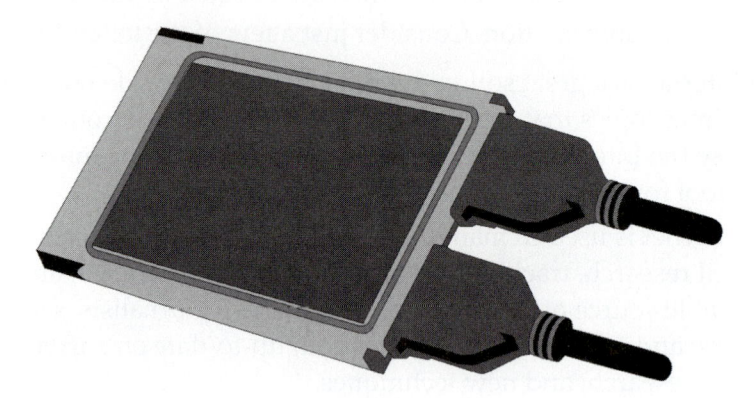

Figure 12.2. You can use a modem to connect to the Internet.

Today most computers come with a modem. Also, you may have a modem that can also function as a fax machine. Connected to the phone line, you can fax documents from your computer.

Modems differ basically in speed, and the speed is measured in how much data is transmitted per second (bits per second, or bps). This measurement is often confused with baud, but baud rate is not really the correct terminology.

Early modems could transmit data at around 300 bps. As modems became more popular, speed increased to 1200, 2400, 9600, 14,400 (sometimes called 14.4K), 28,800 (or 28.8K), and 33,600 (33.6K). The newest modems can transmit 56,000 bps or 56K, which is effectively as fast as this technology will get with existing phone technology.

> **Speed is limited:** You can only go as fast as the device to which you are connecting, and the speed is limited because of phone technology.

To get around the phone-line bottleneck, new modem types have been developed. You can access the Internet via your cable company. To do so, you can use a cable modem. You may also be able to get connected via a special type of phone line called a DSL line. Originally these services were not available everywhere and were pricey. Now this type of access (often called broadband access) is common. Some providers also enable you to connect wirelessly through a satellite. You can check your local cable or phone company to see what type of Internet service they provide, as well as the cost.

The need for speed: You want the fastest Internet connection so that you can display pages and move from link to link without a lot of waiting. Speed for broadband access is measured in kilobytes per second (KBps) and megabytes per second (MBps). The amount of data that can be transmitted is often referred to as bandwidth. Faster connections are referred to as broad bandwidth or high bandwidth.

WEB: To see what DSL services are available, visit the site www.dsl.com.

PICKING A PROVIDER

In addition to a connection, you need a company that provides access to the Internet. This company is called the Internet Service Provider, or ISP. Internet providers are your on-ramp to the Internet; they provide the link to the various networks of the Internet. Your ISP also handles your mail and provides a list of newsgroups to which you may want to join. For these services, you pay a subscription fee.

Many consumers get access to the Internet through an online provider, such as America Online. In addition to providing a link to the Internet, America Online offers its own content and features. With America Online, you can get instant messages, participate in chats, and review content, all within the America Online community. Microsoft Network (MSN) is similar to AOL; you've probably seen TV advertisements about this online service.

While America Online does provide Internet access, it is not a dedicated Internet provider. You can find companies that are just that: Internet providers. You can find national providers, such as EarthLink. You can also find local providers in your area. Also, as mentioned, your cable and phone company probably now offer Internet service. You have lots of options, so be sure to shop around if you are signing up for a new service.

When choosing an Internet Service Provider, it's important to check out these factors:

- What are the fees? Is it a flat fee? Is there a startup fee? Do you have a free trial period? Any extra charges?
- What types of connections do they support? If you have a special connection (say a DSL), your provider must support that connection.
- Is the connection call local? You want a local or toll-free call. If the call isn't local, check out any fees for the actual phone call.
- What help support is provided? Does the provider have phone support? Online support? Does the provider charge for support?
- Do they support multiple e-mail addresses? If you share a computer with a family, for instance, it's best if each person has his or her own unique address. Some sites provide extra e-mail addresses for free; for others you may have to pay a small fee.
- What other services are provided? Some provide Web hosting services so that you can publish your Web pages through the provider. Some even give you free publishing for a page within a certain size (not physical size, but size of the files).

CHOOSING A BROWSER

In addition to the connection and the provider, you need the software to access and display Web pages. The software for displaying Web pages is called a browser, and the most popular browser is now Internet Explorer, which is included as part of Windows.

> Originally Netscape had the biggest share of the Internet market. Enter Microsoft, which by including Internet Explorer as part of Windows, stole most of the market. That was part of the reason for all the Justice investigation into Microsoft in 2000.

Figure 12.3 shows the Internet Explorer program.

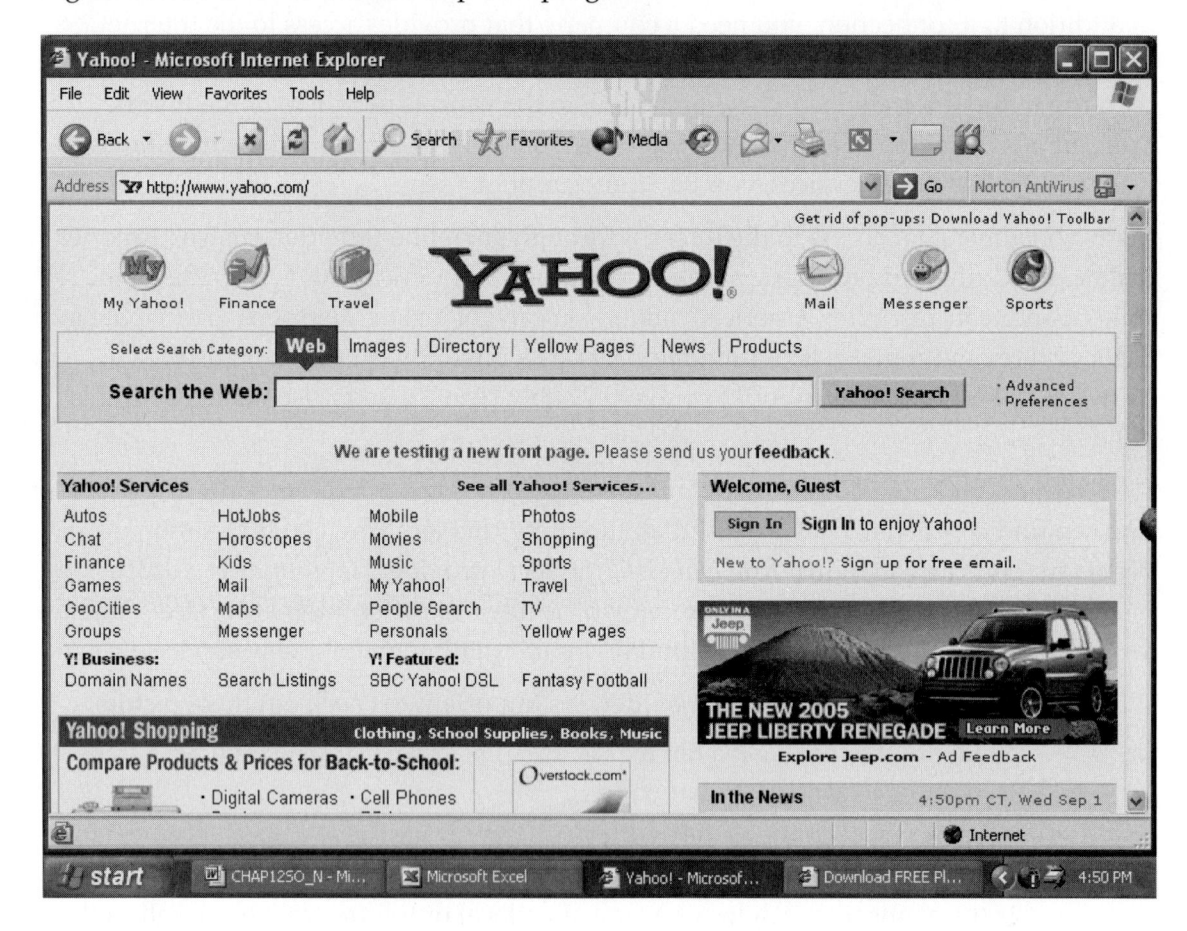

Figure 12.3. Internet Explorer is the most popular Web browser.

In addition to a browser, you need a program for reading mail. If you participate in newsgroups, you need a newsreader. Most browsers now include all of these components in one package. Windows users can send and receive e-mail and participate in newsgroups using Outlook Express (another program included with Windows). You can also find and use other e-mail programs. For instance, a more full-featured version of Outlook Express (called Outlook) is included with Microsoft Office. You can also find other popular mail programs, including Eudora.

SETTING UP YOUR COMPUTER

Once you have all the things you need to get connected, you are ready to get setup. This involves installing any software that is needed and setting up dial-up access to the Internet. You need only do this once, and it does involve entering technical information, such as your username, password, mail protocol, phone number to dial, and other information. Your Internet provider should supply this information to you. You can also use the Internet Connection Wizard (in Windows) to get connected; this wizard leads you step-by-step through the process.

Once everything is set up, you log on. The procedure for logging on will vary depending on your setup, but it usually involves double-clicking the connection icon and entering your username and password. Once connected, you see your browser and your home page (the first page that is displayed each time you log on).

> **Change your home page:** Most browsers enable you to select the home page you want to use. In Internet Explorer, for instance, you can select your home page by selecting Tools, Internet Options. On the General tab of the Internet Options dialog box, type the address of the home page you want to use. Then click OK.

Your home page is your starting point, and most home pages include lots of helpful links. You may even be able to customize the home page. For instance, if you use Yahoo! for your home page, you can set it up to display weather in your area, stock quotes, your horoscope, news stories of interest to you, and so on.

If you have a cable, DSL, or satellite connection, you are always online and don't need to log on and off. Because of this 24/7 connection, you do need to take some security precautions to prevent others from accessing your computer. Lesson 13 covers this topic as well as other security and privacy issues relating to the Internet, e-mail, and computers.

Browsing Web Pages

There's no way you can summarize all the information you can find on the Internet. There are huge telephone-like books that list sites and books that cover specific features, such as finding a job or trading stocks online. If there's something you are looking for, you can most likely find it. All you need is a few basic skills for navigating, and this section introduces those skills.

UNDERSTANDING A WEB PAGE

A Web page consists of text, graphics, links, and other multimedia elements. What you see when you visit a particular site varies from site to site. Some may include video clips or sounds. You may find animations. Some may include cool graphics; others may be mostly text. Many sites include advertisements. Almost all sites include links to other sites. These links usually appear in a different color and are underlined. You can use these links to navigate from site to site, as covered in the next section.

Lesson 12
The Internet

UNDERSTANDING A WEB ADDRESS

A Web site is a collection of pages, and each Web site has a unique address called a URL, or uniform resource locator. Here's the address, for instance, of the White House:

www.whitehouse.gov

Most addresses follow this format. They start with www, which is an indication that the page is a Web page (as opposed to other site types). You might see http:// before the www, but this part of the address is usually assumed. HTTP stands for HyperText Transfer Protocol and is the language, or protocol, used for displaying Web pages.

> **FTP sites:** Another common site you may find are FTP sites. FTP stands for File Transfer Protocol; these sites are used to download information. They usually follow a hierarchical structure, much like documents stored in folders on your hard drive.

The next part of the address is the name of the site. Usually this accurately reflects the content. What's the page for the NBA? www.nba.com. What's the site for CNN? www.cnn.com. Even if you don't know a page name, you can usually take a guess.

The final part of the address indicates the type of network. Here's a quick list of the most common extensions and their meaning:

- com   Commercial
- edu   Education
- gov   Government
- mil   Military
- net   Networking (like your service provider)
- org   Private (usually not-for-profit organizations)

Foreign sites also often include a country code as part of the address. Here's a list of common country codes:

- us   United States
- uk   United Kingdom
- fr   France
- au   Australia
- ca   Canada
- ie   Ireland

Each site has a unique name as does each page. Sometimes an address includes the address name and a page name, as in this example:

www.pearsoned.com/us-school/index.htm

This address is similar to a path to a particular document. Notice that the forward slash is used to separate the site name from the path name. Also, the page (document) name may include an extension. HTM (or HTML) is the most common format for Web pages.

> **Secure sites:** For sites with secure information, you don't need to worry about security. If, though, you are sending information over the Internet (purchasing a product, for example), you can be sure you are doing so from a secure site. Most browsers include an icon that indicates when the site is secure. For instance, Internet Explorer uses a closed lock in its status bar. Also, the path name to a secure site is different; rather than http:// a secure site uses the designation https://. You learn more about security in Lesson 13.

UNDERSTANDING OTHER WEB TERMS

In addition to terms like URL, you'll find other specialized language that deals with specific Internet issues. Here are the most common terms:

- *Plug-in* is a program that adds some extra capability to your browser. For instance, media plug-ins enable you to display videos or play games.

- A *cookie* is a software file that is stored on your computer by a site you have visited. The file keeps track of password information (and other preferences). There's a lot of debate about cookies and whether they are a privacy intrusion. In many cases, they are simply helpful. For instance, if you shop at Amazon, they can keep track of the types of books you like and make recommendations of other titles you may like. They can also store your address information so that you don't have to enter it each time. There are some unscrupulous marketing companies that use the tracking information from cookies to send unwanted advertising, for instance. You can control how cookies are handled in your browser. Check the specific instructions for the browser you use; search for cookies in the online help and then follow the suggestions.

- A *cache* is a temporary storage area. The cache, for instance, can keep track of what sites you have visited and provide fast access to these frequently visited sites. You can control the size of the cache (which determines how much information it can store). Check with the Internet browser you use about how your cache settings work and how to make any adjustments.

- *Encryption* is a method to transmit sensitive information securely over the Internet. For instance, when you use the Internet to shop and send your credit card information, that information is encrypted so that it is secure.

BROWSING USING LINKS

As mentioned, most Web pages include links or hyperlinks, and these links often appear in a different color or are underlined. Sometimes a graphic is also a link. A collection of links, each assigned to particular part of a picture, is called an image map.

> **Check pointer:** You can tell when you are pointing to a link because the pointer should change shape (most often to a hand). Also, the status bar may display the address of that link.

To use a link, you click it. Doing so displays that information. When you click a link, you may be taken to another part of the current Web page, to another set of pages at that site, or to another site entirely. You can click any of the links on this page to go to another site or page. Going from page to page using links is called navigating or browsing or surfing the Web (or Net).

BROWSING USING TOOLBAR BUTTONS

When you are browsing using links, you aren't really sure what you'll see when you click the link. You'll see a page, but whether that page is what you are looking for or contains information you seek is hard to tell until you actually see the page.

To help you navigate, most programs include toolbar buttons to help you move among the pages and sites you have visited. For instance, Internet Explorer includes these toolbar buttons for navigating:

Button	Name	Description
Back	Back	Click this button to go back to the last page viewed. You can click this button more than once to go back several pages.
	Forward	If you've gone back, you can then go forward by clicking this button. If the button is grayed out, you have not gone back, so you can't go forward.
	Stop	If a page is taking too long to display, click this button to stop the display.
	Refresh	To update the information on the page, click this button. Some sites continually update the information. As an example, if you are looking at stock quotes, the prices will continually be updated. You can refresh the page to get the most recent information.
	Home	To return to your home page, click this button.

GOING TO AN ADDRESS

In addition to browsing, you can go directly to a site. This is the fastest method to go to a site of interest, but you must know the site name. You can find addresses advertised in print and TV ads. You'll also find sites in books, such as this one.

Follow these steps to type a Web site address:

1. Click in the address bar.
2. Type the site address.
3. Press Enter. You should see the opening page for that site.

Guess: If you aren't sure what the address is, guess. Most sites try to stick to an easily recognizable name. For instance, the address for MTV is www.mtv.com. If you guess wrong, nothing bad will happen. You may get an error message or you may see a page you didn't want.

SETTING UP A FAVORITES LIST

If you find sites that you return to often, rather than type the Web address each time, you can set up a favorites list. You can then click the site from the Favorites menu or from the Favorites bar in Internet Explorer.

At first, you might have just one long list of favorite sites, but navigating through these lists can be time-consuming. So you may decide to set up folders and store similar sites together. For instance, if more than one person uses your computer, each person may have a Favorites folder with his or her favorite sites listed. As another example, you may set up folders by category (art, shopping, music, news, and so on). The following steps explain how to add a site to a favorites list and how to go to a site listed in your favorites list.

Follow these steps to add a site to the Favorites list:

1   Go to the page you want to add to your favorites list.

2   Click Favorites in the menu bar and then click Add to Favorites.

3   The default name is the site name; you can leave this as is or type a different name (see Figure 12.4).

4   To add the site to the list, do any of the following:

   To add the site to the list (not within a folder), click OK.

   To add the site to one of the listed folders, select it and then click OK. (If the folders aren't listed, click Create in to display the available folders.)

   To add the site to a new folder, click New Folder, type a folder name, and press Enter. Then select this folder for the site and click OK.

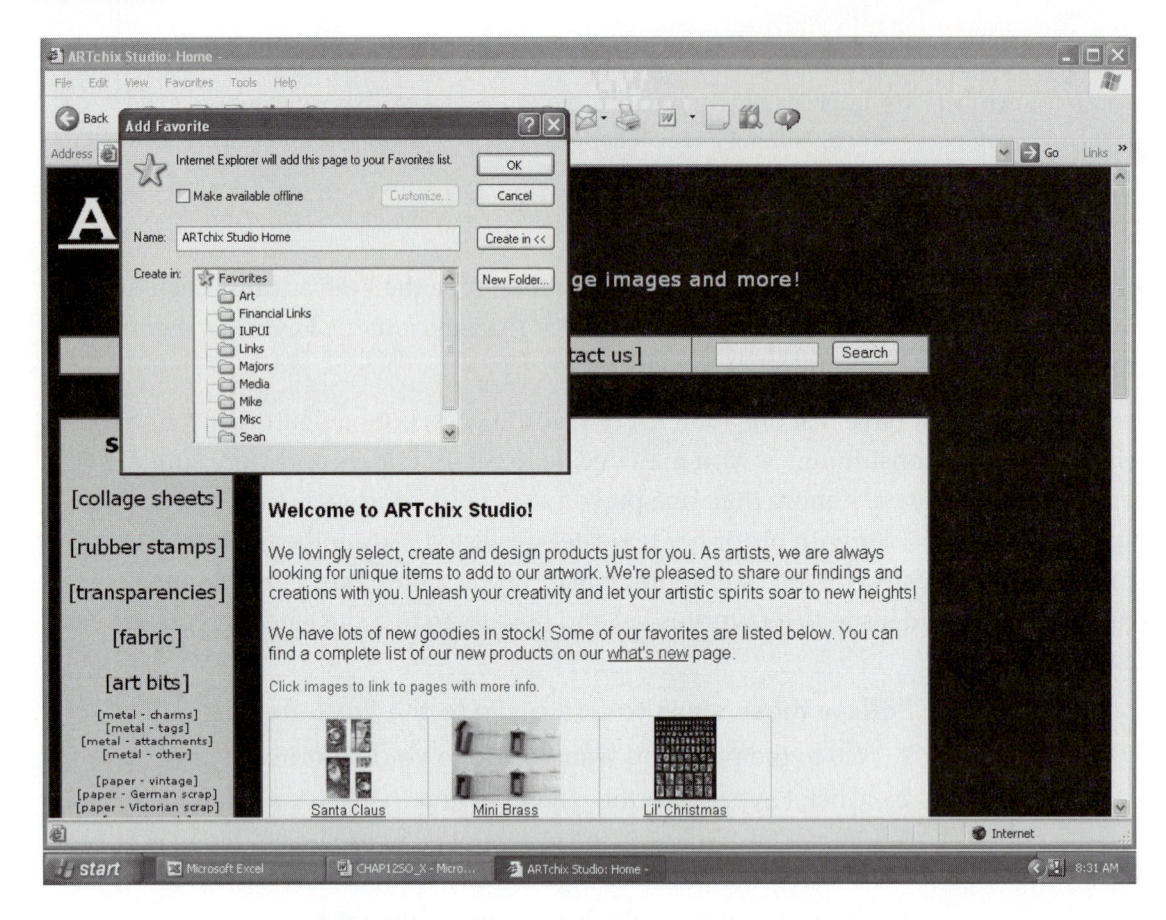

Lesson 12   **Learning Computer Concepts**
The Internet

Figure 12.4. You can add sites to your Favorites list.

Follow these steps to go to a Favorites List:

1. Click Favorites in the menu bar and then (if necessary) click the folder name.
2. Click the site. Internet Explorer displays the selected site.

Organize list: You can organize the list, adding new folders, moving sites to different folders, deleting sites that you no longer want on your favorites list. To do so, use the Favorites, Organize Favorites command.

Follow these steps to move Favorites between folders:

1. Click Favorites in the menu bar and then click Organize Favorites.
2. Select the Favorite to move.
3. Click Move to Folder.
4. In the Browse for Folder dialog box, select where you wish to move the Favorite and then click OK.

VIEWING YOUR HISTORY LIST

Often times in your browsing, you'll find a site that you like, but fail to note its address. In that case, you can view a history list of all the sites you have visited in the past several weeks. You can then use this list to go back to any of these sites.

Learning Computer Concepts
Lesson 12
The Internet

To view the history list, click the History button in the toolbar. You then see the History pane on the left side of the screen. You can expand the list to view the specific sites and pages at a site that you or someone else has visited (see Figure 12.5).

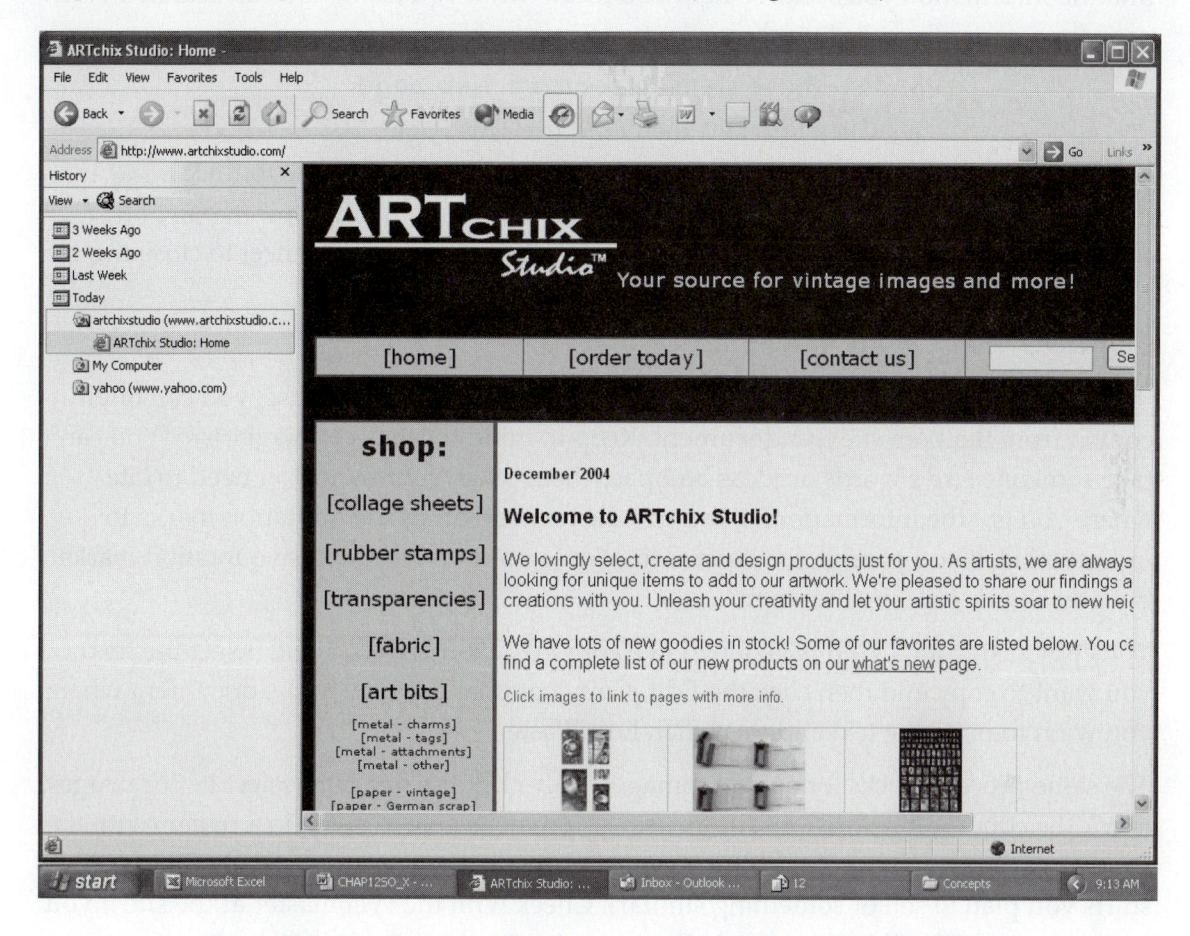

Figure 12.5. You can view a list of sites and pages you have recently visited.

Check browsing: If you have children, checking the history list is a good way to see what sites and pages they have been viewing. Note, though, that you can clear the history list. To do so, click Tools, Internet Options and then click the Clear History button.

Working with Web Pages

You have lots of option with the information you find on a Web page: you can print it so that you can read it later away from the computer, you can save the Web page, you can copy text or an image, you can search for a word or phrase on a page, and you can download files from a site. This section discusses these common Web page tasks.

PRINTING A PAGE

If you are working on a report and find an article of interest, you may want to print a hard copy so that you can read it away from the computer. You print a Web page just like printing any document: click File and then click Print.

Lesson 12
The Internet

SEARCHING FOR TEXT

For pages that contain lots of information, it may be difficult to scan through the text to find the information you seek. To help you locate what you need, you can search a Web page for a particular word or phrase.

> **Follow these steps to search a Web page:**
> 1. Click Edit and then Find (on This Page).
> 2. In the Find dialog box, type the word or phrase to find.
> 3. Click Find Next. Continue to do so until you find the section of the Web page you want. You can then click Cancel to close the Find dialog box.

COPYING TEXT OR AN IMAGE

If you find information you want to quote or an image you want to use, you can often copy it from the Web site to a document. Keep in mind the rules of plagiarism. You can't take someone else's words or ideas and pass them off as your own; you need to cite where you got the information. If you use the text verbatim, use quotation marks to indicate this. If you paraphrase the information, you don't need to use quotation marks, but you should still cite the source.

You copy text from a Web page much like copying text in a document. Select the text you want to copy and then click the Edit, Copy command. Move to the document where you want to paste the text and then click Edit, Paste.

The same process works for copying images, only click the image to select it. For images, check the copyright restrictions for its use. You may be able to use it in a paper (with the source cited), but you can't take image or artwork and then use them freely (like on t-shirts you plan to sell or something similar). Check with the Webmaster at the site if you have any questions about the restrictions on using images.

SAVING A WEB PAGE

You can also save a Web page so that you can view it offline. Depending on the setup of the page (for instance, if it uses frames), the page might not look exactly as it did on-screen. You can save it to a folder on your disk and then display it using your browser or any other program that can display Web pages (for instance Microsoft Word).

> **Follow these steps to search a Web page:**
> 1. Display the page you want to save.
> 2. Click File and then Save As.
> 3. In the Save Web Page dialog box, type a file name for the page.
> 4. Click Cancel.

DOWNLOADING A FILE

Some sites include files that you can download. Music, for instance, is probably the most popular download. You can also download program patches (that fix bugs or security problems in a program), new versions of a program, clip art, and more. The procedures for downloading vary, but the site should provide exact instructions on how to download the file. And if you download a program, you will also need to install it. Again, the site should provide a file with instructions on installing the program.

Searching the Internet

If you know a site name, you can go to that site. You may also find sites of interest as you browse, but if you are looking for a particular site or if you want to see what sites are available for a certain topic, you can search.

To search the Internet, you use a search tool. These tools vary in how they search; you can use search engines, which are large databases, or search indexes. That distinction isn't really that important, and the distinction is somewhat blurred. Some sites, for instance, look for key words and index these as the basis for finding matches. Some sites index hidden tags that identify the site contents (in the Web programming language). Often the search index is automated and done without anyone checking the accuracy of the matches. Other search sites have people review the Web sites and verify how they are indexed. Most sites use a combination of methods to ensure an appropriate match. As a searcher, you should try different search tools as the results from each search site can vary.

BASICS OF SEARCHING

Follow these basic steps to search:

1. Go to the search page. Some start pages include a search feature. Or you can go to any of the popular search sites covered later in this section.
2. Type the word or phrase you want to find.
3. Click the search button. The name of this button will vary.
4. View the results. The results will be a list of links to sites that match your entry. You can click any of these links to go to that site. Some search tools display information to help you decide which link is the closest match. They may have some percentage indicator. You may also see a short description. Some search tools provide reviews of sites. Figure 12.6 shows the results of searching for "U.S. Open Tennis" using the most-popular search tool, Google.

Lesson 12
The Internet

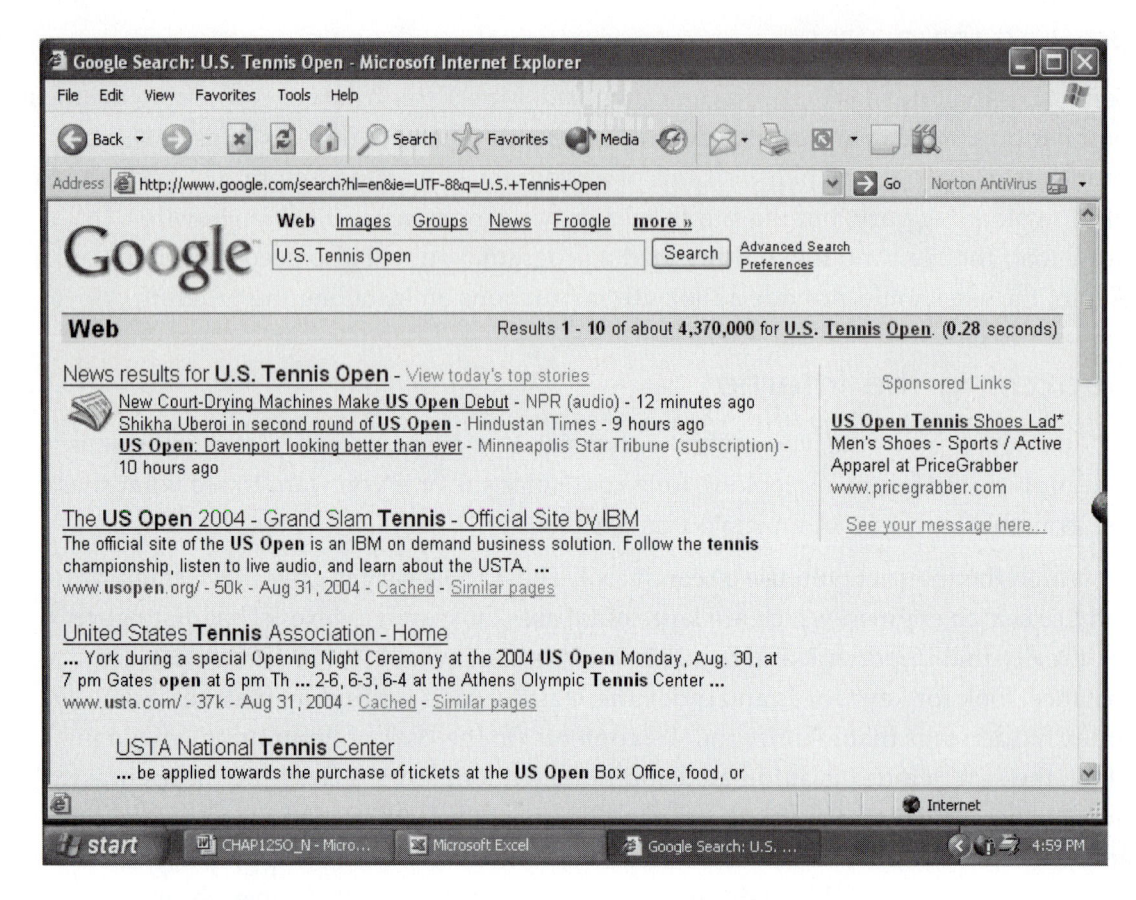

Figure 12.6. You can search for topics using any of the Internet's search tools.

POPULAR SEARCH TOOLS

The Internet is full of search tools, and new ones are offered all the time. Here's a list of some of the most-popular sites and their addresses:

- Google   www.google.com
- Yahoo!   www.yahoo.com
- AltaVista   www.altavista.com
- Teoma   www.teoma.com
- AlltheWeb   www.alltheweb.com
- HotBot   www.hotbot.com

SEARCH TIPS

Finding what you want can be like finding the proverbial needle in the haystack. For the most effective searching, consider these tips:

- If you get too many matches, try narrowing the search by using different words. Also, be sure to pick a unique word or phrase. If you search for too broad of a topic, you'll have too many matches to wade through. For instance, if you search for music, you'll never find what you are looking for. If you search for Celtic music, though, your odds of locating what you desire are increased.

- Try search options. Most tools provide options for refining the search. You may be able to select what parts of the Internet are searched. You can limit searches to match all words entered. Look for a link for search options or something similarly named.

- Use Boolean operators. You can create searches using Boolean operators, such as AND and NOT. As an example, if you search for "Latin" AND "Music" the search will find sites that include both Latin and music (not one or the other). You can find more information about search options by clicking the advanced search link for that particular search tool.

- Use search channels. Some search sites include channels or categories, which you can browse. Looking for travel information? Visit the travel channel.

- Try other search tools. If you don't find what you like with one tool, try another one. The results will vary. You'll also find that you will prefer one site to another.

- Look for people and places. Most tools also include features for finding physical addresses and e-mail addresses. You can also get directions and maps using the search tools and look up businesses in Yellow Page-like resources.

- Check the credentials of the site. Just because information appears on a Web site does not mean the information is accurate. Look for a link called About Us or Company Mission or something similar. Read up on the background of the company to make sure they are providing legitimate and reliable information.

Handling Browser Problems

When you browse the Internet, you may encounter occasional problems that relate to the accessibility of a page, the speed of the display of a page, unwanted advertisements, and restricted access. Generally, you can expect the following problems (and workarounds):

- When you go to a page, you may see an error message (a common error message is a 404 or page not found). This may mean that the site has changed (or been discontinued). Try searching for the site to see if there's a new address. It may also mean that you typed the address incorrectly; double-check your address entry. You may also get a message if the site is too busy. In this case, try again at a different time.

- Also, some pages take a long time to display; this may be caused by your connection speed (if you have a slow connection), the time of day (certain peak traffic times make access slower), and the complexity of the page. Pages with a lot of graphics may take longer to download. If it's a consistent problem, you may consider upgrading to a faster connection such as a cable modem or DSL connection.

- If a page doesn't display correctly, it may be because of foreign characters or missing graphic files. Try clicking the Refresh button to reload the page. If that doesn't work, the problem is most likely with the page itself and there's not much you can do.

- Advertisers often display ads when you go to a site. These may pop-up in windows on top of the Web page or pop-under the browser window. In either case, they can be annoying. Windows has added some features for blocking pop-up advertising, and you can also purchase programs (such as SpamBlocker) specifically designed to block this type of Internet annoyance.
- A more worrisome problem is spyware; this is a program installed on your computer often without your knowledge. It tracks where you go online and then relays that information back to its parent company which can then target you for specific advertising via popups or even spam. You should purchase an anti-spyware program. Then check periodically (not just one time) for spyware and remove it.
- Some sites are restricted. That is, you cannot access them without permission usually in the form of a password. If you have a legitimate reason to access the site, contact the system administrator to see about gaining access.

Summary

- The Internet is a network of networks providing information, entertainment, news, education, and many other types of resources.
- You use the Internet to send e-mail messages, browse the Web, do research, publish information and creative works, and communicate with other users in chats or newsgroups.
- To get connected to the Internet, you need a connection, an Internet provider, and the software for browsing and handling mail and other communications (newsgroups, for instance).
- The most common way to get connected is using a modem. You can then connect via a regular phone line, a special line (such as a DSL line), or a cable connection. The newest way to get connected is wirelessly through a satellite.
- The World Wide Web is a means for distributing information on the Internet. World Wide Web pages contain text and graphics and may also include animations, video, and sound. Web pages also include links (or hyperlinks) to other pages at that site, to other parts of that page, or to other sites entirely.
- Each Web site has a unique address called a URL (uniform resource locator). This address usually starts with www and includes the site name and type of site. For instance, the address to Amazon (a popular online shopping site) is www.amazon.com.
- To go to a site you can type the address of the site in the Address bar. You can use the toolbar buttons in the browser program window to go back among pages you have viewed.
- To find a particular site or to find sites that relate to a certain topic, you can search the Internet. To do so, you use a search tool, and the basic process is to go to the search page, type what you want to find, and click the search button. The search tool then displays a list of matching sites. You can click any of the results to go to that site.

Learning Computer Concepts
Lesson 12
The Internet

Q&A

Multiple Choice

1. Which of the following is not a popular search engine:
    a. Google
    b. Yahoo!
    c. HobNob
    d. AltaVista

2. You can search for text on a Web site using this command:
    a. Search and replace
    b. Search site
    c. Find (on This Page)
    d. Hunt Text

3. To view a list of sites you have recently visited, display this list:
    a. Sites Visited
    b. History List
    c. Archive List
    d. Favorites List

4. Which of the following Web address extensions indicates an educational site:
    a. edu
    b. sch
    c. col
    d. uni

Fill in the Blank

1. The _____ isn't a physical part of the Internet, but a way that information (text, graphics, audio, and video) are displayed.

2. A(n) _____ is a company that provides access to the Internet and for this, you usually pay a subscription fee.

3. A(n) _____ list contains sites that you frequently visit that you have added to the list for fast access.

4. _____ stands for_____ and is the "official" name for a Web address.

Short Essay

1. Name some of the things you need to look into when copying text or images.
2. List some search tactics for finding a match.

LESSON 13: SECURITY AND PRIVACY

Objectives

> ➢ Know how to keep yourself safe
> ➢ Learn about computer crime
> ➢ Keep safe from computer viruses
> ➢ Learn how to browse the Internet safely
> ➢ Learn environmental-friendly computing

Computer Safety

A computer isn't likely to harm you, but there are some potential injuries and hazards that they can cause. Let's start with some issues of your computer and its "health." Then suggestions on safeguarding your health are covered next.

SETTING UP YOUR COMPUTER SAFELY

When you set up your computer, you need to think about its safety and protection as well as your own. For instance, make sure that you position your computer in a safe location. This means making sure that you don't overload power supplies (which could cause a fire risk), that cables are neatly situated so that you don't trip over them and again avoiding fire risk from exposed power cabling, and that the computer has proper air circulation so that it doesn't heat. You should also not place the computer in direct sunlight or in places of extreme heat or cold.

SAFEGUARDING YOUR HEALTH

In addition to the computer itself, you should take some precautions to prevent injury to yourself. Keep these guidelines in mind:

- Working at a computer for long periods of time can cause repetitive stress injuries (RSI), back strain, and eye strain. One way to prevent injuries is use ergonomically designed furniture. Your chair should be comfortable and adjustable so that the monitor is at the proper eye level (by adjusting the monitor or the chair height). This helps avoid eye strain. The chair should also provide proper support for your back to avoid back strain.
- When typing, your hands and wrists should be parallel to the floor. That is, you shouldn't have to bend your wrists up or down too much to properly type. Some keyboards have kickstands that help raise the level. Also, some desks have keyboard pullouts which help properly place the keyboard at the proper typing height. Your chair can also be adjusted for better keyboard typing. These precautions can help prevent repetitive stress injuries (RSI)

such as carpal tunnel. You can also purchase wrist supports as another preventative measure.

- Make sure that your office has proper lighting. This will help eye strain. You may need to purchase an anti-glare screen for the monitor if glare is a problem.
- Use proper posture when you are seated and typing (as mentioned using the proper wrist placement is helpful).
- Another way to avoid injuries is to take frequent breaks, stretching your back for instance and giving your eyes a break from looking at the computer monitor for too long.

KEEPING UP-TO-DATE ON COMPUTER NEWS

Another factor that can help you is to keep up-to-date on computer news. This provides many benefits. First, you can learn about new technology that might make your job easier. You can consider adding to your computer, upgrading to a new version of an operating system, purchasing new software, and so on. You can also stay abreast of any computer security and privacy issues, such as email viruses, legislation that may affect privacy (such as the selling of marketing data gathered through Internet tracking), and other issues.

To keep up-to-date, you may want to subscribe to a computer magazine. You'll find lots of different publications for a multitude of interests (games, for interest or networking or Web marketing). Your best bet is a general computer publication written for an audience that wants information, but who's life doesn't revolve around computers. Go to your local library or book store and browse the magazines. Doing so will give you an idea of the level of detail and complexity on the topics covered.

You can also use the Internet to read about new computer news. You can search for stories or subscribe to online newsletters that provide current information. The Internet also provides lots of ways to connect with others. For instance, you can participate in newsgroups and bulletins, chatting with other users. If you want to get very involved, you may even join a user group that meets in your area. Check your library or local paper for announcements for user groups.

You'll even find computer news in some mainstream publications. For instance, home and family magazines may occasionally include articles of interest to their readers (such as ensuring children's safety when using the Internet).

Computer Crime

Statistics on computer crime are hard to come by. First, it's a fairly new avenue for crime. Second, many defrauded companies don't want you to know that they were compromised. A news story in March 2000 revealed that some 485,000 credit card numbers were stolen from an e-commerce site and then stored on a U.S. government agency database. The banks didn't notify the customers of the threat because the cards were not used to commit fraud. E-commerce sites want you to feel secure in purchasing goods online, so they don't want to publicize breaches in security to cause a panic. (More on these safety issues later.)

Most crimes targeted on the general public are harmless (annoying, maybe, but not destructive). Hackers most often commit these crimes.

HACKERS, CRACKERS, AND PHREAKERS

A hacker is a person that uses his or her extensive computer knowledge to illegally access private computer systems and databases. The hacker wants access for a number of reasons: to show off his or her skills, to play a practical joke, or to simply make a statement. Sometimes the purpose is destructive, but usually a hacker does not gain financially from the attack.

Criminal hackers, often called crackers, do seek to profit from their hacking. They might break into a system to steal credit card numbers or other sensitive data. This type of hacker seeks to defraud a company or industry. For instance, one of the most hunted hackers was Kevin Mitnick, who served 4 ½ years in prison after pleading guilty to computer fraud.

Yet another distinction is phreakers. These hackers specifically target national telephone systems to reroute lines, steal telephone services, elude police, sell wiretaps, and perform other illegal activities. A phreaker, for instance, may bill long-distance calls to another number or sell calling card numbers to others to use fraudulently.

> **Originally all hackers were phreakers:** Initially, communication services were expensive and limited, making them the first target for hackers. The hackers wanted access to this new computer communication line, so they hacked in and stole the services.

SECURITY AGAINST HACKING

To prevent any type of access (criminal or otherwise), companies take many security measures. These range from simple to complex security systems. Here are a few of the security measures used:

- *Passwords*. A basic form of protection is the use of passwords. Passwords help ensure that only legitimate users have access to information and programs.
- *Data encryption*. To ensure that data cannot be obtained, many computer systems encrypt data. Basically, the data is scrambled so that even if the data was accessed, it wouldn't make sense. To understand the data, it has to be decrypted. Most shopping sites use data encryption for credit card information.

- *Firewalls.* A firewall is a system of software and hardware that protects a company's network from outside networks (including the Internet).

Firewall: If you have a 24/7 connection, for instance, through a cable modem, you need to install and use a firewall. Windows XP includes firewall protection, as covered later in this lesson.

SOFTWARE PIRACY

Another computer crime that a common person must safeguard against is software piracy. This is the illegal copying or use of software. For instance, suppose that you purchase a word processing program. You have the right to use this program on one computer and make one backup copy. That doesn't give you the right to copy the disks and give them to coworkers, friends, relatives, or even to use it on another computer at home. Doing so is illegal. Companies license software for a certain number of users; this agreement is called a site license. If users install or allow access to more than the licensed amount, they are committing a crime.

Licensing agreement: When you purchase software, you aren't buying the software but the license to use this software. Most programs have a detailed licensing agreement that you agree to when you install the software (called EULAs for end user license agreements). If you are unsure of when/how you can use the software, review this agreement.

Commercial software is copyrighted and protected by the Software Piracy and Counterfeiting Amendment to the Copyright Act and the Software Act of 1980. Some countries are notorious for not enforcing the copyright act. Purchasing software from such a source is also illegal. Software piracy is a felony offense. It also is responsible for rising costs for end users.

Computer Viruses

A computer virus, like a biological virus, spreads from computer to computer, infecting the computers it comes in contact with. Sometimes the virus is harmless; it might display a message on-screen. Other times, the virus can be destructive (deleting all the files on your hard drive, for instance). A virus works by attaching itself to a "legitimate" file. Once you run this file, the virus is activated and duplicated.

The main concepts about viruses are that:

- Viruses are programs, and you must run the program to be infected. That means you won't get a virus from reading an e-mail message. You may get a virus if that message contains a program attachment and you open that attachment.
- Some viruses are harmless, but others may be destructive.

- When you get infected, you need a program called a vaccine to clean up your system. Deleting the suspect file is not enough because this program has attached itself and made changes to other files that "appear" normal.

- You can take precautions to safeguard your computer from viruses, as covered in the next section.

Like viruses: You can find other types of programs that are like viruses. For instance, a worm is a program that enters usually through a network and then replicates itself. A Trojan Horse looks like a helpful program but instead is destructive. A timebomb stays on the system until a specific date or event; then the timebomb program is executed.

USING VIRUS PROTECTION PROGRAMS

One of the best ways to protect your system from viruses is to use virus protection software, such as Norton AntiVirus (see Figure 13.1). This program scans your system for known viruses, including new programs or e-mail attachments. If a virus is found, the antivirus cleans up the infected system with a vaccine program for that particular virus. You can download updates to protect against new viruses that pop up.

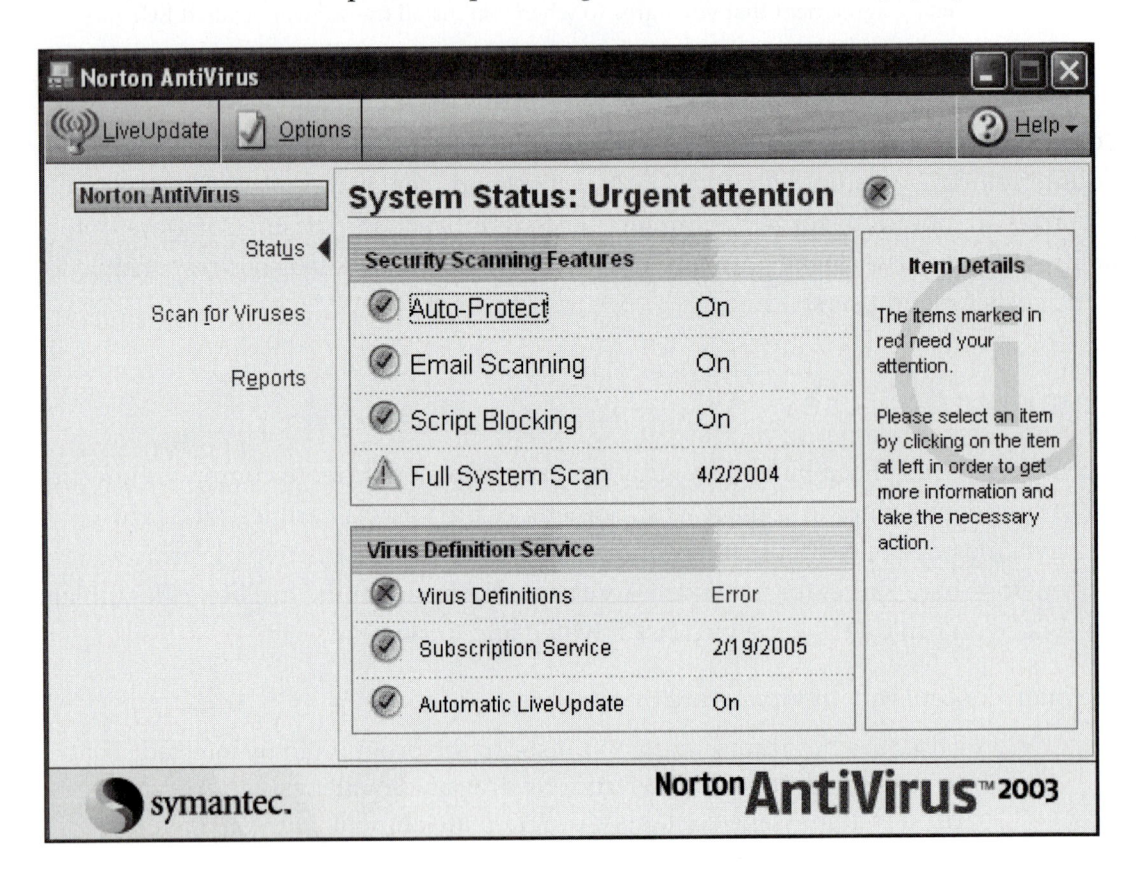

Figure 13.1. You can scan your hard drive for viruses.

Another popular program is McAfee's VirusScan. This program also scans for viruses and then displays any suspected files. If a virus is found, you can use VirusScan to remove and clean up any infected files.

> **WEB:** Visit www.symantec.com to see the various virus and other security software offered by Symantec.

PROTECTING YOUR SYSTEM FROM VIRUSES

In addition to using software, you can follow these tips to protect your system:

- Don't run program attachments unless you check them.
- Don't open attachments from someone you don't know.
- If you use an antivirus program, check for periodic updates on viruses. Usually you subscribe to a service, and then the program periodically checks for new updates via your online connection. You can then keep your virus protection software up-to-date.
- If you do get infected, seek a cure quickly. You can use the Internet to search for information about a particular virus and even get vaccines at nominal costs.
- If you get a floppy disk from someone else, scan it for viruses before you open any files or run any programs on the disk.

USING WINDOWS SECURITY CENTER

To emphasize the importance of security, the newest service release (Service Pack 2) of Windows XP includes the Security Center. You can use this feature to check the status of your computer's virus protection as well as Internet security (covered next). To display the Security Center, click Start, All Programs, Accessories, System Tools, and then Security Center. You can then view the status of the key security elements on your computer (see Figure 13.2).

Lesson 13
Security and Privacy Issues

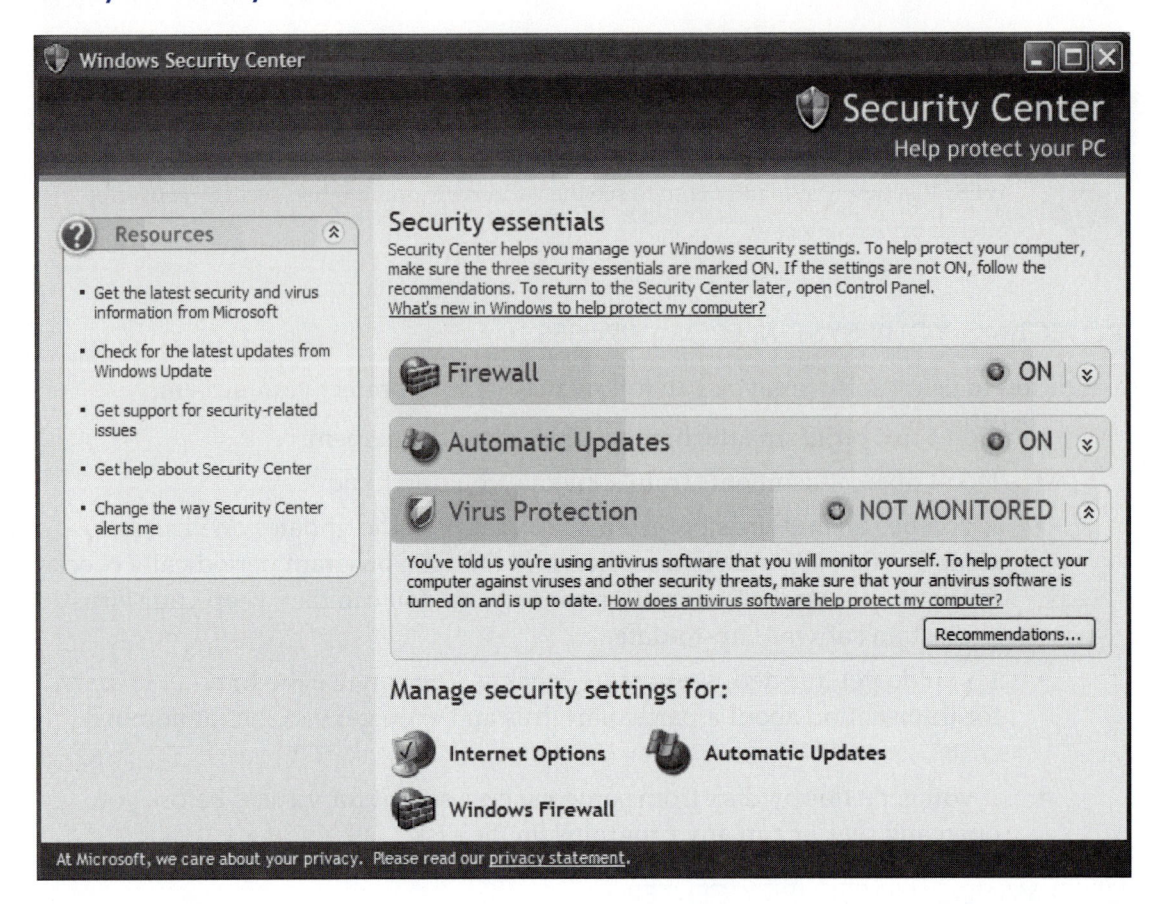

Figure 13.2. If you have the latest release of Windows, you can use the Windows Security Center to review and change security settings.

Getting Security Center: If you don't have the Security Center, you may want to upgrade to the newest release of Windows. As mentioned in Lesson 5, Microsoft periodically releases updates to Windows. If there have been a lot of updates, Microsoft combines them into a Service Pack. At the time this book was written, Service Pack 2 had just become available. You can check out updates to Windows by visiting http://windowsupdate.microsoft.com.

Safe Internet Browsing

In addition to protecting against viruses, you also need to take some precautions when using the Internet. If you have a 24/7 connection, you need to set up a firewall. You may also want to use security programs to block unwanted e-mail (called spam) and unwanted programs (called spyware). Also, if you purchase items online, you want to ensure you are shopping at a secure site.

USING A FIREWALL

One of the conveniences of a cable modem is that you are hooked up to the Internet 24/7; you don't have to log on. On the downside, your computer may be vulnerable to outside attacks. To prevent someone from accessing your computer, you can use a firewall.

Windows XP includes a firewall and it's simple to turn on this feature. The easiest way to do so is using the Windows Security Center (refer to Figure 13.2).

Follow these steps to turn on Windows Firewall:

1. Click Start, All Programs, Accessories, System Tools, and then Security Center.

2. If you don't see ON next to the Firewall option (or you want information about how this feature works), click the Windows Firewall link at the bottom part of the window.

3. Make any changes in the dialog box (see Figure 13.3). For instance, if this feature is not on, select On (recommended).

4. Click OK.

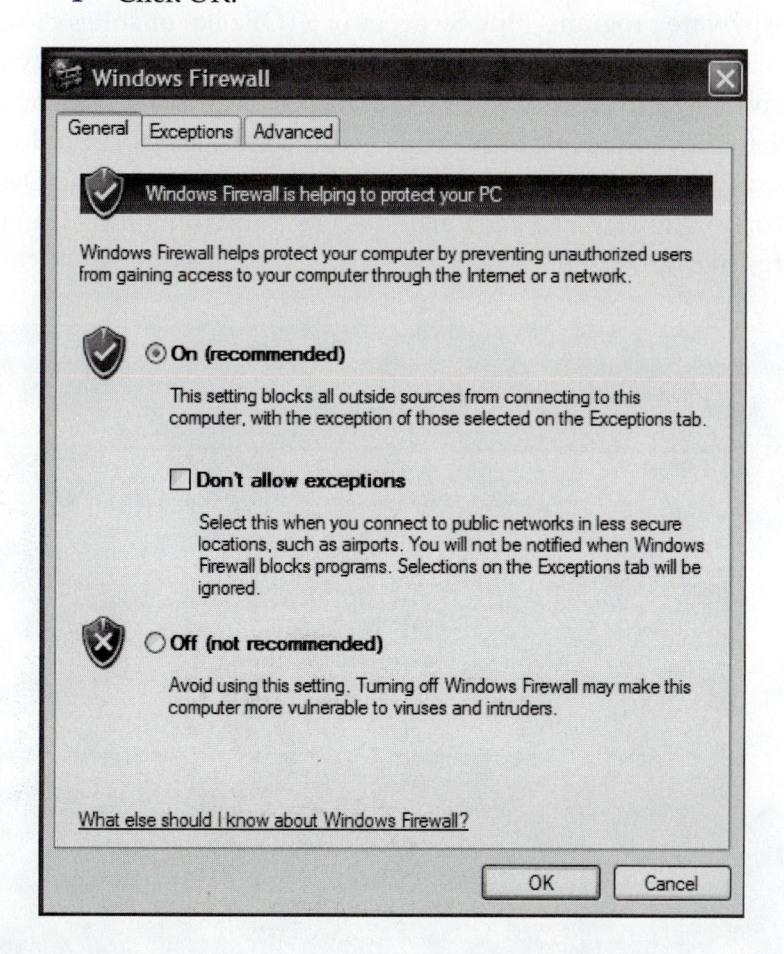

Figure 13.3. Use a firewall to prevent unauthorized access to your computer.

Lesson 13
Security and Privacy Issues

CHECKING FOR SPYWARE AND BLOCKING ADS

Other nuisances of Internet browsing are spyware programs and pop-up advertisements, and often these are related. Spyware programs are installed without your knowledge or consent and track where you go on the Internet. This information is then relayed to other companies. The spyware program is installed automatically when you visit a site. For instance, you may visit a golf site and unwittingly pick up a spyware program. That program may then track what sites you visit and display pop-up ads based on your browsing preferences. The marketing and advertisers argue that this type of program helps them customize ads to suit your interests. But most users don't agree.

In fact, you may be bombarded with pop-up advertisements. These may appear as system messages, or they may appear when you visit a particular Web site. You can easily close the ad windows, but it's annoying.

Windows includes some features to prevent spyware and to block ads. You can also purchase anti-spyware programs (Spy Sweeper or STOPzilla) or suites of security programs such as Norton Internet Security that bundles several features (virus protection, ad blocking, spamware, and so on). As another alternative, you can find some free or shareware versions of programs designed to check for and delete any found spyware programs. One popular program is Spybot's Search and Destroy (see Figure 13.4). You can download a version of this program from http://safer-networking.org/en/index.html.

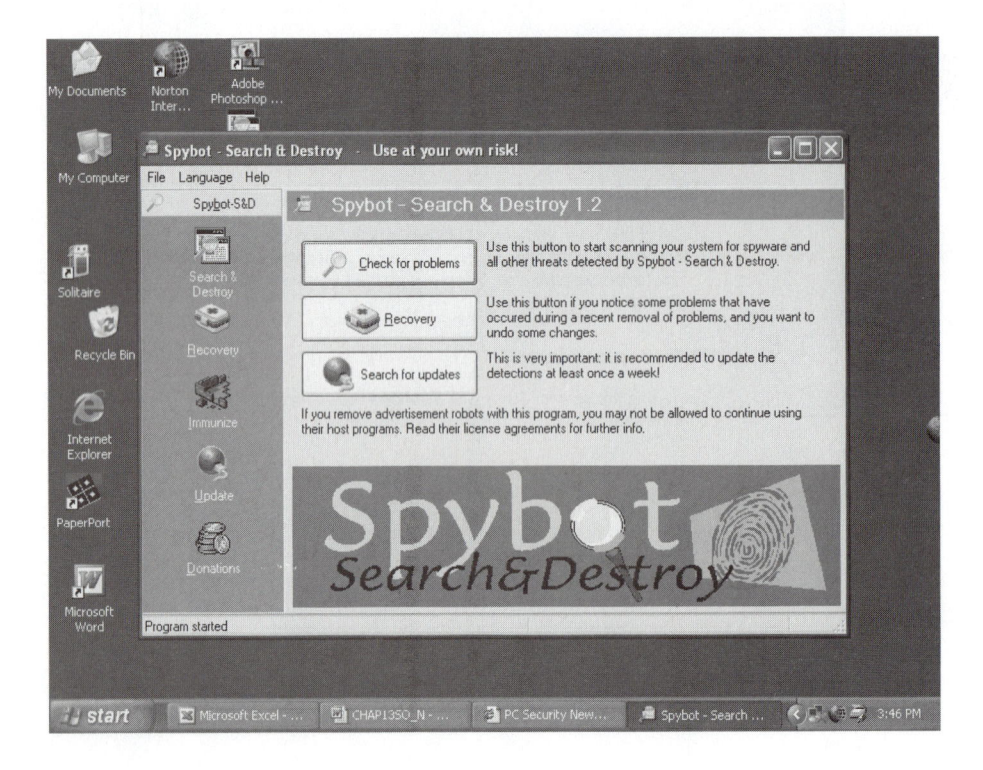

Figure 13.4. You can check for spyware programs and then remove them using anti-spyware programs such as Spybot's Search and Destroy.

AVOIDING SPAM

Once you start visiting sites (and especially shopping online or signing up for contests or polls), your name gets added to the marketing list, and you will see messages in your Inbox for deals, special offers, and so on. This type of e-mail junk mail is called spam.

How do you avoid spam? Some e-mail programs include spam filters where you can automatically place unsolicited mail in a special Junk Mail folder. You can also find spam blocking features in security suites such as Norton Internet Security. Or, you can purchase or download software designed specifically for dealing with spam, such as Spam Inspector and Spam Catcher.

You can cut down on spam by keeping your online information to a minimum. That is, don't give out your personal information at sites. Don't fill in survey forms or participate in contests. And if you order something online, be sure to turn off the automatic e-mail solicitations.

If you receive spam, you can delete the messages. You should also look for a way to get off the mailing list. Usually you respond to a certain e-mail address and unsubscribe.

SECURE SHOPPING

Is Internet shopping safe? For the most part, yes. At least as safe as giving your credit card number and information over the telephone. Most sites use a secure server software (SSL) for transmitting sensitive information such as credit card numbers. The data is encrypted so that even if the data were intercepted, it would not be of any use. The secure site then decrypts the data.

Check the icon: Most browsers use a special icon to indicate a secure site. For instance, in Internet Explorer you see a closed padlock in the status bar when the site is secure.

If you are not sure about a site, check out its policies. Figure 13.5 shows the security information for Amazon.com. You can also consult reviews of the site. For instance, one popular reviewer is BizRate (www.bizrate.com). This company reviews customer service and other features of an online merchant and ranks them accordingly.

Lesson 13
Security and Privacy Issues

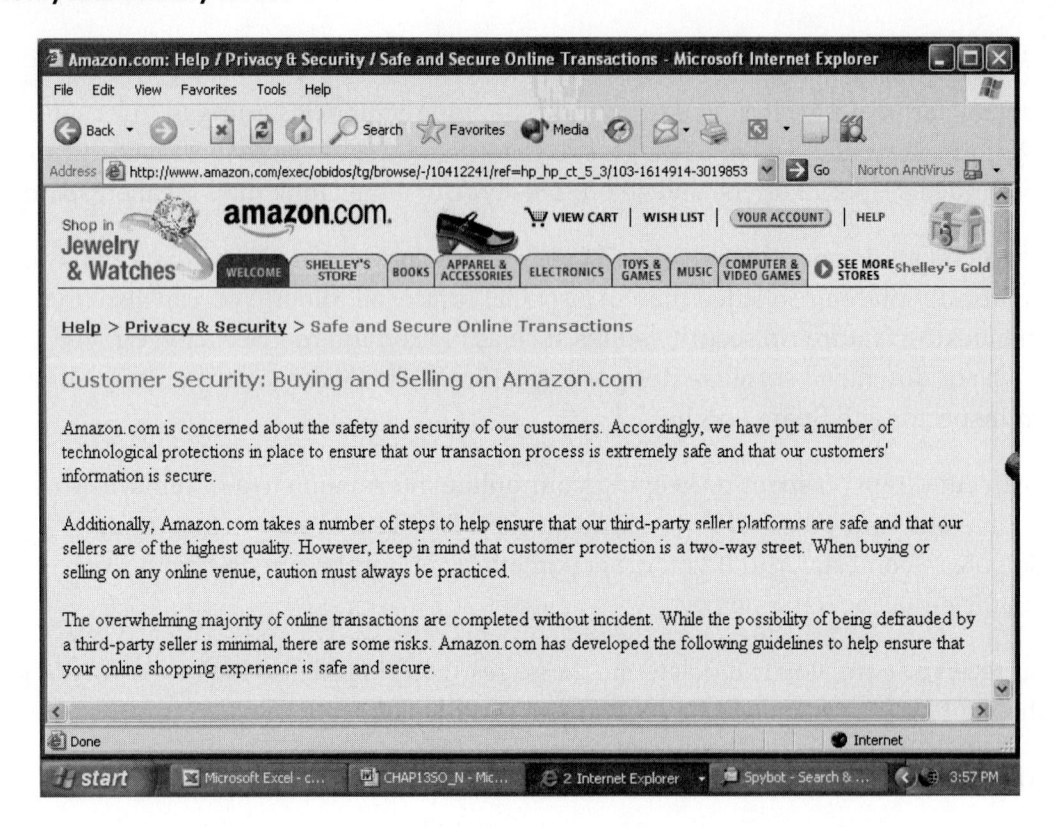

Figure 13.5. Shopping online? Review the store's security procedures.

Still worried: If you are still worried about ordering online, most sites provide access to a toll-free number, a fax order line, or other methods for placing an order.

SAFE BROWSING FOR KIDS

Younger children and even teens may require some set guidelines for Internet access. Some parents may want to purchase and use some type of Internet security software, such as Net Nanny (www.netnanny.com) and CyberPatrol (www.cyberpatrol.com). These programs monitor and may even block access to certain sites. In addition to software, it's a good idea for parents to establish some guidelines for computer use:

- *Don't give out personal information*, including your phone number, address, or school. You should also not give out information about your daily schedule, names of friends or teachers, sports teams, or photos of yourself.
- *Don't ever agree to meet anyone*. Chats and instant messaging are online activities that kids love, but be sure not to give out personal information or to agree to meet anyone, no matter what that person promises. You should also inform a parent or teacher of any offensive activity.
- *Adhere to limits*. It's a good idea to set time limits for online time, especially online chats. If you are the parent, be sure to discuss what things your child can and cannot do, including handling e-mail messages, visiting Web sites, and participating in chats. If you are the child, be sure you know what your restrictions are and stick to them.

WEB: As another option, visit the National Center for Missing and Exploited Children at www.missingkids.com and review its suggestions for online safety.

More options: If you want even more tracking power, you can buy programs for homes and small businesses that will record e-mail, instant messages, Internet activity, and so on. One such program is Spector Pro (www.spectorsoft.com).

Internet Ethics

With the ever-expanding popularity and prevalence of the Internet come not only security concerns but concerns about privacy and censorship. What information about you is floating around the Internet? How do you both provide free speech but also protect against pornography, defamation, and plagiarism?

PRIVACY, PLEASE

The Internet enables you to get information, shop, send e-mail, and more. But what are the associated risks? Who has access to this information? For instance, should someone be able to view the sites you have visited and keep track of your browsing habits? Several companies (using programs such as spyware) track where Internet users go and then build a database of consumer information. These companies then sell this information to marketers.

More privacy acts: In addition to online privacy, you can also find policies and regulations as they relate to computer data. For instance, the Freedom of Information Act gives you the right to request data files that the federal government has on you. The Right to Financial Privacy Act determines what rules federal agencies must follow when they review bank records.

Expect forums, discussions, and possibly some regulation of privacy policies in the future. As of now, you are personally responsible for ensuring your own privacy. To do so, consider these pointers:

- *Don't give out personal information.* You'll come across sweepstake entries, surveys, polls, and other forms that request information. If you submit the information, make sure you know how it will be used.
- *Check for e-mail solicitations.* If you purchase products online or complete surveys, you usually see a checkbox on the form that allows you to accept or decline e-mail solicitations. If you leave the option on, you agree to accept offers for deals, new products, newsletters, or whatever marketing material that site wants to send. If you turn off the option, that company should honor your request to stay off the mailing list.
- *Read privacy policies.* Many sites include a specific privacy policy that explains how they use data they obtain. Check out this policy. Look for a link called Privacy Policy or something similar.

Many sites follow set guidelines for privacy, and the most common are the guidelines established by TRUSTe. In the site's own words, "TRUSTe is an independent, non-profit privacy initiative dedicated to building users' trust and confidence on the Internet and accelerating growth of the Internet industry." It licenses a special seal or logos to Web sites that follow its set privacy principles. This seal "signifies to users that the Web site will openly share, at a minimum, what personal information is being gathered, how it will be used, with whom it will be shared, who is gathering the information, what options the user has, what security procedures are in place to prevent misuse or loss and how users can correct information to control its dissemination."

WEB: Visit the Web site for TRUSTe at www.truste.com to view the current status of computer and privacy issues.

CENSORSHIP

Another issue relating to Web content is censorship. Like privacy, there are no hard and fast rules that apply to Web censorship, but you can find lots of discussion on the topic. Should Web content be monitored? Rated? If so, who should do the rating? What about sites that distribute pornography? What about sites that promote violence?

Again, until specific guidelines are in place, you are responsible for protecting your own interests. Most networks, especially ones at work or at school, will have policies regarding censorship. Do not make the mistake of thinking that anything you send over the Internet is private.

PLAGIARISM, COPYRIGHT, TRADEMARKS, AND OTHER ISSUES

The Internet provides a wealth of content, but just because that information is online doesn't mean it is free for your use. The same issues of copyright protection, trademarking, fair use policy, patent protection, and libel apply just as they do in print and broadcast publishing.

If an item is trademarked, you need to respect any trademark issues as well as indicate the trademark if you include the item in any place (your Web site, for instance). You must also follow any restrictions relating to the patent of ideas or inventions relating to computers or the Internet. If you make critical comments about an individual, you check for any libel problems. You also need to be sure that you don't pass along material that is libelous. Be alert to the possibility of someone else deliberately including incorrect information that harms a person or individual.

Also, the rules of plagiarism still apply: you cannot use ideas and words as your own if they are not your own. If you do, you must cite the source, giving proper credit to the originator of the material. There are several different standards for citing another's work including APA guidelines or Modern Language Association (MLA) guidelines.

As an example, some images are copyrighted. You cannot use them without permission from the artist or publisher. Or you may be able to use them only in a restricted sense. For instance, the Fair Use Policy for Education and Non-Profit allows use as long as the use of that work does not interfere with the rights of the author. If you have any doubts, check with the artist for permission.

> **Netiquette:** The Internet is a community, and while there is no moderator or censor, it does make sense to follow some Internet etiquette (called netiquette).

WORK ETHICS

In addition to ethic standards for personal use, you should also keep in mind that if you use a computer at work, you have certain responsibilities (legally and ethically). Your e-mail is not private, at least according to court decisions. Your employer has legal access to your e-mail and can review it. Also, protect your company's confidentiality. Be sure you do not give out any confidential information about your company either advertently or inadvertently. Even if you delete your e-mail, there is a chance that it may have been saved inadvertently, which could cause some embarrassing situations.

> **Rights at work:** Many people mistakenly believe that their work e-mail or Web browsing is their business, but that's not the case. Most companies have rules about computer use at the office, and companies have the right to read your e-mail as well as track what sites you've visited on the Internet. If you are unsure of your rights, check with your company's human resources department. Most now have specific guidelines included in the employee handbook.

COMPUTERS AND THE ENVIRONMENT

Finally, computers affect the environment, and the main issues are energy consumption and disposing of computer parts (especially monitors). Computers are the fastest growing load of electrical power, and most computers are left on most of the time. Newer computers take advantage of energy-saving features, such as putting the computer and monitor on standby if it is not used for a set period of time. Most companies belong to the Energy Star program, sponsored by the EPA. This program sets the maximum energy consumption for a computer in an idle state. PCs that comply are sometimes called Green PCs.

Another issue is recycling. Recycling supplies relates not to just paper and disks, but also to other computer products, such as toner cartridges and old hardware. Check out the local resources in your area for recycling for more information.

Computer equipment can also be donated to schools or other organizations. Even older computers can be a worthwhile donation. For instance, a technical college may use these computers to learn how to take apart a computer and install components.

Lesson 13
Security and Privacy Issues

Summary

- Computer crime involves illegal access of services, systems, databases, or other computer components. These crimes may be committed for fun or for profit.

- Users that access a computer illegally are called hackers. If the intent is criminal, these users are often called crackers.

- Companies and organizations employ security systems to protect the integrity of the system. These usually involve passwords, data encryption, and firewalls.

- It is illegal to copy software and give or sell that copy. Doing so is software piracy. It is also illegal to purchase pirated software.

- A computer virus is a program or file that infects a system. The purpose may be a prank or some destructive action (such as formatting your hard drive). To protect against viruses, use a virus checker program, such as Norton AntiVirus or McAfee VirusScan.

- The Internet has opened several areas of debate. Two of the biggest concerns relate to privacy and censorship.

- You can shop confidently on the Internet as long as you stick to secure shopping sites; these use secure server software (SSL) to encrypt data. If you are not sure about the safety of a site, check out its security policies.

- E-mail is not private. If you send e-mail from work, that e-mail can legally be reviewed by your employer.

- Most people leave the computer running, which wastes power, one of the environmental issues relating to the use of computers. To deal with this problem, computer manufacturers have started to build in energy-saving features. These computers are Energy Star-compliant. (Energy Star is a program developed by the EPA.)

Q&A

Multiple Choice

1. Hackers that seek to profit from their hacking are called:
    a. Hackers
    b. Phreakers
    c. Crackers
    d. Whackers

2. Internet Explorer uses what type of icon to indicate a secure site:
    a. A closed padlock
    b. A large red circle
    c. The superman logo
    d. A chain

3. This type of software usually installs itself without your realizing it and then tracks and relays your Internet usage back to its parent site:
    a. Snoopy
    b. Spyware
    c. Spam
    d. Ad pops

4. To protect against virus attacks, you should:
    a. Scan all attachments sent via e-mail
    b. Scan disks that you've received from someone else
    c. Don't execute program attachments on an e-mail
    d. All of the above

Fill in the Blank

1. A(n) _____ is a person that uses his or her extensive computer knowledge to illegally gain access to computer systems.

2. _____ is unsolicited e-mail.

3. _____ is the word used to describe the proper and accepted rules, manners, and niceties of using the Internet.

4. If you have a 24/7 cable connection, you should use a _____ to prevent unauthorized access to your computer.

Short Essay

1. Names some ways you can protect your privacy.

2. Explain your computer use rights at work.

IC³-1: COMPUTING FUNDAMENTALS EXERCISES

In this section you will practice key skills for working with a personal computer, including knowledge and use of computer hardware, software, and operating systems.

Objective 3.2: Manipulate and control the Windows desktop, files, and disks

WORKING WITH WINDOWS, HELP, AND APPLICATIONS

1. Start up the computer, and log into the network (if available).
2. Determine the operating system version number.
3. Open the Help system and maximize its window. (Hint: Click the Start button and select Help and Support.)
4. Search the help system for an article that explains how to start the Paint application.
5. Start the Paint application, following the instructions in the Help article you found.
6. Switch to the Help window, and restore it. Adjust its size so that it is approximately half its original height and width.
7. Arrange the Help and Paint windows so that both are visible at the same time. To arrange both windows, right-click on the status bar and select to tile the windows either vertically or horizontally.
8. Close the Help window, and minimize the Paint window.
9. Restore the Paint window, resize it if needed to see the entire drawing canvas, and draw a simple picture using its drawing tools. If you like you can try to duplicate Figure 1 on the next page, or draw something of your own.
10. Save your work as **TestPic.bmp** in the My Documents folder (File, Save). Close Paint when finished.
11. Restart Paint, and then shut down Paint through the Task Manager as if it were a non-responding application (Ctrl+Alt+Delete).

Learning Computer Concepts

IC³-1
Computing Fundamentals

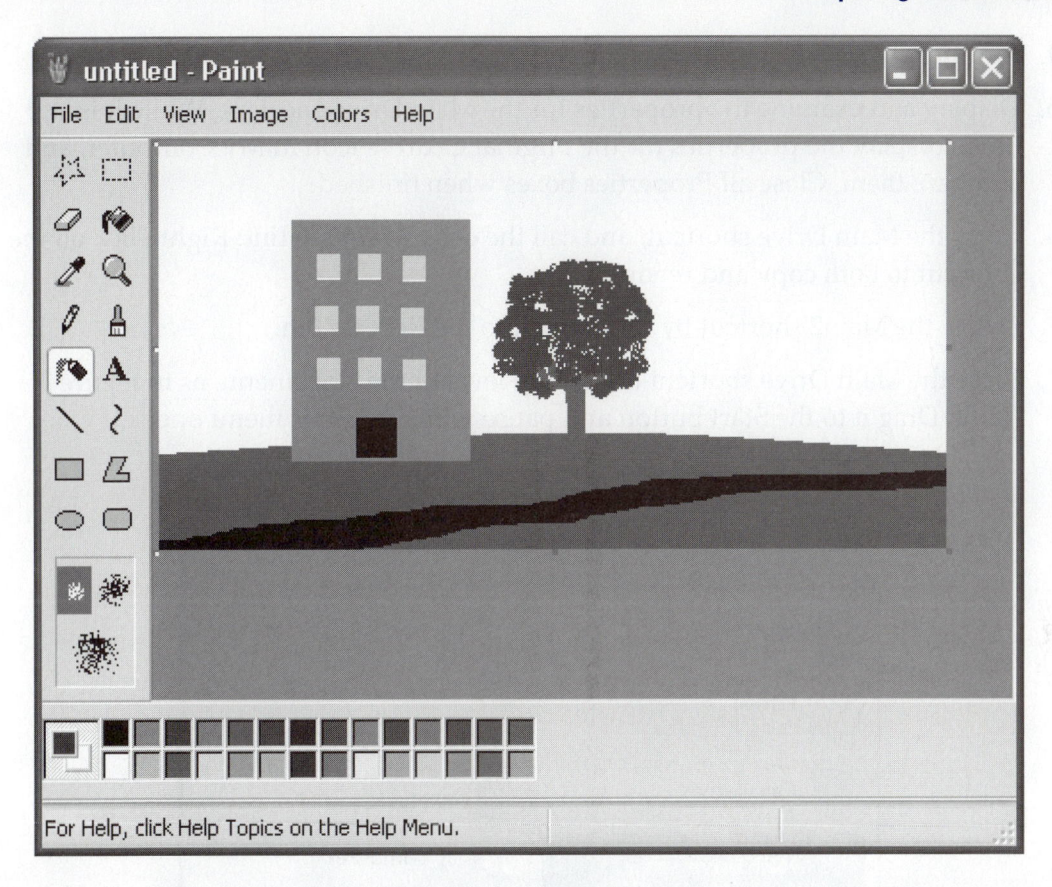

Figure 1: A picture drawn in Paint.

WORKING WITH SHORTCUTS AND PROPERTIES

1. Create a shortcut on the desktop for the Paint application. (Hint: *Right*-drag it from the Start menu.)

2. Open the My Computer window, and identify all the drive icons that appear there. Determine which are for floppy drives, hard drives, CD drives, network drives, and so on.

3. Create a shortcut to the C: drive on the desktop, and rename the shortcut **Main Drive**. See Figure 2. Move the shortcut icon so that it is to the right of the Recycle Bin.

Figure 2: Create a shortcut to the C: drive called Main Drive.

Computing Fundamentals

4. Minimize the My Computer window.

5. Display and examine the properties for the Main Drive shortcut. While it is still open, display the properties for the original C: drive icon in My Computer, and compare them. Close all Properties boxes when finished.

6. Copy the Main Drive shortcut, and call the copy **Main2**. (Hint: Right-click on the shortcut to both copy and rename.)

7. Delete the Main2 shortcut by dragging it to the Recycle Bin.

8. Place the Main Drive shortcut on the top level of the Start menu, as in Figure 3. (Hint: Drag it to the Start button and pause while the Start menu opens.)

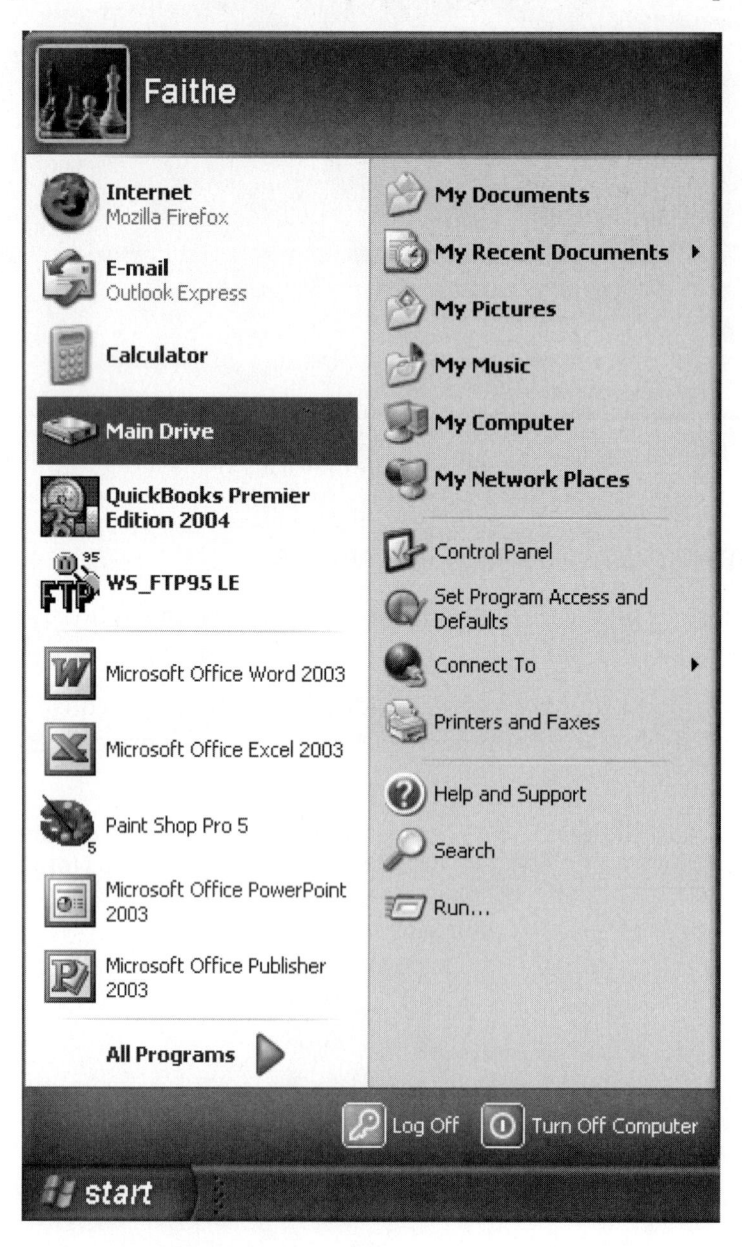

Figure 3: Place the Main Drive shortcut on the Start menu.

Learning Computer Concepts

IC³-1
Computing Fundamentals

WORKING WITH WINDOWS EXPLORER

1. Restore the My Computer window, and click the Folders button on the toolbar to display the Folders pane on the left.

2. Display the list of files and folders on the C: drive.

3. Switch to a Details view of the C: drive's contents and sort the listing by Date Modified, as in Figure 4, with the most recently modified items first. (Hint: Click the Date Modified column header. You will see different files and folders than shown in Figure 4.)

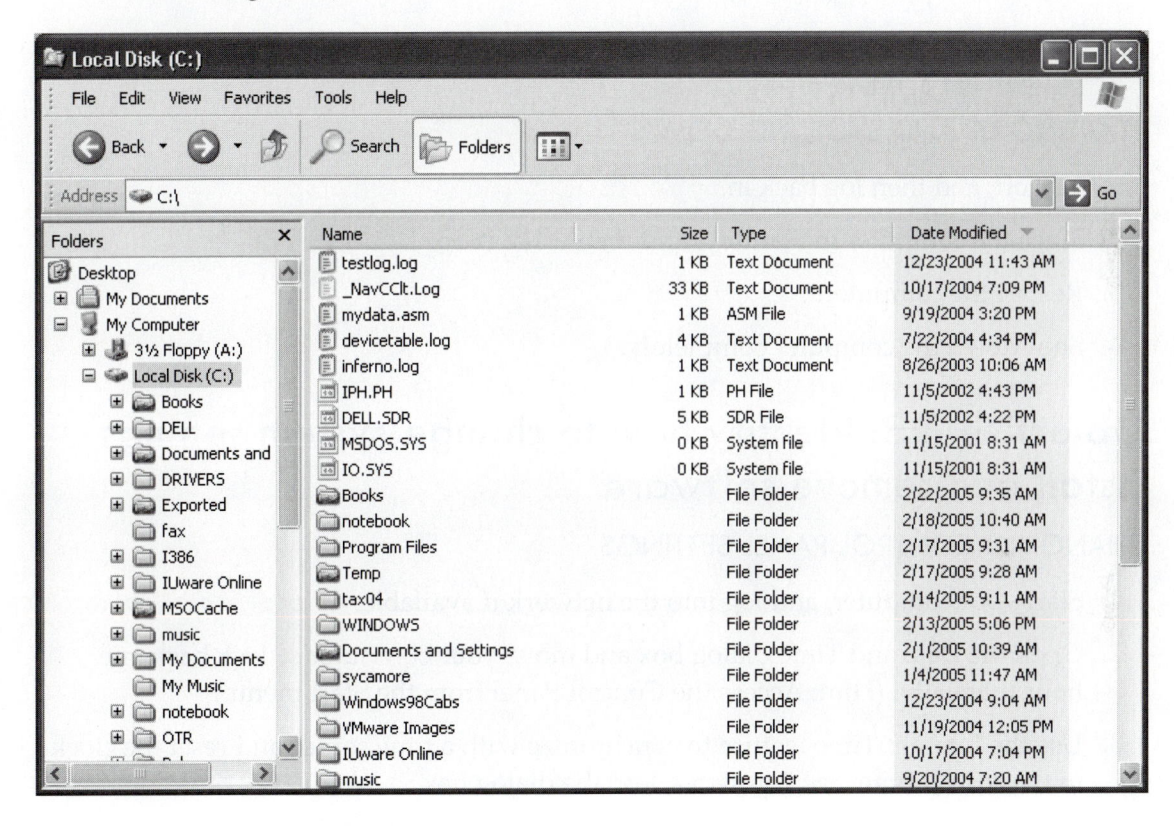

Figure 4: Sort the C: drive's listing by Date Modified.

4. Display the contents of the My Documents folder. Locate the **TestPic.bmp** file and select it.

5. Make a copy of **TestPic.bmp** and name it **Test2.bmp**.

6. Rename **TestPic.bmp** to **Test1.bmp**.

7. View the properties for **Test1.bmp**, and identify the purpose of each one. Set the file to be Read Only. (Hint: Right-click the file and choose Properties.)

8. Try to delete **Test1.bmp**. Then remove the Read-Only attribute from **Test1.bmp**, and then delete it.

9. Create a new folder within **My Documents** called **IC3**, and move **Test2.bmp** into it.
10. Create a copy of the **IC3** folder in **My Documents**, and call the copy **IC3A**.
11. Move the **IC3A** folder into the **IC3** folder.
12. Delete the **IC3A** folder, and then retrieve it from the Recycle Bin.
13. Delete the **IC3A** folder again, and empty the Recycle Bin so it cannot be retrieved. Then delete the **IC3** folder, and purge that file from the Recycle Bin.
14. Format a floppy disk through Windows.
15. Use Search to find all files with a .BMP extension on your hard disk, and copy two of them to the floppy disk.

STARTING UP AND SHUTTING DOWN

1. Log off, and then log back in.
2. Place the computer in Standby, and then wake it up.
3. Restart the computer.
4. Shut down the computer completely.

Objective 3.3: Identify how to change system settings, install and remove software

CHANGING CONTROL PANEL SETTINGS

1. Start your computer, and log into the network if available.
2. Open the Date and Time dialog box and move your computer's clock back one hour manually. (Hint: Access the Control Panel from the Start menu.)
3. Use the Internet Time feature to synchronize with a time server and reset the clock to the correct time. See Figure 5. Close the dialog box.

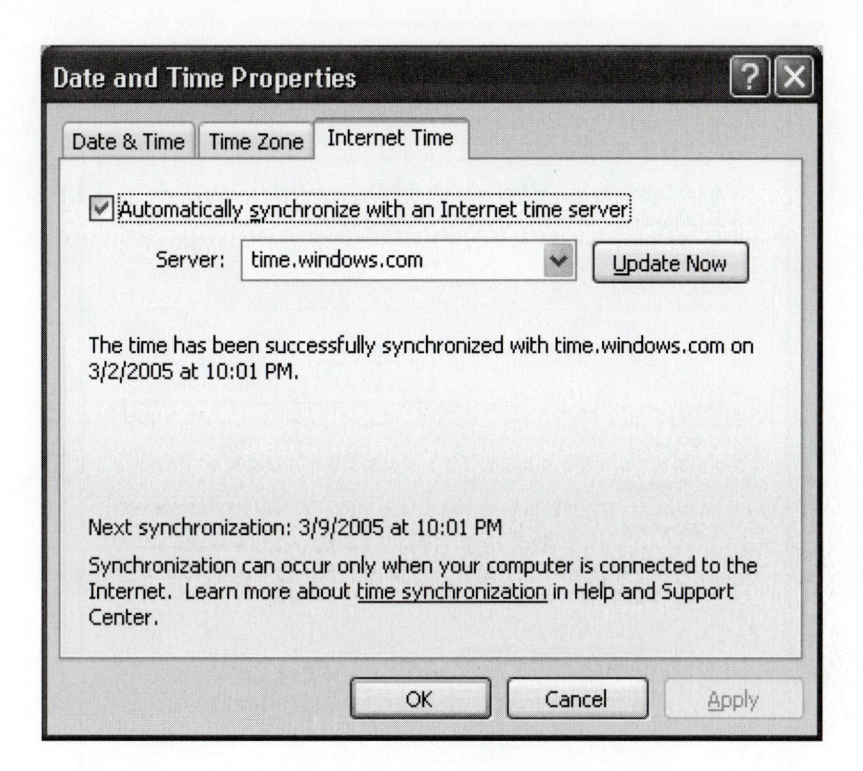

Figure 5: The Internet Time tab in the Date and Time Properties dialog box automatically updates the time.

4. Open the Display dialog box. Change to a different display resolution. For example, if you are currently at 1024x768, change to 800x600, or vice-versa.

5. Change at least three appearance settings in Windows from the Display Properties. Choose from this list:
    - Theme
    - Background image or color
    - Screen saver, and modify its settings
    - Color scheme
    - Style of windows and buttons
    - Effects

6. Using the Sounds and Multimedia controls in the Control Panel, play a sound to confirm that sounds are working. See Figure 6. Adjust the volume setting if needed to hear a sound.

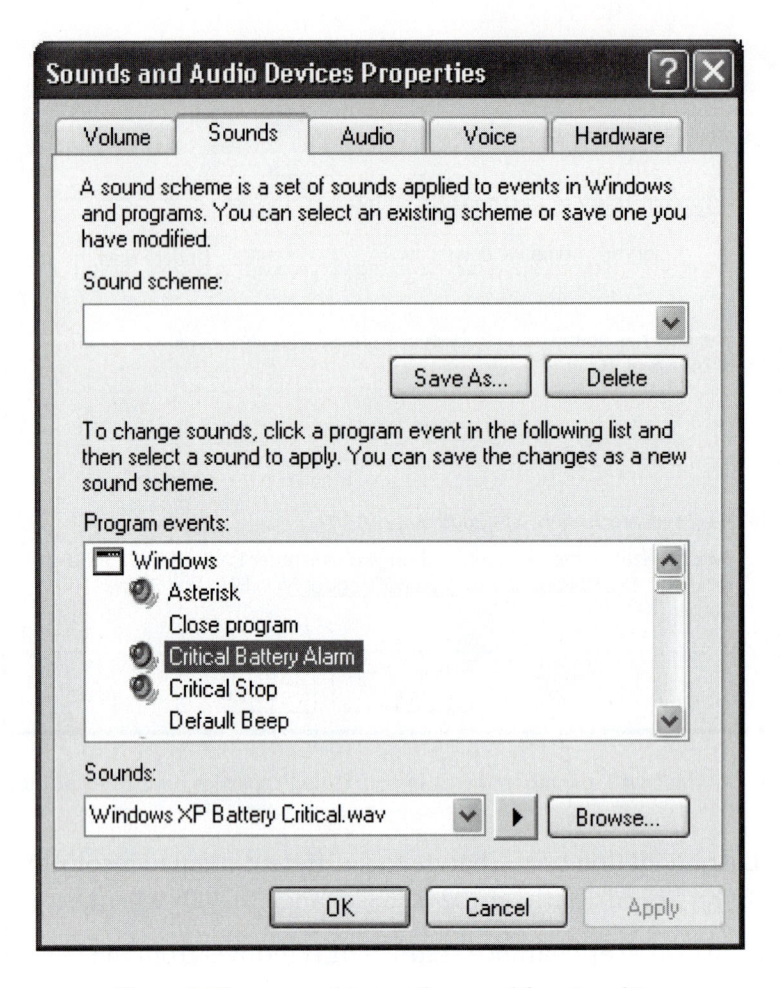

Figure 6: Play a sound to test the sound functionality.

7. In the Keyboard Properties dialog box adjust the keyboard repeat rate.

8. Adjust the mouse pointer movement and double-click Settings.

9. Choose an alternate mouse pointer from the default one.

10. Return your system to its original settings, reversing all the changes you have made in Steps 1-9.

11. Display a list of installed printers.

12. View the Properties box for one of the printers, and print a test page for it.

Learning Computer Concepts

IC³-1
Computing Fundamentals

WORKING WITH SOFTWARE

1. Back up the important files from the My Documents folder to a floppy disk or a writeable CD. If there are more files than will fit on a single disk, back up only as many as will fit. (Hint: You can manually copy the files or use Microsoft Backup. Microsoft Backup will not write directly to a CD.)

2. Install a new application from a Setup CD.

3. Start the new application and confirm that it works.

4. Download and install any updates for the application from the Web (if available).

5. View the list of installed applications through the Control Panel, in Add or Remove Programs, as shown in Figure 7.

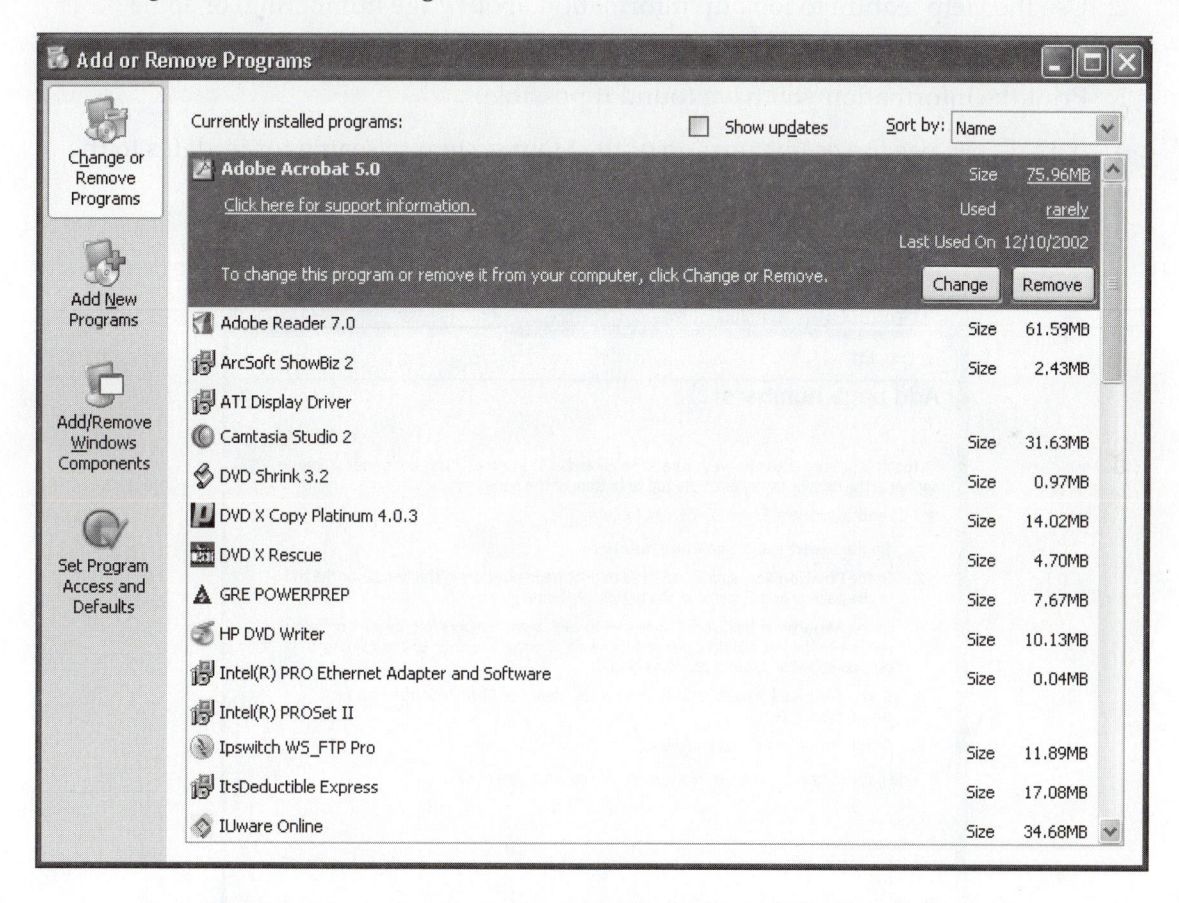

Figure 7: View the list of installed applications. You will have different ones than shown here.

6. Locate the application you just installed and remove it.

7. Shut down the PC.

IC³-2: KEY APPLICATIONS EXERCISES

In this section you will practice key word processing, spreadsheet, and presentation skills.

Objective 1.1: Be able to start and exit a Windows application and utilize sources of online help

1. Start a word processing application, such as Microsoft Office Word. (Hint: Click Start, All Programs, and then locate Word.)

2. Use the Help feature to look up information about page numbering, or some other topic that interests you. Figure 1 shows a typical Help system.

3. Print the information you have found if possible.

4. If available, use the online portion of the Help system to search for updates to the application. If you find any updates available, install them.

5. Exit the application.

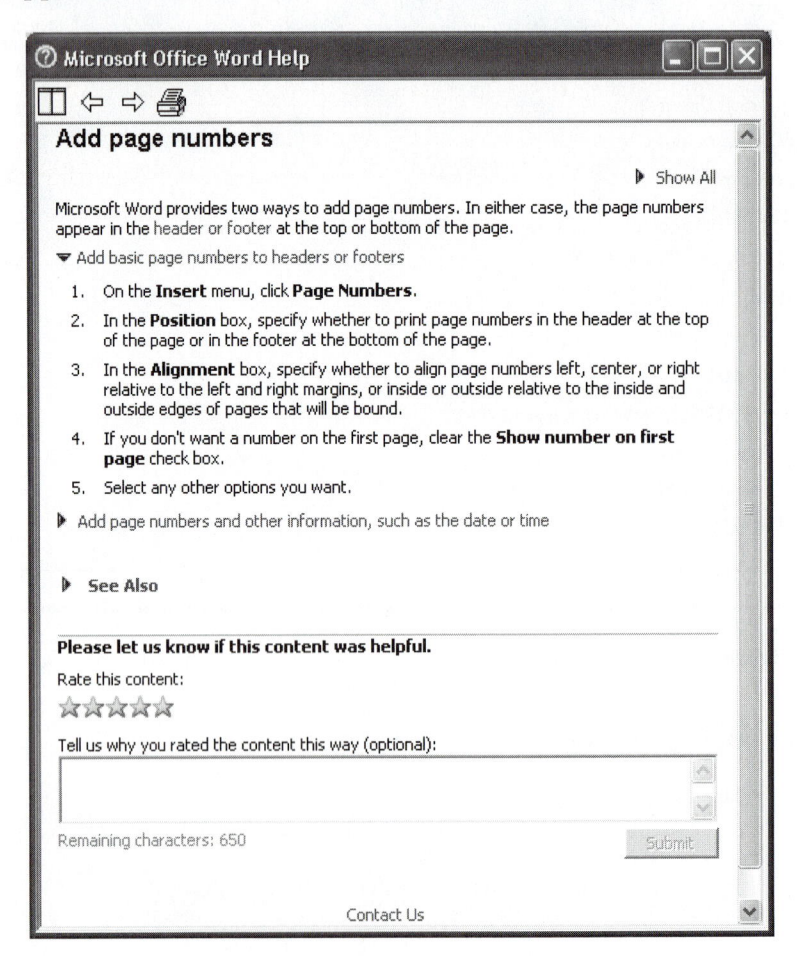

Figure 1: A typical Help system.

Objective 1.2: Identify common onscreen elements of Windows applications, change application settings and manage files within an application

START A NEW DOCUMENT BASED ON A TEMPLATE

1. Start a word processing application.

2. Identify the toolbars that appear by default, and identify several tools on each one.

3. Display an additional toolbar that does not appear by default. (Hint: Right-click on any toolbar and select a new toolbar.) Identify several tools on it, and then hide it again.

4. Start a new document based on one of the Memo templates that came with the application. For example, you might choose the Professional Memo template that comes with Word, as in Figure 2.

5. Save it as **Memo1** to the default save location using the default file type.

6. Change the Zoom (magnification) level to 110%.

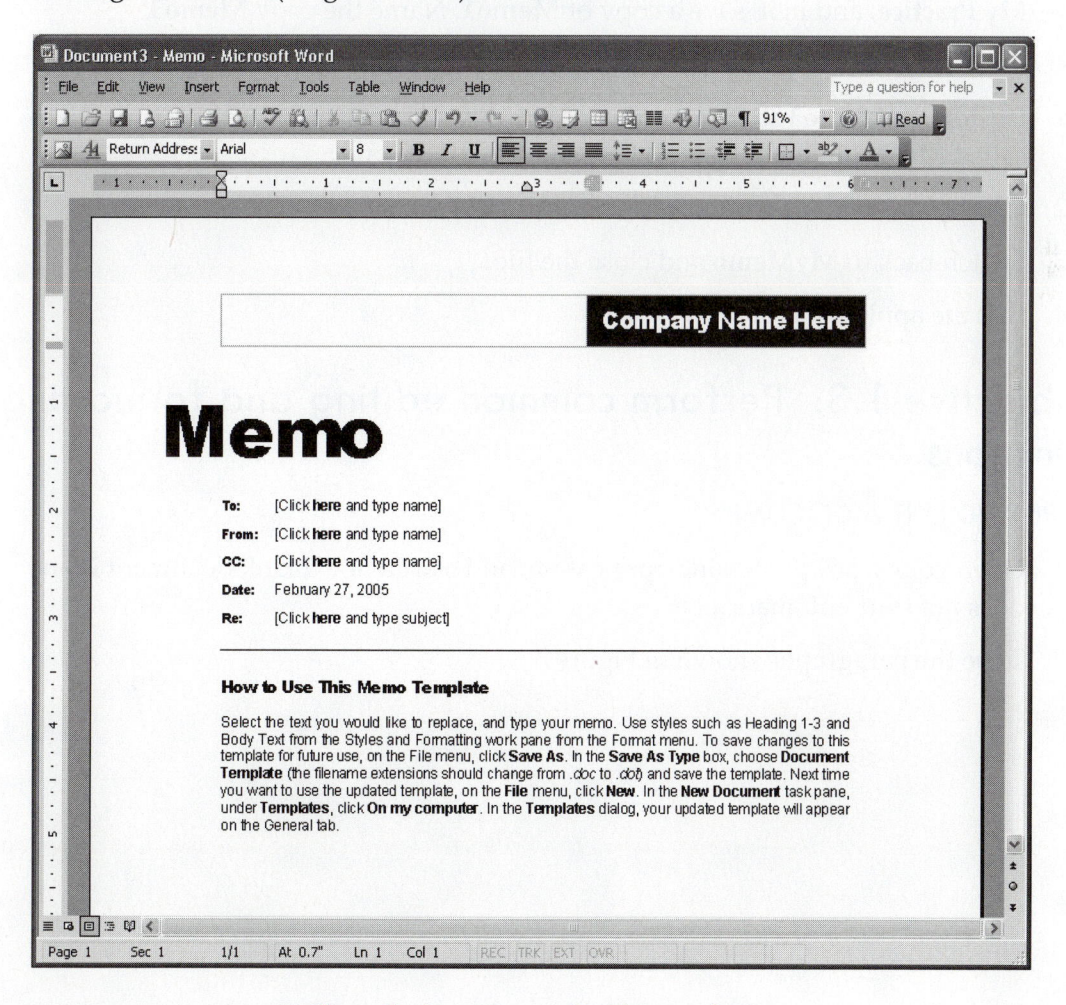

Figure 2: A memo started with a template.

SAVE, CLOSE, AND OPEN DOCUMENTS

1. Insert a floppy disk, or connect a USB flash drive. Save the file as a Rich Text Format file called **Memo2.rtf** to the floppy or flash drive. (Hint: Click File, Save As, and then select Rich Text Format from the Save as type drop-down list.)

2. Close **Memo2** and close the application.

3. From Windows Explorer, display the contents of the default save location (probably My Documents) and locate **Memo1**.

4. Right-click **Memo1** and choose Properties, and make a note of the application it is set to open with by default.

5. Open **Memo1** in the application you used to create it originally. If it is not the default application for that file type, you can right-click the file and choose Open With to select the desired application.

6. If possible, save a copy of **Memo3** to a network location. Name the copy **MemoNet**. Then close **MemoNet** and reopen **Memo1**.

7. Using the Save As dialog box, create a new folder on the Windows desktop named **My Practice**, and in it, save a copy of **Memo1**. Name the copy **Memo3**.

CREATE A NEW TEMPLATE AND SWITCH BETWEEN DOCUMENTS

1. Customize **Memo3** so that it contains your own name, and save it as a template called **MyMemo** in the default template save location.

2. Create a new, blank document.

3. Switch back to **MyMemo** and close the file.

4. Exit the application.

Objective 1.3: Perform common editing and formatting functions

TYPE AND EDIT A DOCUMENT

1. Open your word processing application, and start a new blank document if one does not start automatically.

2. Type the paragraphs shown in Figure 3:

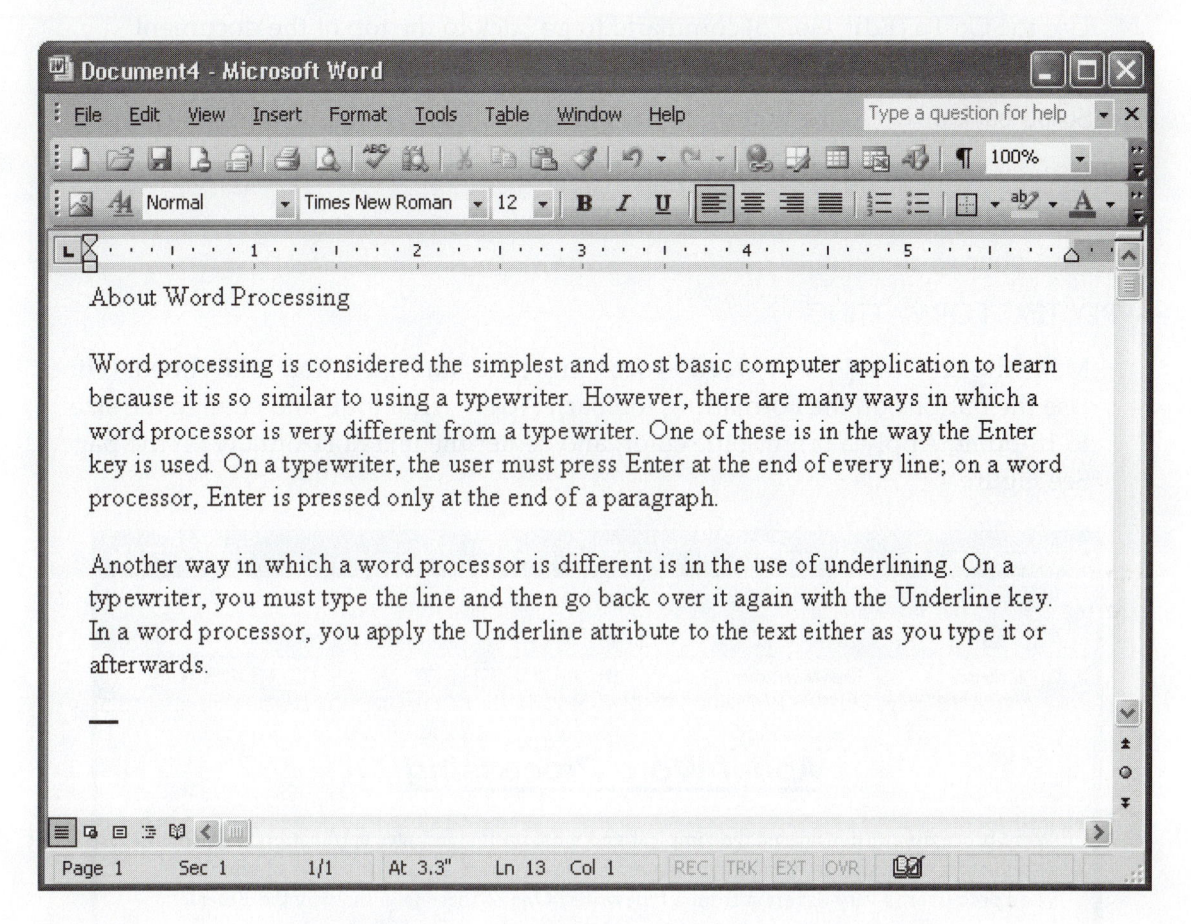

Figure 3: Type this text in your word processing application.

3. Save the file as **Editing1**.

4. Select the entire paragraph and copy it to the Clipboard (Ctrl + C).

5. Start a new, blank document and paste (Ctrl + V) the copy into it. Save the new document (Ctrl + S) as **Original** and then close it.

6. Select the word *user* and press Backspace or Delete to remove it. Then type *typist* in its place.

7. Using Find (Edit, Find), locate the word *many*. Delete it, and type *several* in its place.

8. Replace all instances of the phrase *word processor* with *word processing program*.

9. Use the Undo feature (Ctrl + Z) to undo the replacements; then use Redo to redo them again.

10. Select the entire document (Ctrl+A) and copy it to the Clipboard.

11. Open Notepad, and paste the document. Save it as **Editing2**; then close Notepad.

12. Return to the word processing application and save your work. (The file name should still be **Editing1**.)

13. Copy the second paragraph, and paste it at the bottom of the document six times in a row.

14. Use the Go To (Edit, Go To) command to go back to the top of the document (line 1).

15. Scroll back down to the bottom of the document again using the scroll bars.

16. Use the Undo feature to undo the six Paste operations you just performed. (Hint: The Undo button has a drop-down list.)

17. Save your work.

APPLY TEXT FORMATTING

1. Make the first line (About Word Processing) bold, italicized, and underlined. (Hint: Use the buttons on the Formatting toolbar.) Apply Arial font, and change the size to 18-point. Apply a bright-blue color, and center the text horizontally on the page. See Figure 4.

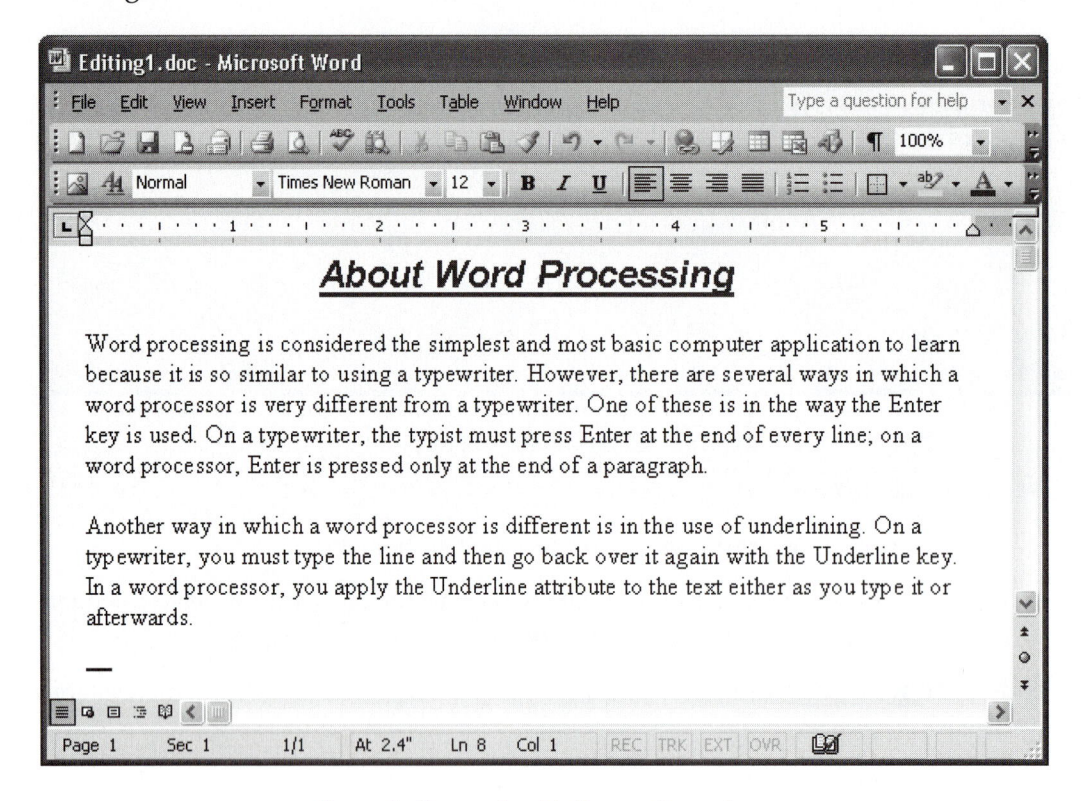

Figure 4: Format the title line as shown here.

2. Type the following text as a new paragraph at the end of the document.

   Yet another difference is in the use of superscript and subscript. On a typewriter, the paper had to be rolled down manually. In a word processing program you can create subscripts such as H20 or superscripts such as 102.

3. Apply a subscript to the 2 in H20, and apply a superscript to the 2 in 102. (Hint: Select Format, Font.) The paragraph should now appear like Figure 5.

4. Save your work.

Learning Computer Concepts

IC³-2
Key Applications

Yet another difference is in the use of superscript and subscript. On a typewriter, the paper had to be rolled down manually. In a word processing program you can create subscripts such as H_2O or superscripts such as 10^2.

Figure 5: The final paragraph should now contain superscript and subscript.

INSERT GRAPHICS AND DRAWINGS

1. Insert a graphic file from your disk into your document (Insert, Picture). You can use any of the bitmap images in the Windows folder or any other image file you like. Set its wrapping to Square. (Hint: Right-click on the picture and select Format Picture. Then, select the Layout tab.)

2. Use the Crop tool on the Picture toolbar to crop the picture.

3. Size the picture so it is exactly 2" wide and maintains its aspect ratio.

4. Position the picture to the right of the first paragraph of body text, as in Figure 6.

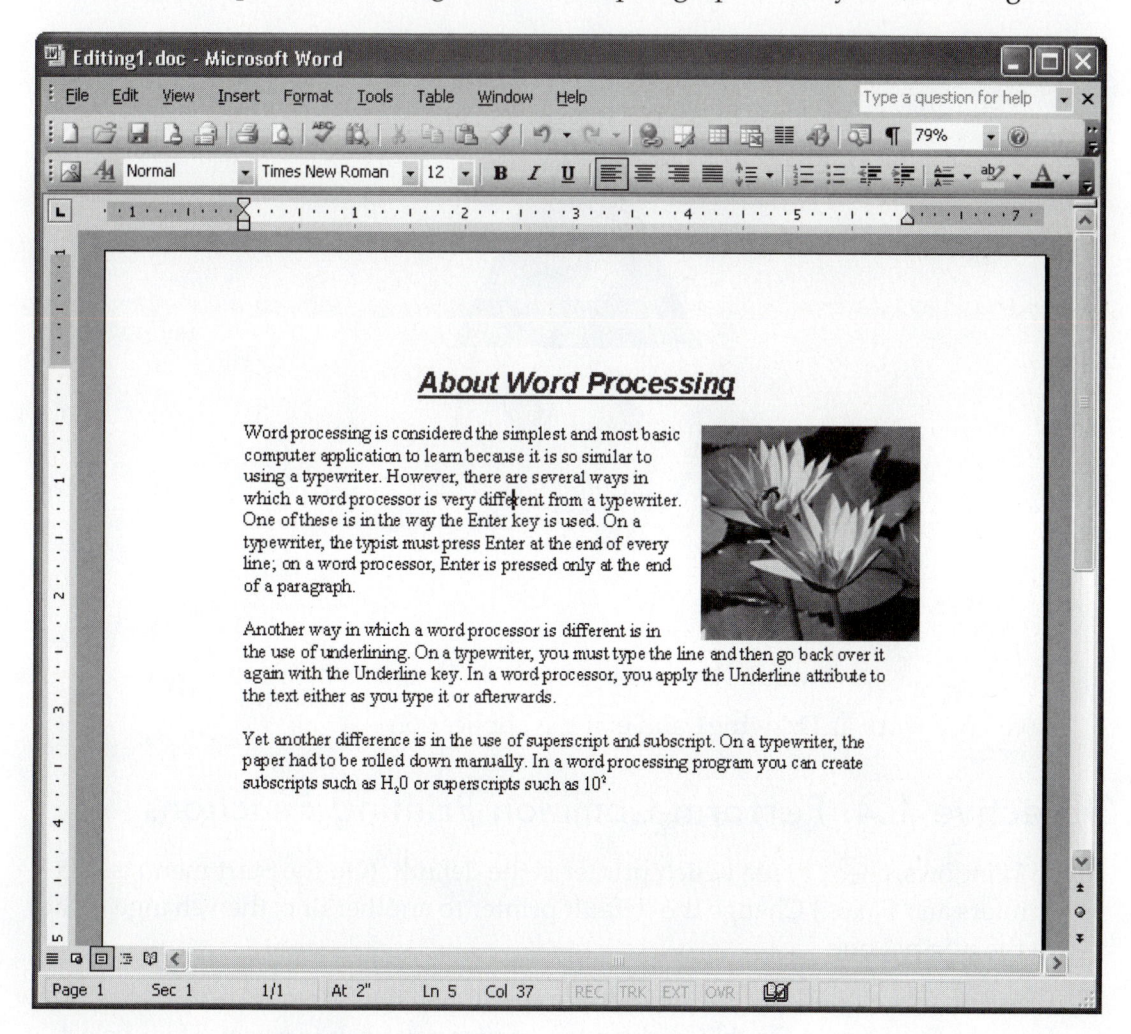

Figure 6: Place a picture next to the first paragraph.

5. Insert a piece of clip art from the Clip Organizer, and place it at the end of the document with Tight wrapping.

6. Make a copy of the clip art (right-click, copy), and place the copy somewhere else in the document.

7. Save your work and close the file.

8. Start a new, blank document, and draw a picture in it using the drawing tools in your word processing program. Include both lines and shapes, and at least four different colors and two line thicknesses. (Hint: Use the tools on the Drawing toolbar.)

9. Layer several shapes on top of one another, and change their stacking order using the Order command (or similar) in your word processing program. (Hint: Use the tools on the Draw menu on the Drawing toolbar.)

10. Group all the layered shapes into a single object, and move them to a different spot. Then ungroup them. Figure 7 shows one example; you can draw anything you like.

Figure 7: Draw a picture next to the first paragraph.

11. Save your work as **Drawing1** and exit the application.

Objective 1.4: Perform Common Printing Functions

1. In Windows, check to see which printer is the default. (On the Start menu, select Printers and Faxes.) Change the default printer to another one; then change it back to the original one.

2. Pause the print queue for the default printer. (Open the Printers and Faxes window from the Start menu. Double-click on the printer you wish to select. Then, select options from the Printer menu.)

3. Start your word processing program, and open **Editing1**.

4. Set the margins to 1.5" on all sides, and set the paper size to Letter if it is not already so (File, Page Setup). Set the Orientation to Landscape, as in Figure 8.

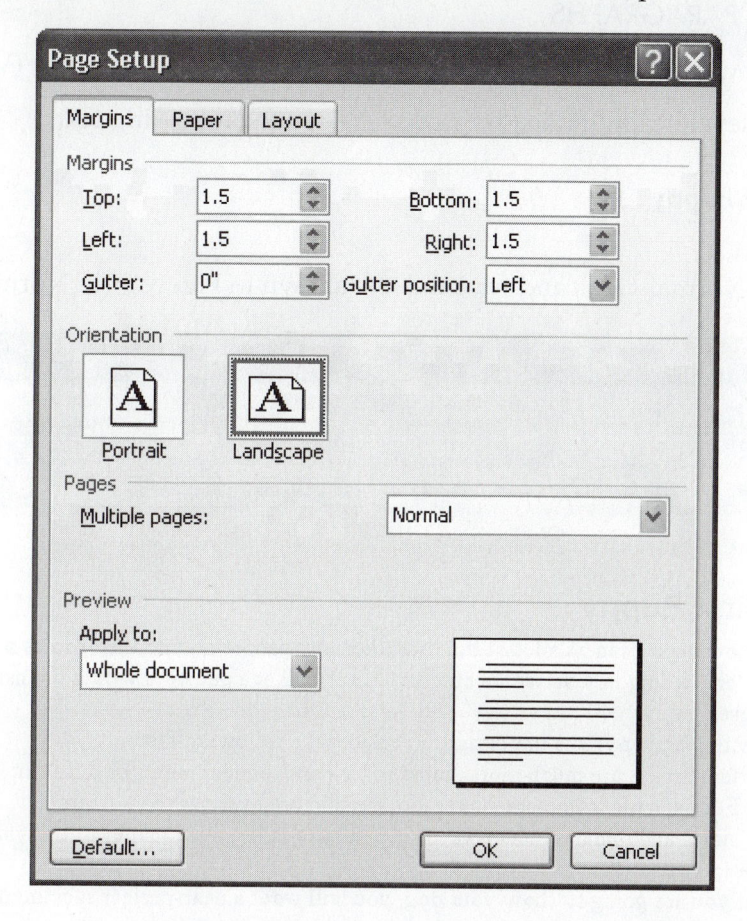

Figure 8: Set the page orientation. (Word is shown here.)

5. Use Print Preview to see how the document will print. Use the magnification feature to zoom in and out. If needed, solve any layout problems.

6. Print two copies of the first page on your default printer. (There might be only one page in total, but enter 1 as the page to print anyway.)

7. In Windows, display the printer's queue and un-pause it, allowing the pages to print.

8. (Optional) If another printer is available, print one copy on that printer.

9. Pause the default printer again.

10. In your word processing program, print the document using all default settings. Then exit the application.

Objective 2.1: Be able to format text and documents including the ability to use automatic formatting tools

FORMATTING PARAGRAPHS

1. Start your word processing application and switch to Outline view (View, Outline).

2. As a first-level heading (Heading 1 style), type the following text:

   Your First Puppy

3. Switch to Normal view, and type the text shown in Figure 9 (in Normal style):

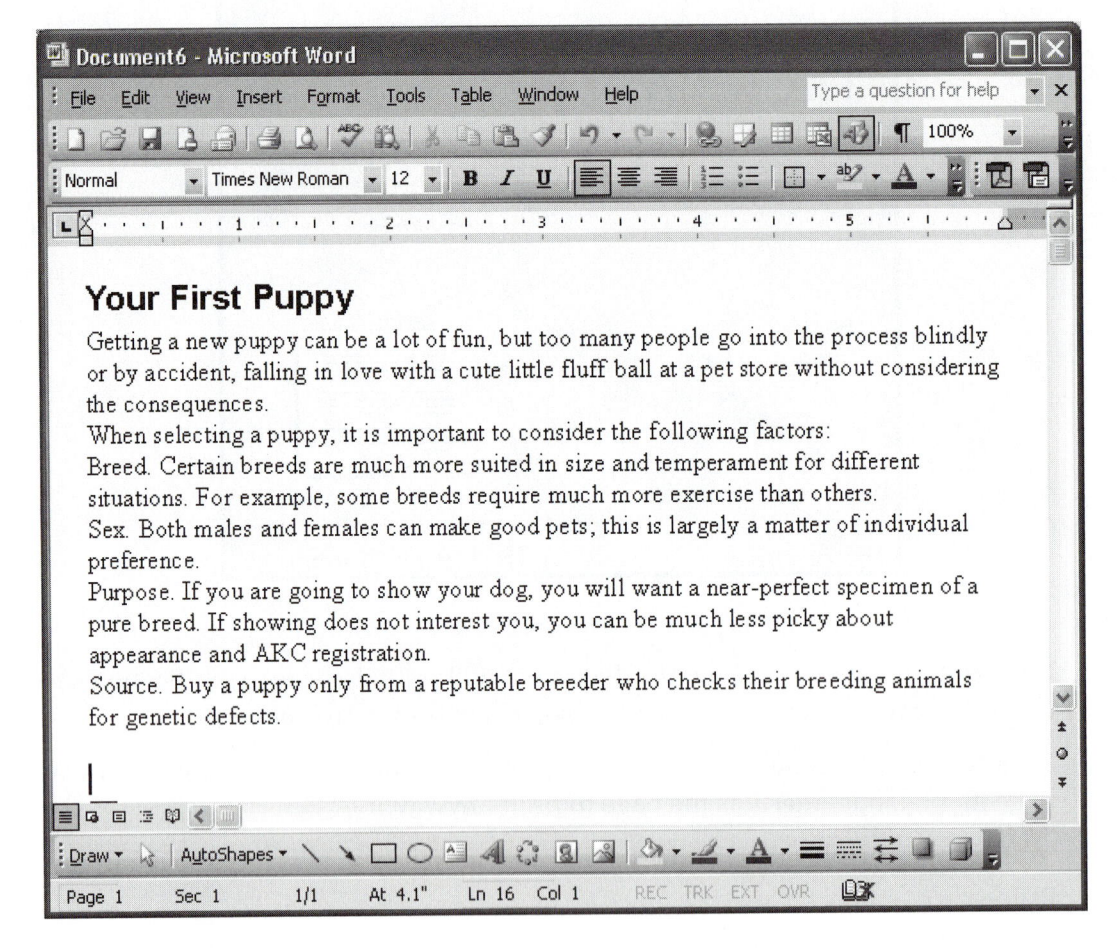

   Figure 9: Type this text.

4. Underline the heading, and create a new style based on the new formatting called **Modified H1**. (Hint: Select the text and then click Format, Styles and Formatting. Then, click New Style and enter information.)

5. Apply a border and light blue shading (Format, Boarders and Shading) to the Modified H1 paragraph, and then modify the style to reflect the new formatting.

6. Display the document statistics (File, Properties), and make a note of the word count.

WORK WITH BULLETS AND NUMBERING

1. Apply numbering to the last four paragraphs. Use the Bullets button on the Formatting toolbar.

2. Change the numbered list to a bulleted list, and choose a different bullet character than the default one (Format, Bullets and Numbering).

3. Bold the first word in the first bulleted paragraph, and then use Format Painter to copy the bold formatting to the first word of each of the other bulleted paragraphs.

4. For the first two body paragraphs (not the bullets), set the paragraph spacing to 12 points of space after each one (Format, Paragraph), and set the line spacing within each paragraph to 1.5 lines. Apply a 0.5" first-line indent to each one.

5. For each of the bulleted list items, set the paragraph spacing to 6 points of space after. At this point it should look like Figure 10.

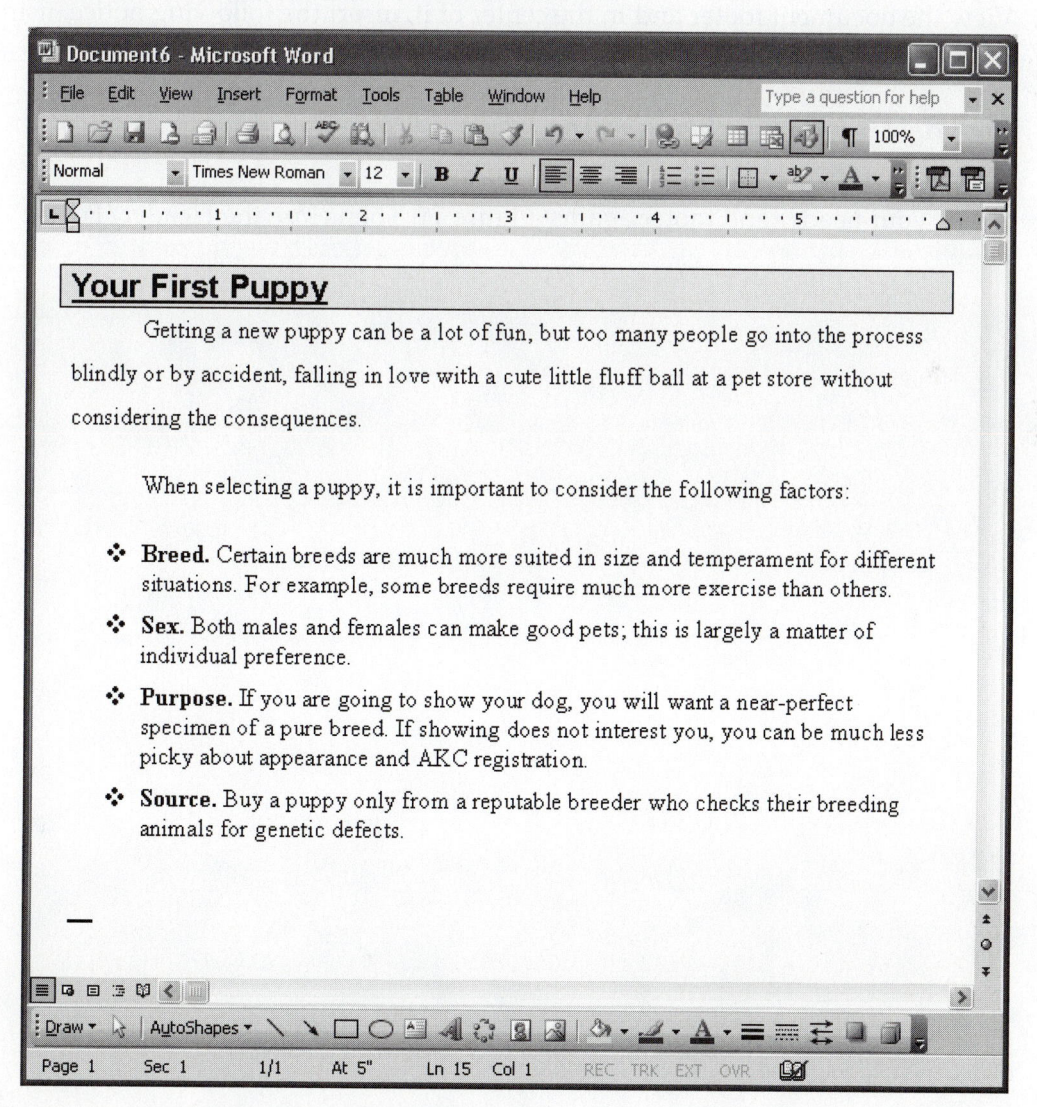

Figure 10: The text after the formatting has been applied.

6. Turn on the display of nonprinting characters, and make a note of the nonprinting symbols you see, such as paragraph breaks, tabs, indent markers, and spaces.

7. Create a page break immediately before the bulleted list (Ctrl + Enter).

8. Delete the page break.

9. Check the document for grammatical errors (Tools, Spelling and Grammar), and fix any that you find.

WORK WITH HEADERS AND FOOTERS

1. View the document header (View, Header and Footer), and insert the code for the current date on the left side.

2. On the right side of the document header, insert the code for the page number and format it as 10-point Arial. Use capital letters rather than digits.

3. View the document footer and in the center of it, insert the following notice, using the Symbol feature (Insert, Symbol) to insert the copyright symbol:

Copyright © Sycamore Services, Inc.

4. Check your header and footer against Figure 11. Then close the Header/Footer view.

Learning Computer Concepts

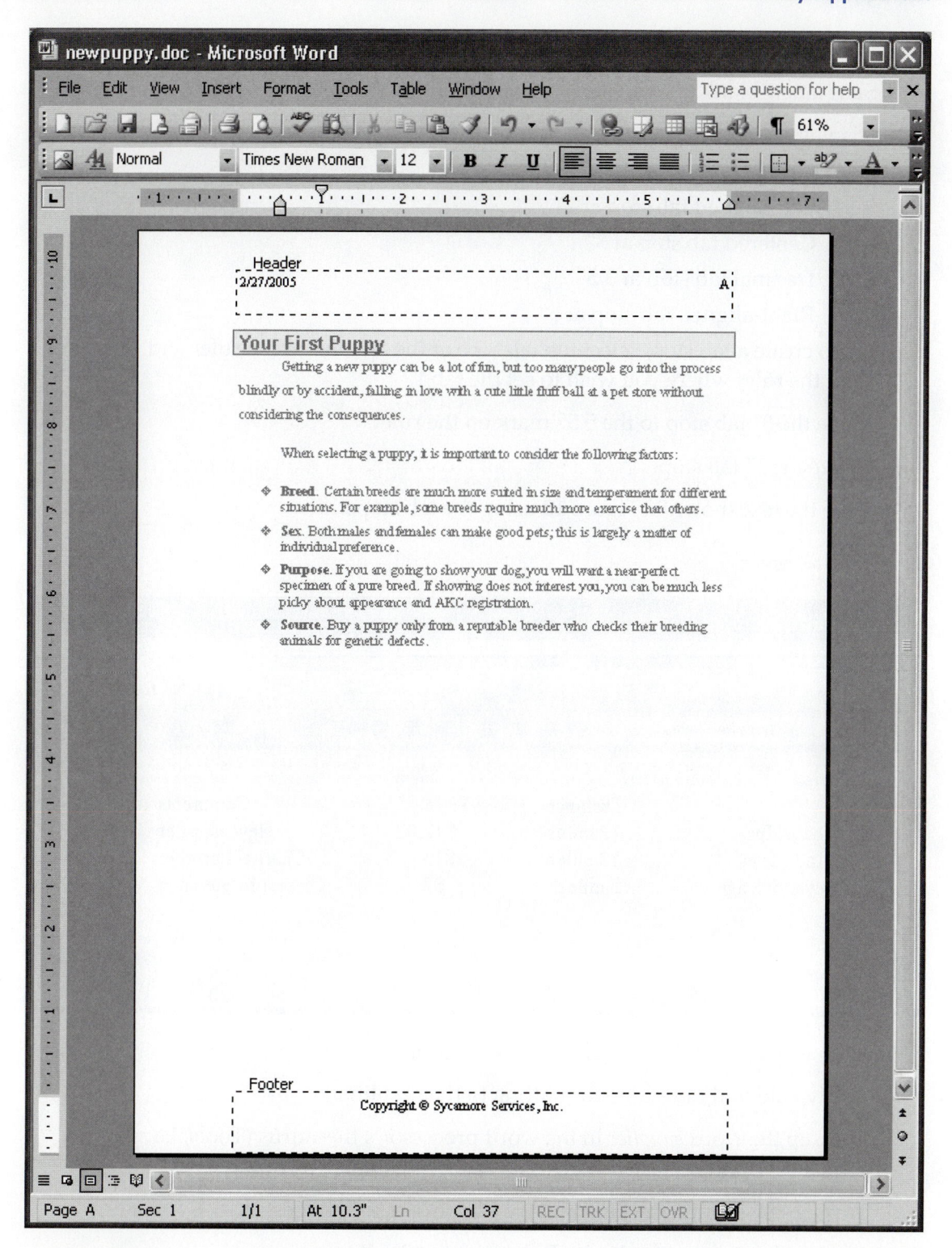

IC³-2
Key Applications

Figure 11: The text after the formatting has been applied.

5. Save your work as **NewPuppy** and close the document. Leave your word processing program open.

Key Applications

WORK WITH TABS

1. Start a new blank document.//
2. Display the ruler.
3. Create the following tab stops in the new paragraph:
    - Left-aligned tab stop at 2"
    - Centered tab stop at 3"
    - Decimal tab stop at 3.5"
    - Right-aligned tab stop at 6"

   (To create a tab stop, select the tab type at the left end of the ruler and then click on the ruler where you wish to set the tab.)
4. Move the 6" tab stop to the 5.5" mark on the ruler.
5. Delete the 3" tab stop.
6. Type the text shown in Figure 12 using the tab stops:

Click to select tab type.

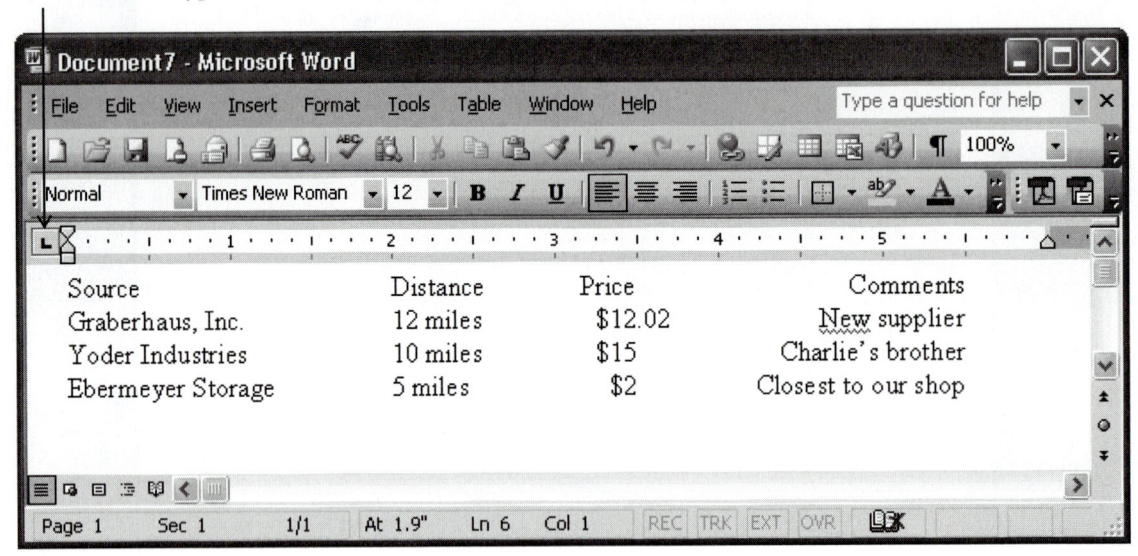

```
Source              Distance    Price       Comments
Graberhaus, Inc.    12 miles    $12.02      New supplier
Yoder Industries    10 miles    $15         Charlie's brother
Ebermeyer Storage   5 miles     $2          Closest to our shop
```

Figure 12: Start with this text.

7. Apply bold and underline formatting to the first line.
8. Look up the word *supplier* in the word processor's thesaurus (Tools, Language, Thesaurus), and replace it with a different, but similar-meaning word.
9. Turn on the change-tracking feature (Tools, Track Changes).
10. Change the distance for Yoder Industries to **18 miles**.
11. Change the price of Ebermeyer Storage to **$2.50**.
12. Attach a comment to Yoder Industries that says **I think this is 18 miles, not 10** (Insert, Comment).

Learning Computer Concepts

IC³-2
Key Applications

13. Display the Comments pane if it does not already appear. (Hint: It displays automatically when you switch to Normal view.)

14. Attach a footnote to Graberhaus, Inc that says **Located in Macon County.** (From the Insert menu, select Reference, Footnote.) Format the footnote as italic 10-point Arial.

15. Turn off the change-tracking feature.

16. Print the document, including comments. (In the Print dialog box, select Document showing markup from the Print what drop-down list.)

17. Accept all the tracked changes except for one: reject the tracked change for Ebermeyer Storage. At this point your document should resemble Figure 13.

18. Save your work as **Suppliers** and close the file.

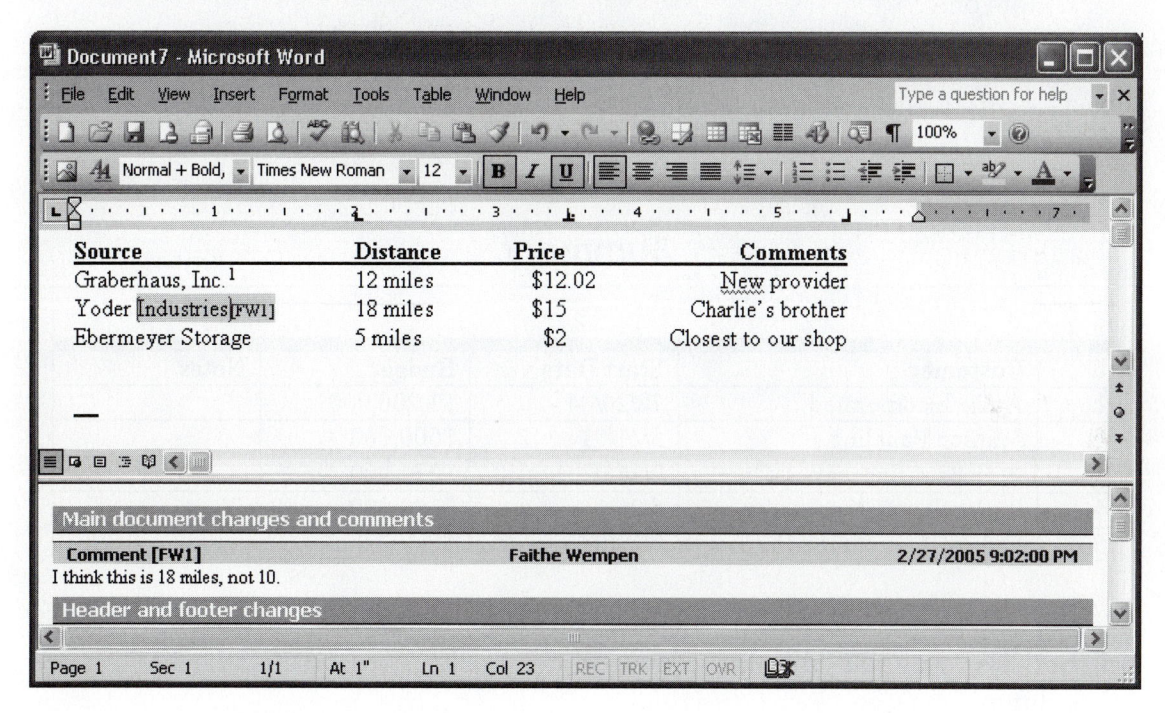

Figure 13: The text after the changes have been made and accepted.

Objective 2.2: Be able to insert, edit and format tables in a document

INSERT AND MODIFY A TABLE

1. Start your word processing program, and start a new document.

2. Insert a table consisting of six rows and four columns (Table, Insert Table).

3. Select the first row, and delete it.

4. Select the third column, and delete it.

5. Insert two new columns to the right of the existing ones.

6. Insert two new rows at the bottom of the table.

7. Merge all the cells in the top row into a single cell, and in that cell, type **Summary**. (Hint: Select the cells, right-click on them, and select Merge Cells.) Format the text as bold 16-point Arial. Set the row height to 1". (Right-click and select Table Properties.)

8. Center the word **Summary** both vertically and horizontally in its cell.

9. Remove the border from all sides of the Summary cell (Format, Borders and Shading), and apply a pale blue background fill to that cell only. (Note: The border may continue to appear as a gray line around the cell if your display is set up to show all gridlines.)

10. Modify the Summary cell's border so that it has a thick black border along the bottom only.

11. Set the width of Column 1 (left-most column) to 0.5" using any method.

12. Type the data shown in Figure 14.

	Summary			
	Customer	Start Date	Budget	Notes
1	Acme Incorporated	12/24/04	$1,200,000	
2	Johnson Paneling	5/21/01	$500,000	
3	Archibald Excavation Co.	2/16/03	$274,000	
4	Lucky Seven Automotive	6/9/01	$100,000	
5	Federal Acceptance Corp.	9/12/02	$2,400,000	

Figure 14: Enter this data in the table after formatting the table grid.

1. Sort the data in the table in Ascending order (Table, Sort) based on the Budget column.

2. Split the top cell (Summary) vertically, creating an additional row (Table, Split Cells). In the new row, enter **Arthur Industries** and change the font size to 12.

3. Remove the bottom border from the Summary cell.

4. Split the table between rows 1 and 2 so that Summary is its own separate table.

5. Convert the Summary table to text (Table, Convert, Table to Text). At this point the table should resemble Figure 15.

6. Save your work as **Arthur** and close the file.

	Summary		
	Arthur Industries		
	Customer	Start Date	Budget	Notes
2	Johnson Paneling	5/21/01	$500,000	
4	Lucky Seven Automotive	6/9/01	$100,000	
5	Federal Acceptance Corp.	9/12/02	$2,400,000	
3	Archibald Excavation Co.	2/16/03	$274,000	
1	Acme Incorporated	12/24/04	$1,200,000	

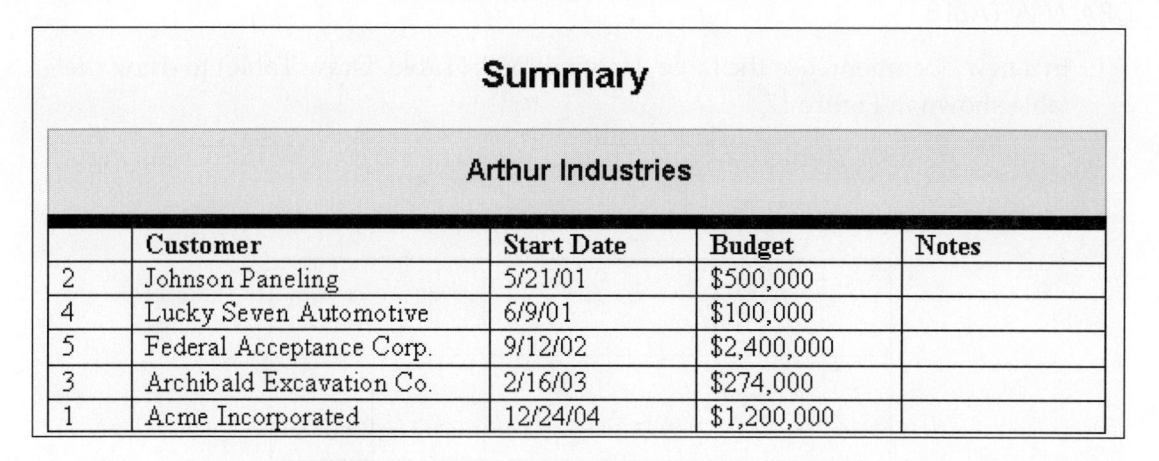

Figure 15: The table after applying the new formatting.

CONVERT TEXT TO A TABLE

1. In a new document, set left-aligned tab stops at 2" and 4" and enter the text shown in Figure 16.

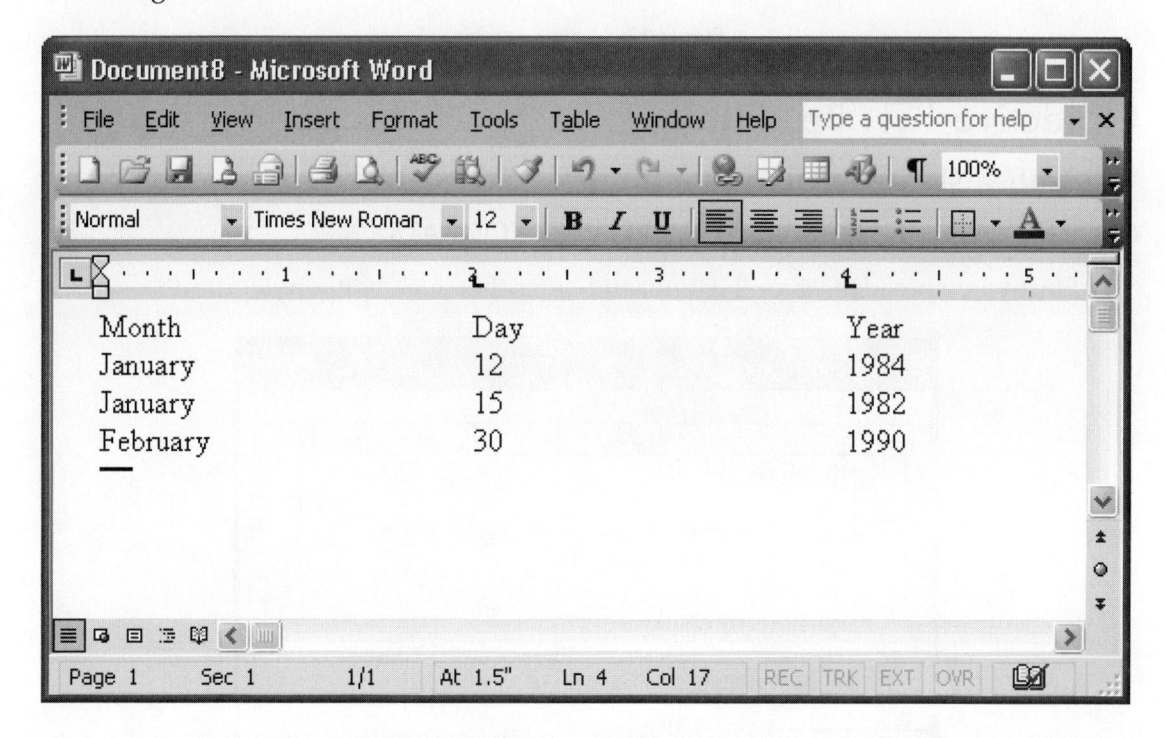

Figure 16: Start by typing this data using tab stops.

2. Convert the text to a table (Table, Convert, Text to Table).

3. Apply an AutoFormat (Table, Table AutoFormat) to the table with special formats applied only to Heading rows.

4. Save your work as **Convert** and close the file.

Key Applications

DRAW A TABLE

1. In a new document, use the table drawing tools (Table, Draw Table) to draw the table shown in Figure 17.
2. Save your work as **tabledraw** and close the file. Then exit the word processing program.

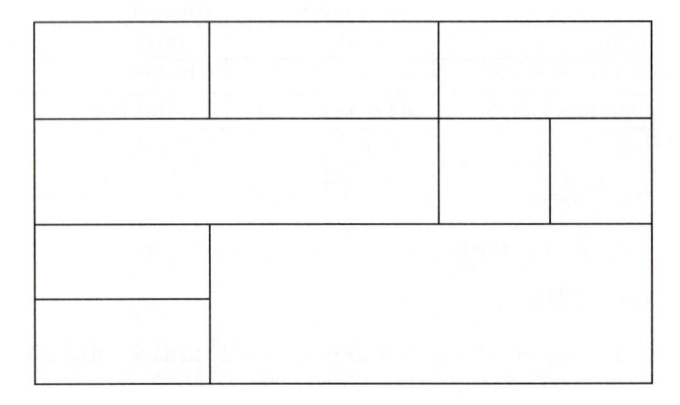

Figure 17: Draw this table.

Objective 3.1: Be able to modify worksheet data and structure and format data in a worksheet

CREATE A WORKSHEET AND APPLY NUMBER FORMATS

1. Start your spreadsheet application, and enter the data shown in Figure 18.

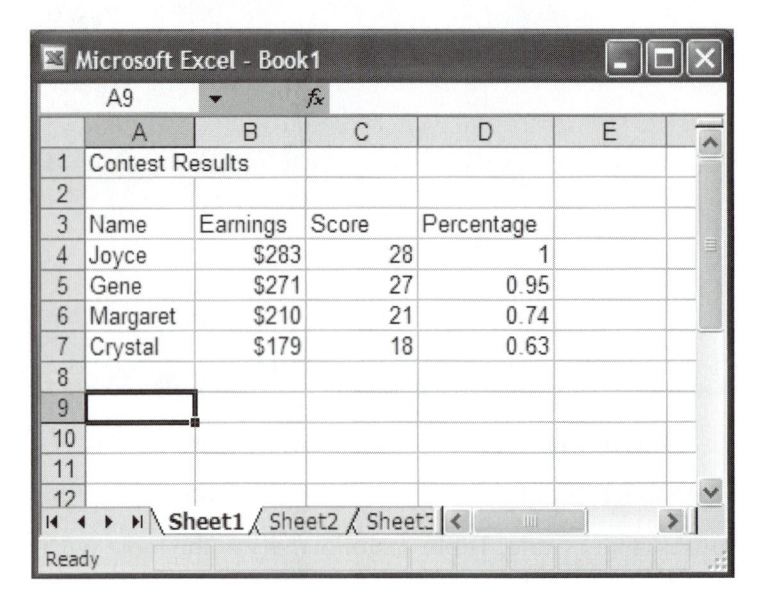

Figure 18: Enter this data.

2. Insert a new column between columns A and B (Insert, Column).
3. Delete row 7 (Crystal's data).

4. Select column C. Move the contents of column C into column B, and then delete column C. (Hint: Select the column, then cut—Ctrl + X—and paste—Ctrl + V—the contents.)

5. Edit A6, changing *Margaret* to **Marjorie**.

6. Select the entire worksheet (Ctrl +A); then deselect it.

7. Select cell A1 and press Ctrl+B to make its contents bold.

8. Select row 3 and press Ctrl+I to make its contents italicized.

9. Select the range B4:B6 and apply the Currency style with two decimal places (Format, Cells).

10. Merge and center cells A1:D1 (Format, Cells).

11. Select the range D4:D6 and apply the Percentage format.

12. Select the range C4:C6 and apply the Number format with one decimal place.

13. In cell A2, enter the current date and apply the mm/dd/yy date format to it.

14. Change the date's format to one that includes the day of the week, and widen column A if needed using AutoFit.

15. Select rows 1 and 2, and set their row heights to 24 each.

16. Delete column C.

17. Insert a new row between Gene and Marjorie with this data:

Albert	$110.00	39%

18. Select A3:C7 and apply an AutoFormat (Format, AutoFormat).

19. Merge and center A2:C2. At this point the worksheet should resemble Figure 19.

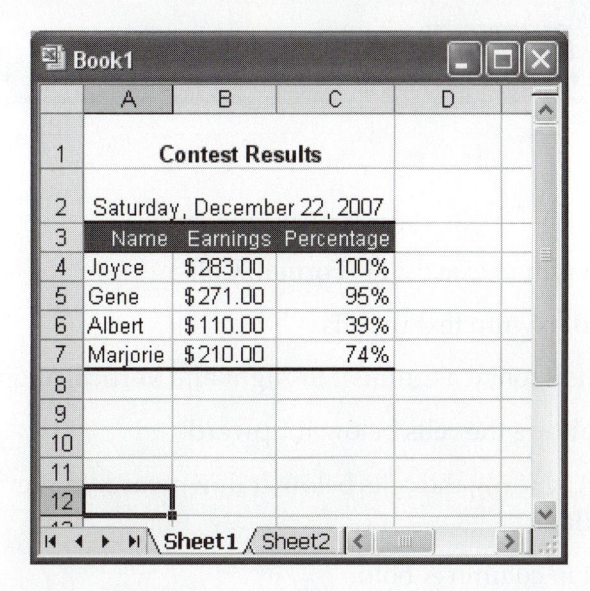

Figure 19: The worksheet after applying the specified formatting.

20. Save the file as **Contest**. Leave it open.

USE FILLS AND CREATE/DELETE SHEETS

1. Start in the Contest file. Rename the Sheet1 tab **Results**. (Right-click the sheet tab and select Rename.)

2. Delete all the other worksheets (right-click sheet tab, Delete).

3. Insert a new worksheet, and rename its tab **Schedule** (right-click sheet tab, Insert).

4. On the Schedule tab, enter **Monday** in A4, and then use the Fill feature to fill in Tuesday through Sunday in cells A5:A10. To use the Fill feature, select the cell and click on the fill handle (the dark box in the cell's lower-right corner). Drag the fill handle down, up, left, or right. Click the AutoFill Options button and select a fill option.)

5. Enter the data shown in Figure 20.

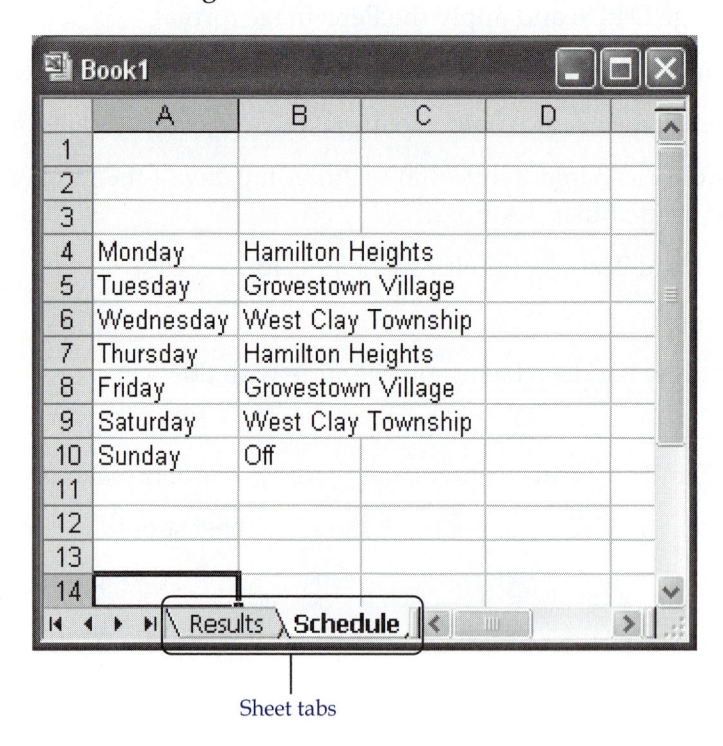

Figure 20: Enter this data.

6. Set column B's width to exactly 11 (Format, Cells).

7. Format column B to wrap text in cells.

8. Set column A's horizontal alignment to Right and vertical alignment to Top.

9. Delete cell B6, shifting the cells below it upward.

10. Insert a cell at B4, shifting the cells below it downward. In the new B4, enter **Grovestown Village**.

11. Make all the text in column A bold.

12. Create a thin blue border around all sides of all cells in the range A4:B10.

13. Save your work. At this point the worksheet should resemble Figure 21.
14. Leave the workbook open for the next exercise.

Figure 21: The worksheet after the specified formatting has been applied.

Objective 3.2: Be able to sort data, manipulate data using formulas and functions and add and modify charts in a worksheet

USE COMMON FUNCTIONS

1. If necessary, open the **Contest** file from the previous section, and display the Results tab.

2. Sort rows 4 through 7 in Descending order by Earnings (Data, Sort).

3. Insert a new row (Insert, Row) between Gene and Marjorie, with this data:

| Maurice | $110.00 | 39% |

4. Sort rows 4 through 8 in Descending order, first by Earnings and then by Name in Ascending order.

5. Enter the labels in column A shown in Figure 22.

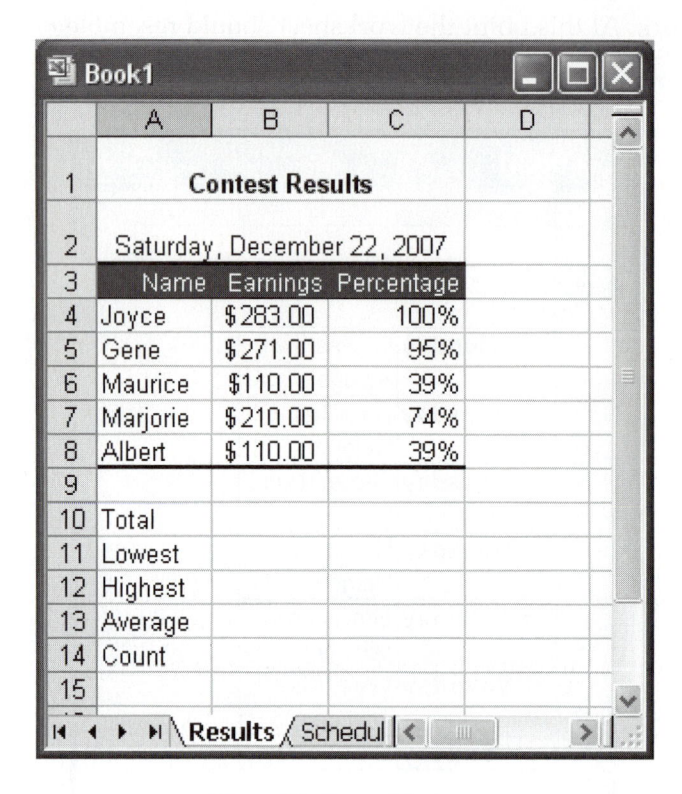

Figure 22: Enter this data.

6. In B10, use AutoSum to total the values from B4:B8. (Select cell B10, and then click the AutoSum button on the Standard toolbar. Check to make sure that the AutoSum marquee surrounds the correct range of data, and then click Enter.)

7. In B11, use the MIN function to show the minimum value in B4:B8. (Select cell B11. Press **=** and then type **MIN**. Type an opening parenthesis [(]. Select the range to be summed, and then type the closing parenthesis [)]. Press Enter.)

8. In B12, use the MAX function to show the maximum value in B4:B8. (Hint: Follow the steps for entering a MIN function, but type **MAX**.)

9. In B13, use the AVERAGE function to show the average value in B4:B8. (Hint: Follow the steps for entering a MIN function, but type **AVERAGE**.)

10. In B14, use the COUNT function to count the number of items in B4:B8. (Hint: Follow the steps for entering a MIN function, but type **COUNT**.)

11. In C4, replace the manually entered percentage with the formula **=B4/B12**.

12. Modify the formula in C4 to use an absolute reference to B12 (B12). (An absolute reference in a formula always refers to the same cell, even if you copy the formula to another location.)

13. Copy the formula from C4 to C5:C8. At this point it should resemble Figure 23.

14. Save your work. Leave the file open for the next exercise.

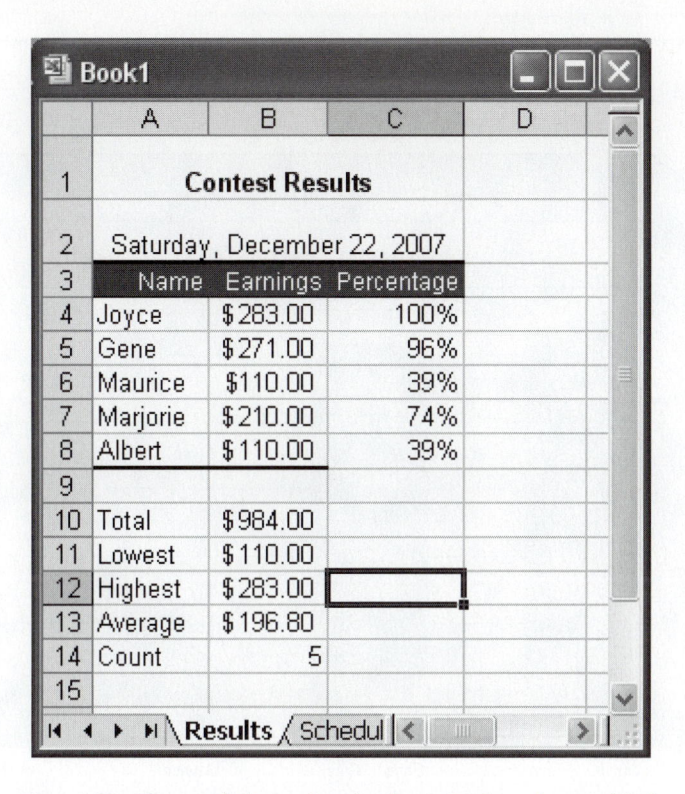

	A	B	C	D
1		Contest Results		
2	Saturday, December 22, 2007			
3	Name	Earnings	Percentage	
4	Joyce	$283.00	100%	
5	Gene	$271.00	96%	
6	Maurice	$110.00	39%	
7	Marjorie	$210.00	74%	
8	Albert	$110.00	39%	
9				
10	Total	$984.00		
11	Lowest	$110.00		
12	Highest	$283.00		
13	Average	$196.80		
14	Count	5		
15				

Figure 23: The worksheet after the formulas have been added.

CREATE A CHART

1. Create a pie chart using the range A4:B8, and place it on its own separate tab. To create a chart with the Chart Wizard, first select the data to chart. Click the Chart Wizard (or, Insert, Chart). Follow the steps to create a standard or custom chart type. Click Finish.

2. Change the chart type to 3D Clustered Column (Chart, Chart Type).

3. Delete the legend, and change the background color (the walls) to light gray. Change the color of the bars to red. Right-click on the chart and select desired options.

4. Change the data range so that row 8 is excluded.

5. Label the vertical axis **Earnings**.

6. Change the vertical axis's scale so that its maximum value is $400.

7. Add the title **Contest Results** to the chart. At this point, the chart should resemble Figure 24.

8. Save your work and exit the application.

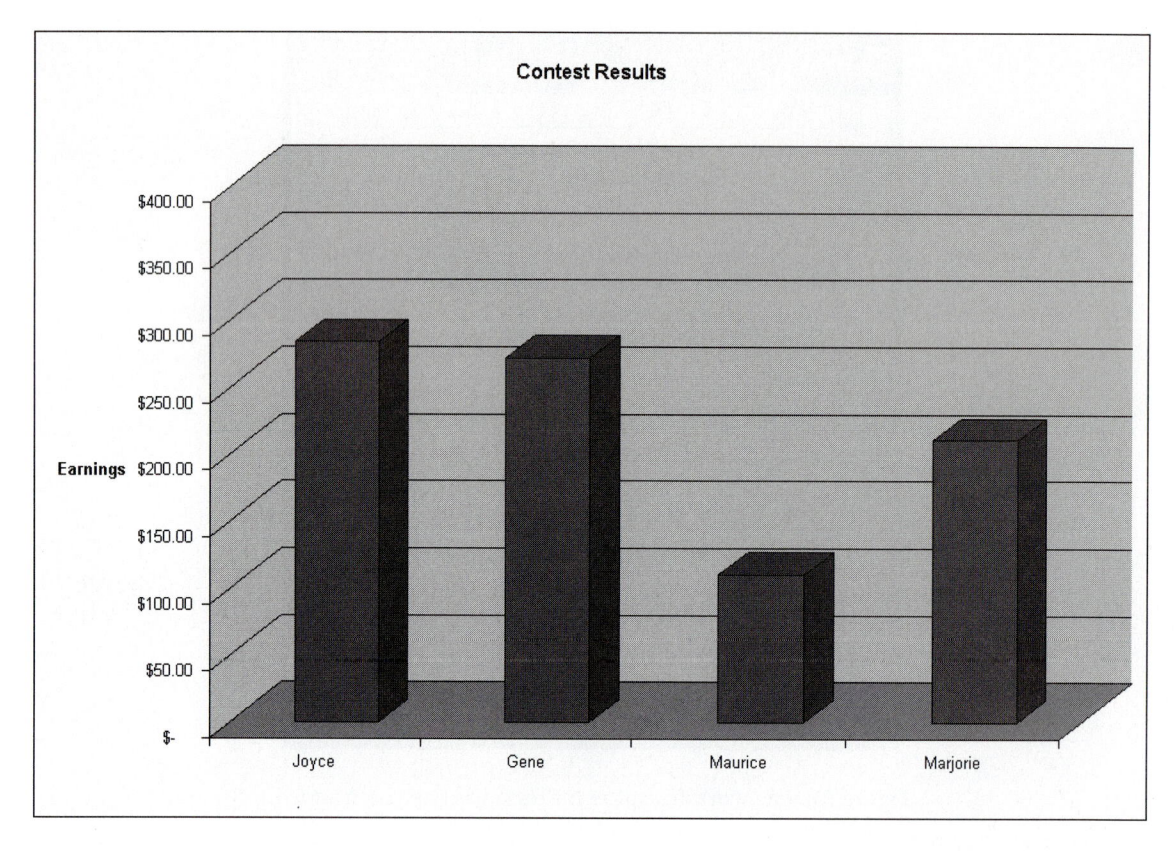

Figure 24: The finished chart.

Objective 4.1: Be able to create and format simple presentations

1. Open your presentation application, and start a new presentation.

2. Apply a design template to the presentation (Format, Slide Design). Choose one with a blue background.

3. Insert a title slide if one does not appear automatically in the new presentation, and type your name and company or school name.

4. On the title slide, insert a piece of clip art (Insert, Picture, Clip Art) that is appropriate for your company or your school, and resize/move it to place it attractively. Figure 25 shows an example.

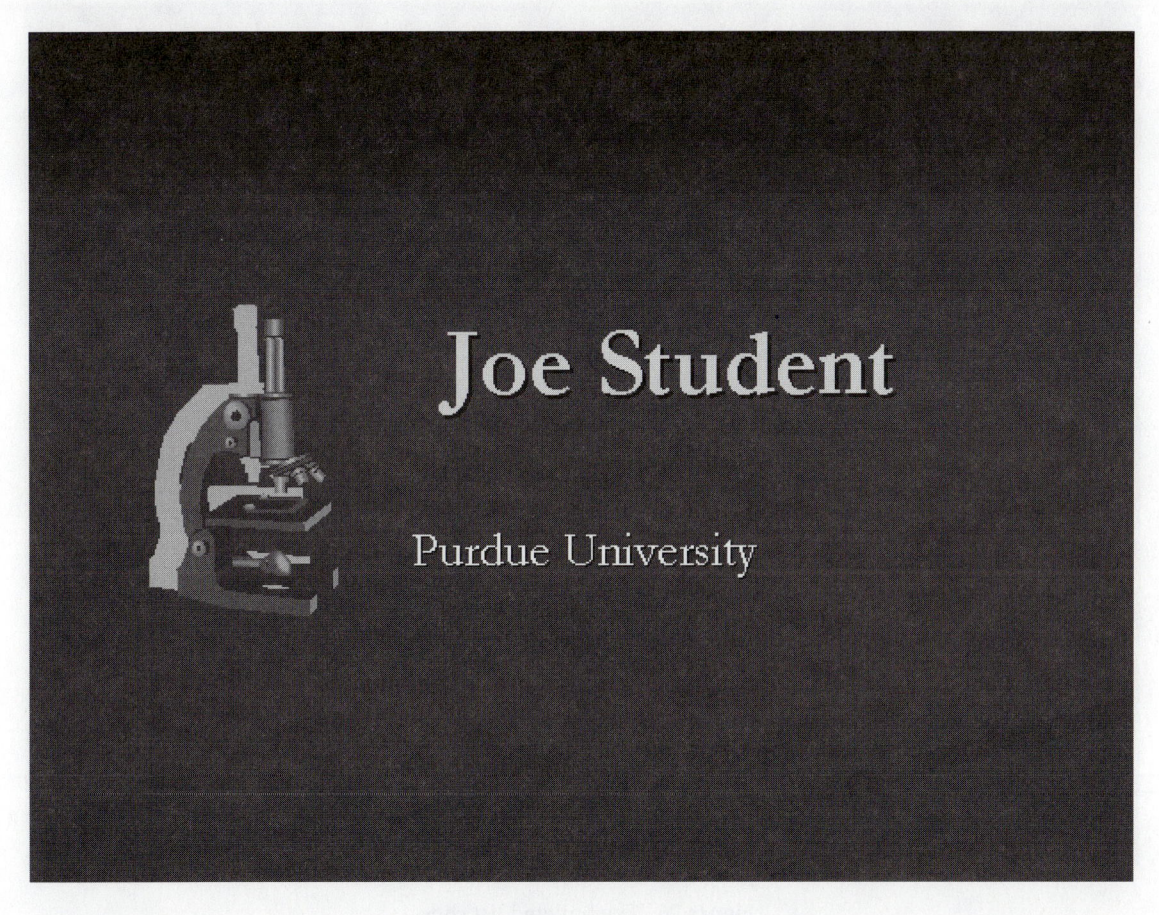

Figure 25: The title slide.

5. Change the title slide's background to a different color (Format, Background), leaving all other slides in the presentation as the original color.

6. Insert a new slide (Insert, New Slide) with a title and a bulleted list. For the title, type **Overview**. Type the following three bullets on the slide:
    - Academics
    - Research
    - Sports

7. Display the Slide Master (View, Master, Slide Master). Draw a small yellow star (using an AutoShape from the Drawing toolbar), and place it in the bottom-left corner of the Slide Master. Close the Slide Master. Figure 26 shows how slide #2 looks at this point.

Overview

- Academics
- Research
- Sports

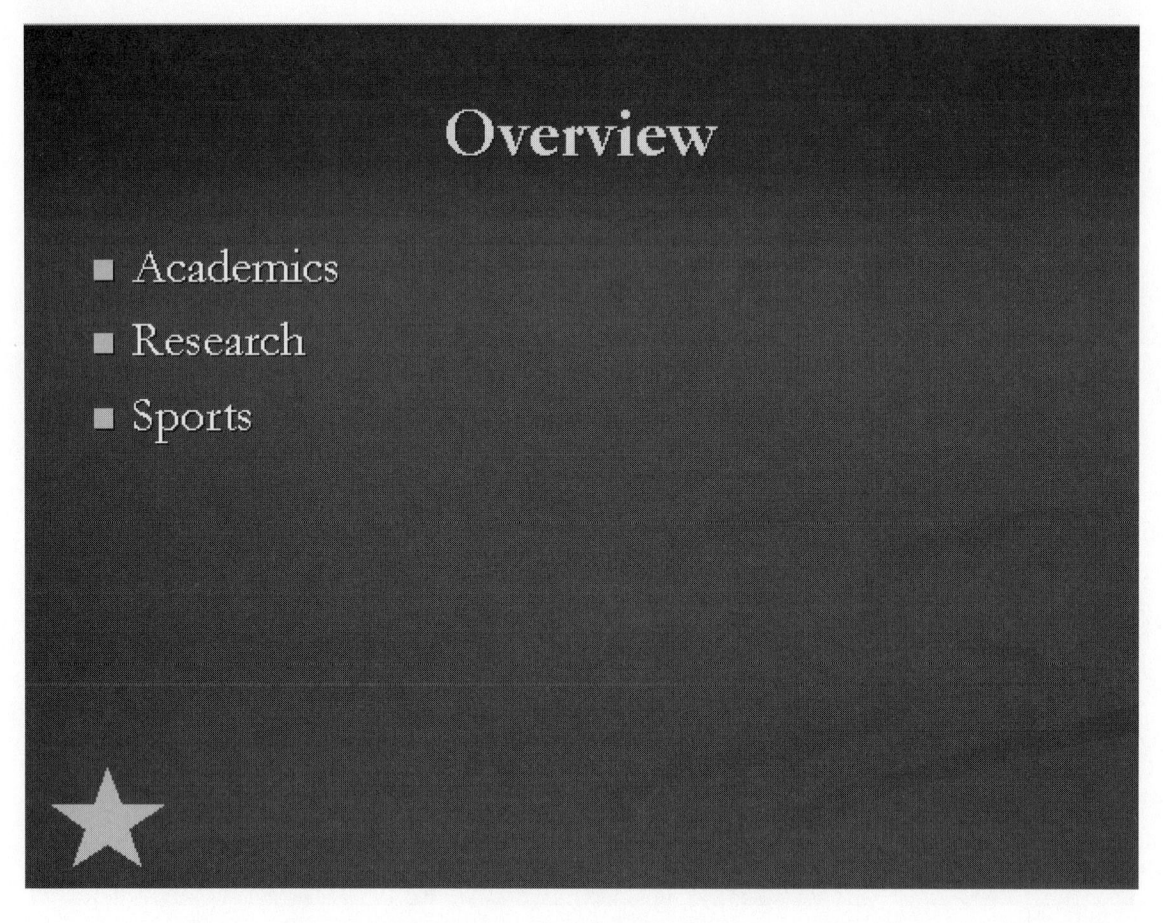

Figure 26: The bulleted list slide.

8. Insert a new slide with a Chart layout. Enter the chart information shown in Figure 27. (Double-click on the chart icon that appears on the chart slide, and then enter the information in the datasheet that appears. Click on the slide to close the datasheet and view the chart.)

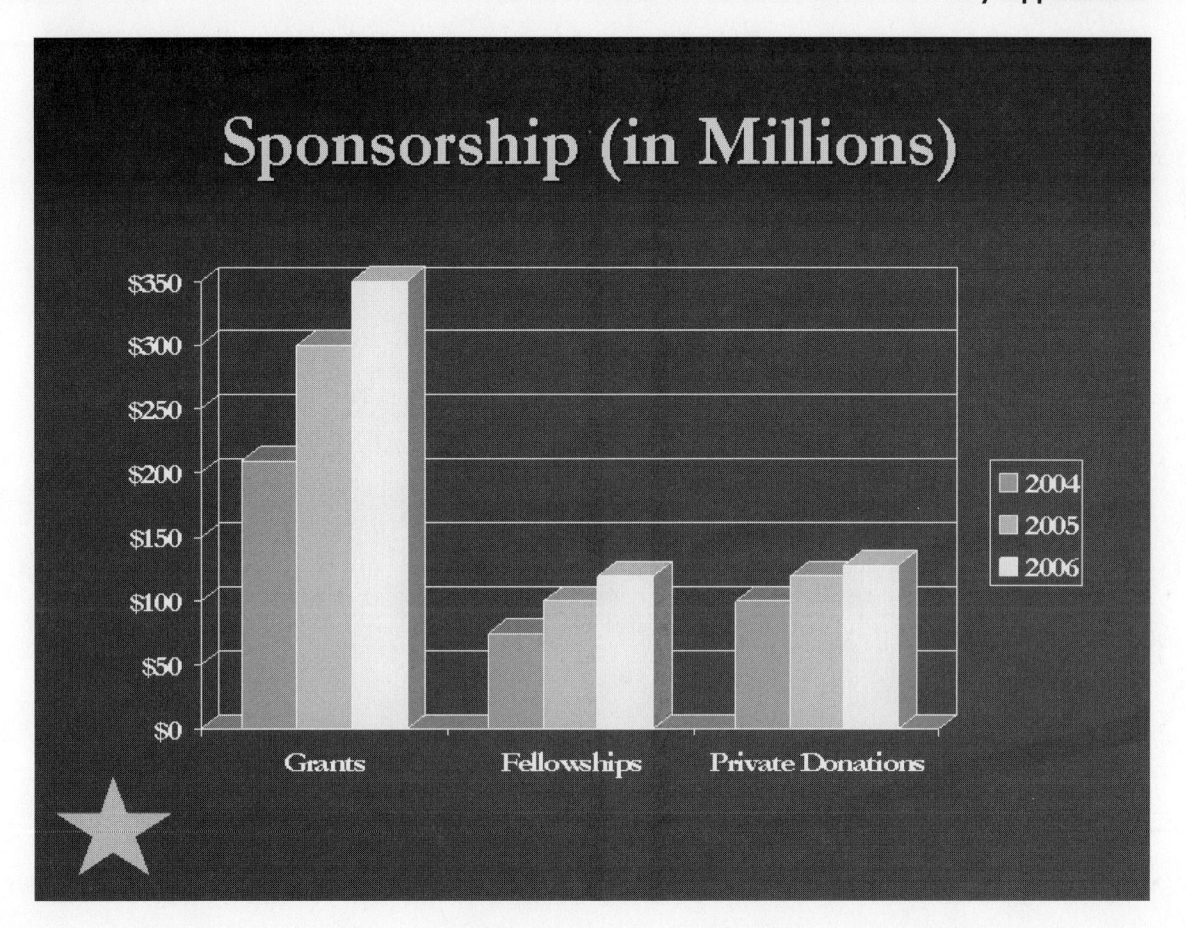

Figure 27: The chart slide.

9. Insert a new slide with a Table layout. Create the table shown in Figure 28, including borders on all sides of all cells. (Double-click the table icon that appears on the Table slide, and then select the table size. Use the Tables and Borders toolbar, which displays, to add borders.)

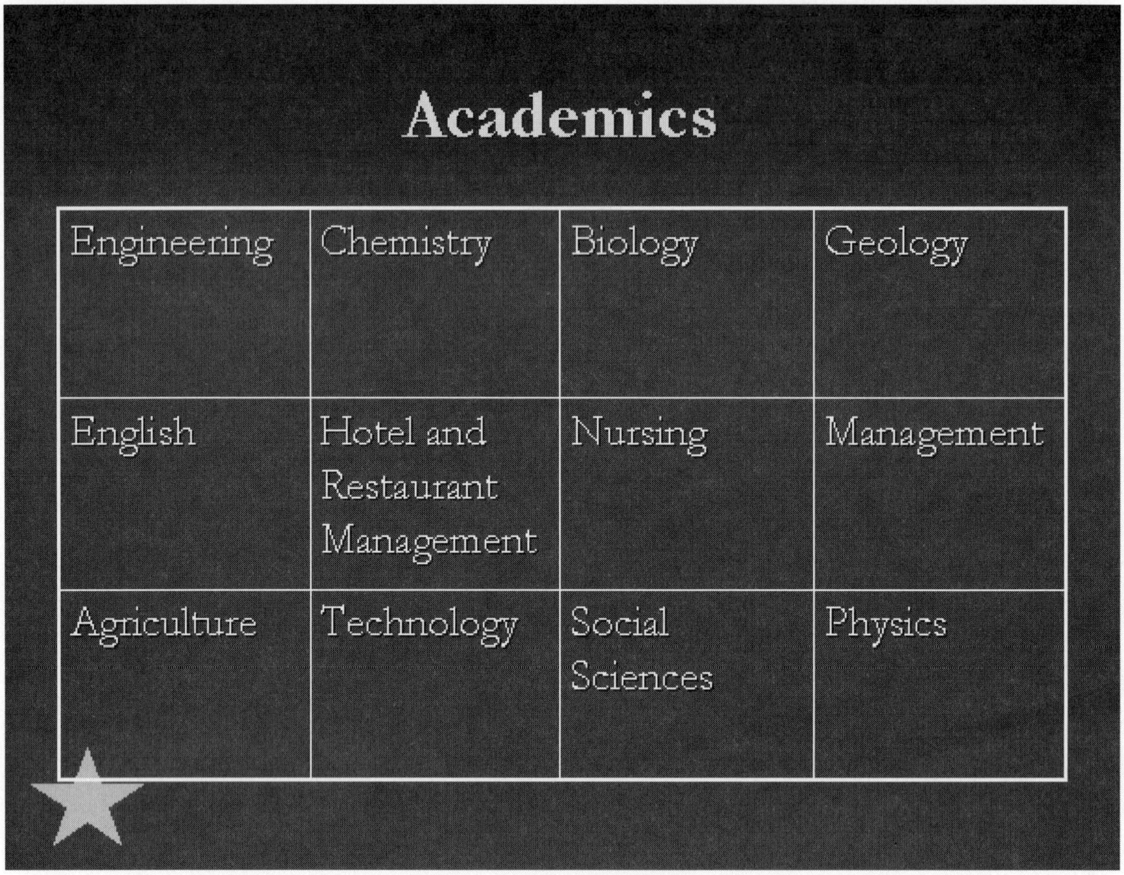

Academics

Engineering	Chemistry	Biology	Geology
English	Hotel and Restaurant Management	Nursing	Management
Agriculture	Technology	Social Sciences	Physics

Figure 28: The table slide.

10. Switch to Slide Sorter view (View, Slide Sorter), and move the chart slide after the table slide. Click and drag the slide to move it. Then switch back to Normal view.

11. Reopen the Slide Master, and apply a Shadow effect to the star AutoShape. Use the Shadow Style button on the Drawing toolbar. Then close Slide Master view.

12. Create a new slide with a two-column bulleted list layout, as shown in Figure 29.

[Slide image: "Sports" with two columns — Football, Basketball, Rugby, Tennis, Swimming, Diving | Gymnastics, Volleyball, Field Hockey, Table Tennis, Ice Hockey, Skeet Shooting]

Figure 29: The two-column list slide.

13. Duplicate slide #2 (Edit, Duplicate), and place the copy at the end of the presentation. Edit the title to read **Summary**.

14. Assign transition effects to all slides (Slide Show, Slide Transition).

15. Print a set of handouts with six slides per page.

16. Annotate the presentation by typing speaker's notes for each slide. (Type whatever text you like.)

17. Print a set of speaker notes pages.

18. Preview the presentation in Slide Show view (View, Slide Show):
    - Go through the entire presentation from start to finish.
    - Jump back to the second slide. (Hint: Right-click on slide, select Go to Slide, 2.)
    - Go to the previous slide.
    - End the slide show (Esc).

19. Save the file as **MyShow** and close the file.

IC³-3: LIVING ONLINE EXERCISES

In this section you will practice key skills for working with the Internet and networking.

Objective 2.2: Identify how to use an electronic mail application

WORKING WITH ADDRESS BOOKS

1. Start your e-mail application. If needed, set up your e-mail account, including configuring the connection to your mail server.

2. Create at least four new entries in your e-mail program's Address Book. (Note: Microsoft Office Outlook has a Contacts list and also access to a Windows Address Book; depending on how the software is configured, they may be separate or linked. You can use either for this exercise.)

3. Open one of the addresses in your Address Book and change the person's name or e-mail address. Figure 1 shows a Windows Address Book entry being edited.

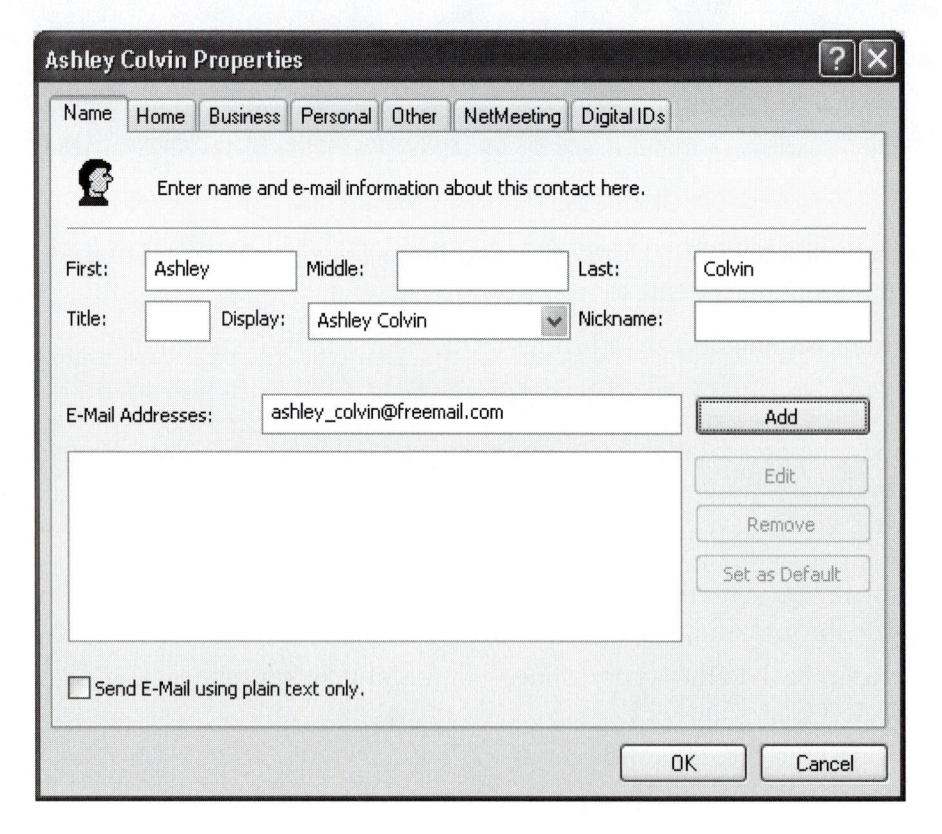

Figure 1: A Windows Address Book entry.

4. Delete one of the addresses in your Address Book.

5. Create a mailing list in your Address Book consisting of three addresses. Name it **MyList1**.

SEND E-MAIL MESSAGES

1. In any text editing program, such as a word processor, create a file containing your full name. Save it as **ForMail** in the My Documents folder. Then close the text editing program.

2. In your e-mail program, begin composing a new message. Address it to yourself, and CC it to one of the people in your address book. For the Subject line, enter **This is Only a Test**. In the body of the message, type **I am testing my e-mail software**.

3. Attach the ForMail file to the message. See Figure 2.

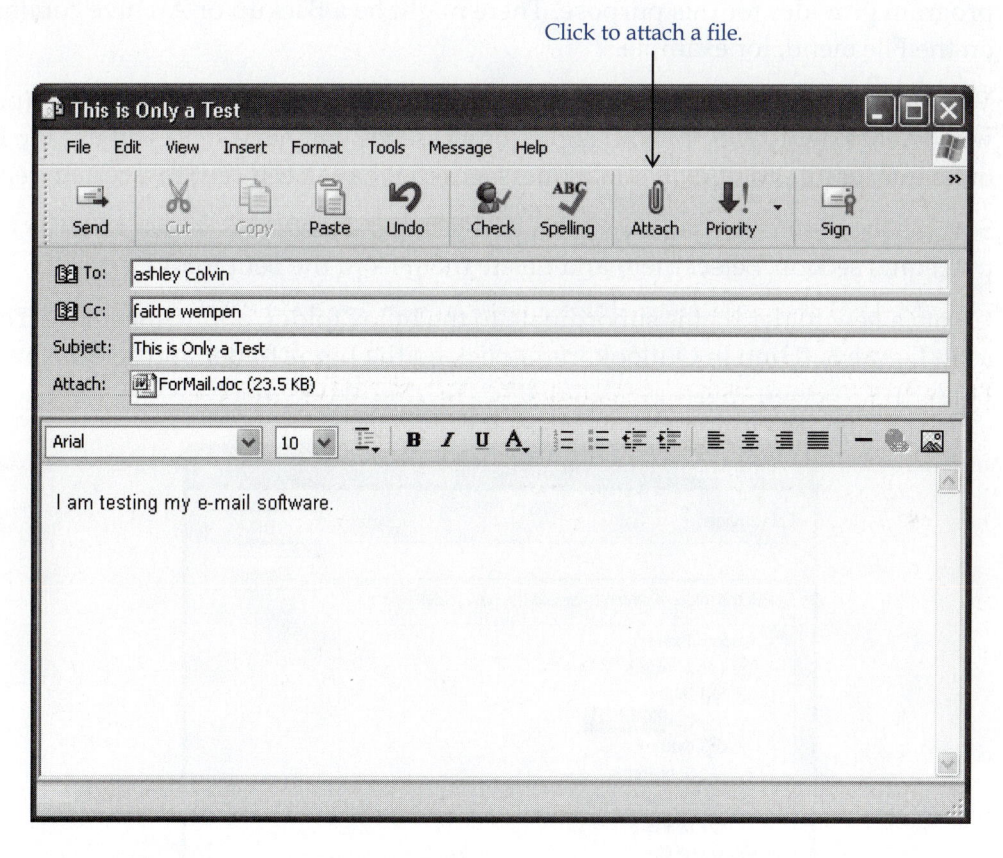

Figure 2: The message, ready to send.

4. Send the message. It goes into your Outbox. If your mail program requires it, issue a Send/Receive command to send the messages from the Outbox. You should receive it back in your Inbox shortly as incoming new mail.

5. When you receive the new message, open it.

6. Open the attachment in your text editing program to confirm that it still contains your name; then close it.

7. Save the attachment to your Windows desktop, and name it **DeleteMe**.

8. Delete the attachment from the desktop.

9. Flag the message for later review, and mark it as unread. (Hint: In Outlook, right-click on the messages to access these options.)

10. Use Reply to All to reply to the message, and in your reply, type Message **received, thank you**. Send the reply.

11. Forward the message to yourself (or someone else), and in your forward, include the comment "**FYI**."

12. If needed in your e-mail program, execute a Send/Receive operation so that the mail is sent.

ORGANIZE E-MAIL MESSAGES

1. Back up or archive the messages in your Inbox using whatever feature your e-mail program provides for this purpose. There might be a Backup or Archive command on the File menu, for example.

2. View the list of e-mail folders in your mail application. Open the Sent folder (or whatever folder is used to hold copies of messages you have sent) and use the Find or Search feature to find all e-mail messages that have been sent to a certain recipient.

3. Sort the list of sent messages by date, and locate the messages you sent in the preceding section. Select them and delete them from the Sent folder.

4. Create a new folder that is subordinate to the Inbox folder, and name it **MailTests**, as in Figure 3. (Hint: In Outlook, right-click on the Inbox folder and select New Folder.)

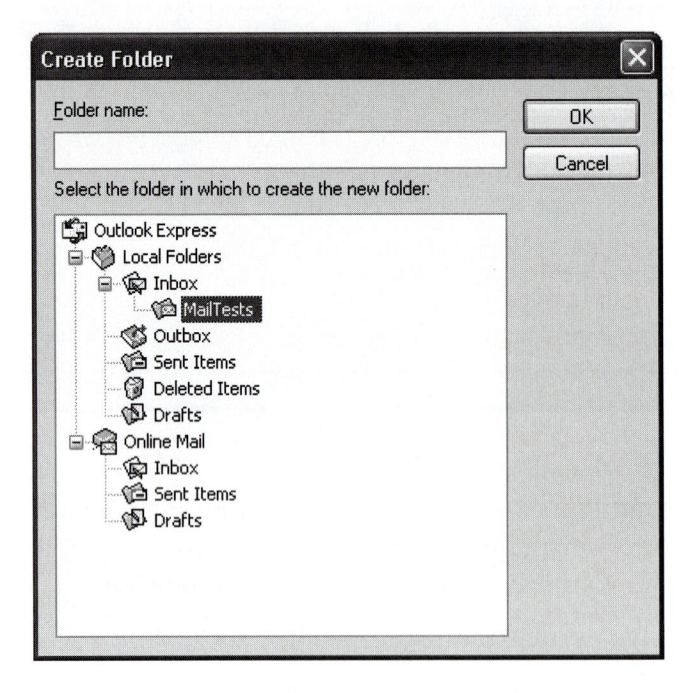

Figure 3: Creating a new e-mail folder.

5. From the Inbox, move all of the messages you have received in the preceding steps into the MailTests folder.

6. Delete the MailTests folder.

7. Close your e-mail application.

Objective 3.2: Be able to use a Web browsing application

1. Start your Web browser application, and navigate to www.phschool.com by typing the address into the Address bar.

2. Navigate through the site until you find a page that spotlights an individual textbook.

3. Save the page as an HTML document on your hard disk (File, Save As). Call the file **PHBook1** and place it in My Documents.

4. Save one of the pictures on the current Web page to your hard disk as a standalone graphic file. (Hint: Right-click on the graphic, and select Save Picture As.) Name it **Graphic1**.

5. Click the Back button to return to the first page; then click the Forward button to move forward again.

6. Close the Web browser application and reopen it.

7. Using the History feature in your browser, return to www.phschool.com.

8. Clear the Web browser's history list (Tools, Internet Options).

9. Set http://news.google.com as the default home page. See Figure 4.

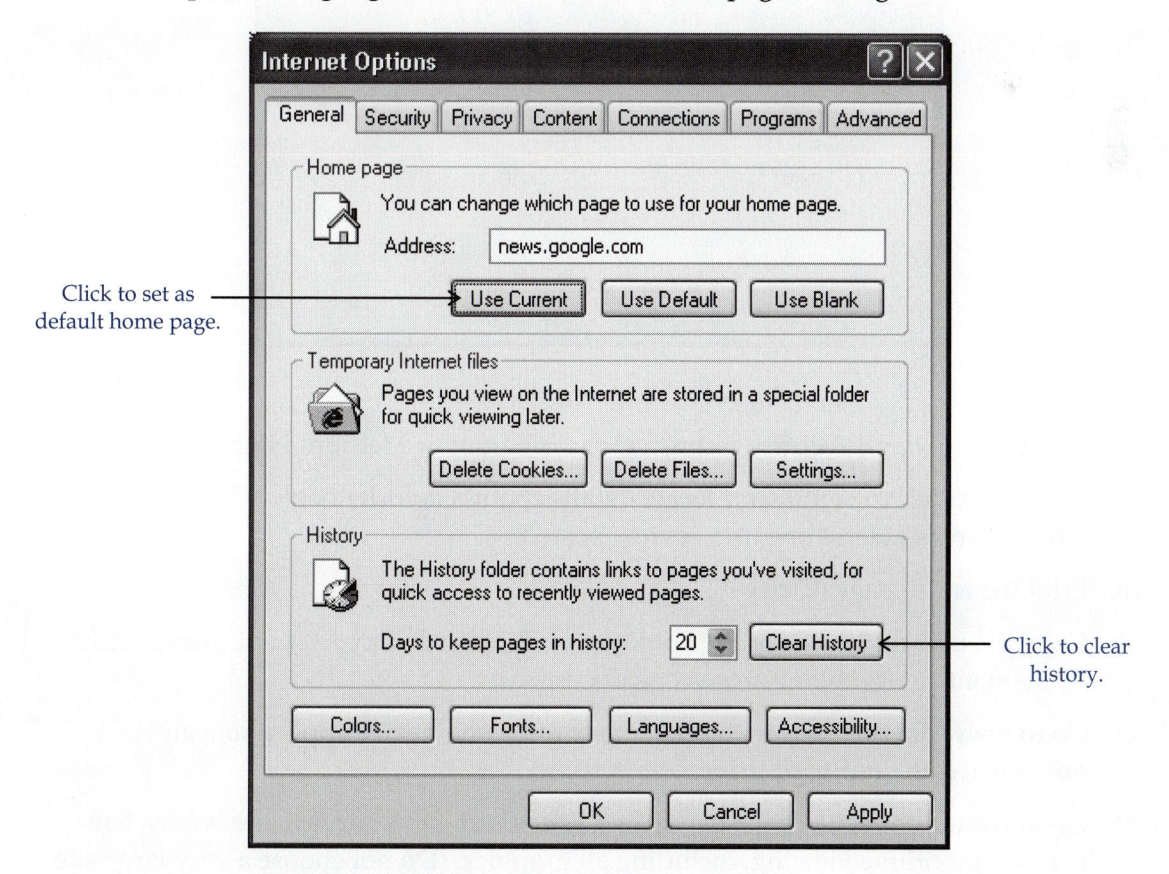

Figure 4: Set the default home page.

10. Go to www.timeanddate.com/worldclock and find the current time in your area.

11. Bookmark the current page (Favorites, Add to Favorites), and name the bookmark **Time**.

12. Create a new folder or category in your browser's Bookmarks or Favorites list, and name the category **Reference**. (Hint: Click Favorites, Organize Favorites.)

13. Move the Time bookmark into the Reference folder/category.

14. Return to your browser's home page by clicking its Home button.

15. Return to the time page using the Time bookmark.

16. Press F5 to refresh the time page's display.

17. Adjust your Web browser's privacy settings so that it prompts you for confirmation every time a cookie is saved to your hard disk. (Click Tools, Internet Options. Then, select the Privacy tab and click Advanced.) See Figure 5.

Figure 5: Configure cookie settings.

18. Set your browser's Security settings to the Medium or Medium High level.

19. Go to www.amazon.com and locate details about a favorite book. Find one for which there is at least one user review posted.

20. Print the entire page (Ctrl + P).

21. Copy the user review(s) for the book to the Clipboard (Ctrl + C), and paste (Ctrl + V) them into a new word processing document.

22. Go to www.download.com. Find an interesting shareware application, and download it to your hard drive.

23. Go to www.yahoo.com and search for a site relating to your favorite hobby. Save that site for offline viewing, including all graphics. (Do not choose a very large site if you have limited hard disk space available or a slow Internet connection.)

Objective 3.3: Be able to search the Internet for information

1. Go to www.google.com and search for a site that contains information about the Shetland Islands, but NOT Shetland Sheepdogs. Use the Advanced Search feature or Boolean operators, such as NOT, AND, or OR.

2. Go to www.yahoo.com and perform the same search. Again use the Advanced Search feature or Boolean operators. Note any differences in the required syntax between sites.

3. Go to www.msn.com and search for information about growing roses.

4. Refine your search to show only results that deal with preventing insect damage when growing roses.

5. Visit several of the pages, and find the one that you think has the best information on it. Print one copy of one page from that site.

6. Close your Web browser.

Introduction

This glossary covers hundreds of the most important computer terms you need to understand and use, including terms about the Internet and World Wide Web. Like other dictionaries, this one presents terms in A to Z order. Along the way, you'll find special elements that highlight key information:

This icon appears beside the name of any term that deals with communications, including networking, connecting computers via a modem, or connecting to the Internet.

Tip boxes like these highlight extra tidbits of information, or ideas and steps to save you time.

This glossary presents command choices by giving the menu name, followed by subsequent command names, all of them separated using the | (pipe) character. So, Insert|Picture|Clip Art means to click the Insert menu, click the Picture command, and then click the Clip Art command in the submenu that appears.

Characters

3.5" disk A floppy disk that has its magnetic storage media encased within a 3 ½" square rigid plastic case. You can copy your computer files onto a floppy disk to create a spare copy of the files or to move files from one computer to another.

A

Abort To stop a program or command before it finishes, often by pressing [V], [Ctrl]+[C], or the Break key on the keyboard. Sometimes, when an operation "hangs," or stalls your computer, it presents a dialog box offering a button you can click to abort the operation.

About dialog box A dialog box you can display to find out what version of a program you're using and to view the registered serial number for your copy of the program. You typically display the About dialog box by choosing the About (*program name*) command from the Help menu in the program.

absolute reference In a spreadsheet program, an absolute reference in a formula always refers to the same cell, even if you copy the formula to another location.

Access (Microsoft Access) This database program, published by Microsoft, enables you to store lists of information, such as a list of customer names and addresses or a list of all the audio CDs you've bought.

accounting software Software you use to perform accounting functions. Business accounting software like Peachtree or QuickBooks typically enables you to track assets, expenses, inventory, and payroll, as well as providing invoicing and reporting features. You can use personal accounting software such as Quicken or Microsoft Money to record transactions for your bank accounts, print checks, monitor credit card balances and investment returns, and review reports such as net worth reports.

active Active indicates that a program window, file window, dialog box, or area within a program holds the insertion point.

Add or Remove Programs A feature in Windows that enables you to install and remove programs more easily. When you use this feature to remove a program, Windows deletes all the program files and cleans the vast majority of references to the program from Windows system files.

To display the Add and Remove Programs Properties dialog box, choose Start|Control Panel, and then click the Add or Remove Programs link (Category view) or double-click the Add or Remove Programs icon (Classic view).

Glossary

address An address, depending on the context, can mean different things. In a spreadsheet program, the address is the location of the cell and is comprised of the cell's column and row. For the Internet, you type an address to go to a particular Web site. This type of address is also known as a URL. For e-mail, you type the recipient's e-mail address in this format (personname@domainname.ext).

Address Book Most e-mail programs, whether used for an internal network or for Internet communication, offer an Address Book into which you can enter the name and e-mail address for each person with whom you correspond.

alignment Refers to how information lines up relative to the document margins or the boundaries of a cell or text box in a document. Figure A.1 illustrates various alignments.

Left-Aligned Text
CENTERED TEXT
Right-Aligned Text
JUSTIFIED TEXT STRETCHES TO FILL THE AREA BETWEEN MARGINS

Figure A.1 Most applications enable you to align text in various ways.

alphanumeric characters Labels, words, or phrases that include both letters and numbers, as in A139X.

alphanumeric sort A sorting method that considers both letters and numbers in a label, word, or phrase. For example, an alphanumeric sort might sort items beginning with punctuation marks or symbols first (!, $, %, or &, for example), then items beginning with numbers. Items beginning with letters are sorted last.

Alt key A key you press in conjunction with another keyboard key to select a command or run a macro. For example, in most applications you can press Alt+F to open the File menu. You can also press Alt in conjunction with one of the Function keys at the top of the keyboard to perform a command or action.

America Online (AOL) One of the world's leading online service providers. Users can log on to share information and e-mail, or connect with the Internet.

animation A moving computer image that combines multiple objects that change in position. You may have seen animated banners and graphics on Web pages, or you may have seen special animated mouse pointers in programs. Numerous programs enable you to create various types of animations and animated objects.

> Animated graphics consume considerable system and video RAM. If your system bombs out when you try to run an animation or if the animation runs in a jerky fashion, you may need to upgrade your system's RAM or video RAM.

antivirus This term applies to any software or software feature that scans your system and files for viruses. Most antivirus programs can also clean or remove the virus from the affected system areas or files. Typically, you can choose to scan for viruses either automatically or manually. Common virus software makers include Norton and McAfee.

append To add information to the end of an existing file or database table.

Apple Computer, Inc. The company that manufactures Macintosh desktop PCs and PowerBook notebook PCs. Apple also makes a popular digital music player called the iPod.

application window The window that opens on the Windows desktop when you start an application. The application window holds a separate window for each file you open and create in the application.

archive Traditionally, this term refers to a specialized backup file created by a backup program. More commonly, however, the term also refers to a special type of file that holds multiple compressed files.

argument A value or text string you include in a programming statement or in a command within a program; the statement or command uses the argument information when it runs. You also use arguments in spreadsheet formulas that include functions. For example, the argument(s) you specify for the SUM function tells the spreadsheet program what values to add or which cells hold those values.

arrow key Literally, the keyboard keys that have arrows on them. Most keyboards offer up, down, left, and right arrow keys, but some also include diagonal arrow keys.

ascending order Ascending order refers to text information alphabetized in A to Z order or numbers ordered from the smallest value to the largest.

ASCII (pronounced as-key) ASCII stands for American Standard Code for Information Interchange. It refers to a standard set of characters that virtually all programs understand. The ASCII character set consists of mostly letters and numbers, but also includes a few symbols and codes for controlling the computer. Many applications enable you to save your files in ASCII or plain text format, which exclude special formatting and characters, but make the files easier for other programs to open.

attribute Windows records key attributes about any file you save, such as its name, how large the file is, the date you created it, whether you've set the file to be read-only (so others can't change it), etc. Within an application, the term attribute describes formatting you apply to text or some other object. For example, you can apply the bold attribute to selected text.

audio Sound produced by your computer or another device.

audio CD An audio CD holds audio data in a format developed for playback via a boom box or your home stereo. Computers also can play audio CDs using audio or CD player software.

autosave The autosave feature on an application will save all open files at a specified regular interval. Then, even if your computer loses power or has a problem, you'll lose only a few minutes' worth of work, rather than a few hours' worth.

B

background The background is what appears on your desktop in Windows. You can change the image or colors used to display the desktop. This term also refers to how tasks are handled. Most computers today can handle multiple tasks simultaneously (multitask). In such a case, the task or application you're currently using occupies the foreground, and the task or application carrying out prior instructions continues operating in the background. Finally, the term background also applies to documents or graphics. You can apply a background color or pattern to many types of files.

Backspace key A keyboard key that deletes the character to the left of the insertion point in a document, spreadsheet cell, or text box in a dialog box.

backup A special type of file that serves as a spare copy for one or more other files. You should backup your work often. You can manually copy your documents, or you can use special backup programs and media to speed the backup process.

bad sector On a hard or floppy disk, a damaged area that can no longer accept data. Normally, your system marks bad sectors so that it doesn't try to write data to them. However, a sector can go bad after the system has stored information in it. In such a case, you can use a utility to try to get the data from the bad sector. These utilities move the data from the bad sector to another location on the disk.

> The primary culprits that cause floppy disk damage include metals, magnets, and dust that can damage the magnetized material on the disk media. Even though a floppy's media is encased in harder plastic, damaging materials can make their way in through the sliding metal cover over the opening on one side of the disk. So, keep your computer area clean, and keep metallic objects like paper clips and magnetized objects away from your floppy and other removable disks.

beta software Preliminary or test versions of a software program, distributed by the software publisher for testing. With the great interest in computers today, eager users seek out many beta software versions. Be careful with betas, though. Installing a beta can prevent other software on your system from working, so you should always back up your system before installing a beta. Many betas expire after a certain number of uses or after a certain time period.

bitmap A method of displaying information on the screen dot-by-dot. Each on-screen dot (pixel) displays a particular color, based on the setting for one or more corresponding bits of information.

bitmap font A font drawn using a pattern of dots, so that the font isn't scalable. If you try to double the size of text formatted with a bitmap font, the computer in essence increases the size of each dot so that you see unattractive jaggies or a stairstep appearance.

bitmap graphic Bitmap graphics, like bitmap fonts, consist of a pattern of colored dots. The file name extensions .BMP, .TIF, and .PCX often identify bitmap graphic files.

bold A formatting attribute applied to characters in an application. Making a selection bold (or applying boldface) turns the characters thicker and darker. Bold formatting can be applied to headings and titles in a document to make them stand out from the rest of the text.

bookmark In a word processor document, you can mark an area in the document by creating an electronic bookmark. Later, you can select the bookmark to jump to that area in the document. In Netscape Navigator's Web browser, you can create a bookmark to note the address for a favorite Web page. You can then select the bookmark rather than typing the full Web address when you want to display that Web page.

boot To start or power up your computer. When you boot the computer, it performs a number of actions to test the system, such as the POST (Power-On Self Test), and loads the operating system so the computer will be ready to accept your commands. A special read-only memory (ROM) chip on the motherboard typically stores the computer's boot instructions.

browser software Software that enables you to view graphical Web pages stored on Web sites on the Internet. The browser loads each Web page, complete with graphics and text formatting. You can click linked text, buttons, or graphics to jump to other pages. Or, you can enter a Web page address to go to that page.

BTW An abbreviation you can type instead of "by the way" in an e-mail message. For example, you might type, "BTW, I received your fax yesterday." You also might see and use other abbreviations like CU (see you) and B4 (before).

bug An error in a program or macro that causes it to stop working, display an error message, return an inaccurate result, or shows some other operating problem.

bullet A dot, box, check mark, or other small graphic used to set off each item in a list, as in:

- Apples
- Pears
- Bananas

button An on-screen shape you click to execute an action in a program. Buttons may be as simple as a rectangle or oval with text in it, or as fancy as a colored image. You often find buttons in dialog boxes or on a special toolbar near the top of the application window.

byte A group of eight bits of information. Because each bit only represents either a 1 (on) or a 0 (off), computers need a combination of bits to define more complex information. Each byte represents a particular character. A *kilobyte* equals 1,024 bytes, a *megabyte* equals 1,048,576 bytes, and a *gigabyte* equals 1,073,741,824 bytes.

> The base-2 math used for bits and bytes results in the actual number of bytes in a kilobyte and megabyte being more than an even thousand (a value identified by the kilo prefix in decimal or base-10 math), million (the mega prefix), or billion (the giga prefix).

C

cable An external connecting wire that carries data between your computer and another device, such as a printer, monitor, network hub, or phone jack. Each cable plugs into a port on the computer. The type of connecting device and the available ports on the computer determine the type of cable needed to make the connection.

calculate To perform a mathematical operation. In most spreadsheet programs, you can manually recalculate the open file so that its formulas reflect results based on the most recent values you've entered.

Cancel button A dialog box button you click to close the dialog box without applying your choices in the dialog box.

Caps Lock key Press the Caps Lock key on the keyboard to begin typing in ALL CAPITAL letters. Press the Caps Lock key again to return to typing in upper- and lowercase letters.

> Most keyboards include an indicator light to tell you when Caps Lock is on. Also note that with Caps Lock on, you still need to press the Shift key to produce certain characters, like !, @, and all other "shifted" characters on the number keys along the top row of the keyboard.

cascade To arrange open windows on the screen so that they overlap like a fanned stack of cards, with the title bar for each window visible. You can then click the title bar for any window to select that window.

case-sensitive In some computer environments or online environments, you must enter commands or addresses using exact punctuation. Often, passwords and user logon names are case-sensitive, too. In such an instance, if you assign a password like *TodaY* to a file, you must enter *TodaY* to open the file, not *TODAY* or *today*.

CD-R A type of compact disc that you can record information to. You can, for instance, create a music CD by copying (or burning) songs from your computer to a CD-R disc (and a CD-R drive). The R indicates that you can only record once; you cannot rerecord information (see CD-RW).

CD-ROM Compact Disc Read-Only Memory disc. CD-ROM discs are about 4.75 inches in diameter and have a polycarbonate wafer coated with a metallic film that holds the data; the wafer and metallic coating together are coated with polycarbonate. One side of the CD-ROM holds printed label information. The metallic coating remains visible through the other side. Each CD-ROM disc holds about 650M of data.

CD-ROM drive A drive that reads—but cannot write to—CD-ROM discs. The CD-ROM drive uses a laser to read the shiny side of the CD-ROM. The laser bounces off *pits* and *lands* in the metallic coating visible on that side of the disc, and the drive reads the reflected light. The reflected light varies in intensity depending on whether it came from a pit or land, and the drive translates each reflection into a data bit that the computer can understand.

CD-RW A type of compact disc and drive that enables you to record and rewrite information to a disc. You can erase a disc and record over the current information. Contrast this type of drive/disc to CD-R which can only be recorded once.

cell The intersection of a column and row in a spreadsheet (worksheet). You can enter text, values, dates, and formulas into each cell. Spreadsheet programs identify each column with a column letter and each row with a row number.

cell address The cell address identifies the specific location of a cell in a spreadsheet (worksheet) using the cell's column letter and row number. For example, the address G15 identifies the cell in column G, row 15.

center To position selected information so its center point is equidistant from the left and right margins of a document or the left and right boundaries of a cell or text box.

central processing unit (CPU) The microprocessor chip that executes commands and controls the data that moves through the computer. The CPU's power defines the capabilities of the PC as a whole. The most popular type of CPU is Intel's Pentium 4 processor.

character When you press a keyboard key (or [Shift] plus another key), the specified character appears on the screen. Characters include letters, numbers, punctuation marks, and other symbols.

chart (also called graph) Representing groups or series of data in a graphical form to clarify how values compare or what trends may have developed over time. Most spreadsheet programs and presentation graphics programs offer charting capabilities. You also can create or insert a chart or graph into a word processor document by copying it from a spreadsheet program into the document. Common chart types include a bar or column chart, line chart, or pie chart.

clear To remove the selected text or object from a file, usually by pressing [Delete] or choosing Edit | Clear in a program. Note that clearing information does not place it on the Clipboard.

click To move the mouse pointer over an on-screen item and then press down and release the left mouse button once.

clip art Predrawn artwork that you can insert into your files. Most major word processors include clip art. You also can buy clip art collections from other resources or download clip art from the Internet.

Clipboard In Windows, a holding area in memory that stores information you cut or copy from a file using the Edit | Cut or Edit | Copy command. You can then paste the information from the Clipboard into another location in the same file or into another file altogether using the Edit | Paste command.

clock An internal clock circuit that generates regular pulses spaced at small intervals. Each pulse represents a single cycle in the system. The computer uses the pulses to synchronize the CPU's activities and information flow in the computer.

close To use a command to remove a file or program from the computer's screen and thus from the working memory (RAM) for the system. Closing a file or application frees up RAM so the computer can use it for other purposes. To close a file in an application, choose the File | Close command. To close an application, choose File | Exit.

Close (X) button One of three buttons at the right end of the title bar for a file window or application window. The Close button has an X on it. You can click the Close button to close the file or application window.

column In a table in a word processor or Web document, a column is a vertical block of cells spanning the whole table height. In a spreadsheet program, a column represents each vertical group of cells.

command button In a dialog box, a button you click to carry out an action. If the command button name includes an ellipsis (...), the command button displays another dialog box. Most dialog boxes include an OK button, which you click to close the dialog box and apply your choices from the dialog box. The Cancel button in a dialog box closes the dialog box without applying your choices.

Command Prompt A Windows accessory that lets you access a DOS-type window and type commands. Click Start | All Programs | Accessories | Command Prompt to display this window.

compress To use a special utility program to reduce the amount of space a file occupies. Compressed files take up less space and transfer more quickly over the Internet or a network. Typically, you compress multiple files into a single compressed file. For example, you can compress ten 100K files (1M of data) into a single file that might only take up 300K.

> You can use Windows Send To | Compressed (zipped) Folder command to compress the selected files into a folder. To do so, select the files and then right-click on the selection. You can then access the Send To command.

compressed folder This is a "container" folder that typically holds the contents of several files. You extract the original files from the compressed file (decompress the file). In Windows, you can double-click a compressed folder icon and then select and copy the files to another drive or folder to decompress them. Some compressed files are self-extracting and have an .EXE extension.

configure To change settings for a piece of hardware or software so that it works correctly when you first install it, or so that it works as you prefer at a later time. For example, after adding more RAM to your system, you need to reconfigure a setting for the system to ensure that it can find all of the new RAM.

Control (Ctrl) key A key you press in combination with other keys to perform a command or make a selection in an application. For example, in recent versions of Microsoft Word, you can press and hold the Ctrl key and click a sentence to select the whole sentence.

Control menu The menu that opens if you click the small icon to the left of the application name or file name in a window title bar. The Control menu contains commands for working with the window. For example, if you click the Close command on the Control menu, Windows closes the window.

Control Panel An area in Windows that you can use to change Windows settings and hardware settings. For example, you can use the Mouse Control Panel to change your mouse settings. To open the Control Panel, choose Start | Control Panel in Windows. You can display the features in Classic view (as icons) or in Category view (as links and listed by task).

copy To duplicate selected text, selected cells, or a selected object, typically using the Edit | Copy command or Copy button.

crash When a computer or program stops working or "locks up." You can try to exit the program that is causing problems from the Task Manager (press Ctrl+Alt+Delete). You can also try to restart by clicking Start and then Turn Off Computer. Click Restart. If the keyboard and mouse have stopped responding, however, you must reset the computer by turning it off and then back on. Do this only as a last resort.

cross-hair pointer A mouse pointer that appears after you select a command or button for inserting an object (like a chart) or drawing a shape in an application. Drag the cross-hair pointer to define the approximate size, shape, and position for the object.

current cell or selection In a spreadsheet program, you click a cell to make it the active cell. If you drag to select a group (range) of cells in a spreadsheet or database table, text in a word processor, or an object in any kind of application, the selection becomes the current selection. Any command or formatting you specify next applies to the current selection.

current file The active file that's ready to accept the next information you type or command you give. The current file holds the insertion point or current selection.

cut To remove a selection from a file and place it on the Clipboard using the Edit | Cut command or Cut button. You can then paste the cut selection to another location using the Edit | Paste command or the Paste button.

Cyberspace The vast online world where users interact and exchange information without physically meeting.

D

data Information you enter into a computer. You can then use the computer to store or manipulate the information.

database A file that holds an organized list of information. For example, a database might list all your audio CDs. The database file divides the list into records and fields. The user could sort the list to find a particular record (CD) listed in the database.

database program A program you can use to compile and manipulate databases (database files).

Date/Time The icon in the Windows Control Panel that you use to reset the actual date and time displayed at the right end of the Windows taskbar.

default The initial or normal setting for a feature or object. For example, most software prints one copy of a file unless you change the default and specify that it should print more than one copy.

defragment When you save a file to disk, the disk drive attempts to write all the information in the file to contiguous clusters on the disk. Over time, as you delete and add files on the disk, the groups of contiguous clusters become smaller, and sometimes the drive has to store different parts of a file in non-contiguous clusters, which fragments the file. The more fragmented files a disk holds, the slower the disk runs. You can run a defragmenter, a utility that reorganizes the information on a disk until every file spans contiguous clusters, enabling the drive to retrieve files more efficiently.

delete To remove selected information from a file, usually by pressing the Del key or choosing Edit | Clear. Deleting information does not place it on the Clipboard.

descending order Text information alphabetized in Z to A order or numbers ordered from the largest value to the smallest.

deselect To remove the check beside a dialog box check box. Or, to click outside selected text, cells, or an object in a document to remove selection highlighting or sizing handles.

Desktop In Windows, the working area or screen background that holds the taskbar, icons, and program windows.

desktop publishing (DTP) Creating publications that integrate text and graphics — typically brochures, newsletters, annual reports, and sales flyers — on a computer. While most word processors offer at least limited DTP features, such as the ability to insert graphics, rules, and other design elements in a document, precise work calls for a separate desktop publishing application such as Microsoft Publisher, QuarkXPress, or Adobe PageMaker.

dialog box If you choose a command with an ellipsis (...) after its name, the command displays a dialog box. The dialog box presents options or choices that you make to control what the command does.

digital camera A camera that saves a still image directly to digital format. You can transfer the images from the digital camera to a PC. Then, as with any other graphic file, you can insert the picture file in a document, print it with a color printer, or include it on a Web page.

disk One of many types of rewriteable magnetic media that holds files created by computer applications. A disk drive reads information from and writes information to the disk. Disk usually refers to floppy disks. Disc usually refers to CD discs.

document A file created in a program.

documentation The instruction books and any online how-to demonstrations that help you use a new PC or program.

domain name The alphanumeric, friendly name for a Web site or other Internet site. For example, www.microsoft.com, www.house.gov, www.writer.org, and www.butler.edu are all domain names for Web sites.

> The suffix for a Web sites gives you a clue about what type of organization operates the site. The .com suffix typically represents a for-profit company, while .org usually identifies the site for a non-profit organization, .gov stands for a government body's site, and .edu stands for an educational entity's site.

double-click To move the mouse pointer over an item on-screen and press the left mouse button twice, quickly.

download To transfer a file from another computer to your computer, usually from an online service or the Internet.

> If you're downloading a file from an unfamiliar online source, it may have a computer virus. You should use virus checking software to scan downloaded files for viruses and remove those viruses.

drag and drop A technique where you drag something to perform a command or action in a program. For example, you can drag a file icon from one folder and drop it onto the icon for another folder to move the file from its original folder to the folder on which you dropped it. In a word processor or spreadsheet, you can drag a selection from one location and drop it into another location to move the selection.

drop-down list A text box in a dialog box or on a toolbar that includes a drop-down list arrow at the right side. When you click the drop-down list arrow, a list of choices opens. You can then click the choice you want in the list.

DVD (digital versatile disc). A type of drive often included on computers or the disc used in that type of drive. DVD drives use a different technique for storing data on the disc and can store a lot more data than CDs. Like CD drives, though, you can find DVD drives that can just read discs (for instance, play a movie). Or you can find drives that can record data once (DVD-R) or drives that can record, rewrite, and erase data on the disc (DVD-RW). The speed for rewriting data is slower than reading or recording.

E

e-mail A message that you send via a network, online service, or the Internet using special e-mail software like Outlook Express. You also can attach a file such as a spreadsheet or graphic to the e-mail message.

e-mail address A unique address used to send and route messages to a particular recipient. Most e-mail addresses follow this format: a unique user name, followed by the @ symbol and the domain for the ISP or company on which the user has his or her e-mail account: username@isp.net.

edit To make a change to information in a file. Many programs offer editing commands on an Edit menu.

embed In OLE, embedding means inserting an object in one application that you created in another application. For example, you can insert a graph created from Microsoft Graph into a Microsoft Word document.

enhanced keyboard Enhanced keyboards include a 10-key keypad to the right of the main group of keyboard keys. Computer users with 10-key skills, such as financial professionals and bookkeepers, can use the 10-key keypad to enter numeric information more quickly.

Enter key Press Enter to start a new paragraph in a word processor or finish an entry in a spreadsheet or database table cell. You also can press Enter in most dialog boxes to close the dialog box and apply your dialog box selections.

error message An operating system or application displays an error message when a problem occurs or when you request an action that can't be completed. For example, you might see an error message if you enter a spreadsheet formula incorrectly. Usually, the error message includes a description of the problem and gives you options for proceeding.

Esc key You press Esc to cancel actions, in most cases. For example, if you open a menu in an application, you can press Esc twice to close the menu and deselect the menu name. You also can press Esc to close an open dialog box without applying your choices in the dialog box.

Excel The Microsoft Excel spreadsheet program, also part of the Microsoft Office suite, leads the spreadsheet market. Like other spreadsheet programs, Excel provides many functions that you can use to perform complex calculations.

Exit The command typically found on the File menu that you use to close a program. The term exit refers to shutting or closing down any application.

expand When you're working with the folder tree in a file window, expanding means redisplaying all the folders and files that have been hidden or collapsed within a particular folder. When you're working with the outlining feature in an application, expanding means redisplaying all the subheadings and body text hidden or collapsed under a particular heading.

extension The extension appears as a suffix on the file name and consists of a dot (.) followed by three characters, as in .EXE or .DOC. The file name extension enables Windows and Windows applications to identify the file type.

external drive Unlike an internal drive installed within the case of your PC, an external drive has its own case and connects to the PC via a cable. Some external drives connect to the parallel port. Others may require that you install a special card to make the connection.

F

FAQ This acronym for "Frequently Asked Questions" refers to a list of questions and answers about a topic provided on a Web site, newsgroup, or as a file that comes with software. Experienced Internet newsgroup participants first compiled FAQs as a reference for new users to prevent the same questions from appearing repeatedly on the newsgroup.

fax software Fax software enables a fax/modem to send and receive faxes. Create a coversheet in the fax software and then attach the file to send. When you send the fax, the fax software tells the fax/modem to dial the fax number specified, send the cover sheet, and send the attached file, page by page. Similarly, faxing software tells the fax/modem to respond to incoming fax calls and store fax pages electronically so you can later view or print them.

field In a database, a field represents a piece of information common to all the entries. For example, if you create a database to list all your audio CDs, the fields might be *Title*, *Artist*, *Genre*, and *Price*.

file A named unit of information stored on a disk. Each application creates a specific type of file. The Word word processor creates document files, each of which has the .DOC extension. The Excel spreadsheet program creates workbook files, each of which has the .XLS extension.

file attachment When you send an e-mail message or newsgroup message, you can send a particular file with the message. This is called *attaching* the file or adding a *file attachment*. You can attach document files, spreadsheets, graphics, or any other type of file.

file size The number of kilobytes or megabytes of information in a file. You may need to know the file size to know if a file will fit on a floppy disk. You also must consider the file size for any file attachment you send via e-mail. Many ISPs will not send (or accept) a message with very large file attachments.

file window When you open a file in an application, it opens in its own window, called a file window. Each file you open appears in its own window and becomes the current file.

> To switch to another open file (and its file window), open the Window menu in the application with which you're working and click the name of the file you want to use. You can also click on the taskbar button for the window you want to display.

Fill Many spreadsheet programs offer a fill feature, which lets you copy an entry from one cell across the row or down the column. Also, in many programs, you can apply a fill, or background, to an object you draw, a selected range, or a selected paragraph.

find A find operation selects each matching instance of a word or phrase you specify. After the program finds the first matching instance, click a Find Next button or choose a Find Next command to select the next match. Most applications provide some type of find or search capability.

> To start a find operation, look for the Edit|Find, Edit|Search, or Tools|Find command in your application.

firewall A system of software and hardware that protects a company's network from outside networks (including the Internet). If you have a 24/7 (cable) connection, you should use a firewall to prevent unauthorized access to your computer.

flowchart This type of chart, often used in programming, illustrates how a process works using different box styles and connecting lines. Flowcharts show how a process branches or proceeds in different directions based on whether the answer to a particular question is yes or no.

folder You can divide the space on any disk into named file storage areas called folders. The folders help organize the information on the disk, because you can save files covering the same topic in a single folder.

Folders list In file and folder windows, you can display a hierarchical list of the drives and folders on your computer. To do so, click the Folders button. Click the plus sign beside a disk or folder to view the folder's contents. Click a minus sign beside a disk or folder to hide the folder's contents.

font Traditionally, a font refers to a particular set of characters in a particular size and style, such as the bold Times New Roman characters in the 12-point size. In most applications today, however, the font choice refers more generally to the typeface, such as Times New Roman. After you choose a font from the Font list, you can choose the size and styling separately.

footer You can create a footer to appear at the bottom of each printed page in a word processor document, spreadsheet file, graphics presentation, or database form or report. The footer might include such information as the file name, date, and page number. Footers and headers help the reader pick up key information about the document from any page.

format When you format selected text or a selected object, you change settings that control the text or object's appearance. For example, you can change the font, size, or color of text. Or, you can apply a colored border around an object and a fill within it.

formula In a spreadsheet cell, you enter a formula to perform a calculation on the values held in other cells. Formulas resemble mathematical equations. You enter an equals sign (=) to start each formula, then use numbers, cell addresses, mathematical operators, and functions to complete the formula. For example, the formula =(C1*5)+C2 multiplies the value held in cell C1 by 5, then adds the value held in cell C2.

FrontPage Use the Microsoft FrontPage software to design your own Web pages.

FTP FTP stands for File Transfer Protocol, a method of transferring files over the Internet.

function In a spreadsheet program, a function serves as shorthand for a more complicated calculation. For example, you can use the AVERAGE function in Excel to average a list of numbers, rather than building a formula to perform the calculation. In programming language, a function typically returns a value on which the program you're creating can then act.

Function keys Sometimes called F-keys, these keys appear in a row above the numbers at the top of the keyboard. Software publishers use the function keys as shortcut keys for accessing program features.

G

G (gigabyte) A gigabyte equals 1,073,741,824 bytes of information, or 1,073M (megabytes.)

grammar checker Top word processing programs can check the grammar used in a document in addition to checking the document's spelling. The grammar checker compares each sentence to a set of grammar rules and highlights any sentence that may violate a rule. You can then decide whether or not to change the sentence.

graphics Electronic still images that you can create and display using a PC are graphics, also called graphics files. "Graphics" also refers to a PC's capabilities for displaying graphical images and data.

grayscale An image using shades of gray in addition to pure black and white to represent shapes and shadows more realistically than a pure black and white image.

gridlines Gridlines separate cells in a spreadsheet, database table, or a table in a word processor document.

H

hard disk The series of magnetic storage platters within a hard disk drive. The hard disk holds the files for the computer's operating system, program files, and files you create with programs.

hard disk drive The hard disk drive holds the hard disk platters. Its read/write head reads the information from and writes the information to the sectors on the hard disk. A hard drive holds the disk platters in an airtight case, making the hard disk data less prone to damage than a floppy disk.

> Remember, you can't save a file to a "drive," the mechanical device that reads and writes disks. You save a file to a "disk," the magnetic media that holds your data.

hard page break A page break that you insert manually in a chosen location in a document, usually by pressing Ctrl+Enter. For example, you could insert a hard page break to create a title page in a document, shifting the body information to the top of the next page.

hardware The circuitry and other physical components that make up a PC's system unit and the devices connected to the system, like the printer, monitor, and keyboard.

header You can create a header to appear at the top of each printed page in a word processor document, spreadsheet file, graphics presentation, or database form or report. The header might include such information as the file name, date, and page number. Like footers, headers give key information about the document on every page.

Help The Help feature in a program explains how to use a feature, provides background information, or supplies definitions. You can display help by choosing Start|Help and Support. In most programs you can find a term by topic, by using an index, or by searching for a keyword.

History list By default, your Web browser keeps a list of Web sites you have visited during recent browsing sessions. To return to a site, you can select the site name from the History list.

Home key Use Home to navigate in programs. You usually can press Home in a word processor to move the insertion point to the beginning of a line. You also can press Ctrl+Home to move to the beginning of a word processor document or to the first cell in a spreadsheet.

home page Sometimes, home page refers to the first page your Web browser loads when it connects to the Internet. More often, it means the main page for a Web site, from which you can connect to other pages the site offers.

HTML The acronym for Hypertext Markup Language, the coding scheme for creating Web pages. Web browser software can read the HTML coding, convert the codes, and display attractively formatted Web pages. While Web page authors used to have to code Web pages manually, more friendly programs like FrontPage enable users to create Web pages using a method similar to creating a Word processor document, where you enter text, apply formatting, and insert graphics.

http:// and https:// These are content identifiers appearing at the beginning of an Internet address, or URL. A content identifier tells you to what type of site the Internet address leads. The http:// content identifier stands for Hypertext Transfer Protocol, meaning any site with an address beginning with http:// holds HTML information, or Web pages. The https:// content identifier leads off the address for a secure Web site.

hyperlink A link you click to display another Web page or document. Most often, hyperlinks appear in Web pages and can consist of specially formatted text, buttons, and hot spots on graphics. You can also insert hyperlinks within the files you create or even within e-mail messages. For example, you can insert a link to a Web page in a Word document or even a link to another file on your hard disk; clicking the link displays the linked Web page or file.

I

icon These small pictures represent files, folders, programs, and features in Windows and Windows applications. Double-click an icon to open the file or run the program.

import To use information from one program in another, completely different program. For example, you might import financial data from Access into Excel.

inbox The folder in your e-mail program that displays newly received e-mail messages.

indent To set one or more lines of a paragraph in from the left or right margin in a word processor document. If you indent the paragraph's first line from the left margin, you create a first-line indent. If you indent the paragraph from the left margin, except the first line, you create a hanging indent. You can also indent the entire paragraph from either or both sides.

insert To add or move text into existing text, or to add a graphic or other object into a document.

insert mode In a word processing program, you use insert mode to insert new text within existing text at the insertion point. Text to the right of the insertion point moves further right to make room for the inserted text.

insertion point The blinking vertical line that appears in a document, spreadsheet cell, database field, or text box to indicate where the next text you type will appear.

install To copy program files from the program disks to your computer's hard disk. Most programs include an installation or setup program that handles the copy process, as well as making certain changes that enable Windows to find and operate the newly installed program properly.

Intel The company that designs and manufactures the most widely used central processing unit (CPU) chips and motherboard chipsets, enabling personal computers to process program instructions.

interface The commands, buttons, graphics, and other program features on your computer monitor that you use to navigate in a program. The interface also provides feedback, such as the page you're currently working with in your document.

Internet The worldwide network of computer networks to which an individual PC can connect for communication and information exchange. Users connect to the Internet to send and receive files and private e-mail, find information from online resources, participate in public message and chat areas, and even shop and transact other business, such as stock market transactions.

Internet Explorer The Web browser software published by Microsoft and distributed with Windows and other Microsoft program bundles.

intranet An intranet is an "Internet within a company," although it may not be connected to the Internet. Intranets are ideal for communicating information to employees, such as new product and inventory information.

italic An attribute or style you apply to text to make it look *slanted*, or *italicized*. In many applications, you can press Ctrl+I to apply italics to selected text.

J

.JPG (JPEG) .JPG (Windows) or .JPEG (Mac) files are types of graphic files typically found on Web pages.

justify A type of alignment that inserts spacing between words and letters to expand each line of text to span between document margins or the sides of a cell.

K

KB This abbreviation, like K, designates a measurement presented in kilobytes.

Kbps *Kbps* stands for *kilobits per second*, or 1,000 bits per second. A 56K modem generally can transfer about 56,000 bps, but some are capable of transferring data at 57,600 bps (with the extra transmission speed provided via data compression and other features).

> The FCC limits data transmission speeds over phone lines. Although some modems can work at 56K, the FCC limits data receiving speeds to 53K, so your modem generally won't connect at a speed greater than 53K on a regular phone line.

keyboard The keyboard is made up of all the letter, number, and character keys that you use to enter information into the computer, as well as special keys that you can use to select commands.

> You can buy ergonomic keyboards that help you hold your arms at more comfortable angles. There are also keyboards with built-in wrist rests to reduce the repetitive-motion injury called carpal-tunnel syndrome.

L

label Text that you enter in a spreadsheet cell to identify data below or beside it.

LAN (local area network) A Local Area Network connects a number of computers so that they share resources on a dedicated file server. A single LAN can serve a few computers or hundreds, but usually the LAN serves only one location or company.

landscape orientation A wide page format that turns the page so that the longer side runs along the top edge. Landscape orientation fits more information on each line or row of the document.

laser printer Laser printers print high-quality hard copies. Laser printers achieve high-print resolutions by using electrostatic reproduction. A fine laser charges areas on a photostatic drum or belt. As the drum or belt rotates, it applies the toner that was attracted to the charged areas to the page. A laser printer offers better print quality than an inkjet printer and also prints faster.

launch Another word for starting an application. For example, "Launch Microsoft Excel" means to start the Excel program.

link Web pages include links (also called hyperlinks) to other pages at that site or other sites entirely (see hyperlinks). Also, in OLE (Object Linking and Embedding), you can paste a linked copy of information from one document (the source document) into another (the target or destination document). When you update the original information, the linked copy updates as well, ensuring that the two files always contain identical information.

list box A list box in a dialog box lists a number of choices. You typically can scroll to display additional choices, and then click the choice you want to apply.

load After you start a program, your computer loads the program into memory. That is, the system transfers the program instructions from the hard disk to RAM. Web browser software also loads a Web page when it receives the page information and displays it on the screen after you click a link or specify a Web address to display.

log in or log on These terms describe the process of providing information to connect to a LAN (local area network) or an Internet connection. For example, to connect with an ISP, your system needs to send your username and password to verify that you have an Internet account. Most communications software make the log on process automatic.

log off When your computer logs off a network connection, it sends information to the server or ISP computer to terminate the connection.

M

M or MB These abbreviations stand for megabyte, a disk storage measurement. Each megabyte is 1,048,576 bytes of data. You also may see MB used to describe data throughput (data transfer) speed, in which case it stands for 1,000,000 bytes. Each M holds 1,024 K, equaling 1,024 x 1,024 bytes or characters of information.

Glossary

macro Creating a macro in a program is essentially creating your own custom command. In many applications, you can record a series of commands and save them as a macro. Then, when you run the macro, the application performs the steps that you recorded.

mail merge The mail merge feature in a word processing program is used to create a mass mailing, including envelopes and mailing labels. The mail merge inserts information from a database into specified locations (fields) in the word processor document, creating one personalized copy of a letter for each record in the database.

mail server The computer and/or software that routes and stores e-mail messages on a LAN or on the Internet. If you connect to the Internet via an ISP, the ISP's mail server sends outgoing e-mail messages and receives and stores incoming messages until you connect and retrieve them with your e-mail program.

margin The white space at the edge of the page around the contents of a printout forms the margin. A page with narrower margins can hold more information.

> Some printers limit the size of the margins you can use in a document. For example, some printers can't print within .25" of the edges of the page and will "cut off" information falling in the unprintable area.

maximize To return a file or application window to its full size.

Media Player The Windows accessory program that you can use to play music and video.

memory The term memory describes any chip in a PC that holds the values and instructions the system needs to run. A ROM (Read-Only Memory) chip holds a set of permanent instructions the system needs to start up. RAM (Random-Access Memory) serves as the working memory for your computer. RAM holds program instructions or information that you've entered into a file but haven't yet saved. Shutting down the computer clears everything out of RAM.

menu A menu lists commands in a program. Each menu groups commands for similar tasks. For example, the File menu lists commands for working with files and the Format menu lists commands for formatting either selected information or the whole file.

menu bar The menu bar lists each of the menus in an application and usually appears near the top of the application window under the window title bar. To open a menu, click its name on the menu bar. To close a menu, click outside it or press Esc twice (to both close the menu and deselect the menu name).

message box A message box looks like a dialog box but appears for informational reasons only (rather than enabling you to choose command options, as does a dialog box). An application displays a message box to inform you when it has finished a particular operation, such as a spell check.

Microsoft Microsoft publishes many of the leading application programs used on PCs today, as well as the Windows operating systems. Microsoft's other products include Office (Word, Excel, PowerPoint, Access, and Outlook), FrontPage, Works, Encarta, Golf, Publisher, and a number of other applications.

minimize To reduce a file or application window to a button on the taskbar.

modem A modem (an abbreviation of MOdulator-DEModulator) converts digital computer information into an analog format and sends it over phone lines. A PC can use a modem to connect with the Internet or to an online service.

monitor The TV-like unit that displays computer information. The video card or display card in the PC draws screen images and then sends them to the monitor for display. Monitors come in different sizes and with other capabilities that determine the quality of the monitor image.

Glossary

motherboard This circuit board holds the essential components of the PC, including the CPU, ROM, RAM, buses, and slots for adapters. The brand and model of motherboard determine what features it includes. For example, some motherboards today feature built-in (on board) networking or video. You can substantially upgrade a PC by replacing its motherboard, CPU, and RAM.

mouse A device that you roll on your desk to move a pointer on the screen.

mouse button A pressable mechanism on the mouse that you use to perform a computer action based on the on-screen mouse pointer location.

mouse pad A portable rubberized pad on which you move the mouse. The ball within the mouse has better traction on a mouse pad than on a slick desk surface, so a mouse pad allows the mouse to operate more smoothly.

> Remember to clean your mouse pad occasionally. A lot of dirt can build up on the mouse ball, causing the mouse to work erratically.

MS-DOS Also called simply DOS, the Microsoft Disk Operating System (MS-DOS) was introduced for personal computers in 1981. MS-DOS controlled basic system operation and let the user give commands to the system.

multimedia Applications or presentations that integrate text, graphics, audio, video, and (often) interactive features.

multitasking This is when a computer executes commands from more than one program at a time.

My Computer The Window's icon or window that you can open to view the various drives and system folders on your computer. You can click Start | My Computer to display this window. If you have a desktop shortcut to My Computer, you can double-click this icon to display the contents of your computer.

My Documents A special Windows folder useful for storing the documents you create. You can click Start | My Documents to view the contents of this folder. Or if you have a desktop shortcut icon to this folder, you can double-click the icon to view the contents.

N

navigate To move around in a file or on the Web. In an application, navigation entails displaying another page, moving the insertion point, or selecting another cell. On the Web, navigating means moving from page to page on a Web site or displaying another site altogether.

netiquette A set of rules for behaving on the Internet such as not sending out junk mail, how to properly reply to a posted discussion, and other niceties. Netiquette helps Internet users treat each other with courtesy and use the Net's resources wisely.

network A group of connected computers that can exchange information. Computers connected to the network may also share central devices, such as file storage, a fast modem or Internet connection, or a printer. Generally, the networked computers are connected via cabling, and network operating software controls the network operation.

network adapter The network adapter card (also called a NIC or network interface card) installs in a PC so that you can connect the PC to a network. Connect one end of the cabling to the network adapter card and the other to a network connection such as a hub.

notebook computer These portable, compact size computers, also called laptops, transport easily and open like a notebook for use. A notebook weighs about 5-9 pounds.

number format In a spreadsheet program, applying a number format to selected cells controls how numbers appear in those cells. For example, if you apply a percent number format, the numbers display as percentages, including the % sign. Choosing a currency format adds a dollar sign and two decimal places.

numbered list In a word processor document, you can number each item in a list, as in a list of ordered steps. Top word processors can number a list automatically for you.

Num Lock key On an enhanced keyboard, you press Num Lock to toggle the numeric keypad at the far right side between typing numbers and working as arrow (insertion point movement) keys.

O

object This term describes any non-text item you insert into a file. For example, a piece of clip art or other graphic is an object that you can select, format, and move.

Office Office, from Microsoft, is the best-selling software suite. The Standard Edition of Office includes Word (word processor), Excel (spreadsheet), PowerPoint (presentation graphics), and Outlook (e-mail and scheduling). The Professional Edition adds Access (database).

offline When a printer is offline it is not ready to receive data. Also, when not connected to the Internet or another online service, your system is offline.

OK button Most dialog boxes include an OK button. Click the OK button to apply your choices and close the dialog box.

OLE OLE (Object Linking and Embedding) technology enables applications to share information and tools. You can copy an object or information from one application (the source application), and insert it as a linked object in the destination (or target) application. Whenever you make changes to the original information in the source document, the destination document changes to match.

online When you are connected to the Internet, you are online. Also, your printer is online when it's ready to receive data; an indicator light on the top of the printer usually lights up when the printer is online and ready.

operating system The software that runs the internal components of the computer, such as Windows or the Macintosh operating system. The operating system software directs information from the keyboard into the system; between the CPU, RAM, and other system components; and from the system to devices like the monitor and the printer.

operators In a spreadsheet program, operators are the mathematical symbols in a formula that specify how the formula should calculate. For example, you can use the + (addition), * (multiplication), / (division), and < (less than) operators, among others.

optical mouse One of the newer types of mice. This pointing device uses a bouncing laser to point and move the mouse pointer. Because it doesn't have any moving parts, this mouse is less likely to develop problems, including dirt getting inside the mouse and affecting its tracking sensors.

option button Option buttons appear in groups in dialog boxes. Option buttons present mutually exclusive options. That is, you can click only one of the option buttons at a time.

outbox The folder in your e-mail program where the e-mail program places messages to be sent.

Outlook and Outlook Express Microsoft publishes these information management programs. Outlook Express is included as part of Windows. Outlook comes as part of the Office suite (or can be purchased separately), and includes e-mail, scheduling, an address book, a to-do list, and journal features.

overtype mode In a word processing program, overtype mode will type over any text to the right of the insertion point. Each character or space you type replaces an existing character or space.

P

page Each printed sheet of information from an application equals a page.

page break A page break in an application is a mark showing where one page ends and the next begins in a printout.

page layout The page layout consists of any settings you make in a file to control the appearance of the printout pages. Settings such as the margins, orientation, and page size affect the page layout.

In many applications, you choose File | Page Setup to access the page layout settings.

paint program A paint program is used to create and edit bitmap graphics. Although you can drag to draw objects like rectangles in a paint program, you have to change individual pixels or dots to edit the image. Windows Paint is a paint program.

Paint Shop Pro This paint program from Jasc software has emerged as a popular and inexpensive alternative to professional programs. Paint Shop Pro offers a number of custom brushes and color effects. It enables you to import and save images in a variety of formats and even to create animated images for Web pages.

palette A palette presents color or pattern choices you can apply to selected text or objects in an application. Click the square for the color or pattern you want to apply to the selection.

pane In some applications, you can split a window into multiple areas called panes. Each pane shows a different part of the file or shows the file information using a different view.

password A secret code that you assign to a file, program, or Windows for security reasons. You must enter the password to open the file, program, or Windows.

paste When you copy or cut information, Windows places the information on the Clipboard. You can then insert that information into another location by pasting it from the Clipboard using the Edit, Paste command.

path Also called the path name, the path identifies the precise location of a file on a disk. The full path to a file might look like C:\My Documents\Memos\Memo.doc.

PC (personal computer) A complete computer system that can be used either as a stand-alone system or connected to a network. A PC includes all the key computer components, including the CPU, operating system, monitor, hard and floppy disk drives, input devices (mouse and keyboard), and a printer. Currently, PCs often come equipped with a modem, sound card, speakers, and frequently include extra devices like a video camera.

PDAs (personal digital assistants) A handheld computer used to store appointments, pictures, notes, contacts, and other information.

.PDF The file name extension for Adobe Acrobat files, often found on the Web. Many types of files convert to the Acrobat format for reading and viewing with the Acrobat reader.

Pentium The name of the most popular computer processor, made by Intel. The most current version of the Pentium is Pentium 4.

PhotoShop This paint program from Adobe enables you to create and work with images. PhotoShop offers professional features for retouching scanned photos and adding special-effects filters.

plug-in Plug-in programs help your Web browser software do something it can't do on its own. For example, the browser may need a plug-in program to play a certain type of video file. Some plug-ins download and install automatically when you need them. In other instances, you will need to download and install the plug-in manually.

pointer The on-screen symbol that moves when you move your mouse.

pointer speed The pointer speed refers to how far and fast the mouse pointer moves on the screen relative to the distance and speed with which you move the mouse.

port Devices plug into a receptacle, or port, on your computer. Most ports are part of an adapter card within the computer.

portrait orientation A tall page format that turns the page so the longer side runs along the side edge. Portrait orientation fits less information on each line or row of the document, but fits more lines of information per page.

power supply The computer's power supply device covers AC power from the wall socket to DC power for the computer's use.

power surge A power surge occurs when the power voltage increases substantially on the power lines coming into your home or within your home.

PowerPoint Microsoft sells the PowerPoint presentation graphics program both as an individual program and as part of the Microsoft Office suite. PowerPoint can import information from Word and Excel and offers a number of features for creating multimedia presentations.

print To send a file's information to the printer, which then creates some type of hard copy output. In most applications, you choose the File | Print command to print.

print buffer A temporary storage area that holds the print queue (information being sent to the printer) until the printer is ready to accept it.

print job When you choose File | Print, set printing options, and then click OK to send a file to the printer, you create a print job for the printer to handle.

print preview Many applications offer a print preview feature so that you can see how a file will appear when you print it. Print preview helps you ensure that pages break correctly.

Print Screen key When you press the Print Screen key in Windows, a graphical copy of the information shown on your screen is sent to the Clipboard. You can paste the image from the Clipboard into a program to save it as a file.

printer A printer connected to your computer makes a hard copy of any file that you specify. The type of printer you connect and install for your system controls your printing options. For example, the type of printer determines the paper size you can use to print.

printer port A port through which you connect a printer to your PC. Printers connect to a PC via a parallel port, a serial, or USB port.

programming language A set of vocabulary, grammar, syntax (command structure rules), organization, style rules, and tools a programmer uses to create programs.

properties In Windows, you set properties to specify the performance of a particular feature. For example, the Display Properties dialog box will display wallpaper or a pattern on the desktop or control how many colors Windows displays.

protocol The rules and standards two devices must follow to communicate via modem, LAN connection, or Internet connection.

Publisher This inexpensive, entry-level page layout (desktop publishing) program from Microsoft allows you to create a variety of documents such as post cards, newsletters, and flyers. Publisher offers a number of wizards to lead beginners through the process of selecting and applying a document design.

Q

QuarkXPress This professional page layout (desktop publishing) program competes with Adobe PageMaker. Quark has long excelled in preparing documents for four-color printing, such as magazine layouts and ads.

query You perform a query in a database program to find and retrieve matching entries in the database. You enter criteria, and the database displays all the records that match.

quit To exit a program. In most programs, you choose the File | Exit command to exit the program.

R

range In a spreadsheet program, a range is a contiguous block of cells. For example, the block of cells that spans from cell C5 in the upper-left corner to cell G10 in the lower-right corner forms the range C5:G10. A range also may refer to a contiguous set of items in other applications, such as a range of pages to print from a word processing document or a range of records from a database.

read When a computer reads information, it retrieves the information from a disk into the system's RAM.

read-only When you mark a file as read-only, you are able to open the file but not change it.

Glossary

Read Me file A program or software component typically comes with a Read Me file that contains necessary information from the software publisher. The Read Me file may be named *Readme.wri*, *Readme.txt*, or simply *Read.me*.

> You should always read the Read Me file for a new program, preferably before you install the program.

reboot To restart the computer, especially after you experience a problem with it or install a new piece of hardware or software.

record In a database program, a record represents one full entry. For example, if you create a database to list all your audio CDs, the full entry for each CD (including the Title, Artist, Release Date, and Price fields) forms a record. You can also use a worksheet to create databases, and each set of information is a record. Finally, the process of using sound or video software to capture digital sound or video. For example, you can use Windows Sound Recorder to record your voice from a microphone.

Recycle Bin The Recycle Bin in Windows holds files that you've deleted from the hard disk. The files remain in the Recycle Bin in case you need to restore them.

> The Recycle Bin icon looks like an empty waste can when there are no files in the Recycle Bin folder. The icon changes to a waste can holding crumpled paper when it is holding some files.

refresh Most Web browsers offer a Refresh button. Click the Refresh button to reload a Web page that didn't display completely or correctly on your system. You may also want to refresh a page to get updated information (such as a page that listed stock prices).

removable disk Also called removable storage, a removable disk drive reads and writes information to a removable cartridge or disk holding a large quantity of information.

reply When you receive an e-mail message, you can click the Reply button in your e-mail program to write a message in response to the received message. If the message was sent to several people, you can click the Reply All button to reply to all of the original recipients.

report In a database program, you create a report to view or print the data in a nicely-designed page format rather than in a plain table.

resolution The resolution for an image or computer screen indicates how large or detailed the image is or how detailed the on-screen display is.

restart Windows offers a command to restart the system. Choose Start | Turn Off Computer. Click Restart.

restore To reduce the size of a file or application window so that it doesn't fill the desktop or the working area within the application window. When you restore a window, you can resize the window or drag its title bar to move it.

restore point A point in time where all your system settings are saved. Windows periodically creates restore points. If something goes wrong with your computer (for instance, after you install a new device), you can go back to a previous restore point and undo the changes.

revision marks Revision marking in a word processing document (and now in some spreadsheet and presentation graphics programs) shows the changes made to a file using markings. The revision marking, or change tracking, feature uses a different color or style to identify changes made by each different colleague or editor with whom you share the file. You can then review each change and decide whether to accept or reject it.

Rich Text Format Files that contain not only the basic data but also basic formatting such as fonts and font sizes. Most word processors and some other types of programs can open .RTF files, allowing you to share information between programs more easily.

right align Aligning information against the right margin, the right side of the cell, or the right side of an object. Right alignment yields an uneven appearance at the left side of a block of text, called ragged left.

right-click To move the mouse pointer over an on-screen item and press and release the right mouse button once.

> You generally click using the left mouse button unless a program instruction tells you to do otherwise or you want to display a shortcut menu.

row A row in a table or spreadsheet consists of all the cells on one horizontal line across the table or spreadsheet.

> To select an entire row in a spreadsheet program, you generally can click the row number at the left side. Drag across multiple row numbers to select multiple rows.

run To start or load a program, or to execute a macro in a program.

S

sans serif A font lacking serifs (decorative cross strokes) on the letters, like **Arial**, **Gill Sans**, **Impact**, or **Helvetica**.

save To name and store a file in a folder on a disk. After making any changes in a file, you should save it again to include those changes in the stored version on file. In most applications, the File | Save command or a Save button on a toolbar will save the current file.

scanner A device that uses light to read an image from a hard copy, such as a photo, in order to convert it to a digital format that you can save on disk, edit, and print.

screen saver A screen saver displays an on-screen moving image after your computer has been idle for a specified period of time. Monitors originally needed screen savers to prevent images from "burning in" to the display material and leaving permanent ghost images. With improved monitors, screen savers are more of a way to personalize PCs.

scroll When you scroll a file, you change the portion of the file that's visible on the screen. For example, if you scroll down in a spreadsheet, you display the group of cells below the previously displayed cells. You also can scroll a list in a dialog box to display other options in the list. Note that scrolling does not move the insertion point or cell selector in a document.

scroll bar You use a scroll bar to scroll through a file. Each scroll bar appears as a long gray bar with an arrow at either end and a scroll box within the bar. You can click either arrow or drag the scroll box to scroll. An application window may offer a vertical scroll bar along the right side; use it to scroll up and down. The window might also offer a horizontal scroll bar along the bottom; use it to scroll left and right.

scroll box This dark gray box appears on a scroll bar. Click on either side of the scroll box to scroll through a screen of information. Drag the scroll box to scroll the document more quickly.

Scroll Lock key In some programs, pressing Scroll Lock will let you use the arrow keys to scroll through a document rather than to move the insertion point or cell selector.

SDRAM Stands for Synchronous Dynamic RAM. One of the most popular types of RAM today and is found in most new systems.

search When you want to look for a particular word, phrase, or value in a word processor, spreadsheet, database, or presentation graphics program, you can perform a search, or a find, to identify matching instances of the word or value. When you're working on the Web, you can perform a search to find Web pages that mention the topic you specify. A Web search engine site will perform a Web search.

search and replace To find a match for a term that you specify and replace the match with other specified information. This feature, called search and replace, or find and replace, helps save time when correcting a repeated mistake in a document.

search engine A Web site that performs a search of Web pages (and in some cases, newsgroups), to find pages with information concerning a specific topic. The search engine displays a listing of links to the pages covering the topic. Click a link to go to one of the listed pages. Each search engine keeps an index of pages registered by Web site operators and uses a slightly different method of matching terms.

> Most Web browsers include a Search button. Click this button to display the search bar and start a search. Many pages also include a search text box and button. You may be able to search just the site or the entire Web using the search features, depending on the page.

serif A decorative cross stroke that finishes off the ends of certain letters, such as the bottom of a lowercase "l" or "f." Serif fonts like **Bookman Old Style**, **Palatino**, and **Times New Roman** work well as body fonts.

server A server computer is the central control point on a LAN (local area network), and stores the networking software and central resources shared by other computers connected to the network. On the Internet, a server computer stores and manages a particular type of information. For example, a Web server stores and transmits Web pages.

setting A choice that you make to control how a program operates or how a command executes. For example, dialog boxes offer settings in programs.

setup Most applications come with a setup program (usually named *SETUP.EXE* or *INSTALL.EXE*) to install the application on your computer.

> When you insert the CD for a new application, your system usually finds and runs the setup program automatically. If not, open My Computer, double-click the icon for the CD drive, then double-click the *SETUP.EXE* or *INSTALL.EXE* file icon.

shareware You can download shareware programs from the Internet and other online resources, or find them on sampler CDs that come with magazines and books. Shareware software operates on the honor system. If you decide you like the shareware and want to continue using it, you need to register it and pay a small fee to the shareware author.

Shift key Pressing Shift on the keyboard in conjunction with another key types a capital letter or a shifted character like @ or *. Shift may also be part of a shortcut key combination that performs a command or action.

Shift-click Press and hold Shift while clicking something on the screen. In a word processor, you can click at the beginning of a block of text to select, then Shift-click at the end of the block to finish the selection.

shortcut menu A shortcut menu, also called a context menu, offers commands that apply to the operation at hand. To display a shortcut menu, right-click the item such as the desktop.

shut down Before you turn off your PC, you should shut down Windows. Choose Start | Turn Off Computer.

soft hyphen Also called an optional hyphen. You insert a soft hyphen into a word that appears near the end of the line. (In Word, press Ctrl+- to insert a soft hyphen.) If you make a change prior to the word with the soft hyphen that will cause it to wrap to the next line, the application will hyphenate the word at the soft hyphen location and only wrap part of it to the next line. Use soft hyphens to avoid short lines of text in a document.

> In the current version of Word, you can use the Tools | Language | Hyphenation command to have Word hyphenate a document automatically.

sort When you sort information, you place it in a new order. You can sort tables and lists in a word processor document, lists of entries in a spreadsheet, or records in a database. Choose a column or field of information by which to sort, as well as a particular sort order. For example, you could sort a list of names and addresses in A–Z order by last name.

space character Enter a space character to separate words and sentences.

> You may have learned in typing class to enter two space characters after each sentence. That is no longer necessary because the font designs compress the space between letters within words, which makes a single space after a sentence a large enough break.

Glossary

Spacebar Pressing the Spacebar key, the long key at the bottom of the keyboard, inserts a space character. Note that some keyboards have a divided Spacebar key, with the right half working like the traditional Spacebar key and the left half working like the Backspace key.

spam Unsolicited e-mail. Some e-mail programs include features for blocking spam. You can also purchase programs specifically for blocking spam.

spelling checker A tool that can check the spelling of every word or entry in a file. The spelling checker compares each word to a dictionary and highlights any word that doesn't match an existing dictionary entry. You can then decide whether or not the word needs correcting.

spinner buttons Spinner buttons, also called increment buttons, appear in a dialog box next to a text box holding a value. Clicking the up spinner button (it has an upward-pointing triangle) will increase the value in the text box. Clicking the down spinner button (it has a downward-pointing triangle) will decrease the value in the text box.

spreadsheet A spreadsheet program presents a grid of columns and rows that intersect to form cells. You can enter text (a label), a date, a value, or a formula in a cell. A spreadsheet formula includes mathematical operators to perform a calculation.

Spyware Programs installed without your knowledge or consent that track where you go on the Internet. This information is then relayed to other companies. You can buy programs that check for and remove spyware programs.

Start menu In Windows, the Start menu serves as the main avenue for starting programs and accessing Windows features. To open the Start menu, click the Start button at the far left end of the taskbar.

start page The first page your Web browser loads when it connects to the World Wide Web. Also called the home page.

start up To boot up your computer. When you start the computer, it performs a number of steps, such as loading Windows, and displaying the desktop.

status bar The bottom of the application window in many programs has a status bar. The status bar often displays information about the open file, such as how many pages it has and the current page number. In some cases, the status bar includes tools you can use to work on the file.

storage Storage is another name for disk space, the area where you store files created in applications. You may see a disk drive called a storage device.

style A style includes a number of formatting settings, such as the font, font size, and alignment. Instead of applying individual formatting settings to a selection, you can simply apply the style. Many word processors, presentation graphics programs, and spreadsheets offer predefined styles, or let you create your own styles.

subfolder A subfolder is any folder within another folder. Each subfolder is one level below the main folder, and appears indented in the tree. You can create subfolders within subfolders.

> To create a new folder or subfolder, open the disk or folder you want to hold the new folder. Click File | New, and click Folder. Type a folder name for the folder that appears and press [Enter].

submenu Some menu commands display a triangle (arrowhead) to the right of the command name. If you point the mouse pointer to such a command, a smaller menu, called a submenu, appears. You can then click a command in the submenu to select a command.

subscript Smaller-sized characters that appear dropped below the normally formatted text. This example illustrates normal and subscript text: Normal$_{subscript}$.

suite A software suite consists of a group of programs that, together, offer a full range of capabilities at a favorable price. At a minimum, a business software suite includes a word processor and spreadsheet. It also typically includes information management or scheduling software. Other types of suites offer database or graphics programs.

superscript Smaller-sized characters that appear aligned above the normally formatted text. This example illustrates normal and superscript text: Normal^{superscript}.

Glossary

support Support, or technical support, means help that you can get from the software publisher of a program that you've purchased or the hardware manufacturer of a piece of hardware that you've purchased. Usually, you can dial a toll-free number for a limited time after your purchase to get free help. Beyond the applicable timeframe, you can purchase additional telephone help by credit card. Most software and hardware manufacturers also offer a Web site that you can consult for technical support information.

surf To use Web browser software to move from page to page on the World Wide Web.

syntax Every type of command you use, formula you create, or query you develop follows rules called syntax. You must follow the correct syntax for the command, formula, or query to work correctly.

system requirements Every application has system requirements that spell out the features a PC needs to run the software efficiently. For example, the system requirements define what type of processor the system needs, how much RAM and hard disk space the program consumes, what version of Windows is required, and any devices, like a modem or a sound card, that the software needs to perform its functions.

system tray The system tray appears at the right end of the taskbar in Windows. It displays the time and the volume control icon. It also may display icons for other items, like the power management features for a notebook. You can often right-click or double-click an icon in the system tray to work with the feature that it represents. For example, you can double-click the time to see a dialog box for resetting the system date and time.

system unit The system unit is the case or box holding the motherboard, CPU, power supply, internal disk drives, and other internal devices of a PC.

T

tab In the leading spreadsheet programs today, every file actually holds more than one spreadsheet, or worksheet. This structure lets each file hold more information and makes it easier to navigate. A tab like a manila folder tab identifies each separate spreadsheet in a file. To select a spreadsheet, click its tab. Dialog boxes with many options also have tabs; you can click the tab to display that set of options.

Tab key In many applications, you can press Tab to navigate. For example, you press Tab to move to the next cell in a spreadsheet or field in a database. In a word processor program, you press Tab to align text to the next tab stop. You can also press Tab to move between the different options in a dialog box.

tab stop A tab stop in a word-processing document is a location (or measurement) that you use to align text. For example, if you set a tab stop at one inch, you can press the [Tab] to align text at that one inch tab stop.

table In an application, a table organizes information into cells formed by rows and columns that are divided by gridlines, much like a spreadsheet. You can insert tables into documents in many word-processing and spreadsheet programs and onto slides or pages in many presentation graphics programs. Most databases use a table format in which you can enter data. In addition, Web pages can display data in a table format. In particular, catalog Web sites often display information in a table format. For example, if you search a Web-based catalog for a type of product, it may display items and prices in a table.

tag When using HTML and XML to create Web pages, you insert codes called tags to specify how particular information should display. For example, you use the </HEAD> tag to identify the page header and the </CENTER> tag to center text. Web browsers read the tags to know how to display the Web page information.

tape backup drive You can connect a tape backup drive to a PC to back up information to cartridges holding magnetic tape. Tape works as a backup media, but isn't as effective as a regular storage media, because tape drives run more slowly and have to access data in the sequence in which it was recorded. In contrast, other disk drives can access information from any location on the disk.

Glossary

task A task is an application or operation on a computer. You can display the Task Manager to see applications and processes that are currently running. To do so, press Ctrl+Alt+Delete. A task also might mean a command or process that you complete within an application to alter a file.

taskbar The taskbar is a bar with buttons and other features that appears at the bottom of the desktop by default in Windows. Each application that you launch in Windows appears as a button on the taskbar. To switch to another open application, click its button on the taskbar.

telecommunications This term refers to using the telephone system to communicate. Telecommunication includes both voice and computer communications.

template You choose a template to make it the basis for a new file in an application. The template provides design elements, such as styles, page layout settings, and graphics. Some templates also provide basic information to help you create a finished document by "filling in the blanks."

text box A text box is a type of option in a dialog box. The text box prompts you to enter information such as a file name when saving a file.

text file A text file contains characters but no formatting. You can use the Windows Notepad applet to create text files, which use a .TXT file name extension. Choose Start | All Programs | Accessories | Notepad to start Notepad. Most applications can import plain text files.

thesaurus Leading word processors offer a thesaurus feature so that you can find a better substitute for a selected word. You may also find a stand-alone thesaurus program that you can use at any time.

.TIFF This file name extension, as well as the .TIF extension, identifies a graphic file in the Tagged Image File Format. .TIFF files are bitmap files. Scanners produce files using the .TIFF format, among others, because it handles color and shading gradations well.

tile To display open windows so that they do not overlap, but instead collectively fill the available working area. For example, if you tile four windows, each window fills a quarter of the screen. In an application, choose Window | Tile to tile windows. To tile open application windows, right-click the taskbar and choose Tile Windows Horizontally or Tile Windows Vertically.

title bar Every window and dialog box has a title bar. The title bar displays the application name, file name, or dialog box name. If the window isn't maximized, you can drag the window title bar to move the window to a new location.

toggle Some commands and dialog box options, such as check boxes, function as toggles, meaning they can be either on (selected) or off (not selected). When you toggle on a menu command, a check mark appears to the left of the command name.

toner The black or colored powder that a laser printer, plain paper fax machine, or photocopier uses to create images on paper.

toolbar A toolbar is a strip of buttons appearing in an application window. You click a toolbar button to perform a command, apply formatting, or accomplish some other operation. Toolbars usually appear at the top of the application window under the menu bar, but they may also appear at the side or the bottom of the window. You can often drag any toolbar to another on-screen location.

toolbox A toolbox resembles a toolbar, but holds items such as drawing tools rather than buttons that perform commands.

touchpad An input device commonly found on laptop computers. You can use the touchpad for the same purposes as a mouse (moving the pointer, clicking, and so on).

trackball A trackball looks and works something like an upside-down mouse. Rather than moving the trackball around on your desk, you move the ball in the center of the trackball to control the mouse pointer.

TrueType font TrueType fonts offers two major benefits: both the computer screen and printer can use the TrueType font, eliminating the need for separately installed fonts and ensuring that the on-screen display exactly matches the printed result; secondly, TrueType fonts are scalable so you can change the size of the text. With older font technology, you had to install a separate font for each text size.

typeface A typeface is more specific than a font. A typeface is a complete set of characters using a particular font, style (bold or italic), and size.

U

underline You can underline selected text or numbers in an application. Many applications offer an Underline button on a toolbar; click the button to apply or remove underlining.

undo This feature allows you to reverse a previous action. In some applications you can undo only the most recent action. In such a case, click an Undo button on a toolbar or choose the Edit | Undo command. In other applications you can undo multiple prior actions. In this case, you can click the Undo button multiple times or click the drop-down list arrow beside the Undo button and use the list that appears to specify the number of actions to undo.

up arrow Pressing the ↑ key on the keyboard moves the insertion point in a word processor document or presentation graphics page up one line, or moves the cell selector in a spreadsheet program up one row.

> Pressing ↑ moves the insertion point to the beginning of the current paragraph, or from there to the beginning of the previous paragraph.

upgrade When you upgrade, you install a newer, and presumably better and faster, version of a software program or computer component. An upgrade may also consist of new or additional components for a system. For example, to upgrade a system's RAM, you add more RAM rather than replacing all the existing RAM.

> When you buy new software, avoid buying the cheaper upgrade version unless you're sure that you have a previous version of the program (or an eligible substitute from another software publisher). An upgrade version won't install correctly unless you're legitimately upgrading from a prior program version.

upload To transfer a file from your computer to another computer, usually to an online service or the Internet. For example, a message you post to a newsgroup might include a file attachment. When you post the message, the attached file is uploaded to the news server.

uppercase Information presented in all CAPITAL LETTERS. Press Shift to type in uppercase.

URL The acronym for Uniform Resource Locator, the address for a Web page (or other resource) on the Internet. The URL consists of several parts. The first is the content identifier: http:// or https:// for Web sites, or ftp:// for an FTP site, for example. The second part is the Web site, as in www.pearsoned.com. The final part is the location, or the path to a particular page, as in /html/order.html.

USB A type of port on your computer. You can use this port to hook up components such as a digital camera, scanner, printer, or special USB drives.

USB Flash Memory drive A new type of portable storage device about the size of a car key. You can connect the device via a USB port and then use it to share data.

user interface The on-screen information that a computer system displays, enabling you to give commands, see the results from commands, and enter information.

user profile Descriptive information about yourself that you enter when you log on to online services, some Web sites, and chat rooms. Other users or the service administrator can look at the information to get an idea of who you are. Web sites and online services might use profile information to market services and products to you.

> If confidentiality is important to you, omit some user profile information. For example, you can give a handle rather than your real name, and leave out information, like your address or e-mail address, to prevent unwanted contact.

V

version A named or numbered edition of a product. Most older software used version numbers to represent different versions, with a full number increase representing a substantial product update and a decimal increase representing a minor update. Now, many software vendors use the year to distinguish different software versions.

virtual memory Windows creates virtual memory to expand a PC's memory capabilities. It uses space on the hard disk as extra memory.

virus A computer program that infects other files and programs. Viruses usually spread when you download files and programs or share files on disk. The virus can destroy files on your system to the point of deleting information or preventing the system from booting.

> Some newer types of viruses called macro viruses can infect files and templates in Word and Excel. Both Word and Excel offer a feature that will alert you if a file that you're opening includes macros and therefore, potentially, macro viruses.

voice recognition Software technology that enables a computer equipped with a sound card to recognize words and commands that you speak into a microphone.

volume The loudness of sound played or recorded by your system. Volume is also another name for a disk.

volume label A volume label is a name assigned to a disk. Windows displays the disk's volume label in the My Computer window, so you can tell at a glance what files a floppy or removable disk holds.

W

Web search To find information on a particular topic on the World Wide Web, you can perform a Web search to find links to applicable pages.

Web site A Web site is a collection of Web pages published by an individual, company, or other organization. The home page or start page for the site contains links to the other pages.

Webmaster The Webmaster is the individual (or group) responsible for maintaining a Web site.

> Often, you can send an e-mail message to a site's Webmaster using an address in the format *webmaster@website.com*.

wildcard A wildcard character can represent unknown characters when you perform a file find or Web search. * for instance is a common wildcard character. If you want to search for all doc files, you could search for *.doc.

window All versions of the Windows operating system present applications, programs, and files in rectangular boxes called windows. Dividing information into windows allows you to switch between applications and files.

Windows Explorer Windows Explorer is a file window with the Folders list displayed. The folders list displays a hierarchical view of all the drives and folders on your drive; you can drag files and folders from one pane to the next to move or copy files.

Windows NT A version of the Windows operating system used on networks. This version provides maintenance features and features facilitating Internet connections that are easy to use.

Windows XP The most current version of Windows. The previous version of windows was named Windows ME (Millennium). There is also a business/network version called Windows 2000 that some older systems may still use.

wireless Wireless devices share information without using wires. For example, if both your notebook and desktop PCs have infrared ports, you can send information between them without using a cable to connect them.

wizard A wizard helps you perform a particular operation, such as creating a new document or setting up an Internet connection. A wizard minimizes an operation into a series of easy choices.

Word The Microsoft Word word processor program anchors the Microsoft Office suite. Word offers a number of templates and wizards to help you create documents, perform a mail merge, or create a table in the document.

word processor In a word-processing program, you can create documents such as memos, reports, and chapters. Word processors offer tools for entering, editing, organizing, and formatting text.

WordPerfect WordPerfect is the word-processing program that's part of the Corel WordPerfect Suite. WordPerfect offers many of the same capabilities as Word. It may be the best choice for users who have used previous versions of WordPerfect, or have many documents created using older versions of WordPerfect.

wordwrap The wordwrap feature automates the process of creating new lines in a word processor. When you enter enough text to fill the current line, the word processor automatically starts a new line.

worksheet A worksheet is the same thing as a spreadsheet. Excel calls each spreadsheet in a file a worksheet, for example.

workstation A workstation is an individual computer (desktop or notebook) connected to a LAN. A workstation also may refer to an extremely powerful PC running software like CAD or UNIX.

World Wide Web (WWW) The World Wide Web is a network of Web server computers that store, organize, and deliver Web pages to users.

write-protect When you write-protect a disk (usually a 3 ½-inch floppy disk), you move a tab on the disk to prevent the drive from writing any new information to the disk.

WYSIWYG This acronym (pronounced wissywig) stands for "What You See Is What You Get." It applies to any display enhancements that ensure that the information displayed on the screen for a file exactly matches its printed output.

Y - Z

Zip drive A Zip drive is a type of removable disk drive that you can add to a PC. Each Zip disk holds much more information than a floppy disk. Iomega makes the Zip drive.

zoom To change a document's size on the screen. Zoom in (or increase the zoom percentage) to make the document look larger. Zoom out (or decrease the zoom percentage) to make the document look smaller.

Index

A

Access/transfer time 37
Accessory programs 108
Accounting software 174
ACT! 83
Address Book
    create 216
Address Books 302
Adobe FrameMaker 86
Adobe Illustrator 92
Adobe SuperPaint 91
Aldus PageMaker 86
Alignment 143
    change 170
Animation 91, 94
Application settings
    change 275
Applications 266
array 194
Artwork 90
Attach files 214
Audience handouts 84, 186
Authorization 198
AutoCAD 93
AutoFormat 171
Automatic formatting tools 282
Automatic references 87
AutoSum 166, 167

B

Baud 234
Binary system 16
B-ISDN 203
Bit (binary digit) 16
Bit/bytes 17
Bits per second (BPS) 202
Blocking ads 258
Blogs 204
Bookmarks 203
Borders
    add 170
Borders and Shading
    add 149
bps (bits per second) 234
Bridge 193
Broadband 202
Brochures and booklets 85
Browser 236
    go to address with 240
    toolbar buttons 240
    using hyperlinks 239
Browser problems 247
Bullets and numbering 147, 283
Business forms 85

C

Cable modem 202
Cables
    File server Lan 192
    peer-to-peer network 196
Cache 19, 239
CAD (Computer-Aided Design) 91, 93
Calculations 78
Calculator 108
Category 5 cable 192
Category 6 cable 192
CD
    photo 93
CD drive 10
    speed 46
    types of 47
CD-R (CD Recordable) 47
CD-RW (CD Rewritable) 47
CD-ROM drive 45
    definition 47
Cell address 161
Censorship 262
Charts 79
    add 293
    create 172, 295
    modify 293
Chat 226
Checkbook manager 96, 174
Chipset 19
Click 56
Client
    File server Lan 190, 205
Client workstations
    File server Lan 191, 205
    Internet 201
Clip art 94
    insert 153
Clip Gallery 3.0 95
Close button
    Windows 107, 114
Cluster 40
Coaxial cable 192
Column/row headings 160
Columns
    insert and delete 164
Combination slide 183
Common functions 167
    in a worksheet 293
Common printing functions 280

Index

Computer
    add-ons 16
    affecting us
        crime 251
    and the environment 263
    benefits using 6
    buying, procedures 24, 26
    crime
        hackers/crackers/phreakers 252
    differences between 15
    drive access 9
    drives 11
    hackers
        security against 252
    handheld 104
    hard drive 37
    hardware 7, 9
    how it works 7
    input 13
    input devices 51
    mainframe 5
    memory 11, 20
    mini 5
    networks 4
    operating system 9, 99
    output 14
    power 16
    power buttons 9
    protect 26
    set up to connect to Internet 237
    size 16
    software 8
    speed 16
    super 5
    system 8
    system types 15
    system unit 8
        inside 11
        outside 9
    terminals 5
    types of 2
    upgrading 25
    uses 5
    virus protection programs 254
    viruses 253
        protect your system from 255
    what is 5
    workstations 5
Computer news
    keep up-to-date 251
Computer safety 250
Consistent design 84
Contacts 80
Content slide 182
Control Panel settings 270
Control Panels 116
Controller 38

Cookie 239
Corel Presentations 84
CorelDraw 92
CPU (central processing unit) 11
Cursor movement keys 130
Customized desktop 102

D

DAT (digital audiotape) 48
Data
    fill 162
    find and replace 134
    protect 27
    select 161
Data encryption 252
Database
    billing 81
    collections 81
    personnel 81
    products 80
    schedules 81
    scientific and other research data 81
    transactions 80
    use worksheet as 173
    what is 79
Database program
    features/benefits 81
    types of 83
Date
    insert 133
DBMS 81
DDR-SDRAM 22
Defragment 39, 40
Demodulator 202
Design or architecture of the chip 19
Desktop 104
Desktop and Web Publishing Programs 85
Desktop Icons 106
    use 85
Dial-up modem 202
Digital camera 58, 60
Digital Images 58
Directories 193
Disk space
    add 26
Document
    close 129
    create new 130
    drawing in 153
    edit 276
    move around in 130
    open 128, 129
    save 126
    type 276
Document area
    word processing 124

Index

Documents
   close 276
   open 276
   print 136
   problems 128
   save 276
   work with 126
Domain 202
Domain names 227
DOS 99
   difficulties 100
Double-click 56
dpi (dots per inch) 66
Drag 56
Drawing 153
   insert 279
Drive 193, 194
   access 9
   DVD 47
   floppy 44
   hard 37
      types of 37
   Jaz 48
   optimize, procedures 43
   problems 30
   SyQuest 48
   tape 48
   types of 10
   ZIP 48
Driver
   problems 31
DSL (Direct Subscriber Line) modem 202
DVD drive 10, 47

E

E-commerce 205
Editing
   common 276
Educational software 96
Electronic card 12
Electronic commerce 205
Electronic mail application 302
E-mail 209
   create and send new .... See
   emoticons 224
   handling 215
   how it works 210
   keep secure 222
   read and respond 211
   send and receive 210
E-mail (electronic mail) 209
E-mail address 209
E-mail etiquette 223
E-mail guidelines 223

E-mail message
   components 210
   organize 304
   send 303
E-mail options
   set up 219
E-mail problems
   troubleshoot 221
E-mail server 201
Emoticons 224
Encryption 239
Entertainment programs 108
Environmental and scientific probes 58
Ethernet ports 11
Expansion (electronic) cards 13
Extranet 197, 198

F

Favorites 203
Favorites list 241
Fiber optic cable 192
File
   download 245
   manage 111
   problems 115
File allocation table (FAT) 40
File management 89
File server 190
File server Lan
   cables 192
   client workstations 191, 205
   hubs 193
   login name 195
   network administrator 195
   network cards 192
   password 195
   printers 191
   server 191
   use 195
File transfer protocol (FTP) server 201
Files
   delete and undelete 114
   move and copy 113
   rename 113
   select 112
   viewing and sorting 111
Fills
   use 292
Financial programs 174
Firewall 190, 193, 198, 253
   use 256
Floppy disk
   care/maintenance 45
Floppy drive 10
   use 44
   vs. hard drive 44

Folder
  create new 112
Font
  change 140, 169
  define 140
Format
  bullets/numbers 147
  character 140
  pages 151
  paragraph 143
Format documents 282
Format text 282
Formatting 140, 150
Formatting functions 276
Formatting marks
  view 147
Formula
  create 164
  how it works 164
Formula bar
  spreadsheet 159
Formula errors
  avoid 167
Formulas 161, 293
Front side bus 19
FTP (File Transfer Protocol) 238
Function errors
  avoid 167
Function keys 52
Functions 293
  what are 165

G

Games and hobbies 96
Gateways 197
GB 37
GIF files (Graphic Interchange Format) 96
Gigabyte (G or GB) 22, 37
Graphic program
  Paint layout 92
Graphical user interface 101
Graphics
  add 153
  insert 279
Graphics and other media 89
Graphics card 64
Graphics files 95
Graphics programs 90
Guest 195
GUI (graphical user interface) 101

H

Hackers/crackers/phreakers 252
  security against 252
Handouts
  print 186

Hard drive 37
  controller 38
  display contents of, procedures 41
  how it stores data 39
  how it works 38
  organizing 40
  types of 37
Hard drive speed (access/transfer time) .. 37
Hard drives 194
Hardware 7
  defined 9
  problems 29
Headers and footers 171, 284
Help 109, 125, 266
History list 242
Home page 88, 237
Hosts 201
HTML (HyperText Markup Language) 88
HTTP (HyperText Transfer Protocol) 238
Hub 193
  File server Lan 193
Hyperlinks 231
  defined 203

I

Icon 101
  Windows 105
ID 195
Image
  copy 244
Information superhighway 203
Input
  devices 51
Insertion point 130
Instant messages 226
Internet 190, 200
  browser toolbar buttons 240
  browser, choose 236
  browsing for kids, safe 260
  browsing, safe 256
  chat 226
  connect to 233, 234
  domain names 227
  e-mail 209
  e-mail emoticons 224
  ethics
    censorship 262
    privacy 261
  go directly to address 240
  history 230
  instant messages 226
  netiquette 227
  news server 227
  newsgroup 227
  plagiarism 262
  provider, choose 235
  search 245

Index

search tools 246
search, procedures 245
search, tips 246
set up computer to connect to 237
shopping, secure 259
spam, avoiding 259
use 202
uses for 232
what is 230
work ethics 263
Internet browser 203
Internet Connection Wizard 237
Internet Explorer 236
Internet or online provider 89
Internet server 201
Internet Service Provider (ISP) 201, 203
Intranets 197
IP addresses 202
ISP (Internet Service Provider) 235

J
Jaz drive 48
Joystick/game devices 57
JPEG files (Joint Photographic Experts
   Group) 95
Junk mail 215

K
Keyboard 8, 14
avoid injury using 53
ergonomic 53
layout 51
use 51
use to move around in a document 52
Keyboard and mouse ports 11
Kilobytes per second (KBps) 37, 46

L
LANs (local area networks) 4
LCD (liquid crystal display) 65
Licensing agreement 253
Line spacing 145
Links (hyperlinks) 89, 231
browsing using 239
Linux 104
log in 195
log on 195
logical units 193
Login name
   File server Lan 195
login procedure 195
logon name 195
Lotus Approach 83
Lotus Freelance Graphics 84
LPT port (printer/parallel port) 68

M
Macintosh 103
Manipulate data 293
Manuals 85
Mapped 194
Margins 151
Maximize/Minimize buttons
   Windows 107, 114
MB 37
McAfee's VirusScan 255
Media slides 183
Megabytes (M or MB) 22, 37
Megabytes per second (MBps) 37
Memory 20
add 26
address 21
cache 23
flash 23
how it works 20
RAM (Random Access Memory) 22
ROM (Read-Only Memory) 22
types of 22
video 23
Menu bar
presentation program 179
spreadsheet 159
word processing 124
Microcomputers 2
Microsoft Access 83
Microsoft Excel for Windows 79
Microsoft PowerPoint 84
Microsoft Publisher 86
Microsoft Works 79
MIDI port 11
Milliseconds (ms) 37
Modem 202
cable 234
card 13
connect to Internet with 234
Modifier keys 52
Modulator 202
Monitor 8, 14, 62
footprint size 64
laptop 65
problems 30
types of/differences 62
Monitor port 11
Monitors
colors 64
display standard 64
resolution 63
size 62
Motherboard 11, 12
Mouse 8, 14
common actions 56
types of 55
use 54

Index

Movement keys 52
   list of 52
MSN (Microsoft Network) 235
Multiple Contributors
   work with 155
Multitasking 101
My Computer
   Windows 105
My Documents
   Windows 106

N

Nanoseconds (ns) 22
Netiquette 227
Network
   how components are organized 193
   what is 189
Network administrators 198
   File server Lan 195
Network cards
   File server Lan 192
   peer-to-peer network 196
Network drives 49
network interface card 203
Network security 198
Network use 195
Networking
   benefits and risks 199
New Document
   start based on template 275
New Template
   create 276
News server 227
Newsgroup 227, 232
Newsletters 85
Node 192
Norton AntiVirus 254
Notebook 3
Notes area
   presentation program 179
Number formats
   apply 290
Numbers
   change look 169
Numeric keypad 52

O

OCR (optical character recognition) 60
Online conferencing 227
Online services 201
Onscreen elements 275
Operating system 9
   DOS 99
   Linux 104
   Macintosh 103
   other 103
   Palmtop 104
   Unix 103
   what is 99
   Windows 99
Outline
   presentation program 179

P

Page
   headers/footers 152
   insert 152
   margins 151
   numbers 152
Page breaks
   insert 133
Page setup 171
Paint 108
Paint (Microsoft Windows) 91
Paint program
   layout 92
Paint Shop Pro 91
Palmtop 104
Paragraphs
   format 282
Parallel port 11
Password 252
   File server Lan 195
Password authentication 198
Patch panel 193
PDAs (personal digital assistants) 3
Peer-to-peer 190
Peer-to-Peer LANs 196
Pen, electronic 57
Performance
   improve 27
Permission 116
   log on 120
Personal computer
   desktop/tower 2
   evolution of 1
   portable or laptop 3
Personal stationery 85
Photo CD 93
Photographs 90
Physical units 193
Pictures
   insert 153
Plotters 68
Plug-in 239
Point 56
Point of sale systems 204
Power fluctuations 26
Powerbook 3
ppm (pages printed per minute) 66
Presentation
   view and edit 185

Index

Presentation program
    features of 83
    program tools 178
    types of 84
    use 83
Presentations
    create 178, 179, 296
    designing 177
    format 296
Print 66
Printer
    color 67
    combination printer/fax/copy machine 67
    differences between 66
    dot-matrix 66
    File server Lan 191
    ink-jet 66
    laser 67
    peer-to-peer network 196
    photo 68
    plotters 68
    ports 68
    problems 31
    supplies 68
PrintMaster 86
Privacy 261
Processing location 192
Processor
    differences between 19
    history of 17
    how it works 16
    manufacturers 20
    speeds of different 18
    types of 17
Program
    accessory 108
    buy 73
    exit 123
    start, procedures 122
    upgrading 74
Program icons
    Windows 106
Program setup 102
Program tools
    presentation program 178
Program tools 123
Programs
    work in 122
Projectors 65
Properties 267
Protocol 238
Proxy server 193, 198

Q
QuarkXpress 86
Query data 82

R
RAM 20
    definition 22
    size and speed 22
    types of 22
Rambus DRAM 23
RDRAM (Rambus Dynamic RAM) 23
Recalculations 79
Recycle Bin 114
    Windows 105
Relational database 82
Repeating commands 131
Reports 82
    Web publishing 89
ROM
    definition 22
Router 193
Rows
    insert and delete 164

S
Scanner
    using 59
SDRAM (Synchronous Dynamic RAM) 22
Search engine 201, 206
Search the Internet 245, 307
Search tips 246
Search tools 246
Sections
    insert 152
Sectors 39
Serial port 11
Server 194
    File server Lan 191
Shade 170
Shared resources 102
Sheets
    create/delete 292
Shortcuts 267
Shorthand expressions 225
Shutting down 270
Sign on 195
Slides
    add text 184
    create 182
    format 184
Small business manager 174
Sneaker net 189
Software 8, 72, 273
    how it works 72
    how to create 73
    install 115
    piracy 253
Solitaire 108
Sort data 82, 293
Sound
    card and speakers 13

Index

Spam 222
Speaker notes 84
   print 186
Special-purpose keys 52
Spelling
   check 136, 215
Spreadsheet
   budget 78
   data list 78
   income 78
   invoice 78
   project management 78
   sales 77
   scientific data 78
Spreadsheet program
   features/benefits 78
   tools 158
   types of 79
   what is 77
   working with 158
Spyware 258
Start button
   Windows 105
Starting Up 270
Status bar
   spreadsheet 160
   word processing 124
Switch 193
Switch between documents 276
Symbols
   insert 133
System information, getting, procedures .. 23
System settings 119
System tools 108
System unit
   inside 11
   outside 9
   power protector 13
   video card 64

T

Table
   add in word processing program 154
   add 153
   convert text to a table 289
   draw a 290
   edit 287
   format 287
   insert 287
   modify 287
Tabs 286
   create custom 147
Tape drives 48
Taskbar
   Windows 105
Tax preparation 174

TCP/IP (Transmission Control
   Protocol/Internet Protocol) 200
Telecommuting 199
Telephone port 11
Telnet 201
Templates 84, 180
   Web publishing 89
Text
   alignment 143
   bullets/numbers 147
   copy 131, 244
   correct 131
   format 140
   format font 140
   indent 144
   line spacing 145
   move 131
   search for 244
   select 132
   type/edit 130
Text Formatting 278
Title slide 182
Toolbar buttons, Web browser 240
Toolbars
   presentation program 179
   spreadsheet 159
   Word processing 124
Touch screen 58
Trackball 56
Trackpad 57
Twin twisted pair cable 192

U

Undo 131
Unix 103
Upgrade
   monitor 26
   processor 26
URL (uniform resource locator) 238
URLs 202
USB Flash Memory Drives 49
USB port 11
Usenet 201
User ID 198
Utility programs 96

V

Values 161
Video camera 61
Video card (adapter) 11, 13, 64
View icons
   presentation program 179
Virtual private networking 199
Virus
   protect your system from 27, 255
Virus and Internet protection software 96
Virus protection programs 254

Index

Virus scanning software 198
Viruses.. 253
Visio.. 92
Voice recognition..................................... 58
Volumes 193, 194
VRAM (Video RAM).................................. 65

W

WANs (wide area networks)................ 4, 197
Web address 238
Web browsing application...................... 305
Web graphics 91
Web link
   insert 214
Web pages.. 243
   browse 237
   print.. 243
   save 244
   understand 237
Web publishing program.......................... 88
   types of... 88
Web site.. 238
Wide Area Networks 197
Window border
   Windows.................................... 107, 114
Window controls
   word processing 124
Window title bar
   Windows.................................... 107, 114
Windows.. 99, 266
   customize... 116
   desktop.. 105
   for Workgroups................................. 102
   introducing 101
   manage files............................ 111, 275
   online help.. 274
   resize/move/close 106
   restart/shut down............................... 110
   troubleshooting................................. 119
   updates.. 103
   utilize sources................................... 274
   versions of 102
   working with...................................... 104
Windows application
   start and exit 274
Windows CE 104
Windows desktop................................... 266
Windows disks 266
Windows Explorer 269
Windows files 266
Windows NT...102
Windows Security Center 255
Wireless access points 192
Wizards 83, 179
   Web publishing...................................89
Word processing
   Checking features 76
   editing features...................................76
   features and benefits...........................76
   formatting features..............................76
   special features 76
   program
      ClarisWorks for Macintosh 77
      Microsoft Works 77
      WordPad 77
      WordPerfect...................................76
   what is 75
Word processing document
   add tables in 154
   edit text in..131
   format text in 140
   select text in....................................132
WordPad..109
Worksheet
   create...290
   create chart in 172
   create formula in 164
   definition..159
   enter data in 158
   enter text/numbers in 161
   format..168
   format data......................................290
   functions 165
   layout...160
   title..160
   use as database...............................173
Worksheet data
   modify 290
Worksheet Data 167
Worksheet structure 290
Workstation
   File server LAN.................................190
   peer-to-peer network 196
World Wide Web (WWW)........................200
   what is...231

Z

ZIP drive.. 10

Notes

Notes

Notes

Notes

Notes

Notes